Decolonization and its Impact

Decolonization and its Impact

A Comparative Approach to the End of the Colonial Empires

Martin Shipway

Blackwell
Publishing

© 2008 by Martin Shipway

BLACKWELL PUBLISHING
350 Main Street, Malden, MA 02148-5020, USA
9600 Garsington Road, Oxford OX4 2DQ, UK
550 Swanston Street, Carlton, Victoria 3053, Australia

First published 2008 by Blackwell Publishing Ltd

1   2008

Library of Congress Cataloging-in-Publication Data

Shipway, Martin.
    Decolonization and its impact : a comparative approach to the end of the colonial empires /
Martin Shipway.
      p. cm.
    Includes bibliographical references and index.
    ISBN 978-0-631-19967-0 (hardcover : alk. paper) — ISBN 978-0-631-19968-7 (pbk. : alk.
paper)   1. Decolonization—History—20th century.   I. Title.

    JV151.S47 2008
    325'.3—dc22

                                                                          2007017676

A catalogue record for this title is available from the British Library.

Set in 10.5/13pt Minion
by Graphicraft Limited, Hong Kong

For further information on
Blackwell Publishing, visit our website:
www.blackwellpublishing.com

Contents

Acknowledgements

It can take longer to write a book than to dissolve whole continental empires. Sometimes it just seems that way. Certainly, in the case of the present volume, there have been times when the author has longed for what Octave Mannoni (1966) called 'The Decolonization of Myself'. In the course of putting this work together, I have received encouragement and supportive criticism from many sources. Not least, several generations of Birkbeck students, many of them with roots in countries whose path to independence is described in these pages, have urged me to transfer my thoughts from my hard drive to their reading lists, meanwhile cheerfully arguing back and putting me straight on some of my more far-fetched or dogmatic hypotheses. Many colleagues at Birkbeck and in the wider academic community have similarly reassured me that my work was valued and would be read (and could I please get on with it). Amongst these, in no particular order, I would mention: Rob Holland, Andy Knapp, Jim Le Sueur, David Killingray, Tony Chafer, Philippe Oulmont, Joanna Bourke, Naoko Shimazu, Hilary Sapire, William Rowe, Sudhir Hazareesingh, Robert Gildea, Julian Jackson, Seán Hand; four of a British quintet of Martins with an interest in France and the French empire, Messrs Alexander, Conway, Evans and Thomas; Peter Catterall and Lawrence Freedman (the editors of the series for which the book was originally commissioned); and a generous and perceptive anonymous reader of a (now abridged) draft manuscript. Recently, MM Sébastien and Jean Laurentie have provided an incalculably valuable personal link (albeit at one remove) with a key actor in my story. Several of those named offered me the welcome opportunity to test my ideas in seminars and conferences at the universities of Exeter, London (Institutes of Commonwealth Studies and of Historical Research), Oxford, Oxford Brookes, Portsmouth, Reading, Salford, Swansea. At various points, I have benefited from periods of official and unofficial study leave, and I am indebted to colleagues in the School of Languages, Linguistics and Culture for bearing with me and tolerating my apparent diffidence in producing some tangible 'research output'; and to the Faculty of Arts, Birkbeck, for a recent research grant. At its outset, the project was supported by a Small Personal Research Grant from the British Academy, which I gratefully acknowledge. Inevitably in a work of this kind, which has induced me to stray far from my 'comfort zone', much has depended on the wisdom, insight and curiosity of the many authors whose names appear in the Bibliography; I hope that not too many of them would be surprised or dismayed by my interpretation of their ideas and research, and none is responsible other than the present author for any lapses of accuracy or judgement which appear in these pages. Many librarians have supported this project, amongst whom I would particularly mention the staff of Rhodes House Library in Oxford, surely one of the most congenial places to work on this or any subject. Blackwells, particularly Tessa Harvey, have consistently shown generosity with deadlines and word limits, and thus patiently brought this project to term. Closer to home, [sentence deleted] Mary Anne, Victoria, Jenna and a resolutely unscholarly feline dynasty have lived through the project and, with a varying mix of love, forbearance, cajoling, complaining (mostly the cats), cold-shouldering (ditto), and attempts at distraction (usually successful), have kept me grounded and not unduly indulged. Mary Anne has drawn on apparently limitless reserves of under-standing and generosity, and this book is dedicated to her. My mother and father gave their unstinting love and support. As ever, I gratefully acknowledge their decades-long loving interest in my intellectual and personal development. Sadly, my father, a man of scholarly and gentlemanly instincts, was taken ill soon after the book went into production, and did not live to see it finally published.

IN MEMORIAM GJS (1926–2007).

MJS, Oxford & London, September 2007

Maps

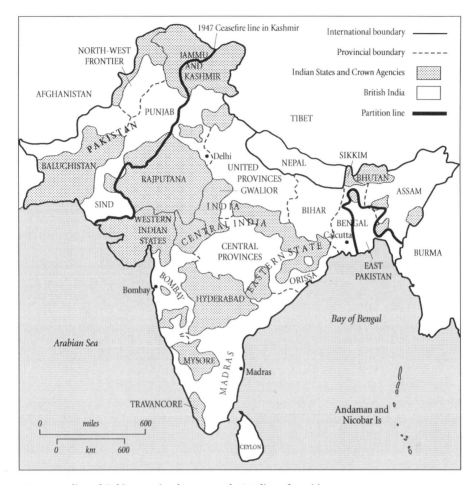

Map 1   India and Pakistan: princely states and 1947 line of partition

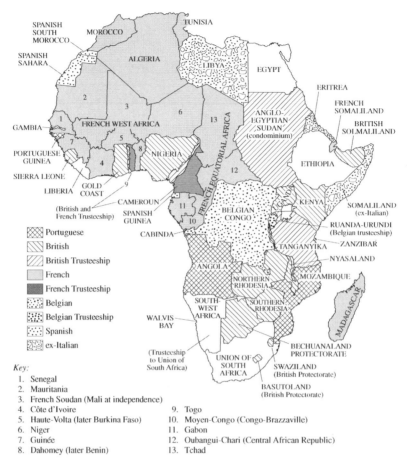

Key:

1. Senegal
2. Mauritania
3. French Soudan (Mali at independence)
4. Côte d'Ivoire
5. Haute-Volta (later Burkina Faso)
6. Niger
7. Guinée
8. Dahomey (later Benin)
9. Togo
10. Moyen-Congo (Congo-Brazzaville)
11. Gabon
12. Oubangui-Chari (Central African Republic)
13. Tchad

Map 2   Africa in c.1946, showing areas controlled by European powers. For names of African states in 2007 with their dates of independence see Appendix, p. 240

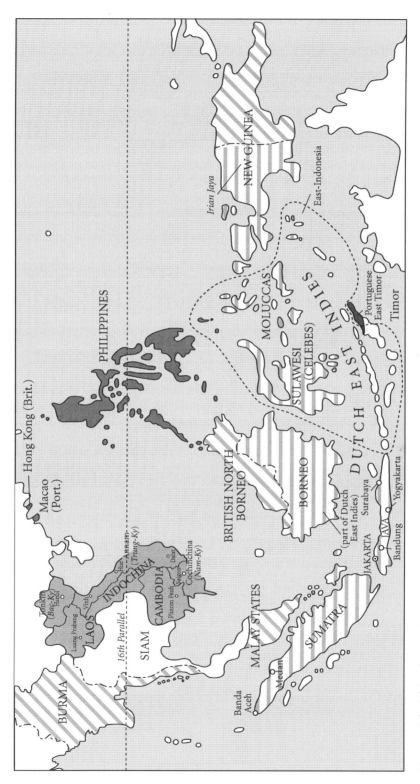

Map 3 Colonial Southeast Asia

Introduction: Decolonization in Comparative Perspective

It is now more than half a century since the first irrevocable steps were taken towards the dissolution of the European colonial empires, and barely more than forty years since all but the most insignificant or obdurate colonial regimes were consigned to some virtual historical junkyard or museum. Revolutions in Vietnam and Indonesia in August 1945, which blocked French and Dutch efforts to recover their colonial possessions from Japanese occupation, were followed in 1946 by the American grant of independence to the Philippines (promised ten years previously), by Transfers of Power in India and a newly created Pakistan in 1947, and in Burma and Ceylon (now Sri Lanka) in 1948. After protracted insurgent campaigns, Indonesia became independent in 1949, Vietnam finally defeated the French colonial power in 1954, and Malaya (subsequently Malaysia) gained its independence in 1957. Between 1954 and 1965, most of the continent of Africa was freed from colonial rule, though the more recalcitrant colonial or settler armies continued to fight on into the 1970s. South Africa alone, which had undergone decolonization of a kind in 1910, maintained quasi-colonial (or perhaps ultra-colonial) structures of rule based on racial segregation until the last decade of the century. A slightly later wave of decolonizations brought independence to a scattered galaxy of smaller nations in the Caribbean and Mediterranean Seas, and in the Indian and Pacific Oceans. For many British commentators, the final, symbolic act of decolonization was the transfer of Hong Kong from British to Chinese rule in 1997, leaving only a few 'confetti' of colonial empire to survive into the new century. But in the main it took only about twenty years for most of the formal structures and institutions of colonialism (though not nearly so comprehensively of their associated mentalities) to be swept away. It is this brief, often violent and intermittently intense period of crisis which forms the subject of this book.

Explaining an international phenomenon as complex as decolonization raises a general problem associated with the shape and purpose of historical narratives, particularly when those narratives have relevance for the contemporary world. Cooper (1996: 6) has summed up this problem: we know the end of the story. Or perhaps, rather, we *think* we do. As with that other global structuring event of the post-1945 world, the Cold War, it is virtually impossible *not* to see decolonization as part of some bigger picture, as the enactment of secular, perhaps even millennial, historical processes, or perhaps as a step towards the abyss. Just as there were those who, however tentatively, saw the 'End of History' in the vertiginous culminating in the fall of the Berlin Wall (Fukuyama 1989),[1] so too the precipitate withdrawal of colonial administrations from Asia, Africa and other parts of the world was seen typically at the time as marking the end of a centuries-long process of European imperial expansion, or more positively (and fleetingly) as the dawning of a new era of relations between the developed and the under-developed worlds. The problem is not simply that such a grandiose version of History-with-an-H may mask the deeper continuities of historical process – and few would dispute that the fundamental structure of North–South relations survived the decolonization process largely intact. It also glosses over the contingency and sheer complexity of major historical crises, and the extent to which the impact of crisis led the actors involved to recast their actions retrospectively in terms of the 'wider' historical picture. Historians have also tended to shape their narratives in such a way as to explain the outcome of national independence and imperial dissolution almost as givens, although the cruder forms of determinism have usually been discounted. Certainly, independence was neither simply wrested by force from the colonizers by triumphant and united new nations, nor was it generously bestowed by wise western statesmen, acting as it were *in loco parentis*, when their charges attained their majority. Nor, whatever else it may have been, was decolonization inevitable in the forms it took. At the very least, it is axiomatic that the precise outcomes of decolonization were rarely ones which anyone had intended, not least because they were brought about according to a timetable that no one had imagined possible.

A further conceptual problem which arises with decolonization more acutely than is the case for the Cold War is that, while the emerging history of the Cold War would tend to support the dictum that history is written by the victors, writing about colonialism and decolonization tends to mirror the structure of the former empires. Thus, working from first principles, decolonization may be seen *either* as a composite of the individual national narratives of each of the hundred or so ex-colonies' paths to independent statehood, *or* as the 'bigger' story of the breakdown of a number of imperial systems against the backdrop of a major structural shift in the international system. The trouble is that neither of these narratives taken on its own is necessarily reliable or complete.

Much of the recent historiography of decolonization has tended to reflect the second of these narratives and thus to favour a top-down or imperial approach, especially when the imperial system under consideration is the British empire. Thus Darwin (1991: 116) rejects the possibility that the decolonization of the British empire might be considered as 'a story of fifty separate chapters'. Similarly, extending this broad approach to a comparative survey of all the European colonial systems, Holland (1985: 1) proposes that decolonization 'happened because colonialism as a set of nationally orchestrated systems (by the British, French, Dutch, Belgians and Portuguese) ceased to possess the self-sustaining virtue of internal equilibrium'. The fact that decolonization took place in such diverse places, and yet over 'so compressed a timescale', suggests to Howe (1993: 11–12) that 'however powerfully determinant local conditions may have been, the procedures of, and pressures on, metropolitan policy making were decisive in the end of Empire'. This argument may be extended to the other colonial empires, particularly to the French, but the concept of a 'Scramble out of Africa' mirroring the process of colonial conquests at the end of the nineteenth century is persuasive. Even the relatively substantial time-lag involved in the Portuguese empire's ragged decolonization, seen throughout the twentieth century as 'marching to a different drummer' (Young 1988: 52), shrinks to insignificance according to all but the most 'in your face' perspectives.

The corollary of this approach is a concern with the overall 'pattern and timing' of decolonization, and with the identification of developments which occurred as part of a clearly identifiable process of imperial dissolution, as opposed to factors which might have had an impact on imperial policy, but which were contained, absorbed or defeated by colonial rulers. This approach tends to discount local factors, such as the rise of anti-colonial nationalist movements or, more generally, the impact of 'colonial politics'. As Holland (1985) puts it, 'ramshackle political coalitions in the underdeveloped world were only one element – and not the most vital – in determining the end to twentieth-century empires'. Although it originated as a way of shifting the perspective of imperial history from the metropolitan centre to the colonial periphery, Robinson and Gallagher's now classic, so-called 'peripheral' or 'excentric' approach to imperialism still attributes much, if not all, of the dynamism and initiative for colonial policy to the imperial power.

The generally accepted landmark according to this approach to decolonization is the Second World War, whose 'corrosive effects . . . at every level of the imperial connection', according to Darwin (1991: 118f.), set off the chain of crises which culminated in the liquidation of the colonial empires. This is not to say, however, that decolonization somehow became inevitable at war's end, because one has to take into account the intense but short-lived reinvigoration of colonial purpose after 1945, the 'revival' of the colonial empires identified by Gallagher (1982), often described as a 'second colonial occupation'. Certainly, Gallagher's preferred metaphors for colonial interaction suggest a wily, resourceful and endlessly energetic colonial power, even to the last:

> Every colonial power sustained itself by shifting the basis of its rule from time to time, dropping one set of imperial collaborators and taking up another. In principle, this process could have continued endlessly. The imperial croupier never found any shortage of colonial subjects ready to place bets with him at the table, although they usually staggered up from the table in some disarray. Certainly in India in 1947, and in Africa in the late nineteen-fifties, there were still plenty of groups ready to try a flutter. (ibid.: 153)

Gallagher's thesis as a whole, in his final, definitive statement of the peripheral approach, is that colonialism was normally a distraction from, or a drain upon, the more serious enterprise of British imperial expansion: in the long view, the British empire in the colonial period may be seen to shift from a world system where influence predominated through a system of informal empire, the preferred mode of British imperialism, to one of direct rule, and to fail in its attempt, in the 1950s and 1960s, to shift back to a system of influence, 'more than British and less than an *imperium*', through collaboration with the new imperial power on the block, the United States (Louis & Robinson [1994]2003).

It should be emphasized that this imperial approach is more a question of geopolitical perspective than of ideology. An account of decolonization may be critical or dismissive of the imperial role in the process, but still consider the question from a top-down perspective. Such is by and large the case for a long tradition of anti-imperial literature, as represented by a chapter in Hobsbawm's magisterial survey of the 'short' twentieth century (1994: 344–71). Certainly the historian of French decolonization would find it difficult to maintain that French policy makers maintained more than nominal control over the process of decolonization in wide parts of the French empire at various moments in the 1940s and 1950s, and there is little to admire in French handling of this process, and yet writing about the French empire in this period, including that by the present author, has tended to mirror the centralizing structure of that empire. More generally, the very phrase 'End of Empire', even when divorced from any sense of nostalgia or apologia, would tend to suggest that global causes must be found for such a strikingly global phenomenon as decolonization or, more tendentiously, that the imperial hand cannot simply have been forced (at least, not by 'ramshackle political coalitions') into something so momentous as imperial dissolution.

Nonetheless, for the most part, one writer's imperial grand narrative looks very like another's imperial apology, and it is a short step from saying that the initiative for imperial change and dissolution was located at the metropolitan centre, to claiming that imperial policy makers decided the manner of their parting, or even that they planned it all along. There is a time-honoured British imperial tradition of accommodating even unwelcome change within an appeal to secular trends, or a 'belief in contingency as a form of destiny – in short, providence – [which] reaches far back into English history' (Boyce 1999: 1). Thus, British 'decolonization' can be dated back to the disastrous loss of the 13 American colonies, taking in the gradual extension of self-government to the settler colonies of Canada, Australia and New Zealand, and the troubled process which led to South African independence (albeit within the imperial system) in 1910, and is reflected even in the shifting and divided constitutional status of Ireland after 1919. British policy makers could thus lay claim to a long tradition of devolving power, which in the mid-twentieth century found expression in the reluctant and ultimately irrelevant promise to accord Dominion status to India and other dependencies, and in the attention paid to the niceties of Commonwealth membership and to the 'invented traditions' of royal protocol in the 1950s.

British claims to foresight and generous paternal wisdom became something of a cottage industry for politicians and officials alike. While Britain's decolonizing prime minister, Harold Macmillan, patented his own brand in such rhetoric, the Colonial Office turned it into a policy, as constitution after Westminster-style constitution was churned out on a rough-and-ready production line. Such 'Whiggish' rationalizations of the end of empire have been reflected more or less uncontroversially in what Twaddle has called the 'Old Commonwealth paradigm' of British decolonization (Twaddle 1986). The corollary of this view is a sense that, somewhere along the way, British policy makers 'lost the plot' and that, just as the British empire could be seen to have been won, as Seeley famously noted, 'in a fit of absence of mind', so also was it lost in an albeit well-intentioned muddle in the corridors of Whitehall (Howe 1993: 11ff.).

It is worth noting that the French counterpart to the British 'Whig' tradition was not simply conjured up by that genius in self-serving rationalizations, President Charles de Gaulle, but constituted a recurrent, if secondary theme in French colonial doctrine, as expressed, for example, by veteran Socialist Prime Minister Léon Blum, reluctantly talking down the *fait accompli* of Franco-Vietnamese hostilities in December 1946:

> According to our republican doctrine, colonial possession only reaches its final goal and is justified the day it ceases, that is, the day when a colonized people has been given the capacity to live emancipated and to govern itself. The colonizer's reward is then to have earned the colonized people's gratitude and affection, to have brought about inter-penetration and solidarity in thought, culture and interests, thus allowing colonizer and colonized to unite freely. (in Shipway 1996b: 94)

However, such claims rang hollow against the dominant unison of appeals to a Republican unity which precluded self-government, but more particularly against the cacophony of almost continuous colonial violence through to Algerian independence in 1962. Indeed, in response to this traumatic mismatch between French national purpose and the catastrophe of Algerian decolonization, it is small wonder that the French nation long chose to remain silent, so that it is only recently that debate over the memories and legacy of decolonization has erupted in France (Beaugé 2005). Even so, French parliamentarians have attempted to steer the debate towards the proposition, bizarrely enshrined in law in February 2005 (and subsequently repealed by President Jacques Chirac), that French colonization had a 'positive role', especially in North Africa (Liauzu & Manceron 2006).

What, then, if decolonization is viewed, *pace* the imperial historians, according to our alternative narrative, as the combined history of individual national struggles for freedom. Here, in at least a hundred 'different chapters', decolonization may more readily be conceived as the culmination of a history of interaction and conflict between colonizer and colonized, externally influenced but nonetheless determined at least in part by internal structures. The imperial historian's concern with 'pattern and timing' gives way to the more complex idea of decolonization as the culmination of a dialectic between colonizer and colonized, or between the various social and political groups within the emerging polity, whether European or indigenous, ruling or ruled, consenting or resistant, traditional or modernizing. Thus there is often a striking difference in emphasis between studies of 'decolonization' which are mostly about the end of empire, and individual national or regional studies presenting a more seamless process of political and social development under colonial rule and beyond. Paradoxically, decolonization as such may be de-emphasized by this approach, either because, as Lonsdale has put it, 'colonialism was a social process which decolonization continued' (in Killingray & Rathbone 1986: 135), or because independence brought an all too brief moment of triumph followed by disenchantment, or accompanied by the awareness that decolonization was merely a stage along the way towards the fulfilment of greater, more satisfying national and international goals.

An implied teleology is perhaps more plausible here, that independence from colonial rule was won by individual colonized peoples united in struggle under their own Nationalist leadership. Few historical processes can have apparently fulfilled the promises of their protagonists so rapidly and completely. But it would be more accurate to say that the scholarly literature is haunted by the ghost of the Nationalist Struggle, rather than possessed by it. Thus, a first generation of writing on decolonization consisted of the manifestos, autobiographies or hagiographies of nationalist politicians themselves, alongside the writings of a self-constituted 'Committee of Concerned Scholars for a Free Africa', as one historian sees the work of western academics in the 1950s and 1960s (Lonsdale, in Cooper [1994]2003: 25). This approach has also been characterized as following a 'Romantic Nationalist paradigm', where the epithet 'Romantic' might be understood as in the 'Wrong but Wromantic' Cavaliers of *1066 and All That* (as opposed to the 'Right but Repulsive' Roundheads in the English Civil War) (Twaddle 1986: 132; Sellar & Yeatman 1930: 63). Indeed, the thesis of fulfilled national promise is one which is almost universally taken as an 'Aunt Sally' to be ritually knocked down by sophisticated professional historians.

It was perhaps to be expected that, from the lofty perspective of imperial decline and fall, little would be made of the role of successor nationalist movements in bringing about the end of empire. Thus Gallagher (1982: 148) argued that in Africa in the 1950s, 'just as in India before it', British policy created the conditions in which mass political parties emerged to generate the 'apparent expression of nationalist demands', thus denying the very possibility that British imperialists, though they might miscalculate, could ever surrender the initiative to their colonized antagonists and collaborators. Darwin (1991: 109) is more generous in allowing that nationalism contributed to decolonization partly through the 'skill and energy with which colonial politicians seized the opportunities for political action which opened up before them'; but even this concession is made within an imperial framework. Such a perspective is less plausibly maintained by historians of French, Dutch or Portuguese decolonization, and even Gallagher concedes that Algerians fought for their freedom.

More surprisingly, the record of colonial nationalists has for long been subjected to extensive critical revision from ostensibly more sympathetic perspectives. The lead was given by the Martiniquan psychiatrist and activist for the Algerian cause, Frantz Fanon, in his posthumously published polemic, *The Damned of the Earth* ([1961]2002) Fanon's coruscating attack on a moribund but still resourceful colonialism reserved a special measure of venom for a collaborating 'national bourgeoisie' taking over the structures of state power from cynically retreating colonial powers which, at the end, 'decolonize so quickly that they impose independence on Houphouët-Boigny' (ibid.: 69).[2] Fanon's at times almost-messianic vision of a decolonization that never was, a violent and cleansing revolution which would establish a post-colonial *tabula rasa*, where formerly colonized 'new men' would enter for the first time into their historical birthright, overlapped with an emerging pessimistic and recriminatory analysis of decolonization as a disguised reinvigoration of imperial purpose. Part of the argument of what came to be known as 'dependency theory', was that formal colonialism had merely shape-shifted into a less costly neo-colonialism, in which the imperialist powers (Americans as well as British and French) now collaborated with a class of 'comprador' capitalists, drawn precisely from that class which had most obviously championed, and in turn benefited from, anti-colonial nationalism, which is to say 'bourgeois' nationalist elites recruited by former colonial rulers. Aside from its function as a comforting explanation, or alibi, for some early national leaders seeking to understand why their own hopes had not been realized (for example, Nkrumah 1965), and notwithstanding the identification of an undoubted structural problem in North–South relations, dependency theory replaced the notion of heroic nationalist agency by a sorrier picture of the former colonized as either dupes or victims of an implausibly efficient conspiracy between prescient colonizers and their new collaborators (Bayart 1993).

The critique of triumphant bourgeois nationalism has become increasingly explicit in more recent debates, so that little now remains untouched of the 'Romantic Nationalist' paradigm. Thus, in the early volumes of the *Subaltern Studies* journal, radical Indian historians focused their attention on the ways in which the Indian National CongressParty, dominated by professional and capitalist elites and fearful of popular revolution, sought to subordinate class struggle to national struggle. The often acute material grievances of Indian peasants and workers, whose perspective was characterized via the Italian revolutionary Antonio Gramsci's notion of the 'subaltern', were thus suppressed, hitched to the bandwagon of Gandhian populism, or glossed over in the interests of national mobilization, while the diverse but misunderstood histories of peasant protest and insurrection under the Raj were appropriated as the prehistory of a determinist 'official version' of inevitable nationalist triumph over the British (Guha & Spivak 1988: 35–6, 37–44).

The final few nails in the coffin of nationalism's reputation have been hammered in by the exponents of a rich and densely argued body of post-colonial theory. A large measure of inspiration for this came from Edward Said's *Orientalism* (1978), which explored the ways in which British and French imperialists and scholars over two centuries had systematically misrepresented the cultures of the Middle East, a secular habit of mind which was then taken over enthusiastically by a new wave of late twentieth-century American imperialists, whose grip on the foreign policy of the world's first 'hyper-power' seems to be showing signs of hubristic abatement as the first decade of the twenty-first century proceeds. Both *Orientalism* and its 'sequel', *Culture and Imperialism* (1993), are presented as histories of, and from within, western culture, but the wider implications of Said's work were rapidly realized. Thus Chatterjee writes of the epiphany which accompanied his first encounter with Said's work:

> I was struck by the way Orientalism was implicated in the construction not only of the ideology of British colonialism which had dominated India for two centuries, but also of the nationalism which was my own heritage. Orientalist constructions of Indian civilization had been avidly seized upon by the ideologues of Indian nationalism in order to assert the glory and antiquity of a national past. So Indian nationalists had implicitly accepted the colonialist critique of the Indian present: a society fallen into barbarism and stagnation, incapable of progress or modernity. (in Sprinker 1992: 194–5)

Chatterjee's (1986) study of Indian nationalism thus charted the ways in which successive generations of Indian nationalists had been constrained to articulate their struggle against British imperialism within the bounds of 'derived discourses' of western-inspired nationalism. Central to this line of argument was the concept of 'power/knowledge', derived from a reading of Michel Foucault. The pessimism of Foucault's studies, examining the processes by which an all-embracing post-Enlightenment state came to exercise control over even the most private and intimate practices and discourses of the individual, seemed to apply all the more forcefully to the cultures enthralled (in both senses: enslaved *and* entranced) by post-Enlightenment western imperialism. The enthusiasm with which Saidian and Foucauldian approaches have been adopted has not gone unchallenged by historians and anthropologists, although this has led to some interesting efforts to establish a new research agenda (Sprinker 1992; Cooper & Stoler 1997). Amongst others, Sumit Sarkar, whose own history of modern India rehearsed many of the arguments of *Subaltern Studies*, has since warned of the political dangers inherent in attempting to wipe clean the historical slate and to return to a state of pre-colonial 'innocence', dangers which are especially pertinent in a wider national or international context of rising religious and cultural fundamentalism (Sarkar 1989, 1997; & in Chaturvedi 2000).

Locating Decolonization in Space and Time

The edifice which awaits inspection by the historian of decolonization thus has an apparently M.C. Escher-like tendency to turn into an optical illusion. In so far as decolonization is written about extensively as a distinct phenomenon, it has often been synonymous with the End of Empire, and the end of the British empire in particular. Conversely, decolonization seen from below has been subsumed into a far wider field of colonial and post-colonial historical study, which tends to elide the moment of decolonization itself, and discounts any suggestion that this moment was more than fleetingly positive. This study attempts to reconcile 'imperial' explanations of decolonization with a comparative approach based on an understanding of the political and social processes of colonialism and colonial rule, and the ways in which those processes culminated in decolonization. Where, then, do we look in order to seek to understand the processes of decolonization? And over what timeframe?

The answer to the first question, or at least the answer that is given in this study, is simple: by triangulating between 'top-down' and 'grass roots' perspectives, and by comparing the various colonial empires, we arrive at that curious entity known in the literature as the 'colonial state'. Since the evolution, structure and composition of colonial states form the subject of Chapter 1, here we consider only how this focus may help to understand decolonization. First, the colonial state is a logical unit of comparison, since the empires themselves were so dissimilar in size and purpose, and since, arguably, only British imperialism was so overwhelming as to be more than the sum of its parts. Secondly, as it turned out, colonial states were in some sense the prize over which colonial governments and nationalist political forces were fighting, competing or negotiating during decolonization; this is suggested not least by the correlation between colonial and post-colonial state boundaries. Thirdly, at this level we may appreciate the complexity of the interaction between colonizer and colonized, between colonial administrations and their chosen or self-selected collaborators and opponents, whom we meet for the first time in Chapter 2. Conversely, reversing the imperial polarities of 'centre' and 'periphery' does not preclude a proper appreciation of metropolitan decision making, for which the colonial state acted as a kind of 'gatekeeper'. Moreover, when it comes to international influences, including the building of an effective international ideological consensus against colonialism, which Darwin (1991: 109) concedes as a further achievement of nationalism, clearly this consensus could not be mediated either by colonial governments or by the metropolitan capitals.

A key reason for focusing on the colonial state is that this may help us with our second question, concerning the timeframe of decolonization. The problem here has been posed with some acuity by Howe, commenting on the 'poverty of historiography' of decolonization:

> ... whilst the acquisition of colonial empires has generally been understood as constituting, or at least reflecting, structural changes – shifts in the *longue durée* – in the world system, most of the literature on decolonization has seen the process purely in the short view of particular events; or in Braudelian terms at best as conjunctural. (Howe 1993: 3)[3]

Where this study risks further disappointing Howe's expectations, however, is in that it locates decolonization precisely at the level of event, or more precisely in a 'twenty years crisis' (to borrow E.H. Carr's label for the interwar period) from 1945. However, neither the *longue durée* nor, particularly, 'conjuncture' can be disregarded. To return to an earlier comparison, whereas the Cold War may be understood as an admittedly large-scale event, the more so because it is now safely over, the grand abstraction contained in the notion of decolonization, or End of Empire, seems to imply some structural shift lasting several lifetimes. Thus Gallagher (1982) traces British imperial decline, revival and fall, along with the workings of a steadily rational British 'official mind', over more than a century from the mid-nineteenth century. Chatterjee (1993) too is prepared to concede the political sphere to the Westernized elites of the Indian National Congress, in favour of a purer Indian national identity located in the private sphere of family and religion.

Interestingly enough, these secular perspectives reflect the imperialist view of change, according to the long vistas and evolutionary timescales of the so-called 'prerequisites' model for imperial development. As Moore puts it parodistically: 'Before India secured self-government it must pass through the stages of evolution that Britain had experienced since the Middle Ages' (1977: 399). Suggesting an even longer timescale, Churchill accused the British government that introduced the 1935 Government of India Act of running 'counter to nature', and of 'trying to put the clock forward without regard to the true march of solar events' (in ibid.). Such perspectives still found utterance in the opposition mounted by British Governors to official proposals for African political development in the 1940s. Until the late 1950s, Belgian administrators sought to apply a Belgian model of building Congolese government up from a strong local base, reproducing the slow evolution of Walloon and Flemish civic government (Young 1965). The French 'official mind' was more straightforward: when, in early 1944, an improvised conference of African governors assembled at Brazzaville under the aegis of General de Gaulle's Free French movement, they ruled out 'the eventual establishment of self governments [*sic*] in the colonies, even in a distant future' (in Shipway 1996a: 35; and see Chapter 5). Even in the 1960s, the empire's *longue durée* remained fixed in the British 'official mind' like an image burned on the retina. Thus, British prime ministers, Harold Macmillan (Conservative, 1957–63) and Harold Wilson (Labour, 1964–70, 1974–6), both came to power resolved to maintain the Empire-Commonwealth or, in Wilson's case, an improbable British frontier on the Himalayas.

The problem with understanding decolonization in terms of the *longue durée* is that, if the Braudelian method may be compared to the use of time-lapse photography to capture the life-cycle of an ancient baobab, then decolonization was the removal of several boughs by a logger with a chain-saw, operating between the exposure of individual frames: now you see them, now you don't. If the camera is speeded up somewhat, however, we move into the Braudel's intermediate stage of conjuncture, at which level we may at least start to pick out some detail in the shorter life-span of the colonial state, if not yet of decolonization itself. In other words, although metropolitan politicians, colonial officials and nationalist leaders alike may have perceived the stakes of decolonization in terms of imperial decline and fall, in fact what was immediately at stake was the survival of formal colonial rule within the boundaries of the colonial state, and that, as it turned out, could be liquidated very quickly indeed: now you see it, now you don't.

The colonial state's essential modernity may be understood in three ways. First, as Hobsbawm (1994: 7) points out, the 'entire history of modern imperialism' may be encompassed within a long lifetime, and though the lifetime he chose was Winston Churchill's (1874–1965), it could have been Mohandas Karamchand Gandhi (1869–1948), Ho Chi Minh (1890–1967), born Nguyen Tat Thanh, the son of an Annamese mandarin, or Joseph Ravoahangy (1893–1970), Malagasy nationalist and scion of the Merina royal dynasty. Official careers also stretched from the early days of conquest in Africa and Southeast Asia to the struggles with anti-colonial nationalism; while many younger officials went on to enjoy 'second careers' after independence, including Pierre Messmer, High-Commissioner in Dakar in 1959, then de Gaulle's Minister of Armies and subsequently Prime Minister (Messmer 1992). A fair degree of continuity may be supposed in the 'official mind' and in colonial officials' efforts to contain and manage colonial disaggregation after 1945; some of these continuities will become apparent in the course of this study.

But, secondly, colonialism may be understood also as modern in a stronger sense, as an integral part of twentieth-century European cultural and political modernism. Thus, Mazower (1998: ix) argues that Europe too was 'in many respects very new, inventing and reinventing itself over this century through often convulsive political transformation'. Whereas we have tended to see European history culminating in the triumph of democracy at the end of the Cold War, for Mazower it is rather to be understood as a 'story of narrow squeaks and unexpected twists, not inevitable victories and forward marches', where the principal drama resided in the near-defeat of democratic values by those of fascism and its authoritarian near-relations (ibid.: xii). By viewing the history of colonialism from such a perspective (although Mazower's canvas is already broad enough, and stretches only fractionally wider in the teasing implications of his title), we may better understand some of the characteristics of colonial rule, and by extension the reasons for its demise.

To return to solar imagery, it would be a truism to state that the zenith of imperial splendour was also the first moment of decline. But given that the colonial empires reached their greatest extent in 1919–20, with the transfer in the Versailles and Sèvres Treaties of former German and Ottoman territories in Africa and the Near East to British, French, Belgian and South African rule, we may observe that placing transferred territories under League of Nations Mandate, while implying that some nations (i.e. Germany) were 'unfit' for colonial rule, introduced an element of international accountability to colonial rule.[4] More generally, the Paris peace process was guided by President Woodrow Wilson's doctrine of national self-determination, which ostensibly applied more widely than to the multi-national empires of Europe. As Füredi argues:

> Since the declaration of the Wilsonian principle of self-determination, nationalism has been accepted as a legitimate vehicle for asserting autonomy. This has presented a problem for the defenders of empire. Since 1919, it has not been possible to mount an intellectual case against the right of nations to self-determination. (1994a: 10)

The Bolshevik Revolution, too, directly challenged the imperial powers as bastions of the 'last stage of capitalism', and in 1919 established the Third International with the aim of actively bringing down those bastions. Moreover, as if on cue, the Paris Peace Conference coincided with the Indian National Congress's first prolonged, if as yet inchoate, challenge to British rule in India, in the 1919–22 campaigns of disobedience. At the same time, Japanese delegates to the Paris Peace Conference failed to secure a Racial Equality Clause in the League of Nations covenant, with far-reaching implications over the next quarter-century (Shimazu 1998). Thus, the modern era of 'institutionalized' colonial rule was accompanied from the outset by the ideological challenge characterized as the 'Moral Disarmament' of the British empire (Robinson 1979).

This is not to argue simply that the colonial states contained the seeds of their own ineluctable dissolution. Rather, colonial rulers were all the more sensitive to the need to legitimate their rule, and were constrained to couch their policy in recognizably modern terms, whether in the domains of administrative structures, revenue generation, labour policy, agriculture, health and welfare, town planning, internal security, external relations or trade. In other words, colonial states were implicitly accepted as normal parts of the modern world, and indeed, they served as 'laboratories of modernity' in many areas of state practice (Wright 1997; Martin 1996).

However, following Mazower, 'modern' does not mean as modern as all that, and the modernity envisaged in the interwar period might have taken a quite different direction – or indeed simply maintained the direction in which it was apparently headed. Thus the interwar European experience tended to reinforce arguments that democracy was 'not for export' outside of Northern and Western Europe, and was probably decadent even there. National self-determination could be equated with the harsh and often violent treatment of ethnic minorities across Central, Eastern and South-Eastern Europe; while nationhood was to British imperial eyes at best a paltry thing, which once acquired, would place, say, the grandeurs of Indian civilization on the same level as, say, 'Guatemala or Belgium'. Turning then to the overseas empires, not only did the ideological sea change of 1919 leave intact the 'civilizing missions' and presumptions of racial inequality implicit in colonial rule, but it was still generally held that 'Civilization', whatever that meant, had to be learnt over 'solar' timescales, and colonial states were instruments for that learning.

Thirdly, however, the colonial state was probably never intended to bear the burden of modern statehood that was thrust upon it. These were, after all, conquest states, their external boundaries defined by international rivalry, their often rickety internal structures and forms of government developed in the aftermath of military occupation, their legitimacy based on technological supremacy. Thus Darwin (1999: 73) describes the colonial state as a 'bundle of districts cellotaped together by colonialism into a dependency', while for Lonsdale:

> The colonial state was, and remained to the end, a conquest state . . . However successful the management of the colonial order was, and however placid the colonial order may have appeared to be, colonial rule always was predicated on the overt or hidden recourse to violence. (Lonsdale 1986a: 235)

The argument here is thus that colonial states were largely cobbled together from other entities with a quite different purpose, some derived from pre-colonial polities, others merely the by-products of imperial convenience, but which retained, as it were, a palimpsest of their origins in conquest. This is not to deny the seriousness of efforts by colonial governments to rule justly or rationally according to their lights, and, as we will see, those efforts intensified in the wake of the Second World War. Rather these efforts might be likened to the process of 'bricolage' described by Lévi-Strauss, for whom mythical thinking is comparable to the work of a handyman (bricoleur) who improvises with pre-existing 'second hand' materials, as opposed to the engineer, who designs everything for the purpose in hand (1962: 30–6). Like Lévi-Strauss's myths, colonial states were in a sense found objects constructed from the 'residues of human works', pressed into service according to a new and rapidly evolving purpose. Looking ahead to later chapters, by 1945 at the latest the colonial state was being subjected to ever more complex iterations of the handyman's craft, and that was even before the question was raised of passing on this improvised creation to new ownership. Indeed, at their most ambitious, the efforts of colonial reformers after 1945 often seemed like an attempt to remake the colonial state from bottom up, to make the shift, in Lévi-Strauss's terms, from bricolage to engineering. The corollary of this, of course, was that colonial rulers wanted to be around for long enough to see their work completed.

Decolonization and the Late Colonial Shift

How then do we articulate the critical shift from 'conjuncture' to 'event', that is, to the short-term political timescales of decolonization? This study does not diverge from the general consensus that this crisis was precipitated by the Second World War, the direct impact of which will be explored more fully in Chapter 3. But it is argued more generally that the War effected a profound shift in the perceptions of both colonizers and colonized concerning the purpose and future of empire. This will be referred to, in shorthand, as the *late colonial shift*, by association with the 'late colonial state', whose 'lateness' derived from its proximity to decolonization (Darwin 1999). This was experienced quite differently by the colonized and by the colonizing 'official mind', but for both it might broadly be characterised as a shift from a view of colonial rule as 'normal' and a stable fixture in the foreseeable future, to one predicated on rapid, possibly violent or radical political change, even if that change was not always immediately conceived in terms of national independence. What therefore chiefly characterized the late colonial state was an unprecedented degree of uncertainty, where the securities of colonial rule – administrative and military control, metropolitan confidence in imperial continuity, but also inaction, stagnation, repression – were superseded by flux, unpredictable change and fresh opportunities to seize the initiative. This is in fact what we mean by 'crisis' – a term which does out seem out of place when the whole colonial scene is surveyed after 1945, notwithstanding some relatively 'trouble-free' decolonizations.

The concept of a late colonial shift has two immediate analytical advantages for understanding decolonization. First, it allows us to cut across the question of whether colonial empire in 1939 was 'still remarkably resilient' (Darwin), or whether the colonial powers had already, like a latter-day court of Belshazzar, been weighed in the balance and found wanting. On the one hand, the 'steel frame' of colonial rule, as described by David Lloyd George in 1922, held firm, and the colonial 'pax' was maintained. Thus, even the Indian National Congress 'had been forced by 1937 to accept a federal constitution of whose long-term effects its leaders were rightly fearful' (Darwin 1991). The Indian case, and also the contrasting cases of interwar nationalism in Vietnam and Algeria, will be examined in Chapter 2. On the other hand, even before the cataclysm of the Second World War, the colonial powers were already having to work harder at colonialism's 'self-sustaining virtue of equilibrium' (Holland 1985: 1), as they confronted the deeper continuities of imperial instability, or of resistance or challenge to colonial rule, or contemplated the sort of policy reforms which were to become commonplace after 1945. Nationalist revolt or more general disorder in the interwar colonial state heralded the beginnings of progress towards independence from colonial rule, as nationalists in India, Vietnam, or the Dutch East Indies flexed their political muscle, while officials in the Central African Copperbelt, the West Indies, French North and West Africa and elsewhere sought to contain increasingly modern-looking social unrest. In other words, although the Second World War precipitated a crisis of far greater magnitude, colonial rule was coming up against its own internal contradictions. Berque's elegant formulation of this idea suggests both impending decolonization, and its inherent unpredictability: '. . . seen as a whole, the Maghreb in 1920 has moved beyond the opening Act. The drama has reached Act Two. But it would not be theatre if it did not leave some surprises for the denouement' (1969: 83).

Secondly, since all parties were now finding their way in an intrinsically open-ended process, the agency for decolonization need not be ascribed solely to the colonial powers or to nationalism. On the colonial side, the late colonial shift replaced the '*bricolage*' of the pre-1939 colonial state with a new sense of deliberate ambition in post-war imperial and colonial planning. Not that this planning was necessarily well-founded. On the contrary, it was typically based on persistent myths of colonial purpose, illusions of imperial strength or metropolitan political will, and on 'fantasy' visions of the colonized and their imagined futures (Cooper 1988; Lonsdale 1990). Nonetheless, it would be anachronistic to apply a simple ideological framework, whereby 'liberals' promoted or acquiesced in 'inevitable' decolonization, while a conservative 'old guard' sought to preserve colonial empire against the odds. According to this view, there probably *were* no liberals in the colonial administrations, since officials to a man (and they were almost all men) in London, Paris, Brussels and The Hague sought to preserve empire in some shape or form, or at the least to manage the process of colonial change over the medium to long term, and in that timescale, as John Maynard Keynes used to say, 'we are all dead' (or in the case of the British 'official mind', safely retired to Bath or Tunbridge Wells).

For political actors on the side of the colonized, encouraged by the outcomes of the Second World War, the late colonial shift was of a quite different order. No hard-and-fast distinction need be made between those who actively 'fought for freedom' against colonial rule, and those who accepted the invitation to the gaming table of Gallagher's putative 'imperial croupier'. Certainly, in a number of instances around 1945, anti-colonial nationalists seized the initiative from a hard-pressed, drastically weakened or temporarily eclipsed colonial regime: India, Vietnam and Indonesia spring to mind. 'Freedom fighters' of divers ideological varieties, and with varying strength of arms and of purpose, figure prominently in several cases. However, the Vietnamese defeat of French forces at Dien Bien Phu in 1954 was the great exception proving the general rule that colonial armies, even after 1945, inflicted military defeat more readily than they sustained it. On the other hand, the translation of military superiority into political triumph proved more elusive to colonial powers after 1945 than it had in earlier periods. More usually, and although many ostensibly 'peaceful' colonial states teetered on the brink of all-out disorder and violence, the colonial 'struggle' after 1945 was primarily a political one that stayed within official bounds, as colonial politicians responded to the challenge of official initiatives for reform or the limited devolution of political representation and responsibility. Moreover, as Cooper observes, the politics of decolonization 'appears less as a linear progression than as a conjuncture' and African political success was 'less a question of a singular mobilization in the name of the nation than of coalition building, the forging of clientage networks, and of machine politics' ([1994]2003: 36). In other words, we will often find ourselves dealing with 'politics as normal', although the 'normality' of late colonial politics proved to be short-lived as colonial states moved towards the endgame of the later 1950s.

After two introductory and complementary chapters, Chapter 1 addressing the pre-1939 colonial state, and Chapter 2 the character and outlook of indigenous political actors within that state, much of the remainder of this study is taken up with a series of case studies, which have been chosen to exemplify, and in part to synthesize, various aspects of decolonization. Faced with a historical process which touched a plurality of the member states of today's international community over the greater part of the twentieth century, the book's scope has been limited in a number of practical ways. First, it has seemed worthwhile to concentrate on depth rather than breadth of coverage. The cases chosen are relatively few in number, and may be seen as paradigmatic in various ways; or their interest may be attributed in part to their relative neglect in the literature of decolonization. These cases will mostly be examined in some detail, and many are covered across several chapters. Secondly, almost all cases are taken from the Asian and African formal empires of the four major European colonial powers: Britain, France, the Netherlands and Belgium. Of those regions excluded from study, the Middle East largely conformed to a different pattern of imperial over-rule and its demission after 1945, while smaller colonial dependencies in the West Indies, Pacific Ocean and elsewhere largely followed the Asian and African empires, in the timing if not in the manner of their decolonization. Thirdly, the timeframe is largely that of the 'twenty years crisis' after 1945, which may be seen as the 'classic' period of decolonization; this excludes 'late' decolonizations such as the Portuguese cases from consideration, but also more recent quasi-decolonization such as the South African transition to democracy or the handover of Hong Kong. On the whole, the 'end of the affair' in each case is the moment of independence, again for reasons of practicality, but also because it was arguably at this point that the bases for comparison began to diverge, as ex-colonial states embarked on their singular national histories. 'Impact', in the title of this book, should therefore not be taken to embrace the whole post-colonial history of the countries studied, but rather the recognition of how the often-convoluted and compressed processes of decolonization contributed to the sometimes surprising manner and suddenness with which formal empire came to an end.

The hypothesis of a late colonial shift is most easily tested in those cases where the Second World War led more or less immediately to decolonization, in South and Southeast Asia. In South Asia, as we will discuss in Chapter 3, British plans to reconcile Indian self-government with the maintenance of British interests were almost fatally compromised, first by the near-collapse of British rule, and secondly by India's chaotic partition into two separate Dominions. British faith in the ultimately meaningless formula of Dominion status within the British Commonwealth is further illustrated by the divergent cases of Ceylon and Burma. Conversely, even in the Southeast Asian dependencies, following the eclipse of colonial rule under the Japanese onslaught of 1942 (also studied in Chapter 3), it will be shown, in Chapter 4, how the European colonial powers attempted to launch their 'return' on the basis of more rational, 'engineered' state structures, and on the negotiation of new terms of engagement between the colonial state and its clients and antagonists; and how the attempt largely failed, not least because of an underestimation of the forces of nationalism ranged against the new colonial state.

Elsewhere, and particularly in Africa, the policies that emerged from post-war planning had a more decisive impact on the shape of the colonial empires, and thus also on decolonization. Indeed, it has been argued, for sub-Saharan Africa as a whole, that the impact of the Second World War was as momentous as that of eventual decolonization (Cooper 2002). This is a subject to which we will return extensively in Chapters 5 and 7. Clearly, African politics in this period was informed by mounting confidence in the possibility of progress towards self-government. However, it would be a mistake to seek to interpret the motivation of ordinary Africans in 1945 in terms of what had been achieved by, say, 1960.

What happened when the channels of 'normal' late colonial politics were blocked off, or the contradictions of colonial rule became too acute, and the late colonial state was forced to respond to armed challenges? In Chapter 6, we examine a number of key cases – Madagascar, Kenya, Algeria, Cyprus – where decolonization was thus dominated by armed insurgency and by the tactical panoply of colonial counter-insurgency. Here, it will be argued, 'lateness' brought not only a new urgency to anti-colonial resistance but also a newly systematic recourse to violence and repression on the part of the colonial state.

Finally, in Chapter 8 we turn to the concept of colonial 'endgame', and to the acceleration of decolonization as it reached a climax at the end of the 1950s. Here we examine not only the reappraisals on the part of the colonial 'official mind' which allowed metropolitan governments and colonial officials to contemplate rapid withdrawal from formal colonial rule, but also the consequences of these reappraisals for the shape and outcomes of decolonization.

Notes

1   The subsequent debate was premised, as Fukuyama's article was not, on the collapse of communist regimes across Central and Eastern Europe over the autumn of 1989.
2   Félix Houphouët-Boigny (1905–93): Ivorian political leader and member of the French parliament, and French minister in the 1950s, first President of Côte d'Ivoire from 1960 until his death.
3   The reference is to the French historian Fernand Braudel's (1980) subdivision of historical time into 'structure', i.e. over the *longue durée* lasting perhaps centuries, 'conjuncture', i.e. the length of economic cycles lasting up to perhaps a century, and 'event'. This article was written in 'this year of grace 1958' (ibid.: 34), a crowded year indeed for *'l'histoire événementielle'* in France and Algeria.
4   For the brief over-extension of British imperial responsibilities into Central Asia in this period, see Gallagher 1982. For the Mandate System, see Chamberlain 1998: 13–15; German territories in the Pacific were transferred to Australia, New Zealand and Japan.

The Colonial State: Patterns of Rule, Habits of Mind

Whatever the future may hold, the influence of the West upon India is likely to decrease. But it would be absurd to imagine that the British connection will not leave a permanent mark upon Indian life. On the merely material side . . . the largest irrigation system in the world . . . some 60,000 miles of metalled roads; over 42,000 miles of railways . . . 230,000 scholastic institutions . . . a great number of buildings . . . The vast area of India has been completely surveyed, most of its lands assessed, and a regular census taken of its population and its productivity. An effective defensive system has been built up . . . , it has an Indian army with century-old traditions, and a police force which compares favourably with any outside a few Western countries. The postal department . . . the Forestry Department . . . These great State activities are managed by a trained bureaucracy, which is today almost entirely Indian. (Thompson & Barratt 1934: 654, in Chatterjee 1993: 14–15)

REG: All right, but apart from the sanitation, the medicine, education, wine, public order, irrigation, roads, a fresh water system, and public health, what have the Romans ever done for us?
XERXES: Brought peace.
REG: Oh. Peace? Shut up! (Chapman et al. 1979)

. . . oxen taxes, taxes on 'chattering pigs', salt taxes, rice field taxes, ferry boat taxes, bicycle or conveyance taxes, taxes on betel or areca nuts, tea and drug taxes, lamp taxes, housing taxes, temple taxes, bamboo and timber taxes, taxes on peddlers' boats, tallow taxes, lacquer taxes, rice and vegetable taxes, taxes on cotton and silk, iron taxes, fishing taxes, bird taxes, and copper taxes. (The 'Asia Ballad', popular in the Tonkin Free School in 1907, in Scott 1976: 95)

Appointed French Minister of Colonies in 1906, Etienne Clémentel is said to have exclaimed: 'Ah, the colonies, I didn't know there were so many!' Aside from what this may tell us about colonial expertise amongst the French Third Republic's legions of parish-pump politicians, Clémentel's professed ignorance also reflected the novelty of the map's message. At the time, although the Algerian agricultural lands and mountains had been divided into *départements* on the metropolitan model in 1848, the huge southern wedge of the Algerian Sahara had only been formally annexed in 1902; the federation of French West Africa (*Afrique Occidentale Française*, AOF), centred on the Government-General at Dakar, was barely more than ten years old, and a second Federation of French Equatorial Africa (*Afrique Equatoriale Française*, AEF) was not established until 1910. The French Republic had only annexed Madagascar in 1896. Laos, the final part of the constitutional jigsaw of French Indochina, was fitted into place in 1897. In 1905, France headed off the German Kaiser's efforts to assert control of Morocco; the Treaty of Fez establishing France's protectorate of Morocco was signed in 1912. King Leopold's personal fiefdom of the Congo was granted to the Belgian state's care on his death in 1908. British, German and Portuguese territories in Africa too were at a skeletal stage of development: one District Officer (DO) in German East Africa (subsequently British Tanganyika) learnt of the Declaration of War in 1914 from his British colleague in Uganda, as there was no telegraph to his command from Dar es Salaam (Iliffe 1979: 119). The Dutch empire was still expanding from its Javanese and Sumatran core to embrace the 'Great East' of the East Indian archipelago. Japan and the United States had recently been admitted to the hitherto European club of colonial powers. The Russian empire, too, had its colonial components, although the Tsar had taken the precaution of selling Alaska, the only part of his empire to be separated from Russia by 'blue water'.

The map's core message lay in the bright and uniform colours of the rival empires. Arguably, Republican concepts of Overseas France or Greater France relied on the impression left by the map of territorial contiguity, stretching from the *Manche* (otherwise known as the English Channel), across the Mediterranean to the Congo or, as General de Gaulle had it in the late 1950s, from Dunkirk to Tamanrasset (in southern Algeria). Portuguese aspirations to a *mapa côr de rosa* (rose-coloured map) in Southern Africa had been foiled by British imperial enterprise (MacQueen 1997: 4). The British thought more in longitudinal terms of an empire 'where the sun never set'. This perpetual sunshine bathed the settler colonies of Canada, Australia, New Zealand, and South Africa, although by this time these were self-governing (South Africa definitively so in 1910). Imperial light also reflected upon areas of informal empire, notably in China and South America, where British influence was determined by trade and investment, or of indirect rule (for example, Egypt); these were more decisive to British power than duly coloured territories in, say, East Africa. But the light burned brightest on the vast Indian empire, which embraced Burma and controlled East Africa, and which exerted a determinant influence on British control of Egypt.

If the pre-1914 imperial map thus reflected the near-culmination of a period of rapid imperial consolidation, its gaudy homogeneity glossed over the reality of colonial state-building, mostly still in its infancy; this forms the focus of this chapter. The European colonial presence was much more fully established in, say, British India or French Algeria, but even here the modern forms of colonial rule in these dependencies only came into being after 1858 in India, when imperial rule was first organized under a Viceroy following the Sepoy Rebellion, and after 1871 for Algeria, where the establishment of the Third Republic triggered widespread revolt by Algerian Berbers; this led as in India to a tightening of administrative structures and to the crushing of further resistance.

Although much of this chapter necessarily relates to the pre-1945 period, we are less concerned here with 'what happened before decolonization', than with identifying approaches and reflexes which still operated, not always fully consciously or deliberately, in the period of the 'late' colonial state. We return first to the colonial map and to the ways in which it shaped colonial rule. Two corollaries of this structure of rule need to be examined in two reciprocal sections, in this and the following chapter: first, the significance of what imperial historians have come to call the 'collaborator system'; and secondly, the issue of control and repression, where the question of that which was to be controlled or repressed forms a large part of the next chapter's focus. We then examine aspects of colonial administrative structure, and in particular the implications of a 'Prefectural' system of rule characterized by a low ratio of rulers to ruled across the colonial empires. Finally, the colonial state may be considered an 'open polity', which is to say open to metropolitan and, increasingly, international influence, whether that process was managed deliberately by a 'gatekeeper' state, or outside the control of the state.

Of particular concern is the outlook of colonialism's 'official mind', a term first used by Robinson and Gallagher (1961), but which also finds an analogy in Lévi-Strauss's near-contemporary work, *The Savage Mind* (*La Pensée sauvage*, 1962). Although the term is often taken as a given, such an approach becomes impossible in a comparative work in which there are many such 'minds' at work. We will therefore address ways in which 'official minds' were formed and reproduced, as well as the doctrines which underpinned their rule, and the ways in which colonial officials adjusted to the demands of modern state practice. But if the metaphor is to be applied fully, it must be assumed that the collective or institutional 'mind' was structured with no less complexity than that of the individual: it functioned partly on the basis of habit and memory, it was sometimes self-contradictory, and frequently irrational. Moreover, this official consciousness was often introverted, that is, although it responded to external stimuli, it was quite capable of planning and debating with a largely theoretical frame of reference to the outside world. Conversely, although its internal equivocations may be of great interest, it was by its actions that it would be judged by the outside world.

Mapping the Colonial State

Seeking to understand colonial rule in terms of lines and colours on the imperial map is like using a space telescope in place of a pair of binoculars: the realities of rule are to be found much closer to the ground than the map allows. Nonetheless, the map is important, not least because of its durability: Clémentel's surprise would have been still greater had he known that, barely two generations later, the map's outlines would survive largely unchanged into the post-colonial world, with only the bitterly contested partition-lines of India, Palestine and Cyprus, and perhaps the 'balkanization' of French sub-Saharan Africa, to mark the transition from administrative boundaries to national frontiers. Following Anderson (1991: 163ff.), the colonial map was one of three institutions, along with the museum and the census, with which the 'imaginings of the colonial state' unwittingly but indelibly marked the formation of the 'imagined communities' of post-colonial nationhood.

The map of Africa reflected perhaps most dramatically the arbitrariness of colonial rule. Straight lines on the map cut across pre-colonial political and ethnic boundaries, usually in favour of far larger entities: African 'partition' was in reality 'a ruthless act of political amalgamation, whereby something of the order of 10,000 units was reduced to a mere 40' (Oliver 1991: 184, in Wilson 1994: 20). Partition created barriers in the mind where none existed in reality: the mapping of the Sahara, especially the massive wedge of the Algerian Southern Territories, tells us more about the French army's influence in Paris (outweighing that of the 'junior' colonial ministry responsible for neighbouring French Soudan, Niger and Chad), than it does about Saharan political geography. Newly created territories were named after geographical features (Niger, Oubangui-Chari, Haute-Volta), much as were French *départements*, and with not dissimilar intent, imposing a new identity rather than admitting pre-existing local identities. Alternatively, they commemorated matters of European significance (Côte d'Ivoire, Gold Coast, Rhodesia), or otherwise reflected the European imperial illusion of creating *ex nihilo*.[1] In 1920, most of German East Africa became the British Tanganyika Territory under League of Nations Mandate; this name, meaning 'muddy village' in Swahili (after the lake), was chosen in preference to Smutsland, Eburnea, Azania, New Maryland, Windsorland, Victoria, Kilimanjaro and Tabora (Iliffe 1979: 247).

Partition typically preceded both the occupation of the territories concerned and the precise determination of boundaries. In the Algerian case, the 1909 Niamey Convention settled the boundaries between Algeria and the two sub-Saharan federations, but even then, these were delimited, rather than demarcated, frontiers: in other words, they were literally drawn onto the map, but left no physical trace on the Saharan landscape, and indeed nothing changed after independence (Brownlie 1979: 26–88). Boundaries between the colonial powers were far more significant than internal ones, and became hostile frontiers in both world wars; this was also the case for the two federations of French West and Equatorial Africa, which came under Vichyste and Gaullist authority respectively from 1940 to 1943 (Chapter 3). Even before that, the French had established an informal system of 'watertight bulkheads' reflecting rivalries between the Interior Ministry and the Army in Algeria, the Ministry of Foreign Affairs, responsible for the Moroccan and Tunisian protectorates, and the Ministry of Colonies (AOF, AEF) (Young 1988: 32–3; Shipway 2002). The colonial powers continued to reorder the African map. German Kamerun and German East Africa were both re-partitioned, with the former divided into French and British Mandated territories, and Belgian Mandated Ruanda-Urundi carved from German-held territory on Lake Tanganyika's western shore. Haute-Volta was absorbed into Côte d'Ivoire in 1931, in order to regulate labour migration from the interior to the coastal plantations; in 1948, Haute-Volta was recreated, largely to suit Parisian party rivalries, rather than administrative rationality (Chapter 5).

These moves set precedents for colonial efforts to make the later colonial state more obviously 'state-like', or eventually to establish units which, when self-government came, might promote the interests of the (ex-)colonial power in the region. Thus the cumbersome and ill-fated Central African Federation embraced the very differently composed territories of Southern and Northern Rhodesia and Nyasaland. Conversely, the French African Federations, which lasted until the late 1950s as late colonial 'super-states', were split into territorial units by Gaston Defferre's Framework Law of 1956. This law reinforced the powers of elected 'national' assemblies and set francophone Africa on the path to a 'balkanized' decolonization (Chapters 7 & 8).

Imperial cartography in Asia was typically based on pre-existing states and empires and on a more widely established imperial presence, but it similarly reflected imperial *raison d'état* and continuity more than local political realities. Here too, spatial boundaries were a European innovation, defining statehood in terms of territorial sovereignty, but also of imperial spheres of influence. This was true even for a state, Thailand, that was allowed to resist imperial encroachment, but whose national boundaries were imposed by surrounding British and French imperialism (Anderson 1991: 170–4). The Dutch imperial presence dated back several centuries in Java and Sumatra, but the Dutch East Indies were extended to carve out a sphere of influence, in response to perceived international pressure in the early twentieth century (van den Doel 2001). French Indochina, so named by French geographers, similarly agglomerated a decades-long process of conquest and annexation (Aldrich 1996: 73–82). The boundaries of both these colonial states subsequently acquired a degree of solidity in nationalist eyes. While Indochina eventually lost the status of 'map-as-logo', in the face of stronger claims to Vietnamese identity (Goscha 1995), Indonesian President Ahmed Sukarno continued after independence to lay claim to a Greater Indonesia embracing Western New Guinea (*Irian Jaya*), until the Dutch relinquished even that vestige of empire in 1963; conversely, expansionism rather than 'irredentism' may better explain Indonesia's thirty-year occupation of the former Portuguese colony of East Timor (Anderson 1991).

The European empires in Asia ostensibly respected at least the outward form of pre-existing sovereignties, but this respect was heavily tempered by *realpolitik*. Thus, the map of the British Raj in India, the most powerful colonial state of all, was inscribed with a long history of imperial conquest, the realization of strategic necessities, for instance the guarding of the North-West Frontier against Afghan and possible Russian attack, and the persistence of rival imperial interests in the form of French and Portuguese enclaves (Pondichéry and the other French Indian Establishments; Portuguese India, now Goa). It also reflected unequal treaties signed with the rulers of the nearly six hundred Princely States, acquiescing to British rule following the 1857 Sepoy Rebellion. Ranging from tiny principalities to the vast domains of Kashmir and Hyderabad, these states constituted some two-fifths of Indian territory where British rule was exercised indirectly by a Resident or political agent. In Malaya, too, British rule was mediated through a complex system of Federated and Unfederated Malay States, established between 1893 and 1909, whose rulers' independence was recognized by the British. Only Singapore and the Straits Settlements, representing the core of British power in Malaya, came under direct British rule. In practice, the Sultans did not enjoy the freedom of political manoeuvre allowed even to the Indian princes, although the British were able to 'pay lip service to the Malay concept of sovereignty', particularly the Sultans' status as religious leaders (Smith 1995). Indochina's five administrative units, Laos, Cambodia, Cochinchina, Annam and Tonkin, concealed a patchwork of protectorates, concessions and only one actual colony, Cochinchina, which thus elected a settler to the French National Assembly. Although the Emperor of Annam retained his throne until 1945, his nominal rule extended only to 'Annam', the central portion of Vietnam: Cochinchina had been ceded to France, which also ruled Tonkin 'on behalf of' the Emperor. Dutch practice with regard to local rulers across the Indonesian archipelago broadly followed that of the French: local sovereigns were treated essentially as agents of the colonial state, although the panoply of courtly and religious ceremony was retained (van den Doel 2001).

The colonial map contradicted any idea of nationhood corresponding to established colonial boundaries, and not only those of rectilinear African cartography. 'India' was claimed as an imperial creation, and emphatically not the domain of a pre-existing nation. By the same token, 'Indians' were portrayed as ineluctably divided against themselves by race, caste or religious community. As the Secretary of State for India, Lord Birkenhead, put it in 1925, it was absurd to speak of an Indian nation: 'There never has been such a nation . . . If we withdraw from India tomorrow, the immediate consequences would be a struggle à outrance between the Muslim and the Hindu population' (in Sarkar 1989: 228). As will be argued, this was in part a self-fulfilling prophecy, since the effect of British policy, if not its intention, was to deepen such communal divisions. The official non-existence of an Algerian nation was all the more forcefully argued because of Algeria's unique status as an assimilated extension of metropolitan territory, according to which 'Algeria is France'. The term 'Algerian' was thus applied generally to all inhabitants of Algeria, and perhaps preferentially to European settlers (to whom we return below), while the indigenous population was labelled variously 'Muslim', 'Algerian Muslim' or 'French Muslim'; indeed as French 'subjects', they did not even appear in French immigration statistics, although large-scale Algerian immigration to the French mainland began in the 1920s (Stora 1993).

Colonial 'divide and rule' policies and attitudes recur in various guises, but it was the map-makers' 'ruling' which initially determined the dividing. The colonial state excluded defeated national or proto-national polities, often for the duration of the colonial period. French officials even in 1945 deployed the historical record of conquest to deny Vietnam's existence, claiming that all five Indochinese 'countries' were geographically, historically and ethnically distinct (Chapter 4). The conqueror of Madagascar, General Gallieni, promoted a powerful narrative of Malagasy history, which cast the French as protectors of the 'coastal peoples' from the dominant Merina people, whose kingdom had been destroyed by the French; fifty years after the annexation, this 'official version' was still being used to explain Malagasy politics, and in particular the 1947 insurrection (Shipway 1996a; Tronchon 1974/1986). As this example also shows, the colonial state embraced and 'protected' favoured minority groups. Thus, Algerians were subdivided into 'Arabs' and 'Berbers', including particularly the Kabyles of the mountainous Algerian hinterland, around whom powerful stereotypes were elaborated (Lorcin 1995). Where the colonial map overlaid pre-existing states, minorities were corralled into quasi-states within the state, such as the Hill States in Burma, or the more informally recognized ethnic minority groups of Indochina, to be protected from more central 'nationalisms' (Christie 1996; Salemink 1995). Berbers and Indochinese so-called 'montagnards' are also examples of minority 'martial races' favoured for recruitment into colonial armies, and typically selected from 'backward' or otherwise peripheral groups, alongside Punjabi Muslims (as opposed to, say, 'effeminate' Bengalis), Nigerian Tiv, Kenyan Masai or the Christian Ambonese islanders of the Royal Dutch Indies Army.

The colonial map also formalized patterns of imperial *bricolage* in its accommodation of migrant communities. These derived from multiple origins, whether resulting from trading patterns located in a regional *longue durée*, or more directly from European imperialism. At its most brutally coercive, 'migration' included the transportation of slaves to the plantation islands of the Caribbean and the Indian Ocean. Even after slavery was abolished by the British in the 1830s, and by the French Second Republic in 1848, its social and economic legacy remained 'the central fact of colonial times' (Young 1988: 39), while a plantation economy ensured that the colonial state remained minimal and problematic. The French so-called 'Old Colonies' were assimilated into the Republic, with voting rights for emancipated slaves; after the Second World War they were more fully assimilated, and thus in some respects decolonized, as '*Départements d'Outre-Mer*' (Overseas Departments) (Chapter 5). But these plantation societies remained vestiges of an older-style colonialism, 'holding operations' (Young, 1988) which the late colonial state would fail to modernize satisfactorily. Emancipation also necessitated a diversified labour pool, leading to further migration, this time of indentured labourers, creating far-flung diasporas, mostly Indian and Chinese in origin. Migrant communities of labourers and traders were a distinctive feature of colonial societies, not only in the plantation colonies, but also in British East Africa, in Fiji and in Malaya. The more 'state-like' the colonial state became, the more these groups were accommodated within the political order. In Malaya, the abortive Malayan Union Policy of 1945–6 attempted to integrate the Indian and Chinese communities within a colonial state which had hitherto favoured the indigenous Malays, whom together they outnumbered (Chapter 4). Colonial censuses played a crucial role in assigning both communal identities within the colonial state and quasi-national identities between states, so that, however artificially, the Chinese subject of, say, the Dutch East Indies could readily be distinguished not only from a Javanese Malay, but also from a Chinese subject of the British Straits Settlements (Anderson 1991). This too could turn into a way of imagining national communities, even if it primarily served to emphasize specific colonial jurisdictions.

The final group of migrants accommodated by the colonial state were European settlers, but here the problems were of a different order. European settlement was a large part of the rationale for colonial expansion, and from the perspective of the British empire, represented something like the imperial norm. Moreover, to the extent that colonial rule was still considered normal across much of Africa after 1945, the concept of white-settled Africa was an important component of that normality, even if South Africa is left out of account. Settlers numbers grew substantially after 1945, much more rapidly than stagnant birth rates allowed, as new waves of emigrants bolstered the already substantial political clout of settler communities in Morocco and Tunisia, Southern Rhodesia and Kenya, Angola and Mozambique: in each of these six countries, settler numbers increased by more than half in the period between 1945 and independence, although only in Portuguese Africa was this a matter of government policy.[2] Even where settler numbers were stable, as in Algeria, or remained a tiny minority, as in French sub-Saharan Africa or the Belgian Congo, they wielded political influence out of all proportion to their number, and British, French and Belgian officials and politicians exercised considerable ingenuity to ensure their continued representation in late colonial constitutional arrangements. Moreover, much as liberal officials or politicians might loath the racial attitudes of settlers, the thrust of late colonial reform favoured them, not necessarily *as* settlers, but as dynamic agents for economic growth. Settlerdom was also supported by British sentimental ties of 'kith and kin' or by myths of a 'Greater France' or a luso-tropical greater Portugal, or Eurafrica, or by the idea of pioneers settling a new 'Far West'. Amongst settler populations, the Europeans of Algeria came closest to white South Africans in their demographic weight and social cohesion (to say nothing of their politics), numbering almost a million in the late 1940s alongside an Algerian population of some eight million. The so-called *pieds noirs* were – not entirely implausibly – coming to regard themselves as possessed of roots, culture and other attributes of a proto-national 'Mediterranean' identity, distinct not only from Algerians but also from the French metropole. They had also established the prerogative to block attempts at even the most cautious of political or constitutional reforms.

Patterns of Rule: the Collaborator System, the 'Thin White Line' and the 'Official Mind'

Colonial rule comes most clearly into focus when viewed at the local scale, and, just as Thomas Hobbes's Leviathan state was a composite of its individual citizens, so too patterns of colonial rule were created from the bottom up, starting at the interaction between the individual colonial administrator and local groups and 'big men', moving up to the level of the colonial state. The discussion here will centre on two inter-related concepts. The first of these is the 'collaborator system', whereby the functioning of the colonial state depended on the collaboration of indigenous groups or local rulers, thus enabling colonial rulers to maintain the benefits of empire while exercising the minimum degree of power consistent with the maintenance of imperial authority. The theme of 'collaboration', its implications for political actors on the side of the colonized, and the objections which may be raised to the term itself, is an important one to which we will return extensively in the following chapter. For the moment, however, it is the colonial side of this equation which chiefly interests us. We therefore consider a further essential principle of colonial rule, encapsulated in the image of a 'thin white line' of European colonial administration (Kirk-Greene 1980). This then leads us to explore the training, outlook and worldview of colonial field officers.

Concepts of collaboration (and, by extension, of resistance) are central to the 'peripheral' or 'excentric' theory of imperialism, and have been deployed to help explain every stage of colonial rule, from conquest to decolonization. Thus, modern colonialism developed from patterns of collaboration on which depended pre-colonial free trade imperialism and the still-preferred British system of informal empire. Formal colonial rule was established where collaborating rulers had ceased to become reliable, perhaps as a result of internal crisis, typically resulting from increased demands by the imperial powers, as in the case of the British occupation of Egypt in 1882, which in turn inspired 'much of the subsequent rivalry impelling the partition of Africa' (Robinson 1972). However, imperial reliance on collaboration soon transcended its origins in the diplomatic expedient of imperial protection. Rather, the designated function of collaborating rulers, landlords and other 'big men' was as agents for imperial interests, for example tax collection, labour recruitment and maintaining local law and order. In essence, as in India, collaboration necessitated a political bargain, according to which revenue was collected without too many questions asked about who paid, while public order was taken for granted by the British without them taking too obtrusive a part in it (Seal 1973: 13). At times of public disorder, or widespread crisis such as the Indian Non-Cooperation movement of 1919–22, the British could persuade themselves that peasant unrest was not primarily directed at British rule, but at the inequities of Indian land rents (for which the Raj could disclaim all responsibility) (Pandey 1988). This was a dynamic system developing over time, as the Raj increased its demands and hence its need for wider systems of collaboration. The links between this system and the development of Indian nationalist politics will be explored more fully in the following chapter.

A parallel argument can be made for British Africa, where collaboration was elevated to a formal doctrine, but here the pattern of change was more imperceptible. The principles of Indirect Rule, which found their most complete expression in Lord Lugard's 1922 treatise, *The Dual Mandate in British Tropical Africa*, were inherently conservative. Drawing on Lugard's experience of conquest and pacification in Uganda and Northern Nigeria, and on wider European perceptions of 'traditional' patterns of rule, these were widely applied in Africa. Lugard noted the vigorous resistance of the Muslim Fulani emirates in Northern Nigeria, and their well-developed systems of taxation and justice, and argued that traditional rulers should be incorporated into the colonial system rather than rejected by it. Although dressed in the admirable rhetoric of modernizing colonial liberalism, Indirect Rule tended to shield the Northern emirates from change, whether that change came from the more intensively colonized South or from within. By the 1920s, Lugard was old-fashioned enough to see his policy as a safeguard against the growing influence of the so-called 'trousered African' of popular imperial prejudice, that is, the mission-educated and 'detribalized' Africans from whose ranks later nationalist cadres would indeed be recruited (Cell 1999).

The orthodoxy of Indirect Rule had been largely superseded well before the Second World War, but even its more liberal successor doctrine of Indirect Administration was arguably founded on a series of 'working misunderstandings' (Dorward 1974). Thus, although British administrative practice was based on extensive ethnographical research, the relationship between colonial ethnography and administration was largely circular and mutually supportive. British efforts to apply Indirect Administration in Tanganyika 'owed much to the Old Testament, to Tacitus and Caesar', but most to modern academic conceptions of African tribes as cultural units 'possessing a common language, a single social system, and an established common law'. The problem in Tanganyika was that these criteria rarely obtained, and that even where they applied, this was largely the result of Tanganyikans' creative efforts to elaborate or invent tribal histories (Iliffe 1979: 322–4; Spear 2003).

The myth of the 'thin white line' certainly suggests the extent to which 'the system worked', relying as it did on an elaborate network of indigenous 'collaborators' in the guise of chiefs and other 'big men', but also subordinate officials, clerks and translators, policemen and troops. Although the very sparseness of an official European presence across colonial territories was commonly taken as evidence of the extent of colonial 'pax' and as an eloquent demonstration of the consent of colonial subjects, the frequency with which the theme recurs suggests an underlying anxiety. The mantra was often uttered at moments of tension, as in the 'somewhat smugly' worded report of the 1935 Commission of Enquiry into labour riots on the Northern Rhodesian Copperbelt: 'To set down two or three British officials at an outstation to rule 100,000 natives, with a handful of police to keep order, is a customary British risk which many years of colonial development has proved to be successful' (in Hargreaves 1996: 10). A similar pattern of revolt and its suppression in 'police actions' which barely register in the records of colonial military action may be found across many parts of an over-extended interwar British Empire in, for example, Mesopotamia and the Southern Sudan. Thus, the Royal Air Force weathered the storm of post-1918 disarmament in large measure because of the capacity it offered for exercising low-level control at long distance (Omissi 1990).

Colonial rule was always a small-scale enterprise, constructed from the base upwards, and with its roots in arbitrary, sometimes brutal, but often fleeting personal contact between individual European officials and the communities they nominally commanded. It was also fundamentally parsimonious: until the last decade or two of development funding from a grudging metropolitan centre, colonies were self-sufficient, reliant on the revenues and labour which the administrators were called upon to extract. Thus, a French law passed in 1900, mirroring British practice, forbade any colonial budgetary drain on the French state, to the extent that French colonial officer cadets were trained at the expense of the Federation to which they were to be assigned; this was only effectively superseded by the introduction of the Investment Fund for Social and Economic Development (FIDES) after 1946 which channelled development funds from the imperial centre for the first time.

At the heart of the myth is the lone District Officer (or *commandant de cercle*, or his Portuguese, Dutch or Belgian equivalent) posted to a remote field station with poor communications to his superiors, whence he toured his district, probably on horseback or by other preferably unmotorized means,[3] and variously commanded, judged, counted and taxed hugely disproportionate numbers of loyal, or at least quiescent, subjects. Practice varied widely between the colonial powers, but field officers were deployed in spectacularly small numbers. Thus, the young Robert Delavignette found himself posted in the early 1920s to the *Cercle* of Zinder, in Niger:

> The *Cercle* ruled over the ten thousand souls in the town and the 135,000 who lived in outlying cantons. There were seven *Cercles* in the territory of Niger, the cultivable area of which was more than half the size of France and had a population of a million souls. Seven *Cercles*, with twenty-one administrators and thirty-nine agents of the Native Affairs bureau: sixty officers in all. And in French West Africa, which was eight times bigger than France and had a population of fifteen million, there were 118 *Cercles*. (Delavignette 1940: 21)

The interwar colonial service in British Africa numbered slightly more than 1,200 men, spread over a dozen colonies with populations of some 43 million spread over more than two million square miles. The Indian Civil Service was staffed by a maximum of

1,250 British officers, for a population (in the 1930s) of 353 million (Gallagher 1982; Cell 1999: 232). These numbers conceal essential differences between areas of direct and indirect rule, nor do they allow for the proportion of indigenous administrators, or for the larger numbers of administrators and ancillary staff at lower levels, both European and local: the 1931 Indian census recorded as many as a million government workers.

Accounts of the 'golden age' of colonial rule almost invariably make a virtuous principle of this arithmetic necessity, and the stock image of the DO out and about with only a walking stick formed an indelible part of colonial mythology. The evidence is typically anecdotal, but builds into a picture of a ritualized expression of authority, as in the following vignette, relating the public schoolboy's reflexes of one DO in Southern Tanganyika:

> D was in the habit of going for a long walk every evening, wearing a hat. When, towards sunset, he came to the point of turning for home he would hang his hat on a convenient tree and continue on his way hatless. The first African who passed that way after him and saw the hat was expected to bring it to D's house and hand it over to his servants, even if he was going in the opposite direction. If he ignored the hat he would be haunted by the fear that D's intelligence system would catch up with him. (Lumley 1976, in Ranger 1983: 216)

Although the cultural referents might vary from empire to empire, the underlying reality was the 'routinization of hegemony' (Young 1988: 48). There was nothing specifically colonial about this prefectural system of rule, which has typically been deployed where 'there were perceived to be threats to the survival of the established regime and/or doubts about the compliance with its directives of significant sectors of the society' (Berman & Lonsdale 1992: vol. 2, 231). In the French case, it represented the colonial extension of the Napoleonic system of rule – still in force in modified form in today's French Republic – where the Prefects were uniformed representatives of the might of the state.

Colonial officers were necessarily versatile agents of government. Of the functions recorded by Hubert Deschamps, relating to his first command in southern Madagascar in the 1930s, most would have been recognized by a British DO:

> The administrator in my time was a Jack-of-all-trades of the bush: sub-prefect, gendarme captain, police commissioner, mayor, tax collector, judge, accountant, road engineer, nurseryman, mapmaker, land agent, customs agent, schools inspector . . . and more besides. He was on his own, in charge of everything, responsible for implementing innumerable regulations. (Deschamps 1975: 121)

By the mid-1940s, a further sub-prefectural role could be added, that of returning officer for the elections and referenda which multiplied in the post-1945 empires. Isolation and the heterogeneity of the societies overseen by these 'kings of the bush' placed a premium on improvisation and autonomous action: Deschamps' office volumes of the *Journal Officiel*, the very symbols of Republican legalism, went largely unconsulted, while British field officers were granted similarly large margins of discretion by their immediate superiors in the Provincial Administration. Personal authority and practical expertise took precedence over specialist administrative skills or close attention to regulations.

Training the Official Mind

The myth of the 'thin white line' invites investigation of the training and outlook of these 'kings of the bush', whose strength of character alone often seemed to hold together their vast, ramshackle domains. Conformity to the job's requirements was ensured via the recruitment process, on the assumption that a shared background and close identification with 'ruling class' values in the mother country would be translated into consistent and effective colonial rule. British colonial officials were overwhelmingly drawn from the propertied middle classes, had fathers who worked in the professions or the service sector (typically the City or senior civil service), probably grew up in the 'Home Counties' of south-eastern England, and followed the traditional privileged path of Public School followed by Oxford or Cambridge. Orthodoxy was further assured by a personalized system of recruitment; thus, one man, Sir Ralph Furse, oversaw recruitment to the colonial service from 1919 until 1948. It is debatable whether the more conventional, and rigorous, British system of Civil Service Selection Boards could have recruited with more consistency than Sir Ralph's 'keen eye for the merits of that admirable class of person whom university examiners consider worthy only of third-class honours' (Furse 1962: 9). Tough, competitive examinations for the ICS, and the more obviously academic criteria for selection to the Colonial Office, as opposed to the 'character' and athletic prowess required in the field, ensured intellectual mettle where it was needed, providing 'a true elite of scholar-official mandarins' (Hyam 1999: 259); the ICS drew on a wider geographic, if not social, catchment area for recruitment, with 'fewer athletes, but more Irish and Scots' (Cell 1999: 232–3).

French officials were recruited with the same aims of shared values and conformity of outlook, even if the methods employed differed substantially. An older generation of colonial officials were recruited rather haphazardly, but by the mid-1920s, the Colonial Corps increasingly consisted of graduates of the National School of Overseas France (ENFOM), which selected via state-run competitions for which students prepared for two years at one of an elite group of *lycées* (state high schools) in Paris and a few other large cities. This placed ENFOM on the same footing as other *grandes écoles* designed to train the state's elite of teachers, engineers, army and naval officers. Significantly, ENFOM was the only *grande école* which specifically trained administrators, before the creation of the *École Nationale d'Administration* (ENA) in 1945, and thus prefigured the 'technocratic' ethos of the present-day Fifth Republic (which often seems to be largely run by ENA graduates, whether politicians or civil servants).

Whereas the more prestigious *grandes écoles* tended to favour the sons (and, far more rarely, daughters) of a social and professional elite, often Parisian, ENFOM cadets in the interwar period (who would reach the highest ranks by the time of independence) were apparently recruited from middle class, less than grand, provincial backgrounds. As one official put it: 'The middle classes . . . have certain virtues which are well known. They make honest, reliable, and generally impartial agents of the State' (in Cohen 1971: 91).[4] French colonial officialdom's values were those of provincial bourgeois Republicanism, with sympathy for the (usually non-communist) Left, or for an emerging doctrine of Catholic humanism. As for the ICS, competitions favoured the Republic's periphery: in the late 1950s, three Corsicans, all called Colombani (two related), dominated Niger's administration (Colombani 1991: 177). Three years at ENFOM contrasted sharply with the 'generalist' British system: cadets studied for a law degree alongside more specialist courses in accountancy, languages, ethnography and, even, in the early days, fencing and horse-riding. Sanmarco criticizes the 'almost infantile conformism' of ENFOM in the early 1930s, preferring the more informal opportunities offered by the libraries and cafés of Paris (1983: 49–50). Nonetheless, he admits that training at ENFOM translated into a formidable *esprit de corps* amongst its graduates, which was a large part of its purpose. Of the 21 governors and governors-general of French colonial Africa who deliberated at the 1944 Brazzaville Conference, all but three were ENFOM graduates, and of those two were already past retirement age.

What then were the values which colonial officials applied to their work in the field? In the British case, we enter here on ground well trodden by contributors to a rich genre of colonial novels. But nothing in the fiction of Kipling (1900), Forster (1924), Cary (1939), Orwell (1935), Greene (1948), Scott (1966–75) *et alii* outdoes the imaginative myth-making and the 'invention of tradition' documented by Ranger (1983), who demonstrates the extent to which British officers drew not only on the neo-traditional forms and rituals of 'Imperial Monarchy', but also on the hierarchies of army, public school and country house. Thus colonized societies could be imaginatively recast according to familiar models of king and subjects, officers and men, school prefects and junior boys, or lords of the manor and retainers.[5] At its heart the ethos of British field officers was Barrington Moore's 'Catonism': 'the anti-rationalist, anti-urban, anti-materialist and anti-bourgeois response of the traditional landed ruling class to the development of modern industrial society' (Berman & Lonsdale 1992: vol. 2, 234). Having been co-opted as at least honorary members of the ruling class, administrators now applied its values in a very different context. Change might be inevitable, but it was to be jealously controlled, preserving the best of a pre-existing, but idealized, rural society. Moreover, true to the 'Whiggish' instincts of a reforming landlord, the rural 'man in a blanket' was to be protected against 'detribalized' urban upstarts, 'professional politicians' or even settlers, when, as happened in the 'White Highlands' of Kenya or in the even more extensively resettled lands of Southern Rhodesia, those interests ran counter to the DO's attempts to create a kind of 'Merrie Africa' (Pearce 1982: 181).

Many of these attitudes had their counterpart in the French outlook, although derived from very different cultural sources. The major distinction between British and French colonial doctrine lay in the French notion of assimilation, according to which French rule aimed to 'assimilate' colonial subjects to French standards of education, social development and, indeed, civilization. As de Gaulle's Commissioner of Colonies, René Pleven, put it succinctly before the Brazzaville Conference (which he chaired), the aim was 'to transform French Africans into African Frenchmen'. This was a rhetorical offshoot of the classic French republicanism that underpinned French efforts, under the Third Republic after 1870, to bring outlying provinces within the enveloping fold of the One and Indivisible Republic. This involved the deployment of the conscript army and the state school system to impose French social and educational norms, and in particular the French language, on peasants and peripheral cultures (Bretons, Corsicans, Provençaux and others) and thus to modernize French society by turning 'peasants into Frenchmen' (Weber 1976).

Assimilation was only one pole in a debate conducted throughout the period of French colonial rule. While assimilationists believed that the universal values of French civilization could be shared by all within a 'France of a Hundred Million Souls', this idea was dismissed as impracticable or undesirable by proponents of the less ambitious and superficially less attractive doctrine of Association, with its underlying idea of a racial hierarchy. This doctrine was derived from the experience of French empire builders, including such authorities as General Gallieni, Marshal Lyautey, founder of the French protectorate in Morocco, or Jules Harmand, who drew on a quarter-century's experience in Indochina. Thus, when in 1941 Félix Éboué, Gaullist Governor-General at Brazzaville, drew up a statement of 'The New Native Policy', he sought to apply to French Equatorial Africa the lessons learnt in Morocco by Lyautey 25 years before. Assimilationist doctrine was largely abandoned by 1919, in favour of a more realistic, less interventionist 'Republican' policy in French Africa (Conklin 1997; Le Sueur 2001: 20ff.). However, although pronounced dead by various colonial modernizers, the doctrine of Assimilation refused to lie down, perhaps because it bulked so large in French officials' ideological baggage. Moreover, policies derived from assimilationist ideas and those inspired by association could sit happily side by side: Éboué's 'New Native Policy' also proposed a statute for so-called 'notables évolués', that is, French-educated Africans who were to be allocated a key role in the projected new colonial order.[6] Notwithstanding heated arguments to the contrary, there was no necessary contradiction between 'associationist' policies and the idea of using French as the exclusive medium of education, as was recommended by Brazzaville, or of administration (since French officers were rarely in post for long enough to learn local languages).[7]

Moreover, French administrators saw themselves as members of a technocratic elite, but also as the sons of peasants. Thus Deschamps' rather Rousseauesque memoirs, published some thirty years after he left the service, offer a close approximation to the paternalism and the rural idylls more readily associated with British myth-making:

> Frenchmen, with rural roots in a more or less recent past, knew the intoxication of landownership, the pride in a well-maintained estate and in the progress brought to it . . . I flourished in these village societies close to my own origins. Having escaped from a limited society and from the gloomy prison of industrial urban life, I returned to my ancestors, while at the same time finding what I had long sought: a taste of exoticism, of difference, of a magical journey in time and space. (1975: 125–6)

In short, assimilation provided a self-justifying myth, and thus constituted the functional equivalent of the 'invented traditions' of British colonial practice, and a parallel fantasy of an idealized and 'eternal' society to be protected against the threat of any but the most organic and incremental of changes.

The District Officer, *commandant de cercle* and equivalents thus constituted the front line of colonial administration, their role legitimated by a tradition with its roots in conquest, their training and ethos grounded in key aspects of metropolitan political culture, their versatility justified by administrative necessity but in turn serving to illustrate the extent, and the benefits, of the colonial 'pax'. Colonial hierarchy was thus built from the base upwards, and policy had also to be mediated through field officers. The almost inevitable consequence was an inbuilt tendency to immobilism: while policy was important both at the establishment of colonial rule, and as it drew to a close, 'In between, the landscape was dominated by a system, not a policy' (Heussler 1971: 576; Berman & Lonsdale 1992: vol. 2, 233).

The Colonial State: an Open Polity?

The concept of the colonial state is a familiar one from the literature but not unproblematic, since in one obvious sense colonies were not states at all, but subordinate units in an imperial hierarchy. While in terms of colonial practice and tradition, colonial governors acted very much as 'proconsuls', and for most practical purposes the colony was the effective unit of government, colonial states might be called open polities (by analogy with open economies), in that they depended ultimately not only on policy directives from the metropolitan capitals, but also on the approval or acquiescence of domestic electorates. The ambivalence to which this gave rise was reflected in various ways, including the structures whereby colonial states were incorporated into imperial systems, but also the way in which a metropolitan political elite and its electoral clientele regarded (and quite often disregarded) the empire.

This ambivalence was reflected in the contrasting imperial frameworks within which a colonial dependency's legal status was established. The British colonial governor's relative freedom of action was assured by the system of 'crown colonies', derived from long experience of dealing with the Dominions of Canada, Australia, New Zealand and South Africa. This system vested law-making powers in a nominated Legislative Council composed of representatives of settler and commercial interests, and chaired by the governor, thus ensuring that each colony retained its legislative identity; in practice, this meant that the last word almost inevitably fell to the 'man on the spot', the governor. In this way the governor was given considerable powers to resist a proposed policy, and Whitehall was obliged to engage in prolonged consultation and, often, revision of its policy proposals. There were also profound differences in administrative culture or mission, so that it was difficult to consider implementing, say, West African policy in East Africa, and *vice versa*. This particularism was to have profound consequences for the pattern of British decolonization, as individual colonies each entered the process of devolving power according to its own timetable and its own tailor-made constitutional arrangements.

At its most extreme, British particularism found expression in a separate Government of India, answerable directly to the King-Emperor. The Viceroy was the grandest of proconsuls, and it is difficult to articulate meaningful comparisons with a case that was so spectacularly *sui generis*, since 'All-India' looked very much like an empire in its own right. There were other separate administrations, too, with their own ethos and traditions, some maintained by ministerial barriers, for example the Sudan, run by a Sudan Service which, for reasons of British Egyptian policy (Chapter 7), was run from the Foreign Office. Others, notably the Cyprus government, maintained autonomy through sheer force of inertia (Holland 1998).

An obvious contrast is suggested with the Republican tradition on which the French based their colonial administration. However, this contrast may be overstated, and substantial differences are sometimes indiscernible in the local impact of the two styles of colonial rule. To be sure, the preferred French administrative model was one of direct rule derived from French conceptions of a strong, centralizing state and the almost sacred doctrine of the 'One and Indivisible Republic', and the impact of principles derived from these was felt at every level. In contrast with British Crown Colonies, the French Republic instituted vast federations in West and Equatorial Africa and in Indochina (and a similar structure was proposed but never implemented in Madagascar), headed by a governor-general who amassed considerable powers, and to whom answered governors of individual territories. Legislative power was exercised not by the governors or governors-general, however, but notionally by the National Assembly in Paris, or more usually by Presidential decree or ordinances enacted by the governor.

In practice, the realities of imperial coordination softened the edges of this pyramidal geometry. Governors-general had a long proconsular tradition to uphold of defying or ignoring Paris, and were still capable in the 1940s and 1950s of presenting the metropole with some alarming *faits accomplis*. Thus although the Governments-General at Hanoi, Dakar, Brazzaville and Tananarive were created in order to coordinate policy between Paris and the colonial periphery, the incumbents were powerful officials who could defy Paris at will. Moreover, there were two significant exceptions to this adapted metropolitan model of the unitary Republic. The first was Algeria, which, since 1848, had been considered an integral part of the 'One and Indivisible Republic'. Although the representative of the state in Algeria was a governor-general, he was appointed by the Ministry of the Interior, and his immediate subordinates were the Prefects of the three *départements* (each subsequently sub-divided into four). Since European needs and interests dominated, the civil administration existed side-by-side with a more properly 'colonial' administration responsible for the majority Muslim non-citizen population. This translated into a corrupt system of indirect rule based on locally recruited '*caïds*' or headmen. The Algerian Southern Territories were governed directly by the Army, and were incorporated as *départements* as late as 1957. The two North African territories of Tunisia and Morocco constituted the second exception, as international protectorates under the treaties of 1881 and 1912, where the Bey of Tunis and the Sultan of Morocco retained notional sovereignty. Since they were governed by the Ministry of Foreign Affairs, the Moroccan and Tunisian administrations were protected to a degree, under an informal system of 'watertight bulkheads', from parliamentary scrutiny or from reformist initiatives originating in other ministries, particularly the Ministry of Colonies. By the same, largely fictional, principle of retained sovereignty, the League of Nations Mandates in Syria and Lebanon were also managed by the Ministry of Foreign Affairs (Shipway 2002; Longrigg 1958).

The efforts of colonial ministries to rationalize and coordinate colonial or imperial policy could often be blocked or resisted by appeals to the greater knowledge and experience of the 'man on the spot'. The voluminous correspondence between ranking governors and metropolitan-based officials was informed by an effective gulf between separate administrative cultures. Simply expressed, pith helmets or ostrich plumes (or the less ostentatious *képi* of the French governor) were greatly to be preferred to, say, bowler hats and rolled umbrellas. But the converse perception in both the British and the French services was more commonly expressed, of a metropolitan-based ministerial staff out of touch with the realities of colonial life. Thus Deschamps, appointed in 1936 as private secretary (*chef de cabinet*) to the incoming Socialist Minister of Colonies, Marius Moutet, confronted a 'cult of incompetence' whereby Parisian officials sought to minimize the influence of officers returning from a colonial posting, for fear that their own control over policy would be lessened (1975: 127–8). An informal tradition of 'beachcombing' allowed members of the British Colonial Service to serve a term in Whitehall, and the regular traffic in the opposite direction by which junior Colonial Office officials spent a year or two overseas, usually in a Colonial Secretariat, went some way towards reducing the cultural gap, although this was inevitably an *ad hominem* solution (Parkinson 1947).

Colonial ministries' capacity to coordinate policy was further affected by their low position within the ministerial pecking order. The British Colonial Office in the interwar period went a long way towards establishing new structures for the modernization of colonial policy through the delivery of technical expertise, establishing functional departments to cover the increasing range of responsibilities in the realms of economic and social policy, a development viewed somewhat wryly by the Permanent Secretary of the period, Sir Cosmo Parkinson (ibid.). In reality, these new departments often merely shadowed the work of separate departments of state or ministries with a different perspective and set of priorities. Paradoxically, as the colonies came to be perceived as more central to British economic prosperity after 1945, the Ministries of Food and Supply would lead the so-called 'second colonial occupation', sometimes against the interests and better judgement of the Colonial Office and Colonial Service, as was the case for the infamous postwar Groundnut Scheme (Iliffe 1979: 442).

One of the paradoxical rules of thumb of colonial administration might thus be expressed as the tendency for the oxygen of influence to become more rarefied nearer the summit of the governmental pyramid. British Colonial Secretaries and French Ministers of Colonies alike tended to be either politicians with little influence within government as a whole, or conversely men for whom the colonial portfolio was a convenient passport to Cabinet rank, but who had little interest in, or knowledge of, colonial affairs. Politicians with a long-term interest in colonial affairs while in opposition, such as Marius Moutet (French Socialist Minister of Colonies, 1936–7, and Minister of Overseas France, 1946–7) or Arthur Creech Jones (British Labour Secretary of State, 1946–50), were a relative rarity. But colonial affairs tended anyway to be the concern of committees, and the major British and French parties each had their contingent of colonial 'experts'. Colonial policy as such thus had relatively little impact on the national political agenda, except, of course, in the event of crisis when the minister or his department could conveniently be blamed.

Notes

1 Slave Coast had disappeared from the map. Except where there are commonly accepted English forms – for example, Algeria, Dutch East Indies, Indochina – colony names are given in the form imposed by the colonizer, especially where there might otherwise be confusion – for example, between German Kamerun, French Cameroun, and the British Cameroons, French Soudan (Mali), vs the Anglo-Egyptian Sudan.

2 Wilson (1994: 125–7) gives the following figures for European settlers in East and Central Africa (to which add the ratio Africans:Europeans): 207,000 in Southern Rhodesia in 1958 (13:1), 72,000 in Northern Rhodesia in 1958 (31:1), 67,700 in Kenya in 1960 (93:1).

3 As Berque (1969: 67) comments, the advent of the motor car severely reduced the contact possible between French officers and their subjects.

4 The 'governor-general of Indochina in the 1940s' is presumably Léon Pignon, High Commissioner in Indochina, 1948–50, a schoolmaster's son from Angoulême. Of the other French officials cited, Delavignette was the son of a Burgundian sawmill manager, Deschamps of a bailiff from Western France; a third ex-colonial memoir-writer, Louis Sanmarco (1983), was the son of an immigrant Italian docker in Marseille. See also Bourdieu 1989.

5 On the British 'public schools' (i.e. private, usually boarding schools), Cell 1999: 233n.; for a subversive post-imperial account, see Lindsay Anderson's 1969 film *If . . .* : the headmaster now sees his charges as future television directors rather than DOs.

6 '*Evolués*' ('evolved persons') was the unflattering term applied to French- or Belgian-educated Africans; '*notables*' were dignitaries or 'big men', originally those to be found in small French towns.

7 On Brazzaville, see Chapter 5. According to one British official in the 1930s, the French aim of 'creating a new race of black Frenchmen' would 'hasten the decline & fall of western civilization', in Ashton & Stockwell 1996: doc. 125 & lxxvii.

Colonial Politics Before the Flood: Challenging the State, Imagining the Nation

Hardly ever have I known anybody to cherish such loyalty as I did to the British Constitution. I can see now that my love of truth was at the root of this loyalty. It has
never been possible for me to stimulate loyalty or, for that matter, any other virtue.
The National Anthem used to be sung at every meeting that I attended in Natal. I then
felt that I must also join in the singing. Not that I was unaware of the defects in British
rule, but I thought that it was on the whole acceptable. . . .

I therefore vied with Englishmen in loyalty to the throne. With careful perseverance
I learnt the tune of the National Anthem and joined in the singing whenever it was sung.
(Gandhi 1926: 142–3)[1]

'Down with the English anyhow. That's certain. Clear out, you fellows, double
quick, I say. We may hate one another, but we hate you most. If I don't make you
go, Ahmed will, Karim will, if it's fifty or five hundred years we shall get rid of you,
yes, and we shall drive every blasted Englishman into the sea, and then . . . you and
I shall be friends.'

'Why can't we be friends now?' said the other, holding him affectionately. 'It's what
I want. It's what you want.' (Forster 1924)

In September 1945, following the August Revolution of the Communist-led Viet
Minh (League for the Independence of Vietnam), banners hung in the streets of
Hanoi proclaiming, amongst other slogans, 'Independence or Death' (Sainteny 1967).
Over the following thirty years, death would indeed be the reward of many hundreds
of thousands of Vietnamese in their struggle for national independence and unity.
And for Anderson (1991: 7), 'the central problem posed by nationalism' is precisely
this, that so many people have apparently been willing to go to their deaths for the
sake of the nation's 'limited imaginings'. Gambling on their own mortality in the name
of political action, Vietnamese revolutionaries probably felt that the odds were reasonably balanced in their favour; and in late 1945 in Vietnam, as will be discussed in
a later chapter, those odds had indeed recently improved immeasurably. A few years
earlier, before the Second World War wreaked its havoc in Southeast Asia, the choices
open to Vietnamese political activists, which no one would have bothered inscribing

on a banner, might more realistically have been rendered: Collaboration, Prison or, if you insist, Death. And these options would most likely not have been expressed, as in 1945, in English, for an international audience represented by observing American military agents.

This suggests a dramatic variant of the late colonial shift, which, it is argued, operated across the colonial world in the wake of the Second World War. However, nowhere did that war create the conditions for decolonization from nothing, nor did post-war anti-colonial nationalism come simply 'out of the blue'. In this chapter, we explore the immediate pre-history of the post-1945 decolonizing nationalisms, and the basis for indigenous political action within the mature colonial state. Later we examine the pre-war state of colonial politics in a number of key cases. The immediate pre-war period saw the introduction of major reform in the British empire, with the passing of the 1935 Government of India Act, and a more gradual shift towards colonial reformism elsewhere, partly as a consequence of a wave of strikes and disorder starting in 1935. France too experienced a brief period of domestic reformism, led by the doomed governments of the Popular Front from 1936, with considerable implications for colonial policy. These developments have sometimes been seen as offering a foretaste of later reforms within the colonial state, before the colonial situation was transformed by the Second World War. The chapter also identifies potential continuities between pre- and post-war colonial politics, including the potential that in the end was not realized. Rather than retelling the determinist narratives of 'growing national consciousness' or of a colonial political 'infancy' under imperial tutelage, the aim here is to offer a synchronic snapshot of a full range of political possibilities as they existed within the colonial state before the crisis period of the Second World War and beyond.

First, we consider India, the biggest and most advanced colonial state, which had moved substantially towards self-government even before the 1935 Act. Experience of nationalist anti-colonial engagement was one of the principal ways in which 'lateness came early' (Darwin 1999) to the Indian colonial state in India. However, the outcomes or timing of Indian decolonization were not preordained by this time; notably, the still hazy concept of 'Pakistan' was no more yet than the utopian brainchild of Muslim idealists – and Cambridge undergraduates at that. Our second, very different, case is that of Vietnam, within the overarching framework of French Indochina, where the Popular Front briefly and partially cleared the channels of indigenous political activity. Despite, or because of, the degree of official control exercised over colonial politics, the singular combination of Vietnamese cultural renewal and revolutionary political engagement was already in place by this time. As already suggested, this did not ostensibly make the prospects for Vietnamese nationalism any less bleak. Thirdly, in the case of Algeria, not even the Popular Front's goodwill was enough to create significant openings for legitimate political activity, given Algeria's peculiar constitutional status as 'part of France', and the determined opposition by French settlers and their political champions in Paris. Nonetheless, the outline of an Algerian nationalist politics can already be discerned, although this was still necessarily a matter of ideological positioning, rather than of concerted political action.

The Limits of Colonial Politics

Before turning to our case studies, we consider a number of underlying themes running through them, relating to the colonial state's centrality in setting the framework for indigenous political action. How does politics emerge in a system where colonial rule is regarded as the 'normal' (or at least, unavoidable) framework for political change? Following Breuilly's influential comparative model (1993: 218–29), this question may be answered in terms of the evolution of the 'collaborator system', from a set of relationships determined, as we have seen, by the circumstances of colonial conquest and consolidation, but which developed into those of a modern administrative colonial state. A convincing case can be made in this way, up to a point, for the political evolution of British India, which saw the Indian National Congress develop from a 'microscopic minority' of urban professionals to a near-hegemonic national movement poised to 'become' the Raj. The problem with treating India from a comparative perspective is that it was more or less alone in developing a proto-democratic political system based on even limited electoral representation under colonial rule before 1939. Elsewhere, the interaction between colonial rulers and indigenous elites remained at a largely pre-political stage of development, as colonial governments did their best, usually effectively, to prevent the emergence of colonial politics – understood as a 'specialized form of action with distinct organization, objectives and rhetoric' (ibid.: 224). The development of colonial politics thus more usually accompanied or followed the transformation of colonial rule associated with the Second World War.

Until that happened, and in this British India was not so very different from other colonial states, the impact of colonial rule on political development was still felt chiefly in the exercise of the repressive mechanisms of police and military violence, summary justice (such as the *indigénat*, or 'native code' of punishments meted out by administrators), surveillance, censorship and prison. A more broadly inclusive notion is needed of what might constitute 'national' politics within the colonial state. Colonial politics, like any other, was the art of determining, and where possible extending, the limits of the possible. For most of the colonial period, these limits were very narrowly defined. Thus, Breuilly's contention that 'the focus of nationalist movements is upon taking over the state', and that therefore 'not all opposition activity under colonial regimes can be regarded as nationalist', begs the question of how sharply the focus of colonial politics could yet be trained on what seemed, before 1945, a distant prospect (ibid.). Even in India, although Congress adopted national independence as its aim on New Year's Eve 1930, the Raj was still preparing for the long term, having recently instituted targets of 50 per cent Indianization of the Indian Civil Service within 15 years, and of the army and police officer corps within 25 years (by 1952) (Sarkar 1989: 283–4, 227). Arguably, the 1935 Act did little to change that perspective. More generally, the prospects for national independence or self-determination were less than tangible, so that claims to national identity or calls for national independence might be construed as morale-boosting battle cries or the inchoate aspiration to a millennial 'brave new world', rather than as realistic expressions of a concrete political programme. Even in India, when, in 1919, Gandhi promised *Swaraj* [self-rule] within a year', he offered little sense of the content of that slogan, and Congress was disinclined to exercise the necessary leadership to achieve anything approaching self-rule in this period.

If the national idea was thus still largely utopian, then perhaps other strategies, institutions or ideological bases for political action offered plausible political futures. Three such strategies suggest themselves in the cases under consideration: the stance of 'moderate' politics accepting the terms of colonial rule; reform and restoration of 'traditional' rule; and the possibility of communist-inspired revolt against colonial rule.

Moderate and 'Mendicant' Politics

Political elites and leaders typically expressed their aims, less as a challenge to imperial rule than as an appeal to imperial rulers for fair treatment within the colonial order. Thus, the moderate politics of the early Indian Congress could be denounced as dishonourable 'Mendicancy'. Its petitions were addressed, not even to the 'sundried bureaucrats' of British India, but to liberal opinion at the imperial centre, in Westminster, and were concerned with issues such as the government's insistence on holding entrance examinations for the Indian Civil Service in London – an enduring and symbolic means of discouraging Indian entrants, but hardly of direct concern to more than a handful (Sarkar 1989: 97–8). Colonial governments could easily rebuff such limited political beginnings. When the mild-mannered African Association in Tanganyika (modelled on the older European and Indian Associations) intervened in 1930 to thank the British Colonial Secretary for not implementing an East African federation, it was warned off political affairs by the governor. Even as the Association evolved through to the mid-1940s, it was arguably still not nationalist, as its programme 'was a series of requests and aspirations and not a direct challenge to the regime'; nonetheless, it represented 'an advance in political consciousness which could subsequently be passed on to a nationalist movement' (Iliffe 1979: 418).

The colonial state thus provided an unavoidable frame of reference for the discursive process by which the nation was progressively imagined. As already suggested, it was axiomatic to imperial rulers that there was no correlation between colonial boundaries and the identity of the people that lived within them, and thus that there was 'no such thing' as India, Vietnam, or Algeria (and certainly no such thing as Mali or Ghana or Tanzania). Apart from his striking argument, already discussed, concerning the impact of key colonial institutions – census, map, museum – on the form of the nation imagined by colonial nationalists, Anderson (1991: 114) also laid emphasis on the intelligentsia's role in this imagining, and the ways in which their lives were shaped by the 'pilgrimages' which they were constrained to follow: perhaps to the metropole in the first instance, but thereafter to 'the highest administrative centre to which [they] could be assigned'. Further, it was the very modernity of colonial states which allowed this development: mobility via imperial transport systems, bureaucratic expansion creating a demand for 'native' clerks, interpreters and policemen, and the spread of modern education.

Few colonial politicians went as far in endorsing the imperial view quite so explicitly as the Algerian pharmacist and political moderate, Ferhat Abbas, who in 1936 famously declared:

> If I had found the Algerian nation, I would be a nationalist and that would not make me blush as if at a crime. However, I will not die for an Algerian fatherland which does not exist. I have looked for it in vain. I have searched history, and communed with the living and the dead; I have visited the cemeteries; no-one spoke to me of a fatherland. You cannot build on the wind. For once and all time we have put aside all clouds and illusions to tie our future firmly to that of France's efforts in our country. What people are actually fighting for behind the word 'nationalism' is our political and economic emancipation. Without emancipation for Algerians, no lasting French Algeria can be established. (in Nouschi 1962: 89)

We return to this argument below, in the context of a debate amongst nationalists (a term which arguably attached to Abbas even in 1936) in 1930s Algeria. The general point exemplified by Abbas is that the political engagement of this burgeoning elite was largely conditional upon accepting to work within the imperial order. However, the terms of that acceptance could change rapidly: only a few years after denying his nation's existence, in 1943, Ferhat Abbas – without needing to blush – put his name to a 'Manifesto of the Algerian People', which formed the basis of his politics over the following decade or more. Within 18 months of the launching of insurrection by the Algerian National Liberation Front (FLN), he had been won over to the radical nationalist cause with all that implied in terms of embracing Algerian national identity, and rejecting the colonial state.

Thrones and Dominions: Uses of Tradition in the Colonial State

The primary role of the Indian princes, whose lands comprised two-fifths of Indian territory, was as collaborators essential to the maintenance of the post-1857 imperial order. It was unlikely that these 'British officers in Indian dress', as Gandhi called them (in Smith, 1995: 12), would don Congress caps and shape-shift into modern nationalists, although some did make the attempt, somewhat belatedly, in the late 1930s. Nonetheless, a view of the princes as 'buffoons who frittered away their lives in self-indulgence' may be qualified: some of the more influential rulers were relatively progressive, many were 'fairly upright, cultured and hard-working' in an age when constitutional monarchy was still a relevant formula for modern government in Europe (Copland 1997: 284–5). The Indian princes also had a crucial role to play – which need not mean they played it well – in Indian constitutional developments to 1939.

Traditional rulers, and through them their courtiers and followers, could lay claim to prestige and legitimacy which still eluded modern nationalist movements. Thus the Emperor of Annam was both the rallying point for prolonged resistance during the 'Can Vuong' ('Loyalty to the King') or Black Flags rising against French conquest, in the 1880s–90s, and the focus for subsequent nationalist attempts to assert imperial, and thus national, autonomy; both Emperor Than Thai in 1907 and the 'boy Emperor' Duy Tan in 1915 were deposed and exiled by the French for this reason. Much depended latterly on the intelligent but irresolute Bao Dai who ascended to the throne in 1932. French official determination to head off the slightest sign of imperial revival was surely a backhanded acknowledgement of the institution's symbolic potency, as was the so-called 'Bao Dai solution' of the 1940s (see Chapter 4). Elsewhere in the French empire the risk was forestalled more brutally. In Madagascar, the *Menalamba* ("Red Shawls") insurrection, following the French conquest of 1896, provided the French commander General Gallieni with the pretext to complete the destruction of the Merina court; Queen Ranavalona was exiled to Réunion, her prime minister executed by the French on trumped-up charges, and the royal tombs ceremonially burnt in a calculated act of sacrilege. Fifty years later, during the 1947 Insurrection, the French administration still feared a Merina revival (Ellis 1986).

British imperial attitudes to kingship were more ambivalent than those of the Republican French, but nonetheless interventionist. Practice varied tremendously between the 'hands-off' approach adopted towards Indian princes and, say, Middle Eastern emirs, and the more formal structures of Indirect Rule in Africa (Smith 1995). Equipped with native treasuries, and with continuing powers to administer justice, the Emirs of Northern Nigeria or the Kabaka of Buganda maintained their power base under Indirect Rule. As recompense for their loss of autonomy, rulers 'strove to gain the title of king, to obtain invitations to British coronations, to dramatize their internal authority with crowns and thrones, British-style coronations and jubilees' (Ranger 1983). British officials sometimes encouraged these aspirations, which joined up with a whole range of 'invented traditions' of monarchy and hierarchical rule imported from British society; often, what now seems inordinate attention was paid to such niceties as the ruler's choice of spouse or the order of precedence at British coronations – both issues over which rulers lost their thrones after 1945 (Smith 1995: 103–4, 195–6).[2] The overarching structures of British rule kept rulers firmly in their place, however, although in post-1945 colonial politics, this too could be a potent source of nationalist discontent. For example, the British high-handed attitude to the Malay Sultans over the short-lived Malayan Union policy was a major factor in the crystallization of post-1945 Malay nationalism centring around the prestige of the Sultans (Chapter 4).

Communists and Nationalists

A plausible alternative to a purely 'national' colonial politics was constituted by the emergence of an international communist movement avowedly promoting colonial liberation. This movement, formally constituted in 1919 as the Third Communist International, or Comintern, offered an ideological framework for analysing the colonial situation, an institutional basis for action, and even a model of how that liberation could work, with the Tsarist empire's transformation into a multi-national Union of supposedly independent Soviet Socialist Republics. The ideological and organizational obstacles to Comintern support for anti-colonial movements came from within. First, the primary focus of Comintern policy was always on the European centre rather than the colonized periphery. This was true whether the Comintern was fomenting revolution in advanced industrial countries or, from 1922, protecting the Revolution in Russia, according to the doctrine of Socialism in One Country (Hargreaves 1993; McDermott & Agnew 1996). The Comintern's approach to colonial nationalists thus reflected that of colonial governments, in its recognition that power and initiative were located at the imperial centre. A partial exception was 'semi-colonial' China, where the Comintern promoted alliance with the Chinese Nationalist Party, the Guomindang, until the violent split and purges of 1926 set the Chinese Communist Party on its distinctive and independent path. Stalin's increasing grip on power in Moscow, consolidated by the Chinese fiasco, further reduced the Comintern to a blunt instrument of narrowly defined Soviet interests.

If anything, the Comintern's Eurocentrism was even more marked after it adopted the United (or Popular) Front doctrine in 1934, which belatedly identified the threat represented by European fascist movements and urged Communist parties to cooperate with former 'class enemies'. This was of particular significance for the French empire, given the formation of a Popular Front government in Paris in June 1936, supported from outside government ranks by the French Communist Party (PCF). Although the Popular Front government adopted a relatively imaginative and liberal approach to colonial reform, this was predicated on the continuance of French colonial empire. Communist support for this approach was expressed with awkward clarity by the PCF secretary-general, Maurice Thorez, who argued that 'the right to divorce need not imply the necessity to divorce', a formula which signalled the beginning of a long and ambiguous relationship between the PCF and colonial nationalists (Moneta 1971; Cohen 1972).

Another, potentially decisive, obstacle to Comintern support of communists in colonial states stemmed from the analysis of their limited 'historical' role in furthering the anti-imperial cause. The starting point for this analysis was Lenin's perception that, given the 'backwardness' of dependent countries, revolutionary initiative lay with 'bourgeois-nationalist movements', and not with an at best emergent working class. This position was modified at early Comintern Congresses under the influence of the Indian revolutionary, Manabendra Nath Roy, who argued that different action might be required in different countries. As he put it at the Fourth Comintern Congress, in November 1922:

> There were colonies with a fairly strong indigenous bourgeoisie, others where capitalism was only in its initial stages, and others that were still quite primitive. Bourgeois-nationalist movements in the colonies were objectively revolutionary, but if they were directed only against the foreign bourgeoisie and not against native feudalism they represented not a class struggle, but capitalist competition. . . . Leadership would have to be taken over by the communist parties when the bourgeoisie deserted and betrayed the national revolution, as they were bound to do. (Degras 1956–65; Haithcox 1971: 11–13, 32–6)

Roy was arguing primarily for India, where Congress had earlier in the year called off its Non-Cooperation campaign rather than lose control of it in the face of spiralling violence, and thus, in Roy's view, effectively 'deserted and betrayed' the national cause. But the Communist Party of India (CPI), of which M.N. Roy was a founder member, was never strong enough to challenge Congress hegemony, and Roy moved progressively into a political wilderness, as he failed in his efforts to forge a truly national alliance, whether in the form of a communist-led Workers' and Peasants' Party in the 1920s, or under the banner of socialist internationalism in the late 1930s (Sarkar 1989).

Roy's arguments, never fully accepted by the Comintern, posed a wider question as to what constituted a valid approach for communists under colonial rule. The 1922 Congress's Theses on the Eastern Question urged communists to steer a tortuous course between an opportunist defence of 'independent class interests' and remaining aloof from working class interests 'in the name of "national unity" or of "civil peace"':

> The communist workers' parties of the colonial and semi-colonial countries have a dual task: they fight for the most radical possible solution of the tasks of a bourgeois-democratic revolution, which aims at the conquest of political independence; and they organize the working and peasant masses for the struggle for their special class interests, and in doing so exploit all the contradictions in the nationalist bourgeois-democratic camp. By putting forward social demands they release the revolutionary energy for which the bourgeois-liberal demands provide no outlet, and stimulate it further. (in Degras 1956–65)

In short, communists could remain, however uneasily or provisionally, within the nationalist movement, but were not *of* it. Moreover, this conscious balancing of class interests against longer-term revolutionary aims was a further implied recognition of a temporarily foreclosed colonial future, since communists had yet to build a mass following through the education of colonial workers and the 'semi-proletarian strata'.

This conclusion bypasses a necessary distinction between communists and anti-colonial nationalists: patently, M.N. Roy and his Comintern colleagues, Nguyen Ai Quoc (later Ho Chi Minh) or the Indonesian Tan Malaka, came to communism via the national cause. Arguably, rigorous adherence to communist tenets could be reconciled with belief in national liberation from colonial rule. It may be wrong to 'characterize Ho Chi Minh or any other major Vietnamese Communist leader as a nationalist': Ho, as early as 1922, 'considered nationalism to be a dangerous siren capable of luring colonized peoples away from communism', and subsequently campaigned effectively (and brutally) against nationalist 'collaborators' (Marr 1983: 320). However, communist ideology may be understood primarily as a way of understanding the colonial situation and acting against it. Crucially, and notwithstanding Roy's or Ho's careers as Comintern agents, or the subsequent distorting effects of the Cold War, this need not imply that the strategies of Indian or Vietnamese communist movements were subordinated to the priorities of 'international revolution' set in Moscow.

Conversely, colonial administrations often claimed, and perhaps even at times believed, that this was the case. Indeed, officials used terms such as 'communist', 'subversive' and 'illegal' as near-synonyms, both in the interwar period, and more particularly once the Cold War began to influence colonial discourse after 1945. Thus, when one Indian proconsul claimed in 1918 that Gandhi was 'Honest, but a Bolshevik and for that reason very dangerous', only the last two words carried effective meaning (Governor Willingdon, in Sarkar 1989: 177).

Collaboration and Resistance

It may be worth briefly revisiting the concept of 'collaboration', which, as argued in the previous chapter, was an essential mechanism of colonial rule. 'Collaboration' is an ugly concept, however, carrying with it the implication of a moral choice by those who collaborated – and for Europeans, it carries indelible but misleading associations with the experience of 1940–4. It is not even terribly accurate, since what is meant is usually a *'convergence of interests* between colonial state and individual groups or classes of colonized society' (Osterhammel 1997: 63, emphasis in text). Thus, Bayart's (1993) persuasive paradigm argues for the 'ordinary' functioning of African politics, centring on the concept of 'extraversion'. This is explained as the tendency of African elites to seek support from the outside world, to their own ends, even if typically on highly unequal terms. Although this has obvious kinship with collaboration, in the emphasis that it places on the relationship between colonial ruler and indigenous ruled elites, unlike the 'peripheral' approach, Bayart's model allows for indigenous initiative and agency, both at the moment of conquest and subsequently under colonial rule and beyond. In other words, whereas for Robinson and Gallagher, the colonial empires were, so to speak, sucked into a power vacuum, for Bayart they were drawn in by a political process stretching back over centuries. Bayart's African extraverts thus exploited the political, technological and cultural resources offered by the colonizer, while resigning themselves to the developing realities of imperial domination. Although his primary focus is on the post-colonial sub-Saharan African state, Bayart's argument draws for its significance on a far longer timescale, and may arguably be extended to a broader canvas.

Thus, although the idea of collaboration is straightforward enough from an imperial perspective, it begs the question of political motivation. After all, collaboration might flow from an acknowledgement of defeat, or from the need to maintain what power and influence were allowed by the colonial state. Thus the Prime Minister of Annam expressed the resignation of *anciens régimes* across the colonial world in 1901: 'Since pacification, everyone has understood that all resistance was useless, and that the best was to accommodate oneself to the new state of affairs' (in Brocheux & Hémery 1995: 92). It might be motivated by the desire to fight colonial rule on its own terms, or the ambition to take over the colonial state from within. Over time, collaborators included traditional rulers, appointed and salaried chiefs, urban intellectuals or business leaders, ethnic or religious community elders, elected regional or national deputies, nationalist party bosses or trades union leaders, even the odd Comintern agent. What then occasioned these periodic shifts in collaborative partnerships? Was the imperial hand never forced, and if the colonial power did choose, was this not by some assessment of relative strength or potential? The collaborative model thus effectively collapses one side of the imperial relationship, telling us about the form of colonial politics, while largely ignoring its content (Breuilly 1993: 158–61). Although consistency dictates that the term 'collaboration' is maintained, its use remains problematic.

And what of those who refused collaboration, placing themselves beyond the colonial pale? For imperial historians, resistance is readily consigned to the oblivion of 'primitive' or 'tribal' revolts, reactionary refusals to accept the inevitable course of history, 'romantic, reactionary struggles against the facts, the passionate protest of societies which were shocked by a new age of change and would not be comforted' (Robinson & Gallagher, in Ranger 1968: 437). Conquest was then followed by peace and order in which the 'thin white line' of the colonial administration was able to rule largely unchallenged.

Resistance to colonial rule should not be dismissed so readily. First, colonial conquest was always part of the background to colonial rule, and the possibility of resistance was often founded in the relatively recent memory of defeat. For example, when Joseph Nyerere toured southern Tanganyika rallying support for Tanganyika African National Union (TANU), he was met with memories of the Hehe people's resistance to German conquest and of the 1905 Maji Maji rebellion:

> The people, and particularly the elders, asked: 'How can we win without guns? How can we make sure that there is not going to be a repetition of the Hehe and Maji-Maji wars?' It was therefore necessary for TANU to start by making the people understand that peaceful methods of struggle for independence were possible and could succeed. (in Iliffe 1979: 519–20)

But *revanche* is a powerful motivating force, and memory of defeat acted as a rallying point for subsequent resistance at the right moment. Thus, the 1896 Menalamba, or 'Red Shawls', insurrection, so called because the insurgents smeared their shawls (*lamba*) with Madagascar's red earth, encapsulated many of the grievances which accompanied colonial occupation for more than sixty years, and inspired the 1947 Insurrection, fought over much the same territory in the eastern forests of Madagascar, and with a similarly hopeless outlook (Ellis 1986; Chapter 6). With a similar regard for historical continuities, when Joshua Nkomo, leader of the Shona-dominated Zimbabwean African Party of Union returned to Southern Rhodesia in 1962, he was greeted by survivors of the Shona and Ndebele revolts of 1896–7 (depicted in Lan 1985). Moreover, it was those who held out longest against colonial control, for example the Balanta people of southern Guiné, who were the 'first and fiercest' to join the wars against the Portuguese in the 1960s (MacQueen 1997: 6, 42).

Secondly, resistance shaped the structures of colonial rule. This was, after all, part of the point of Indirect Rule, not only recognising the power of, say, the North Nigerian emirs, but also allowing the British to step back from early efforts to impose direct taxation, for example, following the Hut Tax rebellion in Sierra Leone. Similarly, the emergence of a French policy of 'association' in West Africa, which followed their efforts to impose direct rule before 1914, owed much to the rebellions which met French recruiting drives to fill the 80,000-strong ranks of *tirailleurs sénégalais* (Black African troops raised in French West Africa, not just in Senegal) who fought on the Western Front (Conklin 1997: 143–51; Michel 1982). In Madagascar, General Gallieni was obliged to modify the so-called *politique des races*, directed against the hitherto dominant Merina ruling caste, because French rule needed their administrative skills more than it needed their complete submission. Right up to decolonization, and especially after crushing the 1947 rebellion (which the French blamed on the Merina), French policy maintained an uneasy balance between accepting Merina collaboration and empowering the other Malagasy peoples (Shipway, 1996a).

The idea of a colonial 'pax' implies a delay occurring between the 'primary' resistance to conquest and the subsequent campaigns of nationalist movements in the late
colonial period. But the more closely the colonial 'pax' is examined, the more spatial
and temporal patches appear in it: like Balzac's magical wild ass's skin, the *peau de
chagrin*, the effective area of colonial control shrank the more demands were made of it.
Thus, 'primary' revolts against colonial rule and their 'pacification' continued well into
the period of consolidation of colonial rule, and encroached on territory supposedly
controlled by the colonial administration. Many parts of Africa escaped effective
control right up to 1914, and sometimes much longer. Parts of Cambodia were still in
a state of 'primary' rebellion against French colonial penetration into the 1930s
(Brocheux & Hémery 1995). In North Africa at the end of the First World War, fully
two-thirds of Morocco was in a state of '*siba*', that is, 'dissidence' or a 'state of flux'
(Berque 1967), and the Rif war of 1925–6 looked very like a delayed war of colonial
conquest by the French and Spanish colonial armies. Further South, the nomadic
Reguiebat clan whose territory lay across the Saharan no man's land of Algeria, Spanish
Rio d'Oro, Morocco and Mauritania, submitted to the French *makhzen* (temporal
authority) as late as 1934. By the late 1950s, the Reguiebat were preparing to transfer
their allegiance to the Moroccan National Army of Liberation, and were only headed
off by a timely show of French force (Chaffard 1967: vol.2; Shipway 2002).

   Thirdly, the distinction between primary revolt and 'mature' nationalism is difficult to sustain even in areas of relatively advanced colonial penetration. Thus,
although colonial rulers saw rebellions such as the 1905 Maji Maji revolt as 'tribal',
it was precisely the effort to transcend the purely local political level which offered
a model to later nationalists (Iliffe 1979; Ranger 1968). For India, one author lists
77 peasant uprisings in the period from the 1857 Sepoy Rebellion, classified variously
as 'restorative, religious, social banditry, terrorist vengeance and armed insurrection'.
The period of the rise and eventual triumph of Indian National Congress is thus
punctuated by guerrilla movements wresting back peripheral regions from British or
princely control, movements such as that of Birsa Munda in the 1890s, or the 'veritable
guerrilla war' conducted by Alluri Sitaraa Raju between August 1922 and May 1924,
a folk hero who spoke highly of Gandhi while considering violence necessary; or the
actions of the Hindustan Socialist Republican Army, formed in 1928, whose key leader
Bhagat Singh briefly threatened to supplant Gandhi, before he was captured the
following year and executed (Sarkar 1989: 43–8, 240, 269). A basic continuity may
also be traced between Indian peasant insurrections before 1900 and the popular
consciousness which underpinned, and indeed often subverted, the initiatives of Congress nationalism or of Communism, such as the 1919 campaign of non-cooperation,
the Quit India insurrection of 1942, or the communist inspired insurrections of
Tebhaga or Telengana which accompanied the Indian 'endgame' in 1946–7 (Guha
1983: 13, 334; Sarkar 1989: 189ff., 388ff., 439–46).

   A more nuanced understanding is needed of resistance to colonial rule than the
simple distinction between 'primary' rebellion and the threat represented by later
nationalisms. Peasant insurrection in India and elsewhere in colonial Asia perhaps
had its African counterpart in a variety of millenarian movements, syncretic Christian
followings and innovations within African religious traditions such as 'witch eradication' movements; these overlapped with 'primary' revolts, were influenced by them,

and in turn continued into the period of 'mature' nationalist mobilization in the countryside (Ranger 1968). Moreover, the features of earlier revolts, which received wisdom perceived as 'primitive', 'atavistic' or millenarian, were often precisely the elements to which later nationalists found themselves drawn when the time came to mobilize mass support for their campaigns. It is to the origins and outlook of mature nationalism, and to its sometimes ambivalent relationship with the colonized masses, that we now turn.

Indian Nationalist Politics to 1935

The Government of India Act of 1935 represented imperial statecraft at its most complex. This was conceivably the point at which colonial state 'bricolage' was transformed into purpose-built constitutional engineering on a grand scale, intended to retain British control of a gradually evolving Indian polity for the foreseeable future. It was the culmination of almost two decades of often intense political struggle, including sustained periods of violence and 'non-violent' disorder, particularly in 1919–22, which perhaps no colonial state after 1945 could have sustained. With hindsight, it may be seen to represent the penultimate stage of a political process which saw the Indian National Congress poised to 'become' the Raj (Brown 1999a; Seal 1973). Thus after its sweeping successes in the 1937 elections, in which Congress ministries were elected in seven out of 11 provinces (with absolute majorities in five), it could credibly claim near-hegemonic national status and set its sights at the last remaining level of politics to be conquered, that of all-India, which the government had so far jealously guarded to itself. As it turned out, 1935 was only a brief intermediate stage on the way to the Transfer of Power little more than a decade later. It would be futile to speculate as to what might have happened had not the Second World War led to the suspension of the Act's full implementation, providing the Congress 'High Command' with the opportunity to order ministers to withdraw from the straitjacket of provincial executive responsibility (Chapter 3). But since it was taken as considerably more than a mere provisional staging post, the brief period following the Act offers a convenient vantage point from which to undertake a brief *tour d'horizon* of Indian politics, to assay its possible futures and those which had perhaps already been foreclosed.

The Indian National Congress had come a long way since its formation in 1885, the loose federation of a 'microscopic minority' of middle-class, mostly English-educated professionals and businessmen – 455 out of 1,200 at the 1888 Allahabad Congress were lawyers – whose careers left little time for politics beyond the annual Congresses, and whose endless articles, speeches and petitions comprised 'a little too much talk about the blessings of British rule'.[3] Alongside this 'Mendicancy', as its critics saw it, a more Extremist politics was emerging, notably around the figure of Bal Gangadhar Tilak of Maharashtra, who declared that 'we will not achieve any success in our labours if we croak once a year like a frog', and seemed already to be moving towards advocating mass passive resistance and civil disobedience (Sarkar 1989: 71).

This still largely parochial Indian politics meshed with the iterations of the imperial collaborator system. As the Raj increased its demands, to pay for the army, for administration or for railways, so it extended the reach of government downwards from the summit of imperial government to the provinces and localities; so also it required ever wider and more reliable systems of collaboration, eventually embracing elections as the most reliable method of all (Seal 1973: 13). Intensifying collaboration had two far-reaching sets of consequences. First, by setting the representative framework for collaboration, the Raj was in part creating the categories by which Indian elites organized themselves. This was already happening through the ten-yearly Census, which, from 1901, sought to classify castes on the basis of 'social precedence as recognized by native public opinion' (Sarkar 1989: 55). The 1909 Morley–Minto reforms took this one step further by creating separate electorates determined by religious community and social class. Colonial knowledge and the exercise of colonial power were closely intertwined here. Although this was a classic device to 'divide and rule', it constrained an elite to compete for the prize of representing these semi-fictional groups – who, for example, *were* 'the Mohammedan Community in the Presidency of Bengal' or the 'Landholders in the United Provinces', both allocated a seat on the Governor-General's Council? Secondly, the gradual creation of a legislative system, eventually extending from local boards to provincial councils to nominated representation in New Delhi, in turn generated a matching structure of politics: the Raj had, in effect, 'cut the steps' by which would-be petitioners were obliged to climb, but it also drove politics upwards to these higher levels (Seal 1973: 12, 14–17).

The British Raj thus played a major role in the process by which the scale of politics moved from the local level, at which collaborator systems operated at their simplest and most durable, to provincial and, ultimately, national levels; it was also deeply implicated in the ways in which 'communal' divisions found political expression. These developments were formalized in the structures of government set up in the 1919 Government of India Act, completed by the Communal Award of 1932, which recognized the communities of Hindus, Muslims, Sikhs and 'Depressed Classes', and in the provisions of the 1935 Act. The principle innovation of the post-1919 system was the introduction of 'dyarchy', by which nominated Indian ministers were responsible to provincial legislatures, elected by a still tiny franchise, for a number of portfolios. As Sarkar (1989: 167) comments:

> [Dyarchy] transferred only departments with less political weight and little funds to ministers responsible to provincial legislatures, skilfully drawing Indian politicians into a patronage rat-race which would probably also discredit them, as real improvements in education, health, agriculture, and local bodies required far more money than the British would be prepared to assign to these branches.

'Responsible government' in the provinces after 1935 differed little from this, although the franchise was extended from one-tenth of the adult male population, in 1919, to approximately one-sixth, about 30 million (Brown 1999a: 432n.). Conversely, central powers were enhanced, and the provincial governor retained special powers (exercised after the mass resignations of late 1939). Although conceived in terms of the 1917 promise of 'the gradual development of self-governing institutions', the Act was silent on a 1929 declaration of Dominion status as the eventual aim of British policy. Far from being a staging post to further reforms, much less an act of imperial demission (although that was how its conservative critics in London saw it), this was intended to draw a line under a limited process of British concessions, and more particularly to 'hold India to the Empire'.

From its largely parochial beginnings can be traced the two broad strategies by which the Congress operated within and against the system created by the British. First, and up to 1920 almost exclusively, it acted as 'a co-ordinating agency within a system of elite politics' (Breuilly 1993: 174), a political home and steering committee for local and provincial politicians working within the structures set in place by the Raj. Outside the great campaigns of non-cooperation in 1919–22 and civil disobedience in 1930–2, and the period of opposition to the war which preceded the Quit India campaign (Chapter 3), these politicians shared the perspectives of their provincial constituencies, as the British surely intended; all-India Congress was an accordingly poorly co-ordinated and poorly financed organization, whose provincial supporters 'stepped nimbly in and out of the all-India organizations, like so many cabs for hire' (Seal 1973: 23). However, notwithstanding the obvious limitations of responsible government after 1935, Congress ministers could demonstrate their executive skills, including management of law and order (Sarkar 1989: 352; Arnold 1992). Electoral success in 1937 seemingly offered an overwhelming endorsement to those on the Right of the party who favoured this constitutionalist strategy.

For the new electorate of 'dominant peasants' (mistakenly selected by the British for their loyalty to the Raj, rather than to an 'elitist' Congress), a vote for Congress in 1937 was not a vote for a safe pair of hands, but rather 'a patriotic duty . . . a vote for Gandhiji' (Sarkar 1989: 347). In other words, electoral success was arguably inconceivable without the often-dominant counterpoint of Congress's alternative strategy, that of all-Indian agitation. At the heart of this strategy were the tactics and ideology, but perhaps above all the charismatic example, of Mahatma Gandhi. Initially, Gandhi was literally an outsider, since his return to India in 1917 after more than twenty years, in London and then as a lawyer in South Africa, left him without a local power base, even in his native Gujarat, the greatest if not the first professional politician whose 'very freedom from the webs of local interests gave [him] a role that went beyond the localities' (ibid.: 178; Seal 1973: 19). He brought with him distinctive tactics, practical dedication to the anti-colonial cause and a philosophy of non-violence, none of which quite squared with Congress doctrine. It would be difficult to overestimate the impact, on a nationalist movement which had shied away from the socially disruptive potential of mass action, of the key Gandhian themes of *ahimsa* (non-violence) and *satyagraha* (soul-force or truth-force, Gandhi's own coinage from Gujarati), involving the peaceful violation of specific laws, the mass courting of arrest, and the soon-familiar *hartal* (commercial and labour strikes), marches and processions (Sarkar 1989: 179–80). Conversely, non-violence could be seen as tailor-made to reassure conservative Congress supporters. Thus, Gandhi's insistence on home-produced weave appealed to industrialists competing with Lancashire-made cotton, even though the symbolic handloom, reflecting Gandhi's anti-modern utopian ideals, was less attractive. Even more controversial was Gandhi's life-long dedication to Indian unity, begun with his work with Indian Muslims in South Africa, and continued with his alliance with the Khilafatist movement (campaigning against the abolition of the caliphate), underpinning the first wave of *satyagraha* in 1919. Many

Congress leaders found it increasingly difficult to sympathize with this fundamental aspect of Gandhian politics.

Gandhi both coordinated the elite of Congress politicians and mobilized mass participation in support of the national cause. Within Congress, Gandhi's campaigns built up a network of local 'subcontractors' who benefited from Gandhi's prestige (Brown 1989). Even outside periods of agitation, for example following the collapse of non-cooperation in 1922, Gandhi's disciples pursued policies of non-political constructive work in the villages or amongst the *Harijans* (Untouchables), as an alternative to participation in the rat-race of provincial politics (Sarkar 1989: 227).

However, Gandhi's populism was not simply of instrumental utility to Congress, as part of a single struggle against British rule. *Satyagraha* was a highly effective weapon in the nationalist armoury, to be deployed at will at moments of British repression, for example, the Rowlatt Bill (which proposed the retention of wartime restrictions), or of British concession such as the 1919 Act which followed – even if, in effect, imperial initiatives thus drove a largely reactive Congress. Thus, Congress's somewhat hesitant involvement in agitational politics was yet another aspect of the party becoming the Raj. However, as Sarkar and others have argued, such a view of Indian nationalism as essentially 'elite' politics fails to acknowledge the impact of the popular response to Gandhi, and the often autonomously developed political purpose of peasant insurrection.

What Gandhi's campaigns could inspire was thus not simply a controlled, 'non-violent' protest by an increasingly nationally conscious Indian people, as conventional nationalist historiography would have it, far less the primitive rabble of imperial nightmares, but a potentially far more thoroughgoing peasant revolt against the imperial order than Congress was prepared to countenance. Thus, when the Rowlatt *satyagraha* turned to violence, and to General Dyer's brutal counter-insurgency campaign initiated by the massacre at Jallianwallabagh, Amritsar, in April 1919, Gandhi called off the movement, admitting to a 'Himalayan blunder'. However, what was the nature of this blunder? To have provoked British repressive violence? Or to have promised *swaraj* (self-rule) within a year, without precisely defining it, thus provoking a popular millenarian response? Or to have underestimated peasant resentment of landlord privileges, intensified by wartime restrictions, without the leadership or inclination to follow through the ensuing popular insurrection (ibid.: 190–4)?

By 1921–2, Gandhi's advocacy of non-violence was deployed openly as an instrument of control, urging peasants to regard 'as friends' the *zamindars* (landlords) against whom they were revolting. Arguably, this had as much to do with undermining highly militant *kisan sabhas* (peasant organizations) as with enjoining non-violence (Pandey 1988: 242ff.). However, Congress activists could exert only limited control over the decoding of Gandhi's message by ordinary people, which ranged from rumours of miracles rewarding believers and punishing doubters, which the nationalist press only refuted when the moral of the story in question was a socially radical one; to the reinterpretation of 'that polysemic word Swaraj' as a call to direct action (Amin 1988). On 5 February 1922, rioters, proclaiming '*Gandhi Maharaj ki jai*' ('Victory for Gandhi's reign'), burned alive 22 policemen in their post at Chauri Chaura in Gorakhpur district, leading Gandhi again to call off the Non-Cooperation campaign.

The end of Non-Cooperation in 1922 drew a line under the possibility of an Indian decolonization process entailing radical social change; there would be no further calls to mass uprising on the scale of 1921–2 until the Quit India campaign in the very different context of 1942. Gandhian tactics were nonetheless successfully redeployed in the Civil Disobedience campaigns of 1931–2. But it was clear in this second period of agitation that Congress too was settling in for a long haul. Thus, Gandhi's 11 demands presented to the Viceroy, Lord Irwin, in January 1931 were addressed to specific grievances relating to the workings of the colonial state, including most famously the demand for the abolition of the salt tax, which inspired Gandhi's 200-mile march to the sea (Sarkar 1989: 283–4). Thus, 'late colonial' Indian politics in this period constituted a cyclical process of agitation, repression and reform, where the outcome of this particular seven-year cycle, from the appointment of an all-European Commission under Sir John Simon in 1928 to the passing of the 1935 Act, represented a consolidation of the British position in India.

Two particular aspects of the Indian status quo in the late 1930s necessitate further comment in view of 'what happened next'. First, we may locate the communal split that would eventually result in Indian Freedom without Unity. British policy had helped generate communal divisions in Indian politics, by instituting separate electorates in 1909, reinforced by the Communal Award of 1932. *Prima facie* evidence of the success of a putative British 'divide and rule' policy came in the 1937 elections which, alongside Congress's sweeping victories, also returned Muslim governments in three Muslim-majority provinces, although not in the North-West Frontier Province (NWFP), where Muslims voted for Congress, or in Punjab and Bengal, where communal demography was more finely balanced. In reality, the picture was more inconclusive. The days of the Congress–Khilafatist alliance were long gone, and although Muslim leaders supported the Congress boycott of the Simon Commission in 1928, Muslims stayed aloof from Civil Disobedience in 1931–2, except in NWFP. But the potential for disunity was greater during periods of nationalist governmental responsibility, when the political spoils were more tangible (Moore 1977). After 1937, communalism dominated Congress politics as never before, as provincial politicians played the Hindu card, either to head off Muslim challenges, as happened in Bengal, or to resist the pressure of the Hindu Mahasabha party, whose new president, V.D. Savarjkar, declared in December 1938 that: 'We Hindus are a Nation by ourselves . . . Hindu nationalists should not at all be apologetic to being called Hindu communalists' (in Sarkar 1989: 356–7).

Although the identities were real enough, however, there was little sense of mainstream Muslim or Hindu politicians playing for the high stakes of the post-1945 period, and all-Indian Muslim politics had little overall cohesion. In particular, the Muslim League fared poorly in the elections, and its leader, Mohammed Ali Jinnah, met with a dusty answer from Congress when in March he sought recognition of the League as sole representative of Muslim interests. It would take the radically altered circumstances of wartime to push the Muslim League into adopting the principle of a separate 'Pakistan', and the prospect of a post-imperial endgame to force its realization.

Secondly, in one respect, the 1935 Act contained the prospect of substantial change to the very framework of the Indian colonial state. This was the provision of a new

Indian Federation to include the princely states, which would thus be represented in the proposed all-India legislature. Although this part of the story has often been glossed over, this reflects more the ultimate failure of the scheme for all-India Federation than its intrinsic importance (Copland 1977: 73). Indeed, briefly, for the first and last time, the princes became principal actors in Indian politics, despite Congress's disdain, and despite being kept at arm's length by the Indian Political Department at New Delhi. Had Federation worked, the Indian endgame of 1946–7 might have taken a radically different course, since not least the balance of power between Congress and the Muslim League would have been quite different (ibid.: 284). The case can be argued too strongly. Although the princes made the original offer of federating with British India, in 1930, the Chamber of Princes, a relatively recent innovation dating from 1917, remained split on the issue, and opponents of Federation were backed by an influential minority of conservative 'Diehards' in London, chief amongst whom was Churchill. Senior British officials, including perhaps Irwin's successor as Viceroy, Lord Willingdon, covertly undermined princely support for Federation. Three years passed before his successor, Lord Linlithgow, made his abortive 'final offer' to the princes in August 1939, by which time Britain was on the verge of war. A key factor in this evolution, which scared off many of the princes, was Congress's reversal of a long-standing policy of non-involvement in the states, culminating in the first campaign of *satyagraha* outside British India in early 1938; this led to mass demonstrations of hostility to princely rule lasting into 1939 (ibid.: 163–74). Hostile Congress involvement in princely politics, and lingering mutual mistrust between the British and many princes, created the background to the abandonment of the princes by the last Viceroy, Lord Mountbatten. The upshot of this complex episode in late colonial politics in India was to ensure the paradox that Britain's most loyal collaborators in India would be deprived of any meaningful role in the Transfer of Power.

Vietnam in the 1930s: Whose Missed Opportunity?

The electoral victory of the Popular Front alliance in France in May 1936, which led to the formation of France's first ever Socialist-led government (including a Socialist colonial minister, Marius Moutet), constitutes a rather different vantage point for considering politics in French Indochina – and specifically in the demographically and politically dominant Vietnamese portions of the Union – on the eve of the Second World War. The Popular Front's success had little or nothing to do with colonial affairs, and its colonial policy may readily be treated peripherally, as showing the movement's good intentions but limited achievements (Jackson 1988: 288).[4] At best, in a longer perspective, the Popular Front was a crucible for the reformist policies that would be implemented in the post-war empire. For those engaged in Vietnamese anti-colonial politics, however, the Popular Front meant simply an all-too-brief phase of liberalism in an otherwise unremitting cycle of limited reform, revolt and repression, before such opportunities as existed in the colonial system in Indochina were radically transformed by French defeat in 1940 and Japanese takeover.

The new liberal phase in French policy in Indochina ushered in by the Popular Front was the exception to the rule of a colonial regime that was unprogressive when not actively repressive. French administrative *bricolage* in Indochina was at a much earlier stage than was the case in India, and the French administration never resolved the ambiguities of its regime in Indochina. Two principal sources of ambiguity may be identified, the first of which concerned the status of the protectorate regimes which retained the pre-colonial monarchies across Indochina except for the formal colony of Cochinchina, but destroyed their budgetary autonomy. Full authority and revenue-raising powers now lay with the Governor-General, who could depose any monarch with the temerity to assert his autonomy, as happened with both Than Thai in 1907 and Duy Tan in 1915 (see above). Vestigial rights of the Emperor's council were removed as late as 1925, and the Emperor's ministers were subject to French veto, as happened with the newly enthroned Bao Dai's progressive Interior Minister in 1932–3, the young Catholic nationalist, Ngo Dinh Diem (Brocheux & Hémery 1995: 86–9, 105–6, 314).[5] The French administration could not abolish the monarchies outright, in part because they might provide the focus for anti-French resistance, as they had done during the conquest, but more particularly because the imperial administrative system of the mandarinate, and its equivalents in Laos and Cambodia, were needed to ensure the maintenance of local administration 'on the cheap'. Thus, outside Cochinchina, the French system was *both* one of indirect rule *and* of direct rule, and the monarchs' protected status was deeply problematic. As one nationalist writer put it in 1924: 'The king is still there, but the Fatherland no longer exists. Without a fatherland, why do we need a king?' (in ibid.: 89) Bao Dai retained sufficient prestige, and enough of a sense of imperial responsibility, to stake out a role for himself as national figurehead, and to be courted in turn by the Japanese, the Viet Minh and the French (Ibid.: 314; Antlöv 1995; Chapter 4). But when the Emperor's 'celestial mandate' came to an end, in 1945, he was just one national contender amongst many; thus, it was as Citizen Vinh Thuy that he would be appointed as 'Supreme Counsellor' by Ho Chi Minh in 1945, and his resumption of his imperial name was honorific when he became 'Head of State' of Vietnam in 1949.

A second set of ambiguities gravitated between the poles of administrative continuity and political progress. The predominance of the first of these reflects in part the relative immaturity of the French regime, barely fully established by the time of the First World War. Since the French empire reached its zenith only after 1918, it had little incentive to introduce political changes, while after 1930, prolonged crisis for both France and the empire imposed a taboo on any change; political immobilism resulted in either case (Brocheux & Hémery 1995: 99). Periods of relative liberalism depended on the initiative of an individual governor-general. Thus Albert Sarraut, appointed twice to Hanoi in 1911–14 and 1917–19, subsequently Minister of Colonies, and still an *éminence grise* in colonial affairs in the 1950s, defined French colonial policy in terms of *mise en valeur*, that is, the utilitarian economic and social development of the colonies (and Indochina in particular) to the mutual benefit of both colonial populations and metropolitan France (ibid.: 291–3). But Sarraut's reforms amounted to grand rhetorical gestures, coupled with grudging openings towards conservative national figures, who could be co-opted to the municipal councils of the three major cities, Saigon, Hanoi, Haiphong, or to the Colonial Council of Cochinchina (Cooper, 2001: 29–40, 109–11). Similarly, the Socialist Governor-General Alexandre Varenne, appointed by the Left Cartel government in 1925, arrived in Hanoi just in time to parole the veteran nationalist activist Phan Boi Chau, recently sentenced to hard labour for life. Varenne's administrative reforms stopped well short of legalizing the formation of Vietnamese political parties. But following his return to parliament, he was instrumental in promoting the doctrinal innovation of an 'altruistic colonization', which underpinned the Popular Front's colonial policy but had few durable applications (Gantès 1999; Marr, 1983: 15–19; Chapter 4).

Against this sterile and repressive background of French political immobilism – disguised by the empty rhetorical trope of a 'moral conquest' – two striking features of the Vietnamese political 'scene' emerged. First, Vietnam was undergoing an astonishing cultural renaissance, as a generation of Confucian literati, who had had to come to terms with the humiliation of conquest, gave way to a 'new intelligentsia', drawn primarily from 'a volatile component made up of shopkeepers, small traders, artisans, clerks, managers, interpreters, primary school teachers, journalists, and technicians' – in short, a colonial petty bourgeoisie. This group was defined less by class than by a state of mind, a willingness to address the implications of irreversible change wrought by French colonial rule. Their numbers were not great, but enough: of an urban petty bourgeoisie of 550,000 people, perhaps five thousand in the mid-1920s, doubling within a decade, had both the requisite education and the inclination to meet in informal study groups, to publish and read newspapers, books and pamphlets, and to debate (Marr 1983: 30–3). There can be no more striking example of the importance of Anderson's (1991) 'print capitalism' to the development of a modern, national consciousness, facilitated and driven by the burgeoning 'new' national print language, *quoc ngu*. Seventeenth-century Jesuit missionaries first developed a Latin alphabet for Vietnamese, and it spread with the arrival of printing presses along with the French conquest from 1861. However, its popularity far outstripped its intended use as a crude instrument of colonial propaganda. *Quoc ngu* was far more accessible than the alternatives, whether French, or the Chinese of the mandarins, or the adapted Chinese script in which Vietnamese had hitherto been transcribed. Offering a direct link between written and spoken languages, it could be read out loud to an illiterate audience, while also promoting literacy (ibid.: 44–53). Its users could put distance between themselves and the languages representing both Vietnam's past enthrallment to imperial China and its present colonial status. *Quoc ngu* literary production during the colonial period up to 1940 included everything from translations of key French and other western works of literature, science and philosophy, re-editions of Vietnamese classics and commentaries on Confucian philosophy, as well as 'home-grown' publications ranging from self-help manuals to political pamphlets to novels and short stories.[6]

Literacy, the development of the language, and the ideas debated and enshrined in the printed word generated great intellectual excitement in their own right. However, they also indicated the need for political action, as intellectuals came under the influence of social Darwinist ideas, suggesting that Vietnam had been defeated because of some deep-seated, but probably remediable, quasi-biological weakness relative to France. Intellectuals moved away from the 'quietude, fatalism, harmony and comforting repetition' of Confucian tradition, and towards Marxist advocacy of dynamic struggle in defence of material self-interest (ibid.: 130–1, 292–302, 315ff.). Although it would be difficult to generalize the ways in which intellectual activity gave way to political action, anecdotal 'before and after' snapshots might include the history teacher, Vo Nguyen Giap, future strategist of the Viet Minh's war against the French, who, not yet thirty in 1936, was treasurer of the Association for Diffusion of *Quoc Ngu* Study; Tran Trong Kim, prime minister of the short-lived government brought to power following the Japanese takeover of March 1945, a primary school inspector and author of a widely read treatise on Confucianism; and the newly renamed Ho Chi Minh, 'probably the most confident practitioner of the new history', and the author, during his wartime sojourn in Tonkinese highlands, of a 236-line poem, typed out on his portable typewriter (and, sadly, now lost), on 'The History of Our Country from 2879 BC to 1942', forecasting independence in 1945 (ibid.: 328, 106f., 284–5).

The emphasis in Vietnamese politics on revolutionary modes of action was the logical outcome of a dialectical contradiction, as this intellectual explosion came up against the strict limits imposed on political activity by the colonial authorities, whose watchword by the early 1930s was summed up by the Governor-General, Pierre Pasquier: 'Stay vigilant, punish, repress' (in Brocheux & Hémery 1995: 310). Certainly, it is difficult to apply Breuilly's model of an emergent national elite seeking to mobilize mass participation, as Vietnam's political class, if it existed, remained fragmented between a conservative, collaborating elite, and the proponents of revolutionary anti-colonialism, the latter kept under close but not always effective surveillance by the colonial *Sûreté* (political police) (Morlat 1990).[7] Individual parties, such as the Vietnamese National Party (Viet Nam Quoc Dan Dang, VNQDD), founded in November 1927 on the model of the Chinese Guomindang, conceived their objectives more readily in terms of insurrectionary violence than mass mobilization. The VNQDD instigated a wave of bombings and political assassinations from early 1929, and then ordered the February 1930 revolt of the Yen Bay garrison in Tonkin. Yen Bay was a disaster for the VNQDD from which it never recovered, except briefly under the Chinese occupation of Tonkin in 1945–6. The insurrection was rapidly broken, the party's known membership was rounded up, and of almost five hundred prisoners sentenced, eighty were executed, 102 condemned to hard labour for life, and 243 deported; more than 500 *tirailleurs indochinois* identified as VNQDD sympathizers were cashiered or transferred to punishment battalions or to Africa (ibid.: 120–8).

Conversely, mass mobilization was very much the point of the communist-inspired risings which broke out soon after, in Cochinchina and across northern Annam, a moment of crisis for French colonialism in Indochina, known collectively as the 'Red Terror'. (Given the scale of the repression, the term 'white terror' might seem more appropriate.) Notwithstanding the 'Red' sobriquet, the hard-pressed insurgent peasantry needed little encouragement from a newly united and poorly coordinated urban-based Communist party. Both regions were fertile but ecologically vulnerable, with a long tradition of rebellion against an oppressive and inflexible colonial tax regime; the Annamese provinces involved, Nghe An and Ha Tinh (Nghe-Tinh), were particularly poor, restricted to a narrow strip of land between the mountains and the sea and subject to fluctuations in rainfall (Scott 1976: 120ff.). The link is striking between the onset of the Depression, marked by the headlong fall in the price of rice from April 1930, and the beginnings of peasant resistance the following month. Although the Cochinchinese revolt was rapidly brought under control by the French authorities, the Nghe-Tinh rebellion soon took on more widespread forms of organization, taking control of rice stocks and local archives, and forcing the flight of local notables and officials; between September and December as many as 31 rural soviets (*Xo Viet*, a felicitous coinage) were declared in the two provinces in January–February 1931. Although Nghe-Tinh was triggered by a wave of strike action around 1 May, and workers were involved in the spread of communist techniques of agitation and propaganda, the party leadership initially kept its distance from local 'adventurism'; soon it felt morally and strategically obliged to back the soviets (Brocheux & Hémery 1995: 307; Marr 1983: 380–5; Scott 1976: 142–9). The Nghe-Tinh soviets were eventually crushed by main force, including aerial strafing and bombing of large demonstrations, and brutal 'search-and-destroy' missions conducted by a Foreign Legion battalion. The movement was not wound up until the end of 1931, by which time it had partially collapsed in conditions of near-famine.

What conclusions may be drawn from this episode regarding the role of communists as an eventual anti-colonial movement? Perhaps least plausibly, the French colonial minister, Paul Reynaud, told parliament that the rebellion was unsurprising given the presence of 'twelve communist armies' in China, and the still recent Communist rebellion in Dutch East Indies in 1926; similarly, the Commission of Enquiry concluded that the insurrection was part of a Soviet plan to disrupt the colonies, given the 'ineffectiveness of their efforts in the European countries' (in Foster 1995: 67–8). These were comforting explanations, suggesting that social peace could be achieved simply through police action against communist infiltrators and their excitable Vietnamese audience. However, the impetus for rebellion largely came from the peasant rebels themselves, with the party following rather than directing the insurrection, and the Comintern had exercised little control over the fledgling party. Indeed, a unified Vietnamese Communist Party (subsequently renamed Indochinese Communist Party according to Comintern rules) had been formed only in February 1930, in Kowloon, under the guidance of Nguyen Ai Quoc, then the Comintern representative for the 'South Seas', uniting three feuding communist groups.[8]

The communists' own lessons of 1930–1 included the need to prepare for the brutal repressive tactics of the French army, and to avoid 'class war', which had pitted poor peasants against richer landowning peasants in many villages. Most of all the party needed to exercise better leadership and to impose tighter discipline, knowing when to retreat in order to consolidate core political gains, and to avoid what one Comintern delegate called 'demonstrationism without a way out' (Marr 1983: 386–7). Although the party rebuilt itself, partly with the help of Vietnamese cadres returning from Moscow, most surviving Communist Party leaders had ample time to discuss these lessons within the confines of Vietnam's well-developed prisons, which 'were to the Vietnamese what the Long March was to the Chinese . . . microcosms of colonial society and universities of revolutionary theory and practice', or indeed one crucial means by which a Vietnamese national community imagined itself (ibid.: 308; Zinoman 2001). From 1930–1, when as many as 10,000 political prisoners entered the system, prisons played an integral part in the cycle of colonial repression and reform. Thus, one significant contribution of the Popular Front to Vietnamese political life was in releasing the detainees of 1930–1; by 1939 the prisons had again started to fill up. There was little sign that a revolution might be possible within six years that might threaten an as yet unassailable French colonial presence.

Algeria: Blocked Reform and Contested Nationhood

'Algeria is France.' When the newly formed Algerian National Liberation Front (FLN) launched its insurrection on 1 November 1954, thus initiating the bloodiest and most intense of colonial conflicts, this was how the then government in Paris explained why the decolonization of Algeria was not an option. What was striking about this idea was that it came, not from supporters of Algerian settlers or the military, but from the modernizing centre-left prime minister, Pierre Mendès-France, who was already playing a decisive role in the decolonization of Indochina, Morocco and Tunisia, and from his Interior Minister, François Mitterrand, whose reputation as a colonial reformer was also not in doubt. Of course, there were substantial conjunctural 'reasons of state' involved, but the idea of Algeria as an integral part of France was a given within the broad mainstream of French political and public opinion. In examining the state of affairs in Algeria twenty years earlier, when arguably the idea of French Algeria barely needed to be defended, the question of how Algeria came to occupy this extraordinary position within the French empire concerns us less than its practical consequences for French policy, in particular the obstacles it presented to the development of a viable indigenous nationalist movement. Indeed, even some of the most thoughtful and influential Algerian spokesmen held that Algeria's 'Frenchness' precluded either the necessity or the possibility of an Algerian national identity.

What was meant by the idea of French Algeria? The process of constitutional assimilation, initiated in 1848, was suspended during the Second Empire (1852– 1870), since Napoleon III declared himself, not without ambiguity, 'as much the emperor of the Arabs as of the French' (in Stora 2001: 5). It reached a climax after the inception of the Third Republic after 1871, and thus coincided with the process of internal metropolitan assimilation by which the Republic transformed 'peasants into Frenchmen'. Algeria's 'Frenchness' allowed the interpretation of French law, particularly property law and laws of nationality, to the exclusive benefit of the settler community. In particular, French courts had systematically used the absence of a clear concept of private landownership under the Ottoman law prevailing in Algeria before the conquest, to allow settlers to acquire some 215 million acres of land in the years between 1871 and 1919. Settler expansion had thus disrupted a complex system of indigenous access rights, destroyed tribal structures and swept away the prerogatives and charitable functions of Muslim religious orders (ibid.: 6–7). Driven from the best land, Algerians had the choice between menial labour on European farms, fleeing to the big cities or to the mountains, or, from the early twentieth century, in a pattern of labour migration still leaving substantial traces today, seeking employment in metropolitan France. European settlement in this 'land of opportunity' had been officially encouraged from the start. After 1871, Alsatians and Lorrains refusing to live under German rule were offered parcels of land, although it was poor peasants from the French Mediterranean and Corsica who were particularly encouraged to emigrate. Immigrants from around the Mediterranean, principally from Spain, Italy and Malta, swelled their numbers, and by the law of 26 June 1889, they were created French citizens en masse; by 1896, these immigrants outnumbered settlers of French origin. By 1954, 79 per cent of these *pieds noirs* ('black feet'), as they became known for reasons that remain obscure, had been born in Algeria. Notwithstanding the great Algerian land-grab, most *pieds noirs* lived in the coastal cities, and 80 per cent of Algerian land was in the hands of some 10 per cent of *pieds noirs*. Members of a substantial Jewish community, some 25,000 strong in 1830, whose presence in Algeria long predated French conquest, were also assimilated as French citizens, by the Crémieux Decree of 1871.[9]

By contrast, indigenous Muslim Algerians were not citizens, but subjects, liable to a range of 'administrative' sanctions, imposed by a Native Code (*Indigénat*) established in 1881 and only finally abolished in 1944. Withholding citizenship rights did not prelude the imposition of Republican duties, however: Algerian conscription was introduced from 1908, in the face of protests from both settlers (who understood its political significance) and Algerians, 173,000 of whom fought in the First World War, half of them volunteers, and 25,000 of whom died. As in sub-Saharan Africa, young Algerians fled into the forests to evade conscription; then, in 1916 in the rugged Aurès mountains (a stronghold also of the 1954 insurrection), they rose up against it, in the first armed revolt against French rule since the 1871 Kabyle insurrection of Sheikh Mokrani (ibid.: 12; Nouschi 1962: 19–25).

After the First World War, Prime Minister Georges Clémenceau implemented a project for Algerian reform he had proposed while in opposition in 1915, in recognition of Algerian war service. Clémenceau's Law of 4 February 1919 did not address Algeria's social and economic inequities, but rather, in the narrowly political field, offered citizenship to a select band of (male) Algerians aged 25 or older, single or monogamous, having a clean administrative record, resident in the same commune in either France or Algeria for two years; and who could claim at least one of the following: military service, literacy in French, land ownership, elected public office, a public service pension, a French decoration, or a French citizen for a parent. Even if someone passed through these 'filters' the Governor-General could still veto his citizenship (Nouschi 1962: 53–4). The 1919 law established a pattern for Algerian reform that would last into the 1950s, whereby an ostensibly restrictive change to the status quo, greeted in indifference by Algerians, would be resisted by outraged settler opinion, and rejected or neutralized in its impact. Algerian opposition came in the 1920 municipal elections, in which Emir Khaled, grandson of Abd-el Kader, the great leader of resistance to the French conquest, established another pattern, by winning the elections, only for the results to be annulled and Khaled declared ineligible (ibid.: 55).

The French champion of Algerian reform in this period was Senator Maurice Viollette, a liberal Governor-General in the mid-1920s who had earned the sobriquet 'Viollette-the-Arab'. Viollette's moment came a decade later, as Minister of State in Léon Blum's Popular Front government, with responsibility for Algerian affairs. Viollette reintroduced an aborted law of 1931, which went beyond the framework of 1919, and in particular proposed to grant citizenship without candidates having to renounce their 'personal status' as Muslims (for example, in respect of marriage and property law). Viollette's plan was still cautious, and would have granted citizenship to an estimated 20,000 Algerians. Although (or perhaps because) it had Blum's full backing, the plan suffered the fate of so much of the Popular Front's reform programme, and never made it into law, although it was only finally withdrawn in

September 1938. Its chances of acceptance were minimal at best, following a concerted campaign in the Parisian and Algerian press, which regarded nationalist support for the plan as proof that it was anti-French in spirit (ibid.: 79–95; Tostain 1999). Its ultimate significance, apart from demonstrating the unlikelihood of successful reform in Algeria, was perhaps that it acted as a litmus test for the various currents of Algerian nationalism, to which we now turn.

Viollette once warned that there were '100,000 Muslims who mattered in Algeria, and that if they were not to be allowed to join the French *Patrie*, they would look for another one elsewhere' (Ageron 1979: vol. 2, 388). This gave a narrowly Francocentric slant to the wider problem facing Algerian reform: the 1919 and 1936 reforms did not go far enough, even if they stood a chance of implementation, and there were limits to the patience even of those 'moderate' nationalists who comprised Viollette's '100,000 Muslims'. By this latter group, Viollette had in mind the French-speaking intellectuals affiliated to the Young Algeria movement, whose views were shared by a Federation of Algerian elected representatives formed in 1927. By the 1930s, their most eloquent spokesman was Ferhat Abbas, the French-trained pharmacist from Constantine, born in 1899, whose denial of the Algerian nation's existence was quoted above. In another article, published in the *Jeune Algérien* newspaper, Abbas gave his own version of Viollette's warning: 'There is nothing in the Holy Book which prevents a Muslim Algerian from being *nationally* French [. . .], and conscious of the demands of national solidarity. Nothing, that is, except colonization' (in Nouschi 1962: 63). Events in the 1930s, not only the failure of the Blum–Viollette Plan, which Abbas and his colleagues naturally supported, but also, for example, the earlier insensitive tub-thumping celebration of the centenary of conquest, in 1930, were thus pushing even the 'intellectually French but culturally Muslim' Young Algerians towards radical, oppositional nationalism.

The diametrically opposed argument to that of Ferhat Abbas may best be summed up in the pithy formulation of Sheikh Abdelhamid Ben Badis (1889–1940), founder and leader of the Association of Algerian Ulama: 'Arabic is my language, Algeria is my country, Islam is my religion' (Stora, 2001: 16). The aims of this Association, formed in 1931, were more cultural than political, and represented an attempt to defend Islam in the wake of the collapse of the Ottoman empire and the abolition of the caliphate. Within Algeria, the *ulama* (doctors of law) opposed the Sufi preachers (*marabouts*) and local religious orders who threatened the purity and unity of Islam, although they were also critical of the French colonial regime for sustaining these institutions. Ben Badis's formula reflected a complex set of overlapping Arabic concepts, none of which exactly corresponded to the western category of 'Nation': *umma* (nation or community of believers), *cha'ab* (people), *watan* (homeland) and *quawmiyya* (nationality) (ibid.). This nonetheless allowed him a clear enough, classically nationalist, position from which to refute Ferhat Abbas's argument:

> History has taught us that the Muslim people of Algeria was created like all the others. It has its history, marked by great events; it has religious unity, a language; it has a culture and customs, which have their good and their bad features. This Muslim people is not France; it cannot be part of France, it does not want to be part of France. As a people, it is separated from France by language, customs and religion; it has no desire to be

incorporated into France. It possesses a fatherland with fixed frontiers; and that is the Algerian fatherland, which extends as far as is recognized. (in Nouschi 1962: 89)

Although the *ulama* supported the Popular Front, and hence the Blum–Viollette Plan, this was conditional upon the long-term creation of an Algeria protectorate, 'that is to say a democratic nation under French protection' (ibid.: 90). Here too was the potential for political radicalization, and Ben Badis's successors would eventually rally to the FLN.

Only one Algerian party in the 1930s combined a consistent campaign for Algerian independence with opposition to the Popular Front government. This was the *Etoile Nord-Africaine* (ENA, North African Star), which from its formation in 1926 until it was eclipsed by the FLN in the 1950s, constituted the principal vector of radical Algerian nationalism. Unlike the elitist Young Algerians or the scholarly *ulama*, neither of whose programmes resonated strongly with ordinary Algerians, ENA was a populist, revolutionary party, although its capacity for decisive action did not square with its radical aims: Algerian independence, the withdrawal of French troops, land reforms, democratic reforms, the creation of Arabic schools, etc (ibid.: 61–2). Characteristic of the party's appeal to poor Algerians was the fact that it was founded amongst Algerian migrant workers in Paris, and drew strength from the migrant labour force right through to the 1950s. Its leader, Messali Hadj, born of artisan stock in Tlemcen in 1898, had served in the army in 1918, and moved to France in 1923. Although Messali received crucial support from the PCF in setting up the party, it was not a communist party, and from its reformation in 1932, it banned PCF members from its ranks. Indeed, from 1935, it was opposed by a separate Algerian Communist Party (PCA), supported primarily by European trades unionists and intellectuals (ibid.). Messali's message was clear to his Algerian supporters, and to the French administration, who initiated a further recurring pattern in Algerian history in 1929 by dissolving ENA, as its programme represented a threat to French sovereignty in North Africa. Reconstituted in 1932 as the Glorious North African Star, by early 1937 it led popular unrest surrounding the Blum–Viollette Plan. On 26 January 1937, it was again banned, this time under the Popular Front's new legislation banning extra-parliamentary 'leagues', designed to combat the fascist threat in France. After Messali reformed the party as the Popular Algerian Party (PPA) in the spring of 1937, and won several seats in municipal elections in Algiers, he was imprisoned for 'reconstituting a banned league' amongst other charges; he was released in 1939, but the PPA and its newspaper *El Oumma* were banned at the end of September. In Algeria, no less than in India and Indochina, it was the war that would create the conditions for a substantial shift in the fortunes of the nationalist movement, although in the Algerian case, not even the war was enough on its own to shift the bases for French colonial rule.

Notes

1   Referring to the period around Queen Victoria's Diamond Jubilee, 1897, when Gandhi was practising law in Natal, South Africa.

2   For example, Seretse Khama of Bechuanaland, deposed in 1952 after marrying an English-woman, which officials feared would excite South African disapproval; the Kabaka of Buganda, deposed in 1953 following a dispute sparked initially by the honours accorded him at Elizabeth II's coronation; and Sultan Ibrahim of Johore's two successive European wives, both granted the title of Sultana against British advice.

3   Sarkar 1989: quoting, respectively, the Viceroy, Viscount Dufferin c.1888, 'no doubt precisely because there were a few signs that it might become less microscopic', 94; and Aurobindo Ghosh, attacking Congress 'mendicancy', 97–8; and see Seal 1973: 17.

4   An exception in focus, if not in overall conclusions, is Chafer & Sackur 1999.

5   Diem's moment was yet to come, as the vehemently anti-French future president of the post-1954 Republic of South Vietnam.

6   As represented by more than 9,000 titles held in the Bibliothèque Nationale, Paris, for the period 1923–42, and by hundreds of periodicals and many more clandestine publications now lost; see ibid.: 47n. & 49–50n.

7   Significantly, the Director of Political Affairs in the Government-General was also *ex officio* head of the *Sûreté Générale*.

8   One of Lenin's Twenty Conditions was that member parties had to be named after the state unit within which they operated.

9   For clarity, the term 'Algerian' is here used to describe those of indigenous Algerian descent, as opposed to European settlers. Throughout the colonial period, 'Algerian' meant simply 'born in, or living in' Algeria, so that, for example, the writer Albert Camus, of mixed Alsatian and Spanish parentage but born in Algeria, might describe himself as 'Algerian'. The Crémieux Decree was rescinded by the Vichy regime in 1940, and restored in 1944. Although by the definition given Algerian Jews were 'Algerian', they were thus drawn into the settler camp, and they dispersed along with the *pieds noirs* at independence.

The Second World War and the 'First Wave' of Decolonization

How may we assess the impact of the Second World War on the colonial empires? The wider argument which forms the background to this chapter is that the Second World War triggered comprehensive changes, over the following two decades and more, in the way the international system was ordered, in the ways in which colonial rule was managed and tolerated, and in the relative standing and prosperity of the colonial powers, such as to make some form of decolonization increasingly inevitable. But what of direct impact? Certainly, in a number of key cases, the evidence of the war's direct impact on decolonization is compelling. Thus, in British India, the Second World War threw up a complex set of opportunities and threats for both Indian political leaders and the British Raj, as a consequence of which India moved decisively into the endgame of decolonization during the war years, although the outcomes of this process were radically different from those either intended or envisaged. Clearly, also, in the Southeast Asian colonies occupied by the Japanese, war created an 'opportune moment' which could be seized by well-placed local political movements, making it difficult if not impossible for colonial powers to recover their position after 1945. This chapter will consider these cases in turn, but we start with a more general survey of the ways in which war impacted on the structures and practices of colonial rule.

Many of the issues raised during the Second World War had been prefigured in the colonial politics of the First World War and the interwar period. Colonial governments had already mobilized men to fight and labour during the First World War, which had had a significant impact on colonial states, many still at a rudimentary state of development when war broke out in 1914. The overall effect of the 1919 settlement was to consolidate and extend colonial rule, despite the ideological challenges of Bolshevism and Wilsonian national self-determination. Nonetheless, the post-1919 crisis had rocked the empires, bringing nominal independence to Egypt and triggering waves of unrest in India which evoked the British official mind's worst nightmares of colonial breakdown. The Depression too had shaken colonial economies by driving down prices and imperilling colonial budgets dependent on tax revenue, disrupted patterns of labour migration, and generally increased the pressures on the colonial state's crucial collaborative relationships. In so doing, it stirred many colonial administrations from their wonted 'masterly inactivity' (Darwin 1999), and generated many of the policies, such as soil conservation, which were to carry through into the postwar 'second colonial occupation'. More generally, it illustrated the point that colonies were not isolated from the world by their imperial protectors, as developments in a nascent 'European Civil War' impacted in the colonies. Colonial governments feared the impact of Comintern policies on emergent nationalist movements, though popular revolt such as the 1931 Nghe-Tinh 'soviets' in Vietnam did not need to be directed by party cadres, much less by Moscow. Fascism too surged out from Europe in the form of the brutal Italian invasion of Abyssinia, which provoked a diffuse, politically inarticulate wave of popular disquiet, characterized by Frank Füredi as an 'Italo-Abyssinian Complex', which worried British officials as far afield as Jamaica (Füredi 1994a: 32). Metropolitan developments could have far-reaching, if ambivalent consequences at the colonial periphery, most notably, as we have seen, the election of a Popular Front government in France in 1936.

Nowhere did the Second World War simply effect radical change *ex nihilo* in colonial states and societies, which were already in a state of crisis, albeit a slow-boiling one: did this represent Robinson's (1979) 'moral disarmament' of the empires, as officials struggled to reconcile the imperial centre's democratic principles with their own autocratic habits of mind; or was it more, as Füredi (1994a: 53) has it, a 'moral collapse' prompted by 'sentiments of anxiety and inner anguish that accompanied the perception that the imperial idea had become irrelevant'? In either case, colonial administrations were already developing the kinds of policy that would be applied more generally in response to the pressures of war. However, war did not necessarily to spell the end of colonial empire. Rather, our starting point is to suggest that the Second World War's primary effect on colonial empire was to determine a new conviction as to the purpose of empire, which was to support the metropole in times of national crisis. This may be understood, first, following Gallagher (1982), in terms of the last great 'Revival' of the British empire:

> Only in war, most clearly during the Second World War, did the Empire approach the otherwise mythical status of a formidable, efficient, and effective power system, prepared to exploit its apparently limitless resources, and actually able to deploy forces throughout the world. (Jeffery 1999: 307)

For the French and the Dutch, too, the experience of defeat sharpened the political focus on an empire, lost in the Dutch case, and for the French partly lost and partly split between Vichy and Free France, whose importance for the prestige and very survival of the metropolitan 'home country' was perhaps appreciated as never before. This sense of purpose in turn infused and informed policy making, or at least planning, for the post-war colonial state. This argument will be taken up in detail in the following Chapters, where we turn to post-war colonial policy making.

But a further point to be made here is that this reinvigoration of imperial purpose was enhanced by the challenge of American anti-colonialism and the more familiar, but less immediately perceptible threat of Soviet anti-imperialism. Britain and France may have 'been there before' in 1919, but this time the ideological threat was accompanied by a decisive shift in the relative and absolute power of the colonial empires as international players, and by the presence of American forces in many colonial possessions, whether as occupying forces in North Africa or in West African and Pacific bases. To be sure, the tide was already turning by late 1942, when Churchill famously declared that he had 'not become his Majesty's First Minister in order to preside over the liquidation of the British Empire', and de Gaulle too could count with increasing confidence upon the restoration of French imperial unity. Even so, by the time of Japanese capitulation in August 1945, the post-war future of colonial empire was still far from clear.

In short, the Second World War represented a decisive watershed for colonial empire, but the metaphor of 'watershed' needs to be carefully nuanced. History cannot be an exact science like physical geography, and whereas in some cases a watershed may be marked unmistakably by a chain of peaks (imperial defeat, foreign occupation, nationalist revolution), more usually the watershed was crossed as if by hiking over open ground with no reliable map or compass to indicate whether the course of events was flowing towards decolonization, or whether merely with the current of imperial policy and control – or both.

Imperial Sovereignty

The first theme to be considered is that of imperial sovereignty, or more precisely the ways in which war threatened the integrity of the colonial empires. While even the Dominion governments of Australia, New Zealand, Canada and South Africa needed to manage the declaration of war 'behind' the imperial mother country with varying degrees of caution, and while the ambiguity of Ireland's constitutional status with regard to the empire led to the Irish Free State's neutrality (Boyce 1999: 70–88), only in India was the Declaration of War itself at issue. Indeed, as we shall discuss below, this was in many ways the turning point at which Indian politics steered decisively towards the 1947 Transfer of Power.

Elsewhere it seemed, for the duration of the Phoney War at least, as if there was no immediate threat to the informal interwar system of 'collective security for empire' (Robinson 1984: 84), in what still seemed an almost exclusively European conflict. Potential points of conflict over colonial territory could readily be identified, although until Italy entered the war on 10 June 1940, these were theoretical rather than actual. Such was the case in the Western Mediterranean, which the French Prime Minister, Edouard Daladier, had toured in January 1939 in order to counter increasingly strident Italian claims to Nice, Corsica and Tunisia (Duroselle 1982: 95). The French protectorate in Tunisia was particularly vulnerable, not only because of its proximity to Italian Libya but also, given the dominant Italian settler community, whose Fascist sympathies were well known. British and French possessions in the Horn of Africa were similarly vulnerable, and Spanish claims for frontier revision in Algeria and Morocco, as well as Italian threats to Chad and British and French Somaliland might also be anticipated (Thomas 1998: 31–2). Proposals for the return of Cameroun and Togo to German rule had been entertained by the British government in 1936 and discussed in Paris, but Hitler was less interested in this curious episode in appeasement than his then Economics Minister, Hjalmar Schacht (Crozier 1988; 1997: 126–9). In the British Cameroons, as in Tunisia, the perceived threat was more internal than external. German Kamerun had been partitioned in 1919, but whereas French settlers had bought out German plantations, a German settler community remained on the British side, and claimed loyalty to the Nazi regime (Ndi 1986: 213). However, the period to May 1940 largely represented 'business as usual', as colonial governments struggled with the aftershocks of the 1930s crisis.

This picture was radically transformed by German defeat and occupation of three colonial powers, France, Belgium and the Netherlands, by Italian entry into the war on the German side, and by the British empire's 'darkest hour'. From the outset, colonial control was a central aim in General Charles de Gaulle's campaign against the German occupation and partition of metropolitan France, although at the time of his famous *Appel* of 18 June 1940, he was completely without resources or territory, let alone the authority and prestige of the Leader of the French State from July 1940, Marshall Pétain. What for de Gaulle was initially only a theoretical proposition, that France could depend on 'a vast empire behind her', worked massively in Pétain's favour, as proconsul after proconsul rallied behind the 'victor of Verdun' and hero of the Moroccan Rif War of 1925. Those proconsuls initially inclined to rally behind de Gaulle were swiftly replaced, as happened with Governors-General Marcel de Coppet in Madagascar and Georges Catroux in Indochina; both became key players in Gaullist colonial administrations. In the Caribbean colonies of Martinique, Guadeloupe and Guyane, the presence of French naval vessels ensured loyalty to Pétain, and the persecution of Gaullist sympathizers. Loyalism to Pétain was reinforced by the 'treacherous' British attack on the French naval squadron based at Mers el-Kébir, in Algeria, on 3 July 1940, and by the less bloody but – for de Gaulle – scarcely less catastrophic Anglo-Gaullist raid on Dakar in September 1940, both of which, along with the British retreat from Dunkirk, constituted mainstays of Vichy anglophobic propaganda for years to come (Thomas 1998: 38–49). For Dutch and Belgian colonial administrations, there was no conflict over loyalty to their respective governments-in-exile in London, although some Belgian settlers entertained the fantasy of a unilateral declaration of settler independence, possibly with South African backing; in the event, Governor-General Pierre Ryckmans integrated the Belgian Congo fully into the Allied war effort in Africa (M'Bokolo 1982).

De Gaulle soon acquired colonial territory, and over the three years to Bastille Day, 14 July 1943, every French colonial dependency switched authority from Pétain to de Gaulle, with the single exception of Indochina, where a Vichyste administration endured, even after the eclipse of the Vichy regime in France, until the Japanese takeover of 9 March 1945. By September 1940, after a series of swiftly executed *coups d'état*, de Gaulle had a territorial base in Africa comprising principally the territories of French Equatorial Africa and Cameroun, and a makeshift capital at Brazzaville; 'I feel how much this land is French', he declared somewhat improbably on arrival at the heart of 'Free French Africa' (26 October 1940, in 1970: vol. 1, 38). Only in Gabon was this process delayed until November 1940, when it was marked by Franco-French skirmishing and the suicide of the wavering governor. Other outlying administrations had little choice but to declare for de Gaulle, given the overwhelming proximity of British territory, as in the tiny French Indian enclaves (total population in 1941,

323,295), or were encouraged to do so by the Royal Navy, as in New Caledonia and Polynesia (Aldrich 1996; Deschamps et al. 1948; Weber 2002).

Surprisingly little actually changed in the running of the colonial state in the wake of what were after all 'palace revolutions, not popular uprisings' (Thomas 1998: 56), in which mostly officials, army officers and small settler communities participated. Different outcomes might have transformed the face of colonial Africa with more immediate effect, for instance had the Dakar raid succeeded (or, indeed, not been launched), or had Tchad been attacked, as planned, by an expeditionary force from Dakar. Military resources were lacking for operations on all but a minimal scale, and there was some logic to the resulting stalemate that lasted for more than two years. Free French territories, largely inaccessible from the sea and therefore economically interdependent with neighbouring British colonies, particularly Nigeria, were incorporated along with the Belgian Congo into an overall Allied African strategy for production and supply, including the crucial air route from West Africa to Egypt. From being a remote backwater, Tchad now constituted a front line with the Axis, providing Gaullist colonial troops with their first battle honours, at Bir Hakeim in the Libyan Desert. Conversely, AOF had acquired a hostile frontier with British Africa, which gave a political edge to problems over labour migration. Although Dakar underpinned Vichy's efforts to act independently of German control, it was isolated and economically stagnant until incorporated into a united Gaullist administration in 1943. More generally, the emergence of a temporary Free French colonial power assisted the 'internationalization' of African colonialism brought about by the Allied war effort in Africa (Kent 1992).

African War Efforts and Hardships

Aside from the longer-term consequences of French political loyalties, the more immediate impact of war in colonial Africa may be measured in military mobilization and the various concerted efforts for economic production. There was no more direct and visceral way in which the colonial state could engage its colonial subjects than through military mobilization, and no more vivid way in which that engagement could be demonstrated than through reports of bravery and sacrifice on the battlefield (Lonsdale 1986b). At the same time, fighting and perhaps dying for France or for the British empire created expectations of reward for soldiers and their dependants, and the likelihood that those expectations would be disappointed, with incalculable but certainly anxiety-inducing consequences for colonial rule.

The deployment of that superb imperial resource the Indian army was a significant factor in both British and nationalist calculations in the Indian endgame. In Africa, however, only the French grasped the double-edged sword of military mobilization with anything approaching eagerness. In 1914–18, France had deployed a 175,000-strong 'Force Noire' of so-called tirailleurs sénégalais, both as a formidable fighting force in its own right, and as a curious secret weapon, since they could cynically be portrayed in racist French propaganda as savage and unflinching on the battlefield.[1] In 1939–40, some 100,000 Black African troops were conscripted, and their numbers reached close to 9 per cent of French army strength (compared with 3 per cent in

1914–18); of these, 24,270 were missing at the Armistice, some 15,000 of them prisoners (including Léopold Sédar Senghor, future president of Senegal). Vichy maintained an army in AOF of some 100,000 to guard against British invasion, and de Gaulle deployed similar numbers from 1943, constituting the core of Free French troops in North Africa, in the Italian campaigns from 1943 and in the July 1944 landings in Southern France. Escaped African PoWs, as well as Indochinese and North African *émigrés*, fought in the metropolitan Resistance. Echenberg (1985: 364–5; 1991) has calculated that, of some 200,000 Africans recruited, perhaps 12 per cent 'could have ended up *morts pour la France*'.

African troops in the British army were at first restricted to the African continent, and thus did not see action until Italian fronts were opened in Ethiopia and Somalia; they later fought in North Africa and Madagascar and in the Far East. Although African volunteers 'overwhelmed the army recruiting centres' in Kenya, and despite reports of African enthusiasm for the Allied cause, for example in the Gold Coast, officials reported a general sense that this was a 'white man's war' and that 'even without African support the British would inevitably win' (Lonsdale 1986b: 120; Holbrook 1985: 349; Crowder 1984). When the war came to Africa, this fact perhaps mattered more to Africans than the experience of those relatively few who fought. In Tanganyika, although 2,358 died of 86,740 Africans enlisted, most were recruited to the pioneer corps or the military labour service; a further 3,861 Tanganyikans were absent without leave in 1945, having escaped from arbitrary impressments (Iliffe 1979: 370).

Official anxieties surrounding the alienation of demobilized troops proved to be largely exaggerated, an extension perhaps of more diffuse anxieties about African 'detribalization'; the anxiety nonetheless translated into policy. Thus, in Tanganyika, 'Only those Africans who had been politically aware *before* they were recruited seem to have picked up new ideas in the course of their service' (Westcott 1986: 154). Ideas were one thing, however, skills quite another: the army was the 'widest avenue for advance' of African skills and, in Kenya, trained 600 teachers and 15,000 drivers, while achieving a 70 per cent literacy rate amongst ex-servicemen, 'a huge addition to the ranks of those with vulnerable expectations' (Lonsdale 1986b: 128). Returning *tirailleurs* were theoretically destined for incorporation into the elite of so-called *évolués*, since military service figured highly amongst criteria for citizenship. However, few sought this distinction, and besides, from 1946, a new French Union citizenship was extended to all irrespective of service, education or property (Chapter 5). French officials' anxieties were realized in the short term by the explosion of unrest amongst angry troops awaiting demobilization. The source of the problem was partly de Gaulle's typically ungrateful *realpolitik* when, constrained by the Americans to accept a ceiling of 250,000 men in the French army, he demobilized African troops and replaced them with white Frenchmen, whose active role in France's liberation he was keen to enhance; the low priority given to repatriating demobilized troops or paying their wages did the rest. *Tirailleurs* rioted at camps in Southern France and outside Liverpool, and disorder culminated in one of the first symbolic acts of post-war French colonial violence in December 1944, at the Thiaroye transit camp, outside Dakar, where rioting was savagely repressed leaving thirty-five dead (Echenberg 1985).[2]

Africa was ultimately more important to the Allied war effort as a producer of food and other commodities. Combat on the African continent enhanced the importance of supply routes, not only from West Africa to Egypt but also from South to North, through the heart of British East Africa. African fronts created demand for African food production, whilst the Battle of the Atlantic virtually wiped out the competition from crucial imperial trading partners in South America. The Japanese invasion of Southeast Asia transformed colonial Africa's economic fortunes even more radically, by cutting off strategic supplies of rubber, tin, fibres and rice. Demand soared for Kenyan and Tanganyikan sisal and for pyrethrum, the basis for insecticides needed for the Far Eastern campaigns to come – these two crops alone earned Kenya 'more than twice as much as the military sales of Kenya's foodstuffs' (Lonsdale 1986b: 120–2) – while African rubber production increased, and Nigerian tin production replaced Malayan. African cotton production also benefited from fluctuations in Indian supplies occasioned by political uncertainties. Even a relatively poor colony such as Gabon could benefit from increased demand for hard woods used in laminates for aircraft production. This massive growth in demand for African production had variable effects on African producers and consumers. The commodity boom brought Kenyan settlers together as a politically cohesive group whom the colonial government could no longer keep at arm's length, while dividing Africans by region, ethnic affiliation or social group – setting agriculturalists against pastoralists, Kikuyu squatters against both landed 'kulaks' and White Highlands settlers, and agricultural producers against urban consumers (ibid.).

The concept of a 'second colonial occupation' refers to the systematic boosting of colonial production in post-war British Africa, but truly that occupation started during the war years, as Africans were arguably exploited more fully than ever before. Indeed, for ordinary Africans, the predominant experience of the period was surely one of hardship, as men were forcibly recruited to serve the Allied war effort while those who evaded conscription or were left behind worked all the harder to maintain domestic production. The numbers involved are uncertain, beyond the 'well over half a million soldiers' recruited by Britain in Africa during the war, most of whom were deployed as labourers rather than combatants, but the scale of civilian labour mobilization is beyond question. In most, if not all sectors of British colonial economies forced labour was deployed extensively (Killingray & Rathbone 1986), and not only for civil and military purposes but also increasingly for private enterprise on plantations and in mines. This reversed the thrust of colonial labour policy going back to the 1930 League of Nations Convention on Forced Labour, in the face of protest in the House of Commons, disquiet in the Colonial Office, widespread evasion and desertion, and in the teeth of the rational argument that forced labour was rarely effective labour. It also represented a retrograde step for the British 'official mind' as it worked gradually towards the idea of an African worker *per se* as opposed to the still prevailing essentialist view of the African as migrant worker tied to his 'tribal' village (Cooper 1996).

All other differences apart, a frank acceptance of forced labour was common to Vichyste and Free French Africa. Although France too was a signatory of the 1930 Convention, the hard realities of forced labour had continued largely unchecked. During the Popular Front period from June 1936, forced labour could not be discussed because it did not officially exist, so governors relied on covert understandings to achieve production targets, and one governor advocated a euphemistic Apostolate of Labour, to educate Africans to the rigours of wage labour. In Vichyste West Africa from 1940 to 1943, these restraints no longer applied, and forced labour was freely recruited to suit the European cocoa planters of Côte d'Ivoire and banana growers of Guinée; Governor-General Boisson could thus exercise some control over the practice by discussing it, as a first step towards limiting it (ibid.: 194). Conversely, the liberal reputation of Free French Governor-General Félix Éboué was tarnished by his forthright approach to forced labour in order to meet ambitious targets for production (M'Bokolo 1982; Lewis 2002). These targets increased from 1943, as de Gaulle sought to punch as close to France's weight as possible in the Allied war effort. It was against this background that the 1944 Brazzaville Conference passed a recommendation to phase out forced labour, although the war effort was to be allowed to run its course (Chapter 5).

Spanish and Portuguese colonial administrations, with no war effort to sustain, but conversely with little compunction about the deployment of forced labour anyway, also profited from the commodities boom through the continued extensive use of conscripted Africans on public works and in private enterprise (Clarence-Smith 1985).

Hardship also meant food shortages as the war dragged on, and disruption and drought led to famine in many parts of Africa and in Madagascar (as in India and Tonkin, see below). 'Famines that kill' were largely a thing of the past across colonial Africa thanks to better government, modern medicine and the advent of motor transport, so that famine mortality had largely given way to 'mere' malnutrition for Africa's rural poor. Even so, perhaps as many as 300,000 died in Rwanda in 1944, and famine was severe in parts of the Sahel (Iliffe 1988: 155–61). The diversion of resources, the depletion of reserves, the dearth of transport, and the absence of conscripted workers from the land indicate slippage in the colonial state's infrastructural development, so that the 'second colonial occupation' in the latter war years represented in some ways a partial return to pre-war conditions (Iliffe 1979: 351). Beyond the cost in human misery, the political impact of these shortages can only be guessed, although famine in Algeria and in Madagascar was an undeniable factor in the unrest leading to the 1945 and 1947 insurrections in those countries (Chapter 6). The short-term official response was one of crisis management, in the form of more labour conscription and the further stretching of resources to head off catastrophe, or, in Madagascar, the promise of special concessions, with little discernible effect.

Notwithstanding the exactions and the hardships of the various war efforts imposed upon colonial Africa, the colonial state system in Africa had worked and proved its worth to the colonial powers. But if the British and French African empires experienced a last great 'revival' as a consequence of the way imperial resources were deployed during the Second World War, the colonial war efforts represented also a revival of older colonial practices, and the temporary suspension of the trend towards colonial reformism of the interwar period.

Southeast Asia: Eclipse of the European Colonial State, 1940–1945

In the European and American colonies of Southeast Asia, the question of colonial sovereignty was thrown starkly into relief by Japan's forcible inclusion of the region within a Greater Asia Co-Prosperity Sphere, first by heavy-handed diplomacy and then by the breathtaking application of military main force. None of the colonial regimes of the region resisted the onslaught; all were eclipsed by Japanese military occupation and superseded by a rapidly improvised Japanese colonial administration which also gave qualified encouragement to local political forces. The only partial exception was French Indochina, where the eclipse started earlier following France's defeat of June 1940, but was only completed by the Japanese *coup de force* of 9 March 1945, which overthrew the increasingly anomalous Vichyste administration. Japanese occupation had several consequences for Southeast Asian decolonization. First, alongside the harsh treatment meted out to their erstwhile colonial rulers, the peoples of Southeast Asia also suffered, whether directly at the hands of the Japanese or from the privations of war. Secondly, although Japanese claims to favour an 'Asia for the Asians' were ambiguous at best, the occupation represented an opportunity for nationalist advancement. As Japanese occupation approached its end in 1945 and was then precipitately terminated following the bombing of Hiroshima and Nagasaki, nationalists in Burma, Indonesia and Indochina seized an 'opportune moment' to take power. Thirdly, the old colonial powers were thus confronted with the prospect of colonial reconquest, indicating the need to recreate the colonial state essentially from scratch.

Only in Indochina did the complete eclipse of colonial rule seem avoidable. Admiral Jean Decoux's regime thus offers a fascinating glimpse of a colonial state kept, as it were, in suspended animation; it perhaps even suggests how post-war Indochina might have developed had the hiatus of 1945 been avoided. Decoux's predecessor as Governor-General, Georges Catroux, was principally charged with exceeding his authority in the concessions he made to Japanese economic and strategic demands during the Battle of France; his inclination towards declaring for de Gaulle only counted further against him (Thomas 1998). Henceforth, Indochina was to supply rice, rubber and other commodities to Japan, and acted as a forward air base. France was required to cease operation of the Yunnan railway to the benefit of Nationalist China. But French humiliation continued under Decoux's leadership, as he was forced, following a brief naval encounter in 1941, to accept Japanese mediation and to accede to Siam's irredentist claims to the two Western provinces annexed by France in 1907 – thus necessitating restoration of the colonial map in 1945–6 (Tønnesson 1991). More generally, while colonial institutions remained in place, or were shadowed by parallel Japanese bodies, most notably the *Kenpeitai* (secret police), French authority was visibly challenged by the presence of twenty thousand Japanese soldiers and by Japanese airpower, while rumours spread of the humiliations visited upon Frenchmen in city streets (Marr 1995).

Under these circumstances, Decoux's policy was surprisingly assertive. Decoux was an enthusiastic Pétainist, claiming in his memoirs that the cult of the Marshall married well with Confucianism, and a frank authoritarian, relishing the relief from the liberal circumspection of the Popular Front, much as did his counterparts in Vichy-held West Africa and Madagascar (Jennings 2002). Abortive communist-led rebellions in Tonkin and Cochinchina in late 1940 were efficiently crushed, while press and intellectual opinion was carefully monitored. After their takeover in 1945, Japanese authorities were suitably impressed by the *Sûreté*'s intelligence networks. Conversely, Decoux sought to mediate French authority through a network of 'sovereigns and notabilities', incorporated into a Federal Council created in 1943, but which met only once (Smith 1972). Decoux was the first proconsul to pronounce the proscribed term 'Vietnam', although in passing rather than as a new policy departure, thus prefiguring the concession made to Bao Dai in 1949 (Chapter 4).

Decoux's authoritarian reformism did not temper indigenous resentment of the French presence, although Decoux may have protected Indochina from the rigours of Japanese occupation, including demands for forced labour. However, neither the French nor the Japanese could head off the devastating famine which hit Tonkin after the shortfall of the September 1944 rice harvest. Aside from long-term structural factors and some diversion of production to 'industrial' crops, French and Japanese stockpiling was a major factor, as was the failure to transport stocks North from Cochinchina, compounded by Allied bombing of roads and railways and the interdiction of coastal shipping. Nowhere else was the impact of famine so catastrophic, casting its appalling shadow over subsequent French, Japanese and Vietnamese manoeuvrings: in all, perhaps a million people died of starvation or disease in a few months, that is, one-tenth of the population of affected areas (Marr 1995: 96–107).

Elsewhere in Southeast Asia the ambiguities of official collaboration were sidestepped by the complete overthrow of European authority. Not even the recently completed imperial fortress of Singapore could resist the Japanese onslaught of early 1942. The sinking of the British battleships HMS *Repulse* and *Prince of Wales* in December 1941, and Singapore's fall in February 1942, the 'worst disaster and largest capitulation in British history' according to Churchill, were above all imperial defeats, so that in a sense subsequent metropolitan criticism of the failures of British colonial rule in Malaya were beside the point (Stockwell 1999: 473–6). The Dutch Governor-General resisted the urge to flee with his administration before the Japanese invasion of Java, in what was seen as an act of statesmanship 'worthy of our traditions and moral mission' (van den Doel 2001: 63). However, deploying a Dutch demolition corps to carry out a 'scorched earth' strategy, destroying oil refineries, bridges and rice-mills, was seen by nationalists as being 'directed more against the Indonesian people than against the Japanese'. Conversely, the establishment of civil front organizations to aid potential Indonesian victims of war was entrusted by the Dutch to the nationalist parties, to the latter's further credit (Touwen-Bouwsma 1996: 7–8).

One by one, starting with Hong Kong on Christmas Day 1941, European colonial states were no sooner defeated by the Japanese, than a policy was implemented amounting to wholesale eradication of the European colonial presence. Principally, this involved the internment and deployment as forced labour of European administrators, soldiers and settlers – 138,000 died or were captured in the defence and fall of Singapore alone – but it extended to removing physical traces of the European presence by changing place names (Batavia became Djakarta), removing monuments, banning European languages in public places and replacing public signs with Japanese. Colonial institutions were simply taken over by Japanese officials, indigenous administrators were promoted, and local traditional rulers were entrusted with a greater, if more subservient, role in the 'indirect rule' of their subjects (van den Doel 2001: 69–70; Christie 1996; McCoy 1980).

Many nationalists were disappointed, initially at least, in their expectation that the eclipse of European colonialism would bring opportunities for national advancement.

Nationalist parties in the Dutch East Indies before the Japanese arrival split between the minority left-wing Gerindo party which saw the anti-colonial struggle as dependent on the successful outcome of anti-fascist war, and the majority Parindra party which believed increasingly in the likelihood of Axis victory, following which the national cause could be furthered. Although there were only scattered preparations to help the Japanese or sabotage the Dutch, Indonesian nationalists were encouraged, in part by Japanese propaganda, to welcome the arrival of the Japanese with the formation of Merdeka ('Independence') Committees.

Once the fighting was over, Japanese occupation authorities disbanded these committees, and made it plain that Indonesian nationalist activities would be tolerated only if subordinated to the Japanese war effort (Touwen-Bouwsma 1996). The nationalist debate was now between those leaders favouring collaboration with the Japanese, such as Ahmed Sukarno, and those who resisted the compromises this entailed, such as Mohammad Hatta and Sutan Sjahrir. Subordination to the Japanese notably entailed cooperating with Japanese demands for labour, as did Sukarno, or becoming associated with the distribution of scarce food supplies – and arguably it was material hardship rather than nationalism which principally exercised the mass of Indonesian opinion during the period of Japanese opinion (van den Doel 2001). Mass paramilitary organizations were formed under Sukarno's leadership, including a 'Labour Service', reaching membership of some two million, but serving Japanese interests (including labour in mines, and the construction of airfields, roads and railways), and inculcating Japanese-inspired virtues.

It transpired also that the Japanese had their own national hierarchy. In January 1943, Japanese Prime Minister Tojo Hideki announced that Burma and the Philippines, but not Indonesia, would be granted self-government under Japanese leadership; Tokyo rejected prospective Malayan independence as late as February 1945. Criteria of political 'readiness' were less significant in these approaches than Japanese wartime interests: whereas Malaya and Indonesia were economically crucial to the Japanese war effort, the occupation of Burma had chiefly negative strategic interest, as a threat to British India. The Burmese government formed in August 1943 under Ba Maw, with Aung San as defence minister, thus gained valuable administrative experience while awaiting the independence struggle that would follow the British return. Indonesian nationalists, by contrast, had to be content with a 'Central Advisory Council', formed in June 1943, succeeded in late 1944 by a 'College of Counsellors', which, 'with a little fantasy', resembled an Indonesian cabinet (ibid.: 73–5).

The Japanese 'Greater Asia Co-Prosperity Sphere' offered the greatest opportunities for nationalists as it approached its end in 1944–5, whether through tactical alignment with the returning colonial powers, or through the Japanese 'scorched earth' approach to the nationalist question. Armed resistance to the Japanese offered a means of gaining political advantage, but this was not guaranteed. The Ba Maw government's switch in allegiance in late 1944 transformed it into an anti-Japanese resistance movement, the Anti-Fascist Organization, subsequently better known as the Anti-Fascist People's Freedom League (AFPFL). Ba Maw branded himself a collaborator by fleeing to Japan, giving the AFPFL's dynamic new leader, Aung San, an unassailable advantage over potential political rivals through his anti-Japanese credentials, established not least in contacts with Mountbatten. The other principal nationalist contender, U Saw, had been exiled to Uganda for pro-Japanese activity in 1941, and thus started with a considerable disadvantage following his return to Burmese politics in December 1945. Burma's pre-1942 political leaders, meanwhile, were obliged to kick their heels in Simla, seat of the Burmese 'government-in-exile', until the governor resumed civil administration in Rangoon (Smith 1988: 48–9).

Conversely, more consistent anti-Japanese resistance movements in the Philippines and Malaya rapidly became isolated. In the Philippines, the only other Southeast Asian colony retaken from the Japanese by force of arms, General MacArthur's portentous promise, 'I will return', was carried out in the company of members of the pre-war Manual Quezon government, to ensure that President Roosevelt's 1935 pledge of independence was honoured with suitable guarantees for continuing American interests. When leaders of the pro-Communist Hukbalahap movement, which had resisted the Japanese since 1942, declared their willingness to work with the Americans, they were arrested, on 9 April 1945 (ibid.: 52).

The Malayan People's Anti-Japanese Army (MPAJA), an arm of the Malayan Communist Party (MCP) whose resistance had received considerable military backing from Force 136 (a branch of the British Special Operations Executive, SOE), was also disposed to cooperate with the returning British, but in the event Malaya was reoccupied without the need to launch the expected armed invasion, codename 'Zipper', against the Japanese. The MPAJA's value as political interlocutors was diminished by the fact that Chinese dominated the movement, who had suffered particular discrimination by the occupying Japanese. This ensured that it could never assume the sort of national legitimacy enjoyed by the Burmese AFPFL, and was seen by the British as representing, at best, one ethnic grouping alongside others. The MCP would eventually relinquish even that limited recognition, in favour of anti-colonial insurgency (Chapter 4).

For the three colonial territories not already recovered by the advancing Allied armies, Indonesia, Indochina and Malaya, the few months preceding the Japanese surrender in August 1945 were a period of tense anticipation, preparation and political manoeuvring. This manoeuvring led to widely contrasting short-term outcomes: communist revolution in Vietnam (but not in Cambodia or Laos); non-communist nationalist revolution in Indonesia; and the virtually peaceful British reoccupation of Malaya. But these contrasts should not disguise the underlying similarities in the situation all three countries faced, and therefore the highly contingent nature of those outcomes. This element of contingency was particularly marked in the crucial period of 'power vacuum' which accompanied the precipitate Japanese capitulation and preceded the arrival of Allied troops (Tønnesson 1995). In the first instance, the 'writing on the wall' for the Japanese in Southeast Asia could be deciphered as offering unprecedented political opportunities for local nationalists, although the Japanese approach to these opportunities was a compound of tactical spoiling in the face of the Allied advance, emotional 'Asianness' and genuine enthusiasm for the prospect of post-war independence for the region (ibid.: 118–21).

In Indonesia, Sukarno still apparently envisaged his political future as tied to the Japanese presence. By mid-1945, he was preparing for a Japanese-sponsored declaration of independence scheduled for September. Even without independence, however, Sukarno and his colleagues were hard at work imagining the constitutional nature of their future state, based on Sukarno's '*Pancasila*' or five principles: nationalism, humanism, democracy, social justice and belief in an almighty God, the latter designed to create a secular state and prevent Islamic control. Also according to these imaginings, pregnant with future possibilities, Indonesia was equated with an eventual *Indonesia Raya* (Greater Indonesia) incorporating Malacca, British Borneo and Portuguese East Timor (van den Doel 2001: 76). Indeed, this latter vision was matched, and in some degree exceeded, by that of radical Malay nationalists favouring a *Melayu Raya* (Greater Malaya) uniting all ethnic Malays, as represented by Ibrahim Yacoob's Union of Peninsular Indonesians (KRIS), formed in July 1945 (Tønnesson 1995: 121). Not for the last time in the decolonization process, colonial state boundaries would prove resilient, and Indonesia's independence was declared without the participation of Malays under British rule. In any case, Yaacob's vision was shared neither by the Malayan Sultans on whom the crucial first steps towards Malayan decolonization would depend, nor by the MPAJA, and Yaacob consequently left Malaya never to return (ibid.; Kheng 1988).

The most dramatic opportunity of this period was offered to, and then snatched away from, the Vietnamese government put in place following the Japanese *coup de force* of 9 March 1945. Having decided, in the face of the advancing American threat, to repudiate by force the Vichyste mortgage on Indochina, the Japanese invited the three Indochinese sovereigns – Emperor Bao Dai of Annam, King Norodom Sihanouk of Cambodia and the Laotian King Sisavang Vong – to declare independence and abrogate all treaties with France. Bao Dai was favoured over Prince Cuong De (who had resided in Japan since 1915), and in this brief period of his career he perhaps least deserved the epithet 'puppet'; indeed, by the time he abdicated in August he had succeeded in reincorporating the French colony of Cochinchina into his empire – a move resisted by the Japanese Governor-General Tsuchihashi, reluctant to overturn long-established structures, and a formidable source of friction with the returning French authorities. Bao Dai's government, headed by the former schools inspector, Tran Trong Kim, was well-intentioned, and spent time 'discussing constitutional problems and matters of national political symbolism'; remarkably, it decreed the use of Vietnamese in all official communications, and even instituted a new orthographic convention to supersede the cumbersome Vietnamese system of diacritics (Marr 1995: 118–19, 123). As in Indonesia, these were more the actions of a government-in-waiting than of a fully fledged national administration, and high-mindedness was no substitute for administrative experience, of which Kim's cabinet was almost totally innocent, nor did it offset the crushing responsibility of organizing relief – inevitably inadequate – for Tonkinese famine victims.

The Japanese-sponsored imperial government was not the sole viable contender for power in Vietnam, but, until it happened, the League for the Independence of Vietnam (*Viet Nam Doc Lap Dong Minh Hoi*, or Viet Minh) seemed scarcely more apt to seize power than did Kim to maintain it. Formed in 1942 by one Ho Chi Minh, whom few yet identified with former Comintern agent, Nguyen Ai Quoc, the Viet Minh's declared aim was national liberation. A skilled diplomat and an inspiring guerrilla leader, Ho was not yet transfigured as the 'revered uncle' of the Nation. By mid-1945 the Viet Minh was a well-armed resistance movement controlling a liberated zone in the mountains straddling Tonkin's border with China; it had good relations with the pro-Guomindang warlord of neighbouring Gwangxi province, and nurtured an intelligence-gathering role for the American China Command. Released political prisoners boosted its ranks, and its raids were replacing those of anonymous 'bandits' in official reports (Marr 1995: 362). Profiting from the weakened Japanese grip in northern Vietnam, its popular support mushroomed over the summer of 1945. It was thus neither geographically isolated nor handicapped as was the MPAJA by its ethnic composition, but in other respects it seemed little different, as its leaders, dispersed since the struggles of the 1930s, gathered for a Congress meeting at Tan Trao in early August 1945. Although confident as a guerrilla force, the Viet Minh was completely untried as a potential national government, and understandably cautious about the likelihood of Japanese resistance to an attempted insurrection (Tønnesson 1995).

August 1945 was a moment in history when nothing happened quite as any of the principal sets of actors expected. Even without knowledge of the horror of nuclear bombardment, the shocked incomprehension of Japanese soldiers and officials at the unprecedentedly swift end to their eight-year campaign across Asia was a major factor in creating the vacuum of power. But even the Allies were caught unawares by the devastating success of the American raids on Hiroshima and Nagasaki. The French and Dutch governments, indeed, had not even been informed of the proposed American raids.

As news of impending Japanese surrender spread in Vietnam, the Viet Minh prepared to take over the colonial capital of Hanoi, sidestepping the well-armed Japanese forces, who retained responsibility for law and order. After a huge rally in front of the Hanoi Opera House, armed groups moved to take control, without bloodshed, of selected official institutions. That night, air-raid covers were removed from streetlights, symbolically lighting up the city for the first time in many years. The following morning, the electricity, trains and buses, telegraph, telephone, water-pumping services and other amenities of a functioning state apparatus indicated a new order, rather than chaos (Marr 1995: 395–401). The scenes in Hanoi were matched by uprisings in cities across Vietnam, from the Northern port city of Haiphong to Saigon, and, crucially, in the countryside: without such support, the revolution might have fallen to Chinese or French arms (ibid.: 402ff.). From the imperial capital of Hue, on 20 August, Bao Dai ordered the formation of a new cabinet, stating that he would 'prefer to be a citizen of an independent country rather than king of an enslaved one' (in ibid.: 439). Three days later, heeding Louis XVI's fate and yet anxious to ascertain that Ho was indeed 'the famous revolutionary Nguyen Ai Quoc' (and not some upstart), Bao Dai abdicated. Two days later, as citizen Vinh Thuy, he was dismayed to receive an offer from Hanoi, inviting him to act as 'Supreme Adviser' to the provisional government; it was unclear whether Ho wished to draw prestige from the former emperor, or to keep him under control, or both (ibid.: 439–53). On 2 September, wearing his trademark khaki jacket and white rubber sandals, his head symbolically protected by a (modern) pith helmet and an (imperial) umbrella, Ho Chi Minh declared the independence of the Democratic Republic of Vietnam (although 'Democratic' may be a later amendment to the official text), with eloquent reference to 1776 and 1791 (Declaration of the Rights of Man and the Citizen), but not 1917. He had an international audience in mind, though only four foreign observers were present, Colonel Archimedes Patti and colleagues from the Office of

Strategic Services (OSS) who had accompanied the Viet Minh down from the mountains; although stern warnings were issued to 'the French colonialists', de Gaulle's envoy, Jean Sainteny, only witnessed the proceedings from the 'gilded cage' of the Governor General's palace, where he was under effective house arrest (ibid.: 532–5; Patti 1980; Sainteny 1967). Tragically, 2 September 1945 marked only the beginning of Vietnam's struggle for independence, rather than its climax.

Endgame of the Raj: From 'Quit India' to Quitting India

What forced the British to quit India as soon as August 1947, and what forced Indian political leaders to accept Freedom without Indian Unity, was the Second World War's impact on the structures and mentalities of British rule in India. War reversed the thrust of British reformist policy in India, and then weakened imperial power and resolve, thereby limiting post-war imperial options. The Transfer of Power, when it came, at bottom suited no one. The war also impacted crucially on ordinary Indians, through the experience of combat and imprisonment, violent insurrection, and the privations of war including famine.

The 1935 Government of India Act represented imperial 'bricolage' at its most impressive. The dyarchical structure of provincial self-government, coupled with overarching British control of 'All-India' concerns including foreign policy and defence, might have offered a prototype for many post-war examples of colonial constitution-making, despite the fact that it was never fully implemented. In the end, however, Partition made it a model to avoid rather than emulate. Conversely, the constitutional framework of the 1935 Act was a most versatile vessel, however flawed or cracked, which could accommodate a variety of British policies after 1935, not only allowing the return to gubernatorial control in 1939 following the resignation of the Congress provincial ministries, but even facilitating a swift Transfer of Power to separate Dominions in 1947. The first cracks were appearing in the framework even before October 1939, but in the event, it was the Viceroy Lord Linlithgow's declaration of war without prior consultation with Indian political leaders, and his feeble October 1939 offer, a repetition of dusty promises of Dominion status in return for wartime cooperation, which provided Congress ministers with the pretext they needed to withdraw from the provincial ministries they controlled.

From an Indian perspective, the Phoney War extended, as it were, until late 1941, as Congress returned to opposition and to its own internal conflicts, while British policy revolved around an effort to 'to take advantage of the war to regain for the white-dominated central government and bureaucracy the ground lost to the Congress from 1937 or earlier' (Sarkar 1989: 376). Even the Muslim League's 'Pakistan' resolution at its Lahore conference in March 1940 can only with hindsight be seen as 'lowering the curtain' on the possibility of Indian unity (Moore 1999: 238).

The swift Japanese advance brought a return to negotiation, with the Mission to Delhi of the Labour minister, Sir Stafford Cripps, newly appointed to the Cabinet in March 1942. Although Cripps had little new to offer, the conventional view of the Cripps Mission has been that a missed opportunity for Anglo-Indian understanding was scuppered by the combined efforts of Linlithgow and Churchill. Recent reappraisal suggests a focus less on the constitutional minutiae than on the more immediate circumstances of wartime policy and opinion in Britain and India (Owen 2002). The Mission was only equivocally supported by the Labour Party, and that backing was based on a mistaken belief, encouraged by Nehru's assurances going back to the late 1930s, that Congress would swing behind an 'anti-fascist' platform of support for the British war effort. The Mission was thus sent on the back of a transitory swing in British public opinion in favour of Indian concessions in the face of the Japanese advance. For their part, Congress negotiators were less concerned by the offer of eventual Dominion status, than by their desire to secure something like Cabinet government for the duration of the war within the proposed Viceroy's Council, in order to exert influence on Indian army deployment, and to negotiate terms in the worst case of Japanese invasion. Quite apart from British distaste for what seemed a treacherous waiting game, this position was unacceptable to the Labour Party leader and foremost Indian expert, Clement Attlee, who had long resisted the idea of Congress gaining power without responsibility to an elected national legislature.

The Cripps Mission failed before a probably already 'unbridgeable chasm' dividing Britons and Indians (Owen 2002: 89). But the last piers of the bridge were kicked away by the All-India Congress Committee session at Bombay on 8 August 1942, which passed a resolution urging the British to 'Quit India', and by Gandhi, whose inflammatory speech on the same day brought him to the brink of renouncing a lifetime's commitment to non-violence (Sarkar 1989: 388–9). At issue, as before, was the relative weight that should be given the Indian cause as against the Allied war effort, but also an estimation of the war's likely outcome; and in late 1942, before the tide of the war turned with the Battle of Stalingrad, it seemed that Congress might soon be treating with the Japanese; this *realpolitik* rather than pro-Axis sympathies, as occasionally alleged by the British, drove the Congress debate. Such high political calculations were outweighed, however, by the 'elemental and largely spontaneous outburst' of insurrection that followed the arrests of 9 August (ibid.: 390). Although Linlithgow informed Churchill that he was confronting 'by far the most serious rebellion since that of 1857' (Mansergh 1970–82: vol. II, 853), many accounts pass rapidly over the 'failed' Insurrection, the containment of which demonstrated by the end of 1942 'that the Raj had not yet lost the will to resort to coercion when necessary' (Butler 2002: 41). That will was not in doubt, and a clampdown had been prepared since September 1939, but the scale of repression and the means employed, including machine-gunning villages from the air, ordered by Linlithgow on 15 August, suggest an almost reckless use of force that was probably unthinkable in peacetime. The insurrection demonstrated the extent of popular anger against aspects of British wartime policy, including economic neglect; the abandonment of Indian immigrants in Southeast Asia after the collapse of Singapore; the blunders of the British retreat before the Japanese, including an apparent 'scorched earth' policy in Assam and East Bengal; and, not least, the ruthless violence of the repression (Sarkar 1989: 391–3). The political range and geographical extent of the insurrection also suggested the potential for a more durable breakdown of British control, as the first wave of urban strikes and unrest gave way to peasant rebellions and a series of short-lived 'National Governments', and to terror campaigns in remoter regions against communications, police and army installations (ibid.: 395). Here surely is a kind of mirror image of the 'defeatist' contingency plans for staged British withdrawal drawn up in 1946 by Linlithgow's successor as Viceroy, Field Marshall (subsequently Earl) Wavell, appointed in October 1943, whose sober, soldierly analyses helped steer the Labour Government towards a more rapid Transfer of Power.

The 'Quit India' resolution prompted the gaoling of Congress leaders, thus removing them from the political equation for the rest of the war and giving greater prominence to the Muslim League, and to Muslims, whose communities contributed Indian army troops out of all proportion to their number. Conversely, not for the last time, imprisonment conferred the legitimacy of heroism on its principal nationalist interlocutors; it also drew attention away from their unremarkable record in office, and absolved them from implication in political controversies surrounding the prosecution of the war against Japan, not least concerning Subhas Chandra Bose's pro-Japanese Indian National Army (INA). By the time Congress leaders were released in early 1945, the political stakes had risen immeasurably for both Congress and the League, while the fundamental issue had now shifted: how to achieve Unity, now that the long-standing demand for Freedom seemed about to be satisfied.

Given the maze of events that led to the Transfer of Power, it is crucial to resist the urge to read the history backwards from Partition. However, nowhere was the shift to a decolonizing endgame more dramatically illustrated than in India, as the agenda was dominated by the increasing certainty of a swift timetable for British departure. The centrality of negotiations according to this accelerating timetable may justify the concentration in much of the literature on 'high politics', but it is easy to neglect the beliefs, values and identities underpinning the various constitutional formulae discussed in the period, or what was at the time an occasionally overwhelming sense of pressure from below.

Of the four principal actors in the Indian endgame – the Viceroy, the Cabinet, the Muslim League and Congress – it was perhaps the first who traversed the greatest perceptual distance in the two years from the end of the war in Asia to the Transfer of Power. Lord Wavell's credentials were impeccable as an imperialist in the intellectual, old-fashioned liberal mould. Transferred from command of the British Army in the Middle East, as Viceroy he oversaw the turnaround of British India's wartime fortunes and brought to term the magnificent Indian war effort. He arrived in India in time to supervise relief for the Bengali famine over the winter of 1943–4, largely caused by the halt of rice imports from Southeast Asia and by the need to feed an enlarged army (Sarkar 1989: 406). From a position of considerable confidence, therefore, in early 1945, Wavell sought to persuade Churchill to start negotiating the promised Dominion Status for India. Wavell favoured a balanced settlement respecting all interests, safeguarding British interests above all, and probably taking years to achieve according to the usual timescales; the process leading to the 1935 Act, after all, had taken six years from the convocation of the Simon Commission. It was thus a rude shock when the June 1945 Simla Conference stalled in the face of the Muslim League's insistence on equal negotiating status with Congress. Indeed, the election of a Labour government in July proved less of a shock as Wavell, after initially 'shifting from the accelerator to the brake pedal' (ibid.: 417), discovered that the new government's outlook, especially that of the prime minister, Clement Attlee, coincided substantially with his own.

However, over the following months, India came to 'the edge of the volcano' (Moon 1973), while London confronted the danger of imperial over-extension, including the policing and feeding of a populous Occupation Zone in Western Germany, and the deployment of Indian Army troops in what looked like the colonial reconquest of Indonesia and Indochina, against Wavell's opposition and the protests of Congress (see next chapter). Peacetime for the Raj meant confronting the fact that, since Linlithgow's concession of 1939, the Indian Army was a direct drain on the British Exchequer, thus reversing India's Sterling balances substantially in favour of India (Cain & Hopkins 1993: 196). Indians were in the majority in the Indian Civil Service, following a decades-long process of 'Indianization', alongside the demoralized, ageing and shrinking ranks of European administrators, with no new recruits since 1939 and little prospect of post-war recruitment (Potter 1973, 1986).

Against this background, what impacted on British attitudes over the following months was the breakdown in civil order across India, as the apparent stirring of old imperial reflexes provoked popular anger and led to fears of army mutiny. In November 1945, following the unwelcome news of Indian army actions in support of the French and Dutch, Wavell ordered the trial, in the symbolically highly charged setting of the Red Fort in Delhi, of combatants in the Indian National Army. Treating these potential heroes of Indian nationalism simply as traitors was a massive miscalculation. The INA's military effectiveness had been discounted by British and Japanese alike, but the psychological impact of any Indian army fighting for national liberation was immense, let alone one which recruited about one-third of sixty thousand Indian Prisoners of War in the Far East (Kratoska 1998: 103–9), whose commander, the veteran Congress leader Subhas Chandra Bose, emphasizing his loyalty to Gandhi, had formed a Provisional Government of Free India in 1943. Unrest and Army disaffection over the winter of 1945–6 culminated in the short-lived strike by Royal Indian Navy sailors in Bombay in February 1946 (Sarkar 1989: 410–11; Gupta 1987). The lessons Wavell derived from this period – that he might lose control of the Army, and that Congress had the power to provoke mass movement or revolution in India – found expression in the 'breakdown plan' which he presented to the Cabinet Mission in May 1946, envisaging a staged British retreat to strongholds in North-western and North-eastern India ('Note for the Cabinet Delegation', 29 March 1946, Moon 1973: 232). Had such a plan been implemented, it is not difficult to imagine a political tidal wave extending far beyond British India. Wavell's analysis was profoundly distasteful to Cabinet, as was the strong-arm alternative he proposed, involving the despatch of five British divisions to keep order. But if Wavell was marked down thereafter as a 'defeatist', the spectre of withdrawal he evoked coloured subsequent British calculations, against the background of spiralling communal violence which the British were powerless to control. It was Wavell's proposal of setting 30 June 1948 as a deadline for British withdrawal on which his successor Mountbatten insisted as the price, along with 'plenipotentiary' powers, for accepting the last Viceroyalty in February 1947.

It was the newest All-India player, Jinnah's Muslim League, whose challenge, in the March 1940 'Pakistan' resolution, set the broad parameters for post-war negotiations. The demand for a distinct territory for Indian Muslims may be interpreted as a bargaining chip, or as providing the League with a political platform which, as a sympathetic Linlithgow suggested to Jinnah in early 1940, had previously been wanting. The League, after all, had been trounced in the 1937 elections, most critically in the Muslim-majority provinces of Punjab and Bengal, and Jinnah's subsequent demands for sole representation of Muslims rebuffed by both Congress and the British. The imprisonment of Congress leaders from August 1942 gave Jinnah the opportunity to enhance the League's political credit through full cooperation with the British war effort; this could not simply be wished away at war's end.

Jinnah, the 'London-trained lawyer, secularist and chain-smoker' (Holland 1985: 61), is conventionally depicted as a saturnine, Machiavellian figure disdainful of Muslim politics, who in his unprincipled intransigence 'no longer questioned the wisdom, viability or aftermath impact of partition but had decided by the spring of 1940 that this was the only long-term resolution to India's foremost problem' (Wolpert 1984: 182; Moore 1999: 238). However, the variable geometry of 'Pakistan' from 1940 onwards needs to be considered here: with full or subordinate Dominion status; with or without a central All-India federal authority and/or British control of foreign affairs and defence; with six provinces as in Jinnah's maximalist territorial claim, or shorn of Bengal and the Punjab, as in Gandhi's 1944 offer, or, as in the final June 1947 Partition Plan, with what Jinnah labelled a 'moth-eaten' Pakistan containing the partitioned chunks of West Punjab and East Bengal. According to Jalal's (1985) 'revisionist' account, Jinnah remained committed to Indian unity but aimed from 1940 onwards to secure an equal say for Muslims in an All-India Union. 'Pakistan' was the vehicle for this campaign, and arguably it served its purpose while Jinnah kept talking, and, ironically, while it seemed that the British would be around to guarantee whichever version of Dominion status was implemented. The crucial factor was therefore British determination to oversee the transition, and to protect a settlement imposed upon Congress. After the failure of the 1946 Cabinet Mission (whose proposals for a federal Union, rejected by Nehru, were close to Jinnah's own continuing vision), that British will to remain seemed to be evaporating. The demand for Pakistan would thus 'either have to become the basis of a territorial demand or vanish into history' (Moore 1999: 240–1). This view of Jinnah the master strategist *and* idealist striving for Indian unity on his terms is persuasive, but in concentrating on the route to Partition, it has also invited the criticism that it neglects cultural and religious ideals embedded in the Muslim separatist movement (Talbot 1999: 261; Gilmartin 2003). Indeed, 'Pakistan' was never simply a bargaining tool, in Jinnah's or anyone else's hands, but also represented one of several mutually exclusive utopias with which Indians imagined a post-imperial future.

The dominant utopia, as it were, was nonetheless that offered by the Indian National Congress, but it is a measure of Jinnah's success that the Congress agenda was also headed by the Pakistan question throughout this period. In the end, of the Congress leadership, only Gandhi remained firmly wedded to the principle of Indian unity – a position not inconsistent with his willingness in 1944 to make concessions to Jinnah, since he did not concede the crucial issue of equal representation – but he became increasingly isolated, and his heroic opposition to spiralling communal violence was on a different level from Congress's sharpening focus on the acquisition of concrete state power.

Two broad reasons may be identified why Congress as a whole thus 'came round' to the idea of Partition. First, at the level of high politics, Congress was always the overwhelmingly likely inheritor of the British Raj, whatever the outcome of negotiations. At first, Nehru dismissed the League as unrepresentative of Muslims, unsustainable without British support, while Pakistan was seen as a mere 'fantasy' (Darwin 1988: 91). But the greater threat represented by Pakistan, or by the variously unwieldy proposals for federation with which Wavell, the Cabinet Mission and Mountbatten, sought to accommodate Jinnah, was not that India would be split in two but that it would be 'balkanized', with not only Muslim-majority provinces encouraged to seek independence but also various Princely states, or such intriguing non-communal entities as a united Bengal or a Pathan state based on the North-West Frontier province, which, though predominantly Muslim, had traditionally supported Congress (Sarkar 1989: 449). This threat was most acute in Mountbatten's short-lived 'May Plan', according to which provinces and states would opt for integration into one or other of two Dominions, or for separate independence. Two Indias were thus arguably better than several, as in VP Menon's proposal which formed the basis for Mountbatten's final 'June Plan' (ibid.: 448). But even at this late stage, Congress leaders thought that Jinnah's 'moth-eaten' Pakistan was unviable, and would soon seek readmission to a united India. This helps explain why they accepted the breakneck countdown to independence within two months of the plan's acceptance, and condoned the fact that the Boundary Commission, chaired by the constitutional lawyer, Sir Cyril Radcliffe, whose main claim to objectivity was that he had never set foot in India (Wolpert 2000: 348), had no time to make its findings public until after the Transfer of Power on 15 August 1947. Though territorial partition was the most visible aspect of this process, the apparatus and institutions of the state had also to be divided 'into bundles of 82.5 per cent for India and 17.5 per cent for Pakistan' (ibid.).

The second broad reason why Congress leaders opted in the end for Partition was that negotiations with the British and debates in the ineffectual interim government of 1946–7 were accompanied and often overshadowed by the threat of a breakdown of order. This may be seen either simply as bloody communal violence, or as the 'counterpoint provided by pressure from below' which, as popular action made British rule untenable, obliged Congress to accept even Partition as the 'necessary price' for avoiding far-reaching social revolution (Sarkar 1989: 414). India's 'tryst with destiny', which Nehru proclaimed at midnight on 15 August 1947 – following Pakistan's declaration of independence the day before – was thus coloured with regret for parallel destinies that were not achieved, and in any case overshadowed by the storm clouds of Partition.

A foretaste of Partition was offered in the sometimes apocalyptic waves of communal violence which from August 1946 swept through Calcutta, Bombay, East Bengal, Bihar and finally Punjab in March 1947. The eventual partition line cut perhaps most deeply across the latter province, which was only 56 per cent Muslim, and where Sikh aspirations to a separate 'Sikhistan' were only likely to be realized in the 'worst case' of balkanization (ibid.: 432; Wolpert 2000: 346). By March 1948 some 180,000 Punjabis had died, two-thirds of them Muslims moving westwards; 6 million Muslims and 4.5 million Hindus and Sikhs were refugees, leaving behind 4.7 million acres of land in East Punjab, 6.7 million acres in the West (Sarkar 1989: 434–45). Although at a steadier rate, the flow of refugees continued in both directions well into the 1950s. In the short term, tragically, it took Gandhi's assassination by a Hindu extremist on 30 January 1948 to achieve a respite in the violence, enabling Nehru to apply the 'leverage of popular indignation' to pull India back from the brink (Wolpert 2000: 355–6).

Amongst those whose interests were discarded were the Princely states, cajoled variously by Mountbatten or by Congress leaders V.P. Menon and Vallabhbhai Patel into accepting an Instrument of Accession. By 15 August, only three states remained outside the fold of one or other of the two new states. In two of these, Muslim princes ruled over a Hindu-majority population in states surrounded by Indian territory; one of these, the Nawab of Junagadh, acceded to Pakistan in August 1947, but was powerless to avoid absorption into India. The ruler of the second, much larger state, the Nizam of Hyderabad, was given a year to August 1948 to accept accession. After the deadline passed, an Indian army 'police action' was launched against Hyderabad, in September 1948. However, the principal aim of this was to crush the Telengana rising, a communist-inspired agrarian revolt which arguably worried Congress more than did the Nizam's intransigence (Sarkar 1989: 445–6). In the third case of Kashmir, a Hindu Maharajah, Hari Singh, ruled a three-quarters Muslim majority. As in Hyderabad, a standstill agreement gave Hari Singh the opportunity to decide between communal and geographic logic (since Kashmir bordered on Pakistan and controlled the headwaters of Pakistani rivers including the Indus) and his own inclination to remain an independent 'Switzerland of Asia' (Wolpert 2000: 353). However, within three months of independence, a de facto partition-within-the-partition was forming, on one side of which Hari Singh acceded to India, while on the other a self-declared Azad ('Free') Kashmir acceded to Pakistan. A UN-sponsored ceasefire line came into effect on 1 January 1949, and remains in place in the early twenty-first century, when the legacy of Partition has occasionally translated into nuclear stand-off between the Raj's legatees.

The Rise and Fall of Dominion status: 'More Ceylons and Fewer Burmas'

The greatest of the colonial empires also had the grandest claims made on its behalf, whether in terms of longevity or freedom. Thus, British politicians contemplated the perspective of 'a thousand years of English history', while the anglophile South African Prime Minister, General Jan Christian Smuts, in an interview with *Life* magazine in December 1942, described the British Commonwealth as 'the widest system of organized freedom which has ever existed in human history' (in Louis 1977: 209–10). British and Commonwealth leaders did not always express themselves so extravagantly; but even without Smuts's 'spin' for the American media, such a rhetorical stance was not simply pandering to a sceptical international audience or providing reassurance for metropolitan political opinion. Central to British imperial self-perceptions was a long tradition of granting or conceding freedoms to dependent peoples whilst retaining them within the bounds of what had come to be known, since the First World War, as the 'British Commonwealth of Nations'.

The key concept was that of 'Dominion' status, but before the Indian Transfer of Power, it had only been applied to the 'White' Dominions of Canada, Australia, New

Zealand, South Africa and, from 1921, the Irish Free State. Finally formalized in the 1931 Westminster Statute, the definition of Dominions provided in 1926 by an Imperial Committee chaired by the former Prime Minister Lord Balfour demonstrated how far the idea had moved away from the original idea of an imperial federation:

> They are autonomous communities, within the British Empire, equal in status, in no way subordinate one to another in any aspect of their domestic or external affairs, though united by common allegiance to the Crown, and freely associated as members of the British Commonwealth of Nations. (in McIntyre 1998: 17)

But although such a definition is helpful (especially to those used to the French tradition of textual clarity in constitutional matters), the tradition which underpinned it was one of considerable pragmatic flexibility. Indeed, the futility of a more ideologically rigid approach had been extensively illustrated by more than twenty years of diplomatic wrangling following the 1921 Anglo-Irish Treaty establishing the Irish Free State. Ireland's 'Dominion' status turned out to be compatible with a Republican constitution, rendering otiose the conception of allegiance to the Crown. When it came to war, the Irish Free State remained neutral, but this was tempered with sympathy for the British war effort, to which tens of thousands of Irish combatants contributed. However, it was clear that the Irish 'pillar' of the British Empire was no longer load-bearing, well before the Republic formally left the Commonwealth in 1949 (Boyce 1999: 70–88).

British reluctance to concede Dominion status to India crystallized in concerns that the British parliamentary tradition was not applicable to India. Thus, Dr John Simon argued, in the report of the Commission he chaired in 1928–30, that parliamentarianism in India was 'a translation, and in even the best translation the essential meaning is apt to be lost': 'The British Parliamentary system has developed in accordance with the day-to-day needs of the people, and has been fitted like a well-worn garment to the figure of the wearer, but it does not follow that it will suit everybody' (in Boyce 1999: 92).

The party system in India never corresponded to the British ideal, but provincial election results in 1937 and 1945 were crucial in winning British acquiescence in what was essentially the expression of communal majorities. The crude geometry of Partition which could be derived from these expressions of the popular will (albeit on the basis of limited suffrage) was instrumental in leading the British government to ignore its qualms on this subject. Aside from these issues of political principle, however, and at the heart of British efforts to preserve Indian unity through a succession of constitutional formulae, right up to Mountbatten's penultimate offer of May 1947 (the 'May Plan'), was the hope that the Indian Army could be preserved as a pillar of imperial defence. Partition thus also decisively undermined Dominion status as a means of preserving imperial interests. In the end, and notwithstanding the great importance which Mountbatten attached to the idea of himself as governor-general of both new Dominions, Dominion status was little more than a face-saving mechanism in which imperial interest was reduced to the preservation of imperial dignity. More practically, it allowed a swift Transfer of Power, which thus took place without further legislation beyond a simple amendment of the 1935 Government of India Act (Darwin 1988: 97).

The contrasting ways in which Burma and Ceylon were handled cast further doubt on the substance of Dominion status. In both cases, the Transfer of Power was accelerated in the aftermath of war and by virtue of comparison with events in India. In Burma, the process was so swift and so contrary to British policy as hardly to warrant the euphemism 'Transfer of Power' (Tinker 1984–5; Smith & Stockwell 1988; de Silva 1997). Burma's pre-war position within the empire was inextricably tied to India, as an economic adjunct, exporter of rice and resentful recipient of Indian moneylenders and migrant labourers. So too was its political destiny tied to that of India, and it was thus set on the road to Dominion status in the 1935 Government of Burma Act, paralleling the Indian Act. From a British perspective, the three-year hiatus of Japanese occupation necessitated a return to direct British rule for a further three years, to December 1948; this was enshrined in legislation in June 1945, which also allowed for the ethnically distinct hill states ('Scheduled Areas') to remain under British control pending their willingness to be amalgamated with Burma (Christie 1996).

British power and initiative were never fully recovered, however. With Aung San's AFPFL the only political force capable of squaring up to rural communism, and with the Burmese police dangerously sympathetic to the AFPFL, military reinforcements to help the British administration to negotiate from strength were never forthcoming – a parallel with Wavell's request for five divisions to maintain order in India is suggested. In early 1947, against the backdrop of a disintegrating position in India, but with no charismatic princely conjuror to pull a rabbit from his viceregal hat, the Attlee government conceded control of important areas of government, including administration of the 'Scheduled Areas', in return for Dominion status. But Aung San, mindful of Nehru's likely insistence on a Republican constitution for India, and mistrustful of any revival of the economic and political subservience represented by 'traditional' links with the empire, refused the allegiance to the Crown implied by Dominion status. The shock of Aung San's assassination in July 1947, along with most of his cabinet, did nothing to impede Burma's progress towards independence (Darwin 1988: 97–101). Thus, in January 1948, Burma became the first colony since 1776 to secede completely from British imperial influence. Underlining the singularity of this move, when India applied for Commonwealth membership as a republic a year later, it was unthinkable that such an application be denied, even though this rendered Dominion status virtually meaningless, and the concept passed quietly out of history, at 'what seemed its moment of greatest triumph', although Ghana and Malaysia both subsequently applied for Dominion status.[3]

Regarded as a 'model colony', Ceylon seemed set at various moments to undergo a model decolonization, as British policy makers promised themselves 'more Ceylons and fewer Burmas' (in Louis 1999: 337; Ashton 1999: 448; McIntyre 1998: 108). Some aspects of the model were certainly worthy of emulation, but the circumstances which allowed concessions and compromises on both sides were fairly exceptional. Universal suffrage, introduced in Ceylon in 1931 in an effort to head off communal violence, had in fact heightened communal tensions, principally between the majority Sinhalese community and the substantial Tamil minority. The presence of significant numbers of Indian Tamil migrant labourers (distinct from Ceylonese Tamils), many having acquired voting rights, acted as a further political irritant which negotiations between the Ceylon government and New Delhi failed to settle. The structure of representative government up to 1946, modelled on the London County Council, was a clumsy system of executive committees to which individual ministers answered. Early in the war, Ceylon was regarded as 'likely to present the most difficult problem with which the Colonial Office would be dealing' (in Ashton 1999: 460). Ceylon acquired a crucial wartime role as a major source of raw materials, providing 60 per cent of Allied natural rubber supplies after the fall of Malaya, and as headquarters of Mountbatten's South-East Asia Command from April 1944. Ceylon's political leaders, headed by the conservative Sinhalese leader Dom Stephen Senanayake, could point to loyal cooperation in the Allied war effort, and in return expected Dominion status and cabinet government. What they were offered by Lord Soulbury's Commission, which reported in October 1945, fell short of Dominion status, though it endorsed the demand for internal self-government, with Britain retaining responsibility for defence and external affairs.

The arguments for Britain conceding independence to Ceylon were fairly compelling for both sides, but even so it took almost two years of negotiation, to June 1947, to persuade the Labour government to strike a deal that might be interpreted by a hostile Conservative opposition as yet a further instance of imperial 'scuttle' (Boyce 1999). Never again were the British likely to find such a ready group of collaborators in the imperial endgame as Senanayake and his Sinhalese supporters, whom Patrick Gordon Walker, Secretary of State for Commonwealth Relations, portrayed as 'extremely rich landowners with local power and influence comparable to a whig landlord's in George III's time'. There was nonetheless a measure of self-delusion in the Commonwealth enthusiast Gordon Walker's view that: '. . . if we treat them strictly as a dominion they will behave very like a loyal colony; whereas if we treat them as a Colony we may end in driving them out of the Commonwealth' (March 1948, in Darwin 1988: 105).

In the decolonizing endgame, mutual interest counted more than 'loyalty'. This was the Colonial Office's first territory to advance to self-government, and working on Lord Soulbury's injunction to avoid 'giving too little and too late', officials were determined to force a satisfactory settlement. Officials were accused of seeking to 'rid themselves of the island and so avoid another Indian problem' (in Ashton 1999: 463n.). Viewed cynically, the CO apparently believed that communal tensions, discrimination against migrant labourers, and rural class war were best left to the local experts. Senanayake's United National Party, formed in 1946, had much to gain from rapid agreement with Britain, in order to bolster support against substantial, but divided, opposition from Communists and other left-wing groups. The interim government devised a system of constitutional safeguards to protect minorities, including a bicameral legislature and representation with weightage for both area and population, to benefit the Tamil and Muslim communities who lived in more sparsely populated territory; even these safeguards did nothing to allay the fears of the Tamil Congress, formed in 1944. Following the February 1947 London Conference on Commonwealth citizenship and nationality, the problem of nationality for Indian immigrants was also effectively shelved for an independent Senanayake government to settle, in legislation which 'effectively removed voters of Indian origin from the electoral rolls' (ibid.: 463). The post-imperial relationship was more satisfactorily managed in terms of defence and external relations, in that Britain preserved base rights including access to the naval base at Trincomalee, and in return acted as a counterweight for Ceylon against India's regional predominance. Dominion status was thus attacked by the communists as an illusory independence, and Ceylon was refused UN membership on a Soviet veto until 1955.

The February 1948 Transfer of Power to Ceylon, renamed Sri Lanka in 1972, was celebrated as a significant step forward for British imperial stabilization after the war, or, more simply, as a 'consolation' (Boyce 1999: 107). Some commentators went further, including one CO official, who hailed the evolving Commonwealth as 'the boldest stroke of political idealism which the world has yet witnessed, and on by far the grandest scale', and for whom Ceylon pointed forward: 'Dominion status for coloured colonial peoples, however sincerely professed as an objective, remained a castle in the air. It has now come down to earth' (in McIntyre 1998: 29).

But on the whole, and notwithstanding all public declarations to the contrary, the three new Dominions, and one lost cause, in the late 1940s were seen by the British 'official mind' as a first step along a much more protracted journey. Certainly, as we shall see in the following chapter, the governors of British Africa could be forgiven for desiring policies which would facilitate 'more Ceylons', but this was to be understood more in terms of internal political development, rather than the 'ultimate' end goal of such development.

Having given ground substantially in South Asia, the British had also conceded ideological ground in granting independence even to countries which were not deemed to be 'ready' (which was the case for Ceylon and Burma, if not for India). Now came the drawing of a line. In December 1949, the Colonial Secretary, Arthur Creech Jones, in a memorandum on 'Constitutional Development in smaller colonial territories', considered that the central purpose of British colonial policy was: 'to guide the Colonial territories to responsible self-government within the Commonwealth in conditions that ensure to the people concerned both a fair standard of living and freedom from oppression from any quarter'.

To this end, a territory had to be 'economically viable and capable of defending its own interests'. By this reckoning, some territories might potentially achieve full independence, some might combine with others to form units capable of achieving viability, while others belonged in 'neither of the two categories'. As he concluded: '. . . it is hardly likely that full self-government will be achieved under any foreseeable conditions (apart from associations with other territories) by any except Nigeria, the Gold Coast and the Federation of Malaya with Singapore'.[4] Thus, British policy had given credence to the idea of a Commonwealth of Nations, to which members belonged as equals. But deprived of any real content, the prize of Dominion status had proved to be little more than a sop to British imperial sensibilities. Conversely, the Empire-Commonwealth was still implicitly divided into hierarchies of 'readiness' and viability, while the old colonial rhetoric of guidance towards 'eventual' self-government was, if anything, reinforced by the need to draw a line, albeit one that would be repeatedly redrawn over the coming decade and more, as timetable after timetable was foreshortened by the accelerating progress towards independence of even the smallest and least 'viable' of states.

Notes

1 They were recruited across French sub-Saharan Africa, not just in Senegal. *Tirailleurs malgaches* were recruited in Madagascar, while *spahis*, *zouaves*, and other North African troops recruited from settler and Algerian communities, were also available for metropolitan deployment.

2 For a mythical rather than strictly historical account, see Ousmane (1985), which climaxes in a visually arresting, but wholly fictional massacre of camp inmates by a squadron of French tanks.

3 McIntyre (1998: 107–9) also notes how, already in January 1946, government departments in Wellington were advised to drop the first two words in 'Dominion of New Zealand' in official documents and letterheads, but without incurring publicity.

4 Porter & Stockwell 1987: vol. I, 302–6; Boyce 1999: 133–4. Federation was considered for territories in Southeast Asia, the Caribbean and East and Central Africa; for British federal experiments in Central Africa, see Chapters 5, 8.

Imperial Designs and Nationalist Realities in Southeast Asia, 1945–1955

With hindsight it is obvious that the Second World War marked the beginning of the end of the colonial empires, whether the matter is considered in terms of ideology or of international power. On the one hand, *res publica Americana dixit* – the emerging Superpower of the United States of America had spoken. The Atlantic Charter, signed in August 1941 by President Franklin Delano Roosevelt and by the arch-imperialist British Prime Minister Winston Churchill, pronounced the 'rights of all peoples to choose their form of government under which they will live'; the Charter was further endorsed on 1 January 1942 by the representatives of 26 Allied nations, describing themselves as the 'United Nations', and including the exiled governments of the occupied European colonial powers and the Free French (Chamberlain 1998: 21). Despite Churchill's protestations that this clause applied only to those suffering 'under the Nazi yoke', the principle it enshrined, derived from the doctrine of national self-determination championed by President Woodrow Wilson after the First World War, would be applied across the colonial empires in the following decades. On the other hand, the major colonial powers emerged from the war in severely straitened circumstances, and, humiliated in Southeast Asia, would even have to recover their colonial possessions from enemy occupation and potential or actual nationalist takeover. These shifts in both ideology and power were dramatically symbolized by the Transfer of Power in India, which represented both a major triumph for the self-determination of a colonized nation (albeit split decisively into two) and a significant loss of power for Britain.

However, the light shed from our own time may throw too much of the picture into deep shadow. By the end of the war, the challenge of American anti-colonialism seemed to have been transmuted, for the moment at least, into US support for the Western Allies, including the three major colonial powers. The cloud of discord on the horizon of relations with the Soviet Union that rapidly grew into Cold War suggested further ways of eliciting American support for colonial empire. Moreover, wartime propaganda campaigns had left their mark on imperial doctrine, and forced a new tone of explicit purposefulness in imperial declarations, in which liberal promises mingled with undertakings to conduct the business of empire with a new degree of effectiveness.

Therefore, when the colonial powers fought their way back into Southeast Asia (or, as in Malaya, came ready to do so), they arrived bearing the fruit of labours by colonial planners in London, Algiers and Paris, and the exiled Dutch administration's base in Australia. In place of the *status quo ante*, colonial restoration indicated a rational reordering of the colonial state. Some planning pre-dated the Japanese occupation, but the aim in each case was to clear away the accretions and improvisations of the pre-war colonial order. Equally, new policy reflected the enhanced role that each dependency had to play within a renewed imperial order. This role could be economic, as in Malaya, whose tin and rubber were considered vital to maintaining the Sterling area. Or it could be a question of international prestige: for French leaders, the 'return' to Indochina was central to the French Union project to recover the national patrimony from enemy occupation. For the Dutch, whose imperial identity was almost entirely bound up in the East Indies, retaining control in Indonesia was seen as imperative for the retention of 'medium power' status, for, as Dutch rhetoric so charmingly put it, the Netherlands did not want to be 'reduced to the rank of Denmark' (van den Doel 2001). Unfortunately for these grand designs, a very different political order was already being inscribed, in Indochina and Indonesia at least, on what officials implicitly imagined as a clean slate; policy thus had to be negotiated with unprepossessing nationalist interlocutors in Hanoi and Djakarta. Although the French and Dutch were initially aided by the military intervention of their British colonial ally, this novel encounter with the increasingly confident revolutions in Indochina and Indonesia shifted the emphasis away from reform. And in Malaya, although a new policy was imposed from the start on the Sultans, political pressures from emergent Malay nationalism soon brought about a complete policy reversal.

In all three cases, the returning colonial power soon found itself defending its policy by force, and only in Malaya would the military challenge prove to be remotely containable. However, as the region was drawn in to American containment strategy in the Cold War, the three colonial regimes became potential buffers against supposed communist expansion. Whereas in Malaya and Indochina, this was achieved by a shift in policy and outlook, in Indonesia, the revolutionary Republic was able to contend with its own communist rebels, and the returning colonial power was found to be expendable. For the Netherlands, this was a veritable blessing in disguise, accelerating Dutch post-war prosperity. For the French Union, by contrast, a protracted war against a resourceful, well-equipped national army fighting for liberation led to humiliating defeat, followed almost seamlessly by an even more traumatic conflict in Algeria. Before turning to our case studies, we first consider the emerging imperial framework into which French Indochina was to be incorporated.

The French Union

French approaches to rethinking post-war empire had no precedents to compare with the British conception of Dominion status. Rather, the French tradition of imperial unity derived from the unassailable doctrine of the 'One and Indivisible Republic'. This contrast was self-consciously underlined by the governors of French Africa who gathered at Brazzaville in January 1944, whose statement of principle, heading their political recommendations, even rendered the offending formula in quasi-English, as if to suggest its alien character:

> Before examining this part of the agenda, the French African Conference at Brazzaville decided to establish the following principle:
> 'The ends of the civilising mission accomplished in the colonies exclude any idea of autonomy, all possibility of evolution outside the French bloc; also excluded is the eventual establishment of self governments [sic] in the colonies, even in a distant future.' (Ministère des Colonies 1945)

Nonetheless, French officials and politicians were as adept at reinventing traditions as were the British, and in the wake of defeat, occupation and the four-year occlusion of the French Republic, they needed to be. The declaration certainly reflected the irreducible core of French imperial thinking, which was that the empire was there to stay; this was arguably not so very different from contemporaneous British imperial thinking. Beyond that, however, it represented only one position in a tortuous internal debate, ultimately resulting in the French Union articles of the Constitution finally agreed in November 1946 (Chapter 5).

Central to the French debate was the proposed incorporation of the empire into a revised Constitution. The plans presented at Brazzaville for a French Federation (subsequently transmuted into the French Union) may thus be set alongside the plethora of variously utopian schemes, covering every aspect of French social and political life, which emerged from the Gaullist movement and the Resistance, most of which bore little relation to the reality of the Fourth Republic after 1946 (Shennan 1989). The federal proposals were largely the work of Governor Henri Laurentie, whose role in the 'rallying' of Tchad to de Gaulle in August 1940 led him to become Governor-General Félix Éboué's secretary-general in Free French Brazzaville. In July 1943, he was appointed Director of Political Affairs in the makeshift Colonial Commissariat at Algiers, headed by René Pleven, and retained this key post in the Ministry of Colonies in liberated Paris.

Laurentie envisioned an overarching, federal structure for the French empire, governed by a High Council and an elected Assembly, with metropolitan France acting as 'first amongst equals'. This implied a presidential regime for France, although Gaullist thinking on this subject was still unclear. Colonial territories were to be classed in a number of categories, broadly including what came to be called 'Associated States', which would enjoy a degree of internal autonomy, and a group of 'Associated' or 'United' Territories, deemed not to have developed the political means to govern themselves. A further option was that territories might elect to become *départements* on the metropolitan model, fully integrated into the Republic. The key to the scheme was this recognition of divergent development, which also doubtless guaranteed its unworkability. As Laurentie explained, in March 1945:

> All French territories are destined to attain their political majority. Some have already achieved this: Morocco, Tunisia, Indochina, New Caledonia. Others have some way to go, and they will remain under the control of the French executive, which will also retain some measure of legislative control. But this executive control will be provisional: the United Territories will evolve as is appropriate in each case, either towards the

assimilated status of Overseas Departments, or towards the status of Associated States.
(in Shipway 1996a: 45)

Aside from rejection by the governors assembled at Brazzaville, French post-Liberation politics played a large part in the scheme's demise. But in any case, the policy quickly became a palimpsest of contradictions and misconceptions. For a start, the pallid official debate was never engaged in a wide enough forum. Brazzaville was supposed to have been a grand imperial conference of proconsuls from across the empire. However, Indochina was excluded, as it was still under Japanese occupation. And Morocco and Tunisia were ruled out of discussion, on the conventional grounds that the protectorate treaties of 1881 and 1912 precluded closer involvement in French affairs. Discussion of Algeria in an imperial forum would have broken an even greater taboo than was the case for the protectorates. France's imperial 'watertight bulkheads' were thus acting as an effective barrier to reformist initiatives, although Rabat, Tunis and Algiers all sent observers to Brazzaville, and French North African officials played a largely obstructive role in subsequent discussions (Shipway 2002). As peace in Europe approached, Indochina became a test case for the new policy, and the term 'French Union' was first used officially in the Declaration on Indochina made by the Minister of Colonies, Paul Giacobbi, on 24 March 1945.[1]

Indochina: From the March 1945 Declaration to Bao Dai

The French Provisional Government's ostensibly bold and, on its terms, generous offer to Indochina was pre-empted by the Japanese takeover of 9 March 1945. The Declaration presented two weeks later by Giacobbi thus looked like a reaction to events, although it had gone through at least seven drafts over several months (Shipway 1996a: 123). It was nonetheless a striking statement of post-war imperial intent, which provided the framework for French actions in Indochina until at least the outbreak of war 18 months later: 'The Indochinese Federation will join with France and the other parts of the French community to form a 'French Union', whose external interests will be represented by France. Indochina will enjoy its proper freedom within this Union' (in ibid.: 60–1).

Although what constituted 'proper freedom' was intentionally vague, Indochina was to have a federal government in which all national communities including settlers would be represented, an elected assembly and a nominated Council of State, a dual system of Indochinese and French Union citizenship allowing access to administrative posts within Indochina and across the French Union, 'compulsory and effective' primary education, economic autonomy in which industrialization would be encouraged.

Two aspects of the Declaration were central to subsequent events. First, the Federation was to be headed by a Governor-General, doubtless a metropolitan appointee, thus underlining French authority. Secondly, Indochina was to be divided into 'five lands . . . distinguished by civilization, race and traditions'. This latter move was an attempt to rationalize the anomalies contained within the pre-war patchwork of kingdoms, protectorates, concessions (Hanoi and Haiphong) and the colony of Cochinchina, with each of the five units within the new Federation enjoying equal status. Conversely, while the aim was to maintain a demographic balance between Laos,

Cambodia and the three highly populated regions (or *ky*) of Vietnam, the separation of the three *ky* was based on a tendentious reading of the historical evidence.[2] It was also contradicted by the Kim government's successful efforts, from March to August 1945, to assert imperial rule over both the Tonkinese protectorate and Cochinchina, an achievement which the Viet Minh were keen to consolidate.

The mismatch between the March 1945 Declaration and the intelligence picture that was gradually being pieced together could be resolved in one of two ways. First, some ministry officials in Paris, headed by Laurentie, came close to favouring limited or qualified independence for Vietnam, but were overruled by more prudent counsel, and by de Gaulle's veto. Secondly, the stated primary mission of the new High Commissioner, who combined the roles of Governor-General and Commander-in-Chief, was 'to restore French sovereignty over the territory of the Indochinese Union'; to ensure compliance, de Gaulle appointed an unswervingly loyal member of his entourage, the aristocratic former Carmelite monk, Admiral Georges Thierry d'Argenlieu (Shipway 1996a: 132–47).

Before splitting Indochina five ways, returning French forces had first to work around the two-way split imposed at the July 1945 Potsdam Conference. To receive the Japanese surrender, the Allies decreed the temporary occupation of Indochina by Chinese troops of the American China Command, and by Mountbatten's South-East Asia Command, divided at the 16th Parallel. In the South, the interpretation of Mountbatten's orders by the British commander, General Gracey, allowed him to provide generous assistance to returning French forces commanded by General Philippe Leclerc, who concluded a brilliant campaign of 'pacification' across Cochinchina and Cambodia in early 1946 (Dunn 1985; Tønnesson 1991). In the North, troops of the Yunnanese General Lu Han were an obstacle to French designs, while awakening secular Vietnamese fears of Chinese imperialism. Thus, although the partition barred the North to French officials, apart from a beleaguered representative in Hanoi, Jean Sainteny, it also provided a lever in French negotiations with Ho Chi Minh. In February 1946, French diplomats secured an agreement for Chinese withdrawal in return for the cession of all French extraterritorial and transit rights in China, including control of the strategically vital Yunnan railway. This then paved the way for Sainteny's agreement with Ho Chi Minh on 6 March 1946, which allowed the return of French troops and officials to Hanoi. However, these Accords were signed only after Sainteny had been pushed to the wall by last-minute armed confrontation between French forces riding off Haiphong and the Chinese military authorities: Leclerc urged Sainteny to do anything to secure agreement, even if that agreement had subsequently to be repudiated, in order to avoid further bloodshed and a military fiasco (Shipway 1996a: 170–1).

The March 1946 Accords offer a glimpse of what a peaceful settlement might have looked like, had it been possible. They even marked a brief moment of French ascendancy in the competitive arena of Asian colonialism, as Laurentie argued:

> We must consider that opinion in Asia is generally hostile to the colonial powers. Britain's difficulties in India, and those of the Dutch in Indonesia, are ample proof of this. It is therefore remarkable that our country should by amicable means have arrived at a definition of common ground with Annamite nationalism. (in ibid.: 174)

The Accords stretched the March 1945 framework to breaking point, by recognising the Republic of Vietnam as 'a Free State with its own government, parliament, army, and finances, forming a part of the Indochinese Federation and of the French Union', and by submitting the question of the three *ky* to a referendum. A final conference was to meet in Paris, Saigon or Hanoi. Worse, prompted by Leclerc's desperate messages, Sainteny also agreed, in an Annex to the Accords, to progressive French troop withdrawals over five years, which would leave Vietnam in Ho's hands. However unlikely it was to be applied in good faith by the French, this agreement enabled Ho to 'sell' the Accords to his more intransigent lieutenants, to whom he explained that he preferred 'to sniff French shit for five years than eat Chinese shit for the rest of my life' (in Karnow 1994: 169). Despite Ho's astute diplomacy, however, the Accords were never accepted, either by the High Commissioner, who played no part in the negotiations, or by the government in Paris, preoccupied with negotiating a constitutional text (shortly to be rejected in the referendum of 5 May 1946). The March 1946 Accords are best understood as a purely tactical agreement, allowing the French a foothold in northern Indochina, and thus ostensibly restoring French sovereignty, but only marginally slowing the descent into violence which more accurately reflected the distance between French and Viet Minh objectives.

In effect, two contradictory versions of Vietnam's imagined future were in contention. Ho Chi Minh presented himself as Head of State in his dealings with French officials, and during his protracted visit to France from June to September 1946, stayed aloof from Franco-Vietnamese negotiations at Fontainebleau, touring France and receiving journalists and sympathizers in his hotel suite in Paris. Meanwhile, at home, the Viet Minh consolidated its regime, reversing the thrust of its six-month accommodation with the Chinese, and re-establishing links with the party's organization in the South. The Hanoi government was no longer constrained to deal with rival nationalist parties, such as the Chinese-backed Vietnamese National Party (*Viet Nam Quoc Dan Dang*), or the League of Revolutionary Vietnamese Parties (*Dong Minh Hoi*), which were both rapidly sidelined, their leaders either suborned or brutally liquidated. The Viet Minh in Cochinchina had never fully followed Ho's strategy, and since September 1945 had been repressed by both Gracey and Leclerc. Their veteran leader Nguyen Binh now stepped up efforts to mobilize a mass following in the South, in preparation for the anticipated referendum on Cochinchina's adhesion to a united Vietnam, and to harass the French in a campaign of continuous violence (Goscha 1995).

By contrast, French policy was one of unremitting hostility to the Viet Minh, and exaggerated respect for the March 1945 Declaration. Saigon's alarming propensity to act independently was justified by the political crises which rocked Paris throughout 1946, starting in January with de Gaulle's ill-tempered resignation as president of the Provisional Government. The March 1946 Accords were seen as a purely local agreement with 'Tonkin', comparable with the agreements signed with Cambodia (7 January 1946) and Laos (7 May 1946), and to be followed by similar agreements with Cochinchina and Annam. The key was Cochinchina, where a provisional government of pro-French notables was being assembled. Having failed to stop Ho coming to Paris, d'Argenlieu almost upstaged the negotiations altogether, by proclaiming the 'Autonomous Republic' of Cochinchina on 1 June 1946. Despite official sympathy for this 'separatist' approach, a Cochinchinese delegation to Paris had failed to impress. Conversely, although officials loathed the 'brutal and puerile' Viet Minh, Ho's national authority was still respected, and d'Argenlieu's parallels between the 'expansionist' Viet Minh and the Nazis fell on deaf ears (Shipway 1996a: 194). Although the Fontainebleau conference almost inevitably failed, Ho returned to Vietnam with an eleventh-hour *modus vivendi* agreed with the Minister of Overseas France, Marius Moutet, in mid-September, which held out hopes of a ceasefire and a referendum on Cochinchina.

By the time Ho returned to Vietnam in October, Saigon officials were moving towards breaking with Hanoi altogether. Saigon's propensity for autonomous action was accentuated by the Cochinchinese government's failure and the suicide of its leader, Dr Nguyen Van Thinh, in early November. Officials were emboldened by continuing political crisis in Paris. Following National Assembly elections in early November, France was without a new government for a full five weeks, and, since neither the Christian Democrat MRP nor the Communist Party could command majority support in the Assembly, it fell to the 74-year-old Socialist leader, Léon Blum, to form an interim all-Socialist administration. During these early skirmishes in France's domestic Cold War, a customs dispute at Haiphong in late November escalated into full-scale naval and aerial bombardment of Vietnamese positions, with an estimated 6,000 casualties. Further clashes occurred at the border garrison town of Langson. Following an apparent plot by the Army and officials to provoke the Viet Minh, local 'self-defence' militia units attacked French defences in Hanoi on 19 December 1946, and the French Army retaliated in a 'strike at the head' intended to destroy the Viet Minh government (Devillers 1988; Tønnesson 1991). After three months of bitter fighting for control of the Hanoi region, the Viet Minh were driven back into the mountains of northern Vietnam, from where they had descended in August 1945, and from where they would wage a guerrilla war lasting until the debacle of Dien Bien Phu in 1954. Although it had not been preceded by anything resembling peace, the French war in Indochina, and the first round in Vietnam's thirty-year war of national liberation, had now begun definitively.

Strikingly, French officials had little apparent sense of failure at this crucial juncture, much less of a widening abyss of irreconcilable conflict. Although the initial French riposte was disappointing, the 'hawks' who had been so impatient for action remained confident of a quick military victory over the Viet Minh. Indeed, this confidence returned intermittently, at least until Mao's victory and the establishment of the People's Republic of China transformed the war beyond recognition (see below). But a relatively optimistic prognosis was shared even by the former commander in Indochina, General Leclerc, a principal advocate of the March Accords, who embarked on a mission of inquiry shortly after the 19 December attacks. As he concluded, while the current military situation was critical, 'the problem for the French Command is much more a question of the longer term': an initial ten-month 'political phase' had indeed failed, but the army only needed to hold out until a new 'constructive phase' could be initiated (in Shipway 1996a: 268–9).

The 'constructive phase' in French policy which came into focus during 1947 was far more acceptable to officials than the doomed Accords Policy. Indeed, the new policy was predicated on the removal of the Viet Minh from the political equation.

This task became easier in May 1947, when communist ministers, having abstained on a March vote over military credits to Indochina, and protested over the despatch of troops to quell the Malagasy insurrection (Chapter 6), were expelled from the government by the Socialist prime minister, Paul Ramadier (who succeeded Blum in January 1947), over their refusal to support his incomes policy. With this possibly unconstitutional act, the French domestic Cold War had begun in earnest. Even so, it was only on 23 December 1947, after various unconvincing peace overtures to the Viet Minh by the new High Commissioner, Emile Bollaert, that the government explicitly excluded the Viet Minh from all negotiations (Dalloz 1987: 118, 122).

The core of the new policy was the 'Bao Dai solution', as the French gradually moved towards installing the ex-Emperor as head of a new Associated State of Vietnam within the French Union. In effect, Bao Dai was to be offered the Vietnamese national unity that had been refused to Ho Chi Minh, but in a version that was tolerable to France. Bao Dai's credit with the French had never been high, as a youthful 'puppet' emperor dividing his time between womanizing and hunting, as collaborator with the Japanese, or as citizen Vinh Thuy, who had abdicated in favour of the Democratic Republic of Vietnam. By late 1946 he had fled to Hong Kong. But French plans to draw on his imperial prestige pre-dated the collapse of the Accords policy, originating with the 'Machiavelli' behind French policy leading to war, Léon Pignon, who, as High Commissioner from September 1948, would be responsible for installing Bao Dai in Saigon (Shipway 1996a: 232).

This was an eminently 'colonial' solution to French policy in the state that French officials now finally agreed to call by its name. But Bao Dai, conversely, was determined to drive a hard bargain, and to secure not only the national unity achieved in 1945, but also, as far as possible, independence. After prolonged discussions and delays, and two meetings aboard French warships, Bao Dai consented to return from his self-imposed exile. On 8 April 1949, he signed agreements with the French President (and President of the French Union), Vincent Auriol, and on 2 July, the State of Vietnam was proclaimed. As Bao Dai understood, his position depended almost entirely on French support, however effectively France succeeded in 'Vietnamizing' the war with the Viet Minh. Whereas Bao Dai had formerly drawn on the prestige of the imperial throne, now he had to rely on the dubious resources of his own personality and intelligence. None assessed these qualities more generously than the British Commissioner-General in Southeast Asia, Malcolm MacDonald, reporting that he was:

> . . . impressed by Bao Dai's personality and capabilities. I had been warned that he is moody and sometimes as a result extremely uncommunicative. He inclines to be so with pressmen seeking interviews and this creates the impression that he is a dull dog. The impression is wrong. I spent the greater part of a day with him and found him talkative, intelligent and charming. He has physical courage, patriotism, and independence from subservience to the French. (28 November 1949, in Antlöv 1995: 248n.)

Bao Dai's very lack of Vietnamese support could be an asset: on his return to Saigon, the police were able to arrest three bomb-throwers, clearly identifiable amidst the sparse crowds of onlookers (ibid.: 249). Meanwhile, the new regime depended on the same pro-French notables who had underpinned the failed policy of Cochinchinese separatism, and who had become no more authentically nationalist in the meantime; for other, more determined nationalists waiting in the wings, such as Bao Dai's former minister, Ngo Dinh Diem, the new regime represented an opportunity to expel the French.

Malaya: From Union to Emergency

British rule in pre-war Malaya was based on even more elaborate governmental structures than Indochina, and efforts to reform that structure had foundered on tradition and vested interests. Reforms proposed by the Malayan Planning Unit (MPU), established in London in 1943 under Colonial Office auspices, were thus also correspondingly radical, and the Cabinet accepted that 'restoration of the pre-war constitutional and administrative system will be undesirable in the interests of efficiency and security and of our declared purpose of promoting self-government in Colonial territories' (in Stockwell 1995: liv). In place of the rickety hierarchy of Straits Settlements (one of which, Singapore, was excluded from the new policy), four Federated Malay States and five Unfederated States, the MPU proposed a Malayan Union, with a strong central government and a common citizenship. The traditional rulers of the nine states were to sign new treaties ceding full power to the Crown. The aim was to rationalize government, not only in order to foster Malaya's economic role as a key dollar earner within the Sterling area, but also to reflect the multi-ethnic composition of Malaya's 'plural society' in which indigenous Malays were the largest minority alongside other communities, most notably Chinese and Indians. In keeping with other colonial planning in this period, the proposed policy was designed to promote eventual self-government, even while enhancing colonial control in a foreseeable future.

Initially, the biggest contrast between the Malayan Union policy and French policy in Indochina arose from greater British strength on the ground, although this did not translate into a smoothly managed British return to Malaya. The British Military Administration (BMA), which assumed political control following the Japanese collapse, had planned for an armed and gradual reoccupation of the peninsula, and was unable to cope effectively with the immediate relief of the whole territory. Dogged by corruption, the BMA's 'administrative cack-handedness' soured an otherwise expectant welcome from many Malayans within the few months which preceded the handover to civil authority, on 1 April 1946 (ibid.: doc 65, lvii; Kratoska 1998). The new policy's introduction was managed in a similarly counter-productive way. Whereas the French government had been forced to declare its hand in March 1945, and then obliged to negotiate in militarily and diplomatically fraught circumstances, the details of the Malayan Union were kept secret, although Mountbatten argued that its progressive aspects might impress non-Malays, and perhaps undercut the Malayan Communist Party (MCP), with whose programme it appeared to coincide (Stockwell 1995: docs 47, 51, 52). In a carefully staged tour, a 'Special Representative of His Majesty's Government' (a splendid nonce title invented by SEAC), Sir Harold MacMichael, visited each of the nine Sultans, starting with the senior and most obviously pro-British, Sultan Ibrahim of Johore. MacMichael acknowledged each as rightful ruler (though the BMA had previously deposed three Sultans for collaboration with the Japanese), and extracted the signed agreement of each to the Union. Sultan Ibrahim signed on condition that Johore retain its constitution, executive council, stamps and flag, suggesting to the British that he had not grasped that the scheme would make his constitution a 'dead letter'; his fellow Sultans readily followed the senior Sultan (Antlöv 1995: 238–40).

British heavy-handedness and the Sultans' acquiescence transformed the Malayan political situation, taking the British by complete surprise. When details of the Malayan Union were finally published in a White Paper in January 1946, criticism came not only from Malayan 'old hands' in London, who, in a letter to the *Times*, identified 'an instrument for the annexation of the Malay States' (in ibid.: 241). More importantly, the Union was attacked by the Malay elite on whom the Sultans depended. In answer to an appeal by Dato Onn bin Jaafar, son of Sultan Ibrahim's Prime Minister (*mentri besar*), himself a state official in Johore, 41 associations representing the Malay Administrative Service (MAS) and aristocratic elites joined and in May 1946 formed the United Malays National Organization (UMNO) (Kheng 1988: 23–4). On 31 March, in Kuala Lumpur for the inauguration of the new Governor of the Malayan Union, Sir Edward Gent, the Sultans were persuaded by Dato Onn to boycott the ceremony, and appeared before a large crowd of Malays.

British backtracking began almost immediately, as first Gent, then the Governor-General designate of Malaya, Singapore and British Borneo, Sir Malcolm MacDonald, began to make the case for appeasing Malay demands. Gent feared Malay non-cooperation, and particularly its exploitation by pan-Malay opinion favouring union with Indonesia. MacDonald provided the broader imperial view, with a slight fantastical spin:

> We must, of course, keep in mind that there are powerful political groupings in Asia which are ready to exploit any weakening of our position i.e. Indian nationalists and Imperialism [*sic*], Chinese Imperialism and especially Pan Malayan Movement led by Indonesians. (25 May 1946, Stockwell 1995: doc. 92 & lx–lxi)

British policy reflected such security assessments, although the threat from Indonesia was exaggerated, and was seen to have receded by January 1948. The British now acted upon the perception that the Malay elites grouped in UMNO, although temporarily hostile as a consequence of Malayan Union, represented a new group of fundamentally conservative collaborators with whom they could do business. On 1 February 1948, the Federation of Malaya Agreement came into force, according to which sovereignty reverted to the rulers. Although Malay political predominance was thus reasserted, British negotiators had insisted on the retention in modified form of some of the principles of Union, such as strong central government and a multi-racial citizenship; in this sense, the British government had 'changed tack rather than changing course' (ibid.: lxi–lxiii).

British acceptance of Federation, with the Malay elite represented by UMNO as partners in reshaping the new colonial state, ostensibly offers a classic example of a colonial power, having abandoned one set of collaborators, the Sultans, under

Malayan Union, adopting another in order to preserve the essentials of imperial rule. But this masks the significance of a profound parallel shift occurring, not only in the structure of British rule, but also in the nature of Malayan – or, more accurately, Malay – politics. Although Malaya under British rule had only ever superficially enjoyed the mythical 'happiness of a land without a history' (Stockwell 1999: 469), pre-war Malay nationalism, and in particular the English-educated elite who served the Sultans, had been accommodated within a highly fragmentary system of Indirect Rule. The most far-reaching pre-war attempt to bridge these divisions was by Ibrahim Yaacob, who, influenced by Sukarno, urged the recognition of one united Malay people, and promoted the ideal of *Indonesia Raya* (Greater Indonesia); this ideal drew considerable encouragement from Japanese occupation (Kheng 1988: 6–7). Yaacob's movement collapsed, however, and Yaacob fled, as Sukarno rejected the short-term realization of *Indonesia Raya*, arguing that the young Indonesian Republic could not fight both the Dutch and the British (although it did fight the British in Indonesia). Not for the last time, the boundaries of the colonial state proved more durable, or perhaps simply more convenient, than the more radical nationalist dreams. But Dato Onn and his colleagues took up the theme of a united Malay people, which helped their campaign to transcend what might otherwise seem the expression of self-interest by the social group standing to lose most from the Sultans' loss of power and prestige. Indeed, this was the culmination of a much longer process of popular disillusionment with the Sultans, who had largely retained only spiritual power under the British, and whose political role had been further usurped by Malay administrators under Japanese occupation (ibid.). A striking feature of the campaign against Malayan Union was thus the popular hostility shown the Sultans, and the fact that, although ostensibly restored by Federation, their role was now increasingly that of constitutional monarchs. Power had decisively shifted into the hands of those politicians with whom the British would eventually negotiate independence, although for the moment UMNO's position was that Malaya was 'not ready' for self-rule (Stockwell 1995).

By imposing a radically new policy, then reversing that policy in favour of Federation superficially resembling the *status quo ante*, the British had succeeded in alienating both Malay and non-Malay communities. As the *Straits Times* put it in June 1948: 'The first [policy] was workable but not very popular, the second was not very popular and so far appears to be not very workable' (in Stubbs 1980: 37). Indeed, although Malayan Union was designed to accommodate Malaya's 'plural society', the Chinese and Indian communities initially showed little enthusiasm for it, but even less for Federation. Apart from scepticism regarding British goodwill, and the sense of many Chinese that their role in fighting the Japanese was being overlooked, the separation of Singapore (from both Union and Federation) disrupted Chinese trade, and increased Malay preponderance within what was now considered Malaya. Even common Malayan citizenship worked against the pre-war practice of 'protection' of communities, and officials in the pre-war Protectorate of Chinese Affairs were dispersed amongst other services, where their expertise as Chinese-speakers was diluted (ibid.: 30–1, 53–4). In late 1947, the Associated Chinese Chambers of Commerce joined with non-Malay associations grouped in the All-Malaya Council of Joint Action in calling a country-wide *hartal*, a general strike derived from the Indian example, for 20 October, which effectively brought Singapore and other commercial centres to a standstill. Although this movement failed to maintain momentum, it did mark a new stage of non-Malay political consciousness, and fed into the deterioration of confidence in British rule.

In counterpoint to these developments, the MCP was seeking the most effective means to oppose the reconsolidation of British rule in Malaya. Its efforts culminated in the violence which in June 1948 provoked the British declaration of an Emergency. It might have surprised the MCP in 1945 as much as anyone that this would turn into Britain's longest post-war colonial conflict, colouring subsequent Malayan decolonization and partly determining its outcome and timing. In contrast to the Vietnamese experience, the opportune moment was not seized in August 1945, although the party's prestige was at its height, thanks to the wartime resistance of the communist-led Malayan People's Anti-Japanese Army (MPAJA). The MPAJA was committed to fighting alongside the British against the Japanese, and was thus as unprepared as the British for the Japanese surrender. Moreover, during the power vacuum which preceded effective British military control, the MPAJA had under-mined its own claims as a force for Malayan unity through the brutality shown by its overwhelmingly Chinese membership against mostly Malay alleged collaborators. This was the MCP's inescapable, paradoxical weakness, that the MCP 'was to remain nationalist in vision but predominantly Chinese in support' (Hack 1995: 86). The 'united front' strategy adopted by the party in 1945 reflected the party's organiza-tional weakness as well as wider international communist strategy. A further singular factor hobbling the MCP's decision-making was that the party's charismatic and all-powerful secretary-general, Lai Tek, was a triple agent, having first served the British Special Branch as he climbed party ranks from 1934, and then the Japanese *Kenpeitai*. Having decimated the party during the Japanese occupation, betraying over sixty senior party members, and sending many hundreds of lower ranks to their deaths, he now provided his original British paymasters with detailed intelligence, while braking proposals for more militant action (Stubbs 1980: 55–6). After Lai Tek's exposure and flight in March 1947, the British lost their principal source of information, and his policy of peaceful agitation was discredited, increasing pressure in favour of armed struggle, and tipping the balance within the party towards more radical, more decen-tralized, but largely untested leadership; the new secretary-general, Chin Peng, was 26, and had been in the party for only eight years (ibid.: 57–8). Meanwhile, MCP control of the unions, an essential factor in the strategy of peaceful agitation, was weakened by new labour legislation (Leong 1992). It was at this point that the party learned of the shift in international communist strategy, agreed at the founding meet-ing of the Communist Information Bureau (Cominform) in September 1947, to one grounded in Zhdanov's new-minted doctrine of 'two camps' (that is, capitalist and 'democratic'), and that, at a meeting of the Central Executive Committee in March 1948, a decision was taken to move to a policy of armed struggle. Although the traditional view was that the party was 'ordered into the jungle' by a Cominform delegate to this meeting, it is more likely that news of the 'two camps' policy merely spurred the MCP to follow its own inclinations (Stubbs 1980: 60).

These decisions were taken against a background of confusion for both the MCP and the colonial authorities, and of considerable violence and lawlessness, doubtless including communists taking matters into their own hands, or driven to robbery and extortion by the party's precarious finances. Indeed, although pressure for an Emergency had been building long before the murders in Perak on 16 June 1948 which prompted the declaration, it nonetheless caught the MCP unprepared. Meanwhile, it remained unclear whether the violence was in fact directed by the MCP, and a further decision to outlaw the party did not follow for a month; by this time, the discredited Sir Edward Gent had been recalled to London, but died as his plane crashed approaching London (Stockwell 1994).

Insurgency did not change the MCP's central aim, which was 'to realize communism in Malaya' and to establish a Socialist Republic of Malaya by destroying the alliance between Britain and its 'feudalist' Malay collaborators (Hack 1995: 86). While this helps us to identify the MCP as properly nationalist, since its aim was clearly that of taking over the state, the MCP/MRLA was hampered in terms of both elite coordination and mass mobilization. This was an organization ill-suited at the outset to jungle warfare, and whose leadership had been substantially weakened by Lai Tek's treachery. 'Armed struggle' dictated new tactics, primarily consisting of attacks on British tin and rubber interests, but the overall objective was now if anything more difficult to achieve, since the party was severed from its urban and trades union roots. Conversely, fighting the colonial state did nothing to help the MCP's essential structural flaw, which stemmed from the overwhelming predominance of its Chinese membership, constituting more than ninety per cent of the total. Although the party had recruited some Malays from the trades unions, and even raised a Malay regiment of the MRLA in Pahang in 1949 (ibid.: 95n.), insurgency awakened unwelcome memories amongst Malays of the MPAJA's chauvinism. Malay suspicions of Chinese motivations also resonated with more general fears of Chinese control of the Malayan economy, while communist ideology made little headway amongst the predominantly Muslim Malays. Conversely, the insurgents' appeal to the Chinese community was diluted by the conservatism of Chinese business interests, which dictated working alongside the British administration. Moreover, MCP support was offset by substantial sympathy for the Guomindang, even after Communist victory in China in 1949. The MRLA was thus thrown back on the – willing or coerced – support of landless Chinese 'squatters' on the edges of the forest, and on the '*Min Yuen*', a network of civilian cells in rural villages, which provided the conditions of ideological mobilization and material support for the insurgent to survive 'like a fish in water', according to Mao Zedong's classic formula. The MRLA's isolation even limited its recourse to the terror tactics of more effective organizations, such as the Viet Minh or the Algerian FLN, since it could ill afford to alienate the populations amongst whom it moved (ibid.). Unlike either of these organizations, the MRLA was also isolated from outside logistical support, while identification with the Cold War 'enemy' made it an easier target. This accumulation of weaknesses made the MRLA almost uniquely vulnerable to colonial counter-insurgency (Chapter 6).

Indonesia: Dutch Reconquest, Indonesian Diplomacy and Struggle

Of the three major European colonial powers in Southeast Asia, only the Dutch failed to reconsolidate their regime. And so, following Indonesian independence in 1949, they faced the dismantling of their principal imperial showcase, a bitter pill sugared, as it happened, by the beginnings of a prosperous post-imperial future. The failure of Dutch reconquest in the Indies has been ascribed to the shortcomings of a liberal Dutch vision for post-war empire, or to their 'conviction that they were still much loved by their colonial subjects' (Springhall 2001: 63). In fact, there are striking parallels between Dutch efforts at policy making in post-1945 Indonesia and those of the British and the French in the region, although the disunited and often-vengeful Dutch did not 'play the game' as well as they might have wished, even in the face of probably insurmountable obstacles – in the protean shape of the Indonesian national revolution. The following account in no sense offers a defence of Dutch policy, but seeks to place the Dutch attempted reconquest more squarely in a regional context, and to suggest that the Dutch failure to stem or control Indonesian decolonization was no more 'inevitable' than elsewhere.

One contrast with British and French policy was that Dutch wartime planning for post-war Indonesia was significantly less detailed. The major statement on the future of the Dutch empire came only one year after Pearl Harbor, in a speech by the exiled Queen Wilhelmina, broadcast (in English) on 6 December 1942. Intended for an Allied audience, and apparently serving its primary purpose of appeasing the US president (Thorne 1979: 218), it also provided a broad framework for post-war Dutch policy, and to this end was rebroadcast in September 1945. The Queen announced that a post-war conference would be convened for joint consultation on the changes needed in the structure of the three parts of the Kingdom (i.e. the Netherlands, the Indies and the Dutch Antilles). Assenting to the principles embodied in the Atlantic Charter, she promised: '. . . a Commonwealth in which the Netherlands, Indonesia, Surinam and Curaçao will participate, with complete self-reliance and freedom of conduct for each part regarding its internal affairs, but with the readiness to render mutual assistance' (in Yong 1982: 200–2).

The speech lent itself to a liberal interpretation, and was glossed in terms of 'full self-government' by one of its principal authors, the then Dutch Minister of Colonies, Hubertus van Mook. However, it was the opposite, unitary idea of Commonwealth (very different from the British conception of the term) to which the majority of officials and politicians subsequently appealed (ibid.: 28–30). The speech is thus perhaps best understood as a rather more adroit equivalent of the French declaration at Brazzaville banning 'self governments'.

By the time the first British cruiser arrived off Djakarta, on 15 September 1945, the gulf was already massive, and widening daily, between Dutch expectations reflected in the Queen's speech and the reality of revolutionary Indonesia. Even more critically than in Indochina, the Dutch had a virtually blank intelligence picture of political developments over the crucial preceding few months, for want of the logistics required for information gathering (agents, submarines, Allied support . . .). They thus extrapolated from pre-war experience, in which nationalist revolution had no place, and, no doubt, from their own prejudices, but also from the misleadingly easy occupation of New Guinea and the Eastern archipelago by Australian troops, who had promptly handed over authority to the Netherlands Indies Civil Administration (NICA).

For his part, van Mook, reinstated in 1944 as Lieutenant Governor-General, the post he occupied in 1940-2, seems at first to have believed that the Indonesian 'rebellion' could be quelled by the supply of Australian food and textiles, to offset wartime shortages, and that a swiftly restored *pax neerlandica* would allow Dutch-sponsored self-government, supported by a silent majority of Indonesians. According to the prevailing Dutch view, shared for the moment by van Mook, the Republican government established following Sukarno's 17 September declaration of independence was 'illegal', Sukarno was a 'Quisling' to be shunned, and the *pemudas*, the youth groups so central to the revolution, were Japanese-trained extremists. Moreover, the Dutch took time to appreciate the impact of Japanese occupation, impeding communication between the islands, and varying markedly across the archipelago. While the Japanese military presence and political control had been relatively light in Java, the heartland of both Indonesian nationalism and Dutch colonialism, the occupation had been more intensive in Sumatra, which was central to Japanese economic strategy, and especially in Borneo and the 'Great East' (Sulawesi, Bali and the Eastern archipelago), which had been controlled by the Japanese Navy (Reid 1974). This pattern was broadly reflected in the relative ease with which the Dutch re-imposed control in Borneo and the 'Great East', compared with an effective, if often cruelly harsh, Dutch military occupation of most of Sumatra; conversely, in Java, it took the two 'police actions' of 1947 and 1948 for the Dutch to gain more than a foothold, by which time the show of force did more harm than good to the Dutch cause.

Van Mook's steep learning curve as architect of evolving Dutch policy left many colleagues and most Dutch politicians far behind – dangerously so for the more realist, concessive policy he progressively championed. Two sets of factors assisted van Mook's education. The first arose from the precarious military situation in Java and from the ambiguities of British policy. As over Indochina, the plans for the Allied military administration of Indonesia had been subject to last-minute changes: on 15 August, the date of the Japanese surrender, Indonesia was transferred from the American-led South West Pacific Area to SEAC, hitherto responsible only for Sumatra (with a view to the projected Malayan landings). The British commander, Lieutenant-General Sir Philip Christison, had little time to prepare for his command, and only three divisions of Indian Army troops. In contrast with General Gracey's robust approach to the Viet Minh in Saigon, Christison unintentionally conveyed the impression that he was prepared to recognize the nascent Republic at Dutch expense. In early October, inspired by successful negotiations with Aung San in Burma, Mountbatten told van Mook that he was only prepared to allow Dutch troops to occupy areas where internment camps were located if van Mook agreed to hold talks with Sukarno; in return, Mountbatten promised British recognition of the Dutch as the sole authority in Indonesia (Yong 1982: 42–3). Meanwhile, tensions were running high following the undisciplined violence of those small numbers of Dutch and Ambonese troops of the Royal Dutch Indies Army (KNIL) who had returned from internment or from exile. On 18 November, Christison banned all further Dutch troop landings in Java (ibid.: 53). But ironically, the worst conflict was between Republican forces and the British, in the 'Battle of Surabaya'. When local *pemudas* violently resisted British occupation of the key East Javan port in late October, Sukarno intervened to impose a ceasefire. But after the murder of the British commander, Brigadier Mallaby, British troops laid waste the city, two-thirds of which they reoccupied in three days from 10 November; in all, fighting lasted over three weeks, against the heaviest Indonesian losses of the entire revolution (Reid 1974: 52–3). This was the last decisive British show of force in Indonesia. A fortified British territorial base in Western Java, which might have helped re-establish Dutch authority on the island, never materialized (Yong 1982: 64–5). Henceforward, desperately over-committed in Europe and the empire, the British encouraged Dutch–Indonesian negotiations in advance of the disbanding of SEAC, in November 1946, and the consequent British withdrawal.

The second set of factors impelling the Dutch towards negotiations stemmed from Republican consolidation. The battle for Surabaya was a founding moment of the Indonesian 'struggle' (*perjuangan*), which galvanized solidarity between the cautious Republican leadership in Djakarta and the more militant *pemudas*, but which inspired violent social upheaval across Indonesia (Reid 1974: 54–7). More immediately, an internal power struggle culminated in the formation on 14 November of a govern-ment led by the 36-year-old Sutan Sjahrir, whose youth and firm wartime stance on collaboration endeared him to the *pemudas*, even while Sjahrir himself recognized the greater national authority invested in Sukarno, who remained as president. In his manifesto, published on 10 November, Sjahrir attacked nationalism's xenophobic and reactionary tendencies (as evinced by Hitler, Franco and Chiang Kaishek, but not, explicitly, Sukarno), and pleaded for a fully international approach to revolution, based on Indonesia's dependence on a predominantly capitalist world. While attack-ing rural 'bureaucratic feudalism', he condemned violence against traditional rulers, as well as against Ambonese, Chinese and European minorities. A further manifesto signed by Vice-President Mohammad Hatta on 1 November, but inspired by Sjahrir, rejected Dutch sovereignty in the light of the Atlantic Charter and the 1942 debacle, but promised to assume government debts, and to return all foreign-owned property (ibid.: 69–71). Although acting from long-held conviction, Sjahrir could hardly have made himself more acceptable as a nationalist interlocutor for any but the most reactionary Dutch officials, or in the eyes of British and international opinion. His prominence in negotiations was all the more marked after the Republican leadership accepted the invitation of the Republican modernizer, Sultan Hamengku Buwono IX, to move the capital to Yogyakarta, in December 1945, in order to escape the depreda-tions of Dutch troops in Djakarta (Antlöv 1995). Sjahrir's period in office lasted until June 1947; the policy of *diplomasi* would last even longer, although the opposing ideal of *perjuangan*, with its associated notions of social revolution and '100 per cent Merdeka' (independence), held considerable popular appeal, particularly amongst the *pemudas*, on which soldiers and politicians could draw at moments of crisis.

Once the Dutch government accepted the need for negotiation, van Mook pro-vided the substance. Even before Sjahrir's nomination, on 6 November, van Mook's first proposals conceded the Indonesian right to self-determination, while omitting to mention the Republic; these proposals were swiftly rejected but were anyway over-shadowed by events in Surabaya (Yong 1982: 51–2). Two main elements to van Mook's evolving negotiating position required resolute argument against tough Dutch opposition. First, recognising that Java and Sumatra could not be held by force, he proposed a switch in Dutch focus to Borneo and the 'Great East'. This went against Dutch economic interests and effectively reversed three hundred years of policy con-centrating on Java; it was vigorously opposed by the Dutch military. Although the

Minister of Colonies argued that *neither* Java *nor* the 'Outer Territories' should be abandoned, van Mook maintained a focus on the periphery rather than on the Republican-held centre. Indeed, given the prevailing view of Dutch efforts to 'divide and rule', or to encircle the Republic, it is worth underlining the policy's origin in Dutch powerlessness, and a qualified willingness – bitterly contested in some Dutch quarters – to recognize Republican *de facto* jurisdiction over Java and Sumatra (ibid.: 54–63).

The second main element of van Mook's proposals, following on from this, was the idea of a federal United States of Indonesia (USI), which took shape in the November 1946 Linggadjati Agreement. Van Mook's conceptual breakthrough came with his adoption of the Franco-Vietnamese Accords of 6 March 1946 as a possible model for the USI (ibid.: 76f.). In place of the unitary Kingdom of the Netherlands (or the Commonwealth idea), the Franco-Vietnamese model suggested, first, a Union between the Netherlands and a federal Indonesia, and, secondly, recognition of the Republic as a state within an Indonesian federation. It was the top layer of this structure which presented the greatest problems for metropolitan acceptance, since it implied constitutional revision, but there were also serious objections to any recognition of the 'illegal' Republic.

A hiatus now intervened as the Netherlands approached its first post-war general elections in May 1946; as in France, matters other than colonial affairs preoccupied Dutch voters. Indonesia was one area in which the new government, led by the Catholic Party, could demonstrate its 'progressive' credentials. Negotiations were thus resumed, but a Commission-General composed of senior politicians went East to conduct proceedings, and to sideline the autocratic 'Indies man' van Mook, who nonetheless maintained his influence (ibid.: 80–3, 85–6). Sjahrir's delegation was as keen as the Dutch to secure swift agreement: three Dutch divisions landed in Java in this period, and Republican leaders feared a bloodbath in the absence of agreement before British troops withdrew on 30 November. Sukarno entered into the negotiations after they moved to Linggadjati in Western Java, and an Agreement was initialled on 15 November, subject to approval by the Netherlands and Republican governments. It was not signed until 25 March 1947, after the Agreement was narrowly interpreted by the Dutch government, in an Elucidation designed to secure parliamentary approval. For its part, the Republican leadership enhanced a reputation for integrity by simply accepting the agreement without comment (ibid.: 93–9, 203–5).

At the heart of the Linggadjati Agreement was a projected federal Indonesia, composed of three elements: the Republic of Indonesia (chiefly Java and Sumatra), Borneo and the Great East. Its roots went deeper than Dutch acceptance of military weakness in Java, embracing a paternalist pre-war vision of a multi-ethnic East Indies accommodating all races, including Europeans and mixed-race Eurasians, under benevolent Dutch guidance (ibid.). Even before Linggadjati, van Mook had organized a series of conferences to establish the non-Republican parts of the Federation. First, in June at Molino, in South Sulawesi, he secured acceptance of the federal principle from delegates from the Outer Islands, mostly representing the feudal nobility who stood to lose most from Republican control. The second conference, in October, was intended for non-Indonesian minorities, principally Eurasians and Chinese. And a third conference in December 1946 was intended to establish the other member states of the federation; but, in the absence of delegates from Borneo, only the Great East state, Negara Indonesia Timur (State of Eastern Indonesia, NIT), was created (ibid.: 86–93, 99–102).

Comparison with the Franco-Vietnamese Accords highlights the fundamental weakness of the federal concept. Whereas the Indochinese Federation was divided along lines which had some historical basis, however factitious, the USI's federal boundaries were suggested by the archipelago's geography, but arose largely arbitrarily from the after-effects of Japanese occupation and the disposition of Dutch and Republican forces. Within parts of NIT, Dutch control had been established by brute force, for example in Southern Sulawesi, where a determined terror campaign, led by the infamous Dutch commander 'Turk' Westerling, had eradicated *pemuda* influence in early 1946, at the cost of several thousand lives (ibid.: 38f.; Groen 1994). Throughout its three-year existence, NIT leaders were drawn to Republican influence, and sought to maintain Yogyakarta's goodwill; even Dutch-nominated delegates favoured the red-and-white Indonesian flag and the Indonesian anthem. Dutch policy also tolerated some pro-Republican political activity, partly to signal Dutch liberal intentions to the outside world, partly in the mistaken belief that the Indonesian people would 'choose order and reconstruction in cooperation with the Dutch to the desperate freedom of the Republic' (Reid 1974: 118–19). However, as Dutch influence receded or was neutralized, many areas of NIT strongly backed the Republic. Thus, Dutch efforts to impose federation only resulted in a stronger impulsion towards national unity at independence (ibid.: 161–5). Indeed, although the Dutch imposed the USI structure at independence in December 1949, a unitary Republic promptly superseded it on 17 August 1950.

It was typically those areas which had established Republican ascendancy most forcefully by their own efforts which also resisted unification with the Republic. For example, in Aceh in Northern Sumatra, Muslim *ulemas* led a bloody social revolution in late 1945 eliminating local traditional rulers; from the early 1950s, this was the site of persistent revolt against central government (ibid.: 167–8; Christie 1996). Ethnically or socially distinct groups had many reasons to seek autonomy and an identity separate from that of Indonesia; but as in Borneo, which formed five separate states, the units of the tripartite federation were simply too large to serve the purpose. Although NIT maintained its cohesion, the federation demonstrated an inbuilt tendency to balkanization, which, though far from van Mook's original design, soon became its overriding feature. This was most marked after the first Police Action of July–August 1947, which created a shield – the so-called 'van Mook line' – behind which new states could emerge in Java and Sumatra. By the end of 1948, the nascent federation numbered 15 self-declared states (not including the Republic), of which five (East Sumatra, South Sumatra, Pasundan, East Java and Madura) were in territory allocated to the Republic under Linggadjati. Puppets they may have been, held aloft by the strings of Dutch support, but in number and purpose they served only to discredit the puppet-master.

Perhaps the most obvious similarity between Linggadjati and the Franco-Vietnamese Accords lay in the ephemeral understanding engendered between the Dutch and the Republic. Even before the Agreement was signed, in March 1947, Dutch officials were preparing for the first Police Action, launched on 20 July. The aim of this was unclear, beyond securing key economic resources in Sumatra (plantations) and Java (coal and oil installations); this was rapidly achieved. However, a strengthening hard line in The Hague suggested that nothing could be definitively settled without the overthrow of the Republic, and even van Mook took up this idea when it became clear that the Republic was not going to give up quietly (Reid 1974: 112–13). In the end, the Dutch heeded the UN Security Council's call for a ceasefire at the end of July. Dutch territorial gains were nonetheless striking, although the van Mook Line, declared at the end of August, was somewhat misleading, as it joined up the furthest points of Dutch advance encircling the Republican strongholds of Central Java, rather than representing the extent of real Dutch control. Pockets of Republican control thus remained behind the line, and irregular Republican forces were able to move through nominally Dutch-controlled territory – here too parallels with Indochina are suggested, where French forces could hold the arteries of communication but not surrounding territory. The van Mook Line formed the basis for the UN-sponsored agreement signed on board the USS *Renville* in January 1948; this allowed van Mook to pursue federalism to its logical limits. The sense that the Dutch had secured an undeservedly good deal in the Renville Agreement was offset by the assurance that political control behind the line would have to be approved by internationally supervised plebiscites; more generally, international supervision was a powerful guarantor of the Republic's survival (ibid.: 114).

International interpretation of events in Indonesia, as much as their internal logic, was to prove decisive over the following 18 months. This became clear as a communist threat emerged to the Republican government's authority. A range of Marxist-oriented parties including the Indonesian Communist Party (PKI), Socialist Party and others identified with the policy of *diplomasi*, and in December 1946, together with the organization of socialist pemudas (PESINDO), had formed a Sayap Kiri (Left Wing) coalition to support Linggadjati; this coalition had persisted even after Sjahrir's fall as prime minister in July 1947 (ibid.: 95–8). The Renville Agreement was a step too far, however, and in February 1948, Sayap Kiri, in opposition to a moderate nationalist government led by Hatta, was transformed into a People's Democratic Front (FDR), which repudiated Renville in favour of *perjuangan* and social revolution, and promoted strikes across Republican-held territory. This shift leftwards was reinforced by the unilateral Soviet announcement in May of an exchange of consuls with the Republic, previously negotiated in January but shelved by the Hatta government. In August, the veteran communist leader, Musso, returned to Indonesia from Russian exile dating back to the 1926 communist rebellion; he had briefly returned in 1935, to establish an underground PKI network (ibid.: 131, 136). As in Malaya, local radicalization was encouraged by the new communist 'two camps' doctrine. Although out of touch with Indonesian politics, Musso assumed leadership of the PKI, and the FDR accepted his call to merge with the PKI behind a radical 'New Road' policy; a number of FDR leaders declared their hitherto secret membership of the underground PKI. On 18 September, PESINDO units based at Madiun, in Central Java, seized the town on their own initiative. Sukarno responded with a call to arms against the Madiun *coup*, which he portrayed as a bid to replace the Republic with a Soviet government. Musso replied in kind, effectively sanctioning the *coup*, and accusing Sukarno and Hatta of being the 'slaves of Japan and America' (ibid.: 136–44). In the ensuing mini-civil war, the *coup* was ruthlessly crushed, thousands of its supporters were executed, Musso was killed in skirmishing, and other FDR leaders were captured at the end of November before they could surrender to the Dutch; three weeks later, they were summarily shot. The key point of the episode was not simply that the Republic reasserted its crumbling authority, or that it refused the military support offered by the Dutch, but that it demonstrated its anti-communist credentials to international opinion, and particularly to American observers.

The second Dutch Police Action, launched on 19 December 1948, achieved almost the exact opposite of its apparent aims, although, as in 1947, these were not clearly defined, and chiefly reflected Dutch frustrations, compounded by a rightward drift at home. Significantly, van Mook's influence was finally ended in October, when he was replaced by the former Catholic Party Prime Minister, Louis Beel. Dutch military objectives were again achieved swiftly: this time, Dutch forces went straight for the head, occupying Yogyakarta on the first day, capturing all major Javan towns within a week, and most Sumatran centres by the end of December, with only Aceh offering substantial resistance. The Republican government in Yogyakarta faced 'the most acute choice between *diplomasi* and *perjuangan*; between faith in international opinion or Indonesian strength'; opting for *diplomasi*, Sukarno and the cabinet allowed themselves to be captured, rather than fleeing to the hills, relying on the presence of a UN Good Offices Committee lodged just outside the city to guarantee their safety, and to champion the Republic's cause (ibid.: 149–52). Again, the Dutch acquiesced in UN calls for a ceasefire, but intermittently fierce guerrilla warfare continued across Java and Sumatra for much of 1949. The Police Action's apparent aim was to suppress the Republic in the hope of incorporating Republican territory into the federation on Dutch terms. Dutch overtures to prominent figures, notably the Sultan of Yogyakarta, were firmly rebuffed, however, and the federal state itself was weakened by the resignation of the NIT and Pasundan governments in protest at Dutch actions. The UN Security Council stood firm on its insistence that the Republic be restored, and on 6 July 1949, the Sultan of Yogyakarta welcomed the Republican leadership back to his capital. Although negotiations proceeded at a Round Table Conference which gave separate representation to the Republic and to the federal states, in practice the Dutch faced a largely united front. The Dutch transfer of sovereignty to a Federal Republic of Indonesia on 27 December 1949 was followed by the unitary state achieved the following August. The Netherlands' hard-won consolation prize was Western New Guinea (Irian Jaya), where a rump colonial administration pursued a 'second colonial occupation' of enlightened welfare colonialism and economic development, until this too was claimed back by President Sukarno in 1963 as a 'lost' portion of Indonesia (van den Doel 2001).

Diplomacy played a key role, but an ambivalent one for both sides in this terminal phase of Indonesia's decolonization. Although *diplomasi* was a triumph for Sukarno and the Republican government, this was at considerable expense to their internal authority. Not only had the Left coalition, which for much of the revolutionary period had supported international negotiation, been destroyed by the Madiun episode, but the army was strengthened enormously by the guerrilla warfare of 1949, and abandoned all-out struggle against the Dutch only with extreme reluctance. It is not difficult to see significant portents for Indonesia's future in these outcomes.

The Dutch, conversely, emerged bruised and humiliated from the Indonesian endgame, largely through their own choices. In the end, imperial withdrawal was determined, and indeed dictated, by international actors, primarily the UN backed to the hilt by the United States. However, the Netherlands had a lucky – and prosperous – escape, especially when compared with the dismal French experience in Indochina, where war in mid-1949 still had five years to run. Great significance attaches to the United States' control of Marshal Aid as an implied instrument of persuasion. Indonesia was included in negotiations for the European Recovery Programme from its inception in 1947, and the US State Department was apparently prepared to condone Dutch actions which might steer the Republic away from communist influence (van der Eng 2003). However, the Madiun episode demonstrated the Republic's ability to deal with communists on its own account. When the second Police Action was launched, the Economic Co-operation Agency which managed Marshall Aid announced the suspension of the Indonesian portion of Aid for the duration of military action, and in February 1949, the US Senate was narrowly dissuaded, by Secretary of State George Marshall's intervention, from voting to suspend all Marshall Aid to the Netherlands until the *status quo ante* had been restored. However, and notwithstanding the US Congress's hostility to European colonialism, the proposed amendment was largely motivated by senatorial objections to the principle of Marshall Aid, with the Indonesian case exemplifying the programme's alleged iniquities. The threat of suspension was more a catalyst in bringing Dutch political opinion round than a 'blunt instrument of United States power'. Indeed, by February 1949, the Dutch cabinet had accepted the case for accelerating the push towards decolonization. Officials argued that, given the likelihood of an anti-communist Indonesian regime, its economic importance to the Netherlands could best be preserved by acquiescing in Indonesian political demands, which would best ensure the 'maintenance and in the near future the recovery of our investments in Indonesia' (1 February 1949, in ibid.: 132). Thus Marshall Aid and military aid continued, the Dutch surrendered East Indies debt at independence, and were spared the expense of financing Indonesian recovery from their own coffers; in short, Dutch post-war recovery was hugely facilitated by the decision to go ahead with Indonesian decolonization. Small wonder that French opinion turned to the Dutch example when squaring up to an otherwise unimaginable end of empire.

Indochina: a Front in the Cold War

Like Indonesia, Indochina 'decolonized' in 1949, largely because of the Cold War, but whereas the Dutch were granted the boon of rapid withdrawal, the French were condemned to fight on until the ultimate humiliation of Dien Bien Phu. The first part of this proposition is a tendentious, but not unfounded way of interpreting the Paris Accords on 8 March 1949, which gave 'independence' to the State of Vietnam, with Bao Dai as Head of State (Zervoudakis 2002: 44). Arguably, little was left of the French colonial state in Vietnam, or in the neighbouring 'Associated States' of Laos and Cambodia, and still less of the grandiose Indochinese Federation envisaged in 1945. However, there was no single successor state in Vietnam, but rather two claimants disputing the attributes of statehood and international recognition, divided not so much according to territorial control – since Vietnam's political map up to 1954 was constantly shifting – as by opposing ideological perspectives and competing claims to legitimacy. The Franco-Vietnamese war broke out of the colonial framework, not because of the constitutional fictions behind the March 1949 Accords, but because of massive shifts in global strategy culminating in Mao Zedong's victory in December 1949, the establishment of the People's Republic of China (PRC) on Vietnam's Northern borders, and the United States' assumption of the role of France's paymaster.

The impact of Chinese victory on French morale was not long in coming, in a series of French military reversals in late 1950. Evacuating the exposed Northern border garrison of Cao Bang had long been mooted, perhaps too publicly.[3] When it took place, in October 1950, Giap's forces were trained and ready; in one of their first conventional engagements, they destroyed four battalions of elite troops, leaving 4,800 men dead or wounded along the colonial highway (Route Coloniale 4) from Cao Bang to Hanoi (Dalloz 1987: 172–5). Other garrisons were evacuated, joining up the Viet Minh heartlands of the North (Viet Bac) and the 'liberated' zones of the Red River delta, and threatening Hanoi itself. Cao Bang brought Indochina into the Parisian headlines for once, and in parliament, Pierre Mendès-France, who would eventually end France's involvement in Indochina, argued that things had gone too far *not* to negotiate with Ho Chi Minh. For, as he argued:

> It is the overall conception of our policy in Indochina which is wrong. . . . It is a fact that our forces, even with the support of local troops, are unable to bring about a military resolution, especially since the evolution of the Chinese situation, and it is a fact that our policy of making feeble concessions, and then withdrawing or denying them, has failed, and now, alas, will increasingly fail, to rally the mass of the Vietnamese people to our side. (19 October 1950, in ibid.: 183)

In the event, the Assembly vote approved government policy, and Antoine Pinay's government appointed General Jean de Lattre de Tassigny as France's most effective high commissioner and military commander of the war – like General Templer in Malaya, his effectiveness came in part from his combining the two roles.

De Lattre's tour of duty was cut short by his illness and death from cancer barely more than a year after his appointment in December 1950 – the '*Année de Lattre*' – and in a further cruel twist, his only son, Bernard, was killed in action in October 1951. In that time, de Lattre shaped the principles of French strategy in ways that remained largely unchanged after his departure, wanting only his 'panache and charisma' (ibid.: 191; Clayton 1992).[4] On the battlefield, de Lattre checked Giap's advances in a number of brilliant engagements. Rejecting all talk of abandoning Tonkin, he ordered the construction of a line of concrete blockhouses, of which 900 were eventually built, to protect civilians and impede mass attacks, and instituted a new tactical concept of mobile combat groups able to respond quickly to the Viet Minh. He developed the use of paratroops for more rapid deployment in isolated regions, in ways that pointed towards the innovative use of helicopters (when France could afford them) in Algeria (Clayton 1994: 61; Zervoudakis 2002: 48–54).

He proved just as adept a politician as a commander, developing French policy in two crucial directions. The first of these was 'Vietnamization', which supplied manpower on the battlefield, while instilling some metal into the Bao Dai state. De Lattre worked to secure reinforcements from France, but Europe always came first, especially with German rearmament commencing under the auspices of the European Defence Community (EDC), which made its first tentative steps in 1950. Sending the conscript army was never really an option in Indochina, although in 1954, Mendès-France threatened to send in the *contingent* if he failed to secure a settlement. North African and sub-Saharan African *tirailleurs* were widely used, but the Foreign Legion, 45–50 per cent of whose legionaries were Germans, attracted more criticism in France, particularly from the Communists (Michels 2002). Creating a Vietnam Army, as opposed to integrating Vietnamese troops into the French expeditionary corps (CEFEO), was an obvious solution, but it was only initiated after Cao Bang, and it took time to build up troop numbers, and to train an officer corps at the Dalat military academy created in October 1950 (Dalloz 1987: 194). The Vietnam Army reach its full strength of 151,000 men only in 1953, when total CEFEO strength reached almost 450,000, facing perhaps 400,000 men in Giap's regular, regional and local forces; in that year, it was announced that, whereas in 1946 French soldiers had sustained 88 per cent of CEFEO casualties, that figure now stood at only 17 per cent, with Vietnamese casualties at half the total – by this grisly criterion at least, Vietnamization was working (Clayton 1994: 74).

Secondly, the war was increasingly 'Americanized'. This too can be dated back to 1950, in a process of Cold War alignment initiated by Communist China's recognition of the DRV on 16 January, followed by the Soviet Union on 30 January, and by American and British recognition of the three Associated States on 7 February. However, the US hesitated to provide direct aid for France's involvement in a conflict still tainted with colonialism, and though France received both Marshall Aid and military aid under the North Atlantic Treaty, this could not be diverted outside Europe. Everything changed with the Pyongyang government's strike against South Korea on 25 June 1950, followed two days later by President Truman's pledge of support for South Korea, but also for Taiwan and Indochina. The first military and medical aid, along with a military mission, soon arrived in Saigon (Dalloz 1987: 176–81). Visiting New York in September 1951, de Lattre rallied American opinion to the French cause, or rather to a cause he claimed was no longer French, but that of liberty in Asia, Europe and the world. By late 1952, American financial and military aid was meeting half the costs of the war; by 1954, this figure reached 80 per cent (ibid.: 195–6). Aid did not automatically translate into arms where they were needed, however, and shipments were often delayed by 'red tape' or by the precedence taken by US needs in Korea. With copious Chinese supplies, often of American arms captured from the Guomindang or in Korea, Viet Minh units were often better armed than the CEFEO, with consequent effects upon French morale. Moreover, the well-equipped American presence in Saigon came not so much with strings attached, as with a determined effort to cut the strings tying France to the Associated States, whom, as the American Minister Resident made plain, the US government would far rather supply directly (ibid.: 197–8; Zervoudakis 2002: 49–50).

However, if France now stood as proxy for American containment, the DRV was transformed even more radically. Chinese aid allowed Giap to develop a war of movement engaging the regular troops of the People's Army of Vietnam (PAV), more than the classic insurgency tactics or terrorism of the war's earlier phases. Chinese involvement also brought a tightening of political structures and ideological control. In March 1951, the Communist Party, formally dissolved into the Viet Minh in November 1945, reformed as the Workers' Party of Vietnam, or Lao Dong (Dang Lao Dong Viet Nam), to which some 24 per cent of soldiers belonged by 1953, and the Viet Minh was dissolved into the Lien Viet (Hoi Lien Hiep Quoc Dan Viet Nam, or People's National Front of Vietnam). Alongside party structures, traditional associations of age group or occupation complemented elaborate local government hierarchies, leading French intelligence officers to formulate a largely erroneous theory of totalitarian 'parallel hierarchies' (Ageron 1995). Although party ideologues, notably Truong Chinh (an alias translating as 'Long March'), deployed the Maoist propaganda of 'revolutionary war', this never transcended the reality of a people's war to free Vietnam from foreign occupation, notwithstanding the 'Land to the Tillers' programme of land reform instituted in 1953. The DRV's political reach was considerable, particularly in the Tonkinese Red River delta, where an estimated 5,000 of 7,000 villages were in DRV hands in 1953, represented as red dots on the French army's 'smallpox map' (ibid.; Dalloz 1987: 214–16).

Meanwhile, the State of Vietnam was shrinking into irrelevance, and Bao Dai was losing all authority over a fissiparous confederation comprising Catholics; nationalist and ultra-nationalist parties; and religious sects doubling as well-armed baronies, the Buddhist Hoa Hao and the bizarre, syncretic Cao Dai. These various factions increasingly viewed their destiny as lying with an American alliance. The wider French Union was also apparently disintegrating, as both Laotian and Cambodian regimes sought to shore up their position with something more closely approximating to independence. Although Laotian and Cambodian royal authority was firmly anchored in the traditions of a continuing monarchy, unlike the ex-Emperor Bao Dai's, both kingdoms were riven with internal conflict and threatened by communist insurgencies allied to the Lao Dong: the Pathet Lao and the FUNC (National United Front of Cambodia). By 1953, Giap was also shifting his strategy northwestwards to embrace Laos, and between them Vietnamese forces and their allies soon controlled the mountainous Vietnam–Laos borderlands. In one of the more obscure decolonizing endgames, while Laos had little choice but to sign a treaty, in August 1953, 'reaffirming its membership of the French Union', Prince Sihanouk of Cambodia held out for seven months in 'internal exile', threatening to ally with the DRV, unless Cambodia was accorded the equivalent status to India within the Commonwealth; by the beginning of 1954 a form of independence had been agreed. The State of Vietnam was not far behind, and the Declaration of 28 April 1954 announced two forthcoming treaties, one according Vietnamese sovereignty and independence (this time, perhaps for real), the other establishing cooperation between the two countries. The system of the Associated States within the French Union had thus officially crumbled to nothing (ibid.: 203–12). When the treaties were signed, on 4 June, a more drastic endgame had already climaxed with the fall of Dien Bien Phu a month before.

The outcome of eight years of war came to depend upon the French defence of a small town enclosed by forested hills near the Laotian border, 300 kilometres from Hanoi, whose name is synonymous with devastating imperial defeat. Its location explains the French occupation in October 1953, intended to defend Laos from Giap's strategic shift away from Tonkin. Its isolation suggests the difficulties of defending it, since reinforcements and supplies came along one road through difficult terrain, or via the rapidly constructed airstrip; it was barely within range of French fighter planes flying from Hanoi. Long supply lines should equally have prevented Giap's forces from seriously threatening the defenders within their strategic 'hedgehog', as such rapidly improvised, bristling fortresses were known. However, French intelligence gravely underestimated the PAV's logistical capabilities, which brought 60,000 troops and heavy artillery to the surrounding hills, arduously supplied by lorry, by 'coolie-bicycles' and by legions of porters. Giap's political case for massive Vietnamese forces rested on the shift in the international situation brought about by the Korean cease-fire in July 1953, which brought the prospect of Chinese reinforcements in Vietnam, and the planned peace conference at Geneva. French policy had also shifted towards engineering an 'honourable exit' from Indochina; and General Henri Navarre's mission as Commander in Chief from May 1953 was to seek such an opportunity, although Dien Bien Phu was hardly what he had in mind. The garrison troops thus found themselves besieged by massively superior numbers, and when Vietnamese guns opened fire from their camouflaged shelters, they took out French guns and ultimately destroyed the airstrip. France's last hope was for raids by American B29 bombers flown from Okinawa, but a cautious President Eisenhower vetoed the plan. (An American offer of two atomic weapons was never seriously considered.) French fortified positions were overwhelmed one by one by inexhaustible waves of troops sustaining massive casualties. Defeat on 7 May 1954 could hardly have been more crushing: the garrison of 15,000 men was lost, of whom 3,000 were killed, 10,000 taken prisoner and 2,000 mostly local recruits deserted. Giap could hardly have hoped for better timing, as the Geneva Conference commenced the Indochinese part of its agenda the following day (Clayton 1994; Dalloz 1987; Zervoudakis 2002).

Dien Bien Phu did not end the fighting in Indochina, but it destroyed the last vestiges of French determination to continue the war. Joseph Laniel's government struggled on, surviving two confidence votes in May before succumbing to a third on 12 June. In retrospect, this was wasted time at Geneva, and by early June even Georges Bidault, Christian Democrat Foreign Minister in a succession of governments since 1945, was moving towards the idea of Vietnamese partition, although this was a concession that Pham Van Dong, representing the DRV, was so far not prepared to make (Dalloz 1987: 234–7). Laniel's successor was Mendès-France, who showed he meant business with two dramatic moves. First, although Communist *députés* offered their support for the first time since 1947 to an incoming prime minister, Mendès-France only accepted a majority which excluded the Communist vote. Secondly, he promised a settlement at Geneva within a month, failing which he would resign, having first committed conscript troops to the conflict.

Partition, initially proposed by the conference chairman, British Prime Minister Anthony Eden, was now accepted in principle, and Soviet and Chinese pressure was brought to bear on Pham Van Dong; indeed, the DRV delegation accepted it as a better basis for eventual unification than a 'leopard spot' plan reflecting actual control by the two sides. While the French proposed the line of the 18th Parallel, effectively containing the DRV within its Tonkinese stronghold, the DRV counter-proposed the 13th Parallel, which would restrict the Bao Dai state to Cochinchina. The last-minute agreement of the 17th Parallel reflected a significant French gain over the 16th Parallel used for the temporary partition of 1945–6, since the imperial capital of Huê and the military base at Tourane (later Danang) fell on the 'right' side of the line. Laos and Cambodia were to be evacuated by French and DRV forces, although Pathet Lao forces retained provisional control in two Laotian border provinces. The Final Declaration of the Conference, agreed just within Mendès-France's deadline, and made public on 20 July 1954, held that the 'military demarcation line' was strictly provisional, and the detailed accords provided for Laotian and Cambodian elections in 1955, and Vietnamese elections by July 1956; the latter were to elect a unified Vietnamese government. Although the Accords were watertight enough, the Final Declaration went unsigned, as the US delegation refused to sign an agreement alongside China; the US government merely 'noted' the Accords, while undertaking not to modify their terms. The Accords were also repudiated by the new Saigon government, led by the vehemently anti-French, pro-American (and anti-Bao Dai) Catholic nationalist, Ngo Dinh Diem. The projected Vietnamese elections thus never took place, Diem remained in power until the CIA arranged his assassination in 1963, and Bao Dai, manoeuvred out of power by Diem in 1955, lived in comfortable exile on the French Riviera, until his death in 1997. Vietnamese reunification was only achieved in 1975 by force of North Vietnamese arms, following more than ten years of massively destructive and ultimately fruitless American military engagement in Vietnam.

For France and for the remaining colonized world, this was a decisive turning point, marking the definitive French retreat from Asia, and pointing towards decolonization elsewhere in the French empire. Geneva was followed in April 1955 by the Bandung Conference at which the non-aligned world, led by India, Indonesia and Yugoslavia, lent its moral weight to the anti-colonial cause. Following his triumphal return from Geneva, Mendès-France's next stop was a surprise visit to Tunisia, where, in the Declaration of Carthage on 31 July, he announced French recognition of Tunisian autonomy and readiness to transfer power (Thomas 2000: 59–60). Although he refrained from a similar *coup de théâtre* in Morocco, he created the conditions which led to Moroccan independence two years later. Mendès-France made too many enemies to remain long in office, and fell from power in February 1955, but his legacy may also be traced in the 1956 Framework Law which set the Federations of sub-Saharan Africa on the path to autonomy (Chapter 7). Over Algeria, he was less successful, as reforms instituted by his Interior Minister, François Mitterrand, were overtaken by the insurrection of 1 November 1954; Dien Bien Phu undoubtedly played its part in inspiring the fledgling Algerian National Liberation Front (FLN). France might have resolved never again to enter into the violent maelstrom of colonial war. While perhaps as many as half a million died fighting the French, CEFEO losses in Indochina amounted to 20,000 metropolitan Frenchmen, including 1,900 officers – the equivalent of an entire year-class of officer cadets killed every year – alongside 11,000 foreign legionaries, 15,000 Africans, 46,000 Indochinese; of the thousands held prisoner in horrifying conditions, the return rate was some 40 per cent for Europeans, 50 per cent for North Africans (Dalloz 1987: 234–7). With the FLN's insurrection, less than three months after the ceasefire in Vietnam and three weeks after French withdrawal from Hanoi, the cycle had restarted in Algeria. For many French soldiers this seemed another round of the same conflict against the same enemy, whom many referred to as 'Viets'.

Notes

1   'Union', unlike 'Federation', was compatible with the 'One and Indivisible Republic', and had the additional benefit of paying sentimental homage to the Soviet Union.
2   Population in 1945: Laos, 1.5 million; Cambodia, 4.6 million; Annam, 6 million; Tonkin, 10 million; Cochinchina, 4.6 million (Chamberlain 1998: 9). The Vietnamese names for the three *ky*, called *bo* since 1945, translate simply as North Region (*Bac Bo*), Central Region (*Trung Bo*) and South Region (*Nam Bo*).
3   General Revers had recommended evacuation the previous year in a highly critical report, which was leaked in the so-called 'Generals' Affair'; the idea was shelved, partly because of Revers's disgrace.
4   General de Lattre, like Leclerc before him, was posthumously created Marshal of France.

5

Shifting Frameworks for Change: The Late Colonial State in Africa

> We are in the midst of colonial crisis. Feelings of disillusionment, disaffection, defiance, and hatred are so general as to be dangerous. Our counterweight is a feeble one: the apathy of the colonial masses can never offset the nationalism which is being born or proclaimed across the empire. Nationalism is finding expression at the exact moment when our only hope of keeping the Empire is to undertake a massive operation to capture hearts and minds. Providing we make substantial sacrifices here and there, we can hope to reaffirm through renewal the bonds that unite France to her overseas territories. For want of real power we must deploy different weapons. (Governor Henri Laurentie, Note, 20/21 June 1945, in Shipway 1996a: 74–5)

The Second World War did not, as it did across South and Southeast Asia, propel the colonial powers in Africa into the endgame of decolonization. However, although sub-Saharan Africa was mostly marginal to global wartime strategy, the impact of war across the continent was nonetheless profound. At the level of the colonial state, this impact came from the wider politics of the war, the nature of the enemy and from the perceived might and influence of Britain's and (Free) France's uncomfortable new wartime Allies. This prompted a wide-ranging debate – albeit for the most part an internal debate conducted *in camera* by the colonial 'official mind' – which questioned the terms, if not yet the fact of African colonial empire. But as we have seen, the war also had a profound material impact on the lives of ordinary Africans, who, when they were not induced to fight or to produce for the Allied cause, often went hungry; and who, more positively, were inspired by the war to believe in the possibility of change.

It has been suggested that the wartime period, embracing the decade of crisis in Africa to the late 1940s, constituted 'as important a break point as the moment of independence' (Cooper 2002: xi). At the time, indeed, a continuum could be traced between the momentous shifts taking place in the Asian colonial empires and a general wave of discontent sweeping across colonial Africa, which left few major African colonial centres immune from unrest or organized protest. This has been identified as the 'radical moment of anti-colonial politics', for which 'probably the most important

single radicalising factor was the novel conviction that things did not have to continue along the old lines' (Füredi 1994a: 36–7). General strikes in Lagos and Dakar in
1945 lasted 44 days and two months respectively; miners went on strike in the copper
mines of Northern Rhodesia and in the South African gold mines; in Southern
Rhodesia a railway strike in 1945 was followed by a general strike in 1948; in 1947
there were general strikes in Mombasa and Dar es Salaam. In 1947–8, a strike closed
down the railways in French West Africa more or less completely for five months.
There were riots in Buganda in 1945 and across French North Africa in 1944–5.
Strikes and unrest typically marked the continuation or revival of disputes going
back to the 1930s, but with greater urgency and better organization. Labour unrest
and consumer boycotts in the Gold Coast culminated in the Accra riots of February
1948, the knock-on effects of which set Britain's 'model colony' on the road to self-
government. Armed insurgencies in Madagascar, Kenya and Algeria, the focus of
the next chapter, were all rooted in the immediate post-war crisis.

In retrospect, it is clear that the terminal phase of colonial rule in Africa had begun.
Some writers have thus seen decolonization as simply postponed or retarded by the
colonial powers' failure to recognize that their moment had passed (for example,
Lewis 1995). With an eye to the Transfers of Power which followed in quick succession in the decade or so from the mid-1950s, the lead-up to independence can appear
as a regrettable – if fortunately brief and, in much of Africa, relatively peaceful –
prelude to the inevitable outcome of national self-determination. A persuasive, linear
history of African decolonization can readily be constructed, according to which a
new generation of African leaders mobilized mass discontent in the increasingly
unstoppable cause of national liberation. Thus, in post-war Africa, trades unions
and political parties proliferated, giving a first taste of direct, anti-colonial political
engagement to men such as Kwame Nkrumah, Jomo Kenyatta, Nnamdi Azikiwe,
Léopold Sédar Senghor, Félix Houphouët-Boigny and Ahmed Sékou Touré, who
would lead their countries to independence. By 1945, some were already calling for
independence. In 1943, Azikiwe, journalist and future president of Nigeria, called
for Nigerian self-rule within 15 years of the end of the war; Nigeria duly gained its
independence in 1960. At the Fifth Pan-African Congress, which met in a Manchester
suburb in October 1945, Nkrumah, fresh from ten years of studies in the United
States, demanded 'complete and absolute independence' for West Africa. Within twelve
years, this is what he achieved for Ghana (Flint 1999; Hargreaves 1996: 88–9).

The problem with such a history is that it effectively focuses African decolonization
on a single, culminating endpoint, the moment of independence, whether this is
viewed as nationalist triumph, or as an anti-climactic, but artfully stage-managed
series of imperial retreats, the lowering of imperial flags saluted by minor royals or by
the emissaries of General de Gaulle. In either case, African decolonization appears as
an incidental by-product of a 'bigger' process of imperial decline and fall. The end
of African empire thus fits into a mere half-paragraph, the outcome of a 'policy of
prophylactic decolonization' designed to head off new left-wing regimes within the
more pressing international context of intensifying Cold War (Hobsbawm 1994: 221).
The crowning irony, of course, is that this linear history then leads seamlessly into
a counterpoised history of rapid disillusion and chronic disaster, which is the usual
history of the post-colonial African state.

How may we account more fully for the brief, but crowded period intervening between the post-1945 crisis of colonial authority and the moment of African independence? In this chapter, African decolonization is considered, not simply as a climactic moment, but as a social and political process, albeit an often-chaotic process with largely unplanned outcomes. The starting point for this discussion is the proposition that the impact of the Second World War in Africa brought about a progressive, paradigmatic shift, not initially in the facts of imperial control, but rather in the terms of colonial rule, and that that shift was matched in a countervailing shift in the expectations of ordinary Africans and their political leaders. The effect of this dialectical confrontation was that the political struggle for decolonization was played out in an arena that was itself in the process of rapid and continuous transformation.

At the epicentre of this shift in the African political landscape was the 'late colonial state', whose lateness connoted *not only* an intermediate stage on the way to independence *but also* a decisive stage in setting up new possibilities for the eventual outcome of independent statehood – even if officials imagined that outcome as lying in some distant future. On the colonial side, it is argued, a fundamental shift was taking place in the efforts of the 'official mind' to set colonial rule in Africa on a proper footing, to engineer the late colonial state on surer foundations than the *bricolage* of earlier colonial rule had allowed. The motivation was a varying cocktail, which included Churchillian resolve ('What we have we hold' – a sentiment which translated readily into the other languages of European colonialism in Africa), but also high-minded liberalism, the pragmatic desire to improve the management of imperial resources, and deep anxiety in the face of imperial decline. The aim, however, was not simply to hold on to the colonial state through minimal reform, but rather to complete it, transforming it into a more effective instrument for development, while at the same time anchoring and legitimating its activities through as extensive a system of political representation as was consistent with continuing colonial control. What had not shifted in the first instance was the expectation on the part of colonial officials – whether in London, Paris, Dakar, or Accra, much less in Lisbon or Brussels – that they would remain in control, at least in a future foreseeable in 1945, that the pace of change would be managed, and that the outcomes would be beneficial to the maintenance of imperial interests and continuity.

So far, so imperial. However, this late colonial shift was not restricted to only one side of the eternal colonial dialectic. Rather, it is suggested, the nature of the colonial interaction itself was shifting critically, as not only colonial officials and their imperial masters but also Africans, their leaders and representatives, reacted to radically changing circumstances and to each other. Initially, colonial planners debated their official versions of Africa's future in a vacuum. Although the shock to the system after 1945 was not nearly as great as in South or Southeast Asia, the post-war 'radical moment' exposed the new schemes to the oxygen of political reality, ripping through painstakingly elaborated constitutions, discrediting schemes for top-down, carefully controlled, incremental reform, and forcing the pace of economic and political development.

This chapter focuses on the ways in which official liberal, but still fundamentally colonial, assumptions were challenged and effectively set aside, in two key sets of cases, comparing contrasting but convergent developments in British and French West Africa, and one partial exception to the rule, in British Central Africa. The first British cases are those of the Gold Coast, regarded somewhat complacently by the British as a 'model colony', and Nigeria, Britain's most complex and populous African dependency. Already in 1945, these were the two most politically 'advanced' colonial states in British West Africa (and, indeed, in the whole of colonial Africa north of the Zambezi). In both, initially cautious British reforms were transformed by a political process which, by the beginning of the 1950s at the latest, was pointing inexorably to self-government and independence; by the same token, these two cases, especially that of the Gold Coast, set a powerful example for colonies elsewhere on the African continent and beyond.

Secondly, we will consider the great French federations of French West Africa (AOF) and of French Equatorial Africa (AEF), where France's grandiose project to 'transform French Africans into African Frenchmen' was taken up and transformed by African political leaders, trades unionists and other social and political actors. Starting from very different doctrinal and institutional traditions, which were mirrored also in the contrasting rhetoric and strategies of anglophone and francophone African political actors, the two sets of cases also reveal striking parallels. Just as British officials assumed a model of controlled, gradual evolution towards eventual self-government, but were 'jumped' into a far more rapid process of concessions, French officials imposed a limited conception of political representation, contained within a rigid constitutional framework, and found themselves contending almost from the start with a potentially boundless 'politics of demands'.

In both sets of cases, we start by considering the terms of the official debate on African reform. In the British case, this remained a largely internal debate, but French discussions quickly broke the rather limited bounds of the so-called 'Brazzaville policy', to be swallowed up into the wider constitutional debates that gripped French politics at the Liberation.

The final case to be considered is an apparent oddity according to the argument presented so far, for in the three Central African territories of Southern and Northern Rhodesia and Nyasaland, British policy makers were contemplating a quite different model for late colonial political and social development, and equally found themselves 'jumped' into a more rapid process of constitutional evolution than they had at first allowed. The difference, of course, was that the prime movers in the making of the Central African Federation were European settlers. By the end of our period, stretched somewhat further into the 1950s than the other cases (although in this as in the other cases, the story will be taken up in a later chapter), a settlement had been reached which here too apparently, but in this case deceptively, pointed towards self-government and independence.

A Developmentalist Welfare State

First, we consider the late colonial state's striking innovations in its role as an economic and social actor. Crucially, and effectively for the first time, this role was supported by metropolitan funds. Development and welfare were key themes in the late colonial state's 'legitimating discourse', as the official mind sought to justify colonial rule to an international and metropolitan audience, but also to colonial subjects (Young

1994: 211). The theory, of course, was already in place, as was indeed (of more importance perhaps to the British official mind) the legislative precedent. The Colonial Development and Welfare Act (CDWA) of 1945 thus built on the foundations of its predecessors, the 1929 Colonial Development Act, which provided limited funds, all earmarked for the benefit of British industry and employment, and the 1940 Act, the first to mention 'Welfare' in its title, but which was scuppered by bad timing (Ashton & Stockwell 1996). This time around, the CDWA had a new political will behind it, arising from Colonial Office reformism backed by the new Labour government, and a greatly enhanced budget, providing for £120 million over the ten-year life of the Act (Hargreaves 1996: 104).

French officials worked from earlier conceptions of colonial *mise en valeur* (lit.: valorization) developed by the formidable ex-Governor-General of Indochina, Albert Sarraut, but never properly implemented. Now, doctrine became reality, as the Law of 30 April 1946 established an Investment Fund for Social and Economic Development (FIDES). Here too, development funding reversed the earlier principle of funding colonial development exclusively from colonial budgets. Internal revenues nonetheless continued to fund the bulk of the colonial state's expenditure: FIDES expected the colonial state to match metropolitan funding at a rate set initially at 45 per cent, met through public borrowing from an agency set up for the purpose, or from taxation (Hargreaves 1996: 102). The post-war commodities boom ensured that, although taxation continued to bite, the pre-war system of heavy fiscal extraction now gave way to one where Africans could expect to see benefits for their pains (Young 1994: 214). Indeed, the Belgian Congo managed to fund its extensive welfare programme almost entirely through revenues and private investment, with no equivalent of the British and French development funds.

Colonial development and welfare could readily be interpreted as an attempt to exploit African material and human resources more effectively to imperial advantage. This was explicit in the utilitarian doctrine of *mise en valeur*, which saw health and education as contributing principally to the effectiveness of the colonial workforce (Cooper 2001: 29–40). Moreover, as we have seen, both Britain and France *needed* their colonial empires as never before, not only as part of a claim to continuing status as international powers, but also as a crucial basis for economic recovery following the Second World War. In order to work for the empire, therefore, the colonial state had above all to work more efficiently. This resulted in what has come to be seen as a 'second colonial occupation', a concept originally applied to East Africa, but of much wider application (Low & Lonsdale 1976: 13). But the occupiers were administrators and technicians, newly recruited to the ranks of the colonial service, or deployed by more specialist agencies to support new welfare services, or to boost production. Although they came to colonial development as enthusiastic modernizers, armed with a new form of 'civilizing mission', they were often deeply resented, as they urged drastic measures to eradicate 'swollen shoot' disease in Gold Coast cocoa plantations, or 'sudden death' syndrome in Zanzibar's clove trees (Hyam 1992: xlviii). In Kenya, this was when 'the empire first reached the villages', as a Development and Reconstruction Authority imposed contour terracing, using compulsory labour recruitment, usually of women (Atieno Odhiambo 1995: 25). Alternatively, policy makers bypassed Africans altogether: the infamous Groundnuts Scheme, sponsored by the

Ministry of Supply (against the advice of the Colonial Office), sank £36 million in a catastrophic attempt to use European labour and machines to farm 'virgin' (that is, barren) Tanganyikan bush country on a massive scale, to meet a worldwide shortage of food oils (Iliffe 1979: 440–2; Hyam 1992: xlvi–vii).

The new emphasis on development and welfare showed that colonial officials were thinking in the long term, but there were potential short-term pitfalls. In the Belgian Congo, generous welfare provision lay at the heart of the Belgian administration's 'Platonism', Hodgkin's name for the benign, technocratic paternalism of Belgian 'philosopher-kings', which almost entirely eschewed political development (Hodgkin 1956: 52). By the late 1950s, on the eve of its precipitous decolonization, the Congo had established, almost from scratch since 1945, a system of primary education catering for 70 per cent of school-age children, and boasted colonial health services that were 'the best in the whole tropical world' (Young 1994: 212). Around 64 per cent of FIDES funding went towards high-prestige, capital-rich projects for infrastructural development, such as the Office du Niger, a large-scale irrigation project to produce cotton in the Niger Basin, launched in the 1920s, which by the 1950s still only extended over a fraction of its intended area; or the Palace of the Federal Grand Council of AOF, opened in 1957, by which time it had become redundant through the territorialization of French African politics enshrined in the 1956 Framework Law (Chapter 7; Hargreaves 1996: 102–3; Chafer 2002: 271–2). The 'beneficent rain' of FIDES, falling as it did on the cities and on these spectacular projects, left the interior undeveloped much as before (Deschamps 1975: 125–6). Meanwhile, projects for colonial industrialization, which might have made for development of a different order, remained stillborn (Marseille 1984); not until de Gaulle's Constantine Plan for Algerian development, in 1958, did industrialization figure plausibly in French projects, by which time it was definitely too late. The opportunities for propaganda arising from these projects were of course amply, if often fancifully, exploited: an official publication of 1953 claimed that the Office du Niger had 'pushed back the desert and turned a desolate region into an oasis' (Bancel & Mathy 1993: 224). By the mid-1950s, however, this propaganda was starting to backfire, as metropolitan commentators started to question whether this 'beneficent rain' should not rather be irrigating metropolitan France's own efforts at domestic reconstruction.

The Reformist 'Official Mind' in British Africa

Official rationales for reform and the parameters of a reforming agenda for British Africa were already in place well before 1945. The 1938 publication of Lord Hailey's monumental *African Survey* signalled a willingness to rethink the tenets of British colonial policy. Hailey's ideas were taken up by a newly appointed Colonial Secretary, Malcolm MacDonald (son of the Labour leader and former Prime Minister Ramsay MacDonald), who called for a 'seething of thought' in the Africa Division of the Colonial Office; however, the committee work given over to this intellectual effervescence did not survive the more pressing events of the summer of 1940 (Ashton & Stockwell 1996: vol. 1, lii, doc. 57). MacDonald championed the 1940 Development and Welfare Act, but also commissioned Hailey's further enquiries in Africa, presented in a compendious 1942 report, but only widely circulated by 1944 (Hailey 1980). Hailey's report has been portrayed as a 'kind of organic blueprint for the colonial reform movement', but this was perhaps less because of any particular boldness or originality than for its exhaustiveness, and for its balanced conclusions, 'thus winning approval from opposing factions' (Flint 1983: 407; Pearce 1984: 81; Hargreaves 1996: 64).

In this late wartime period, the emphasis of Colonial Office officials still fell on furthering the colonial development and welfare, culminating in the 1945 Act. The impetus for political reform is largely associated with Andrew Cohen, the 'ardent Fabian reformer' who became head of the Africa Division in 1943. In April 1946, Cohen stated what he saw as a twofold problem. First, there was no 'up to date policy of native administration', even while officials faced 'a rapidly increasing political consciousness among Africans, a rapid extension of the educated class and the special problem of returned soldiers'. And secondly, the Colonial Office and Colonial Governments had 'to a large extent lost the confidence of our administrative officers, especially the younger ones' (Hyam 1992: vol. 1, doc. 40). Cohen and Arthur Creech Jones, Colonial Secretary in the Attlee government, now proposed to establish the machinery for a redefining policy (ibid.: doc. 44). This took the form of a series of consultations: first, a summer school for colonial officials took place at Cambridge in August 1947; secondly, the centrepiece of the plan was the African Governors' Conference held in November 1947; thirdly, this was followed up with a conference in September 1948, to which unofficial and official members of the various African legislative councils were invited (ibid.: xxx). The regional focus of the meetings was subsequently repeated for the West Indies and the Pacific (ibid.).

The African Governors' Conference agenda demonstrates the redefined policy's scope, with reports on general political development, constitutional development, local government, the Colonial Service, agricultural production, marketing policy for colonial exports and education (ibid.: doc. 59). Great things were expected of the new policy, grandiloquently portrayed by one official as a 'world-wide experiment in nation-building' (H.T. Bourdillon, May 1950, in ibid.: doc. 72, & xxix). But if the stakes were high, the methods to be employed were more down-to-earth:

> Africa is now the core of our colonial position; the only continental space from which we can still hope to draw reserves of economic and military strength. Our position there depends fundamentally on our standing with Africans in the mass. And this depends on whether we make a success of African *local* government. (F.J. Pedler, 1 November 1946, in ibid.: doc. 43)

This emphasis on local government is a common thread running back to Hailey's *African Survey* and beyond. The point was to recast local administrations as more modern, representative (if not 'democratic') and accountable structures. This meant that existing structures now needed to be rationalized: larger units, such as the larger Northern Nigerian emirates or the kingdom of Buganda (both archetypes for the policy of Indirect Rule), would be brought 'properly in touch with the people themselves', while 'small and poor tribes' were brought together in effective local government structures (ibid.: docs 59, 40). A distinction was drawn between the chief as traditional 'leader of the tribe', and his official function as 'the agent of the Central

Government'. Officials detected signs of the 'disintegration of tribal influence', and foresaw the eventual 'complete breakdown of the tribal system', under the impact of urban growth, the emergence of a 'new middle class based on wealth and education', and labour migration. So-called 'de-tribalized Africans', regarded in the past as 'a class by themselves requiring special treatment', were now seen as representative of an emerging social norm (ibid.: doc. 40, 217). As will be seen below, there was thus a surprising overlap between official attitudes in this regard and that of a modernizing nationalist such as Nkrumah, whose campaign in the Gold Coast was based, in part, on hostility to the traditional institutions of chieftaincy.

What is perhaps most remarkable about these official deliberations was the proposed schedule for reforms, to be managed in stages into a measurable future. In the past, the implicit model for change had been that of English history going back to the Norman Conquest; officials now recognized that change would occur much more rapidly than that (R.E. Robinson, n.d. 1947, ibid.: doc. 49). Conversely, the largely unspoken counter-example was India, where the government was perceived as having too readily surrendered control to 'unrepresentative' nationalists. The question was therefore how to bridge the gap between the local or 'tribal' level and the colonial state, which educated Africans, like the Indian Congress before them, were seen as intent on capturing. The answer, first developed by Hailey and by officials in the West Africa Department, was a series of stages towards eventual self-government, with the bottom-up development of local government structures mirrored by a top-down incremental development of territorial representative government.[1] At the African Governors' Conference, four stages were envisaged for the latter process, the aim being, as Cohen wrote: '. . . [to] establish a broad framework within which the political development of the African territories can take place with the minimum of friction, the maximum of good will and the greatest possible degree of efficiency' (Agenda Report, doc. 59, 204).

Many African territories had already reached the first stage, whereby an Executive Council, responsible to the governor, divided its responsibilities into a number of portfolios, held by officials, but within a structure pointing towards eventual cabinet government. In a second stage, portfolios passed to unofficial members, who became increasingly responsible to the Legislative Council, with the governor retaining final authority; this stage too had been reached in some parts of Africa. In a third stage, held to be 'a considerable way off', some unofficials became ministers, as the governor increasingly surrendered responsibility to a properly elected Legislative Council. This could only occur when the 'local government machine' was much more efficient; when the 'chain of responsibility from the centre to the people' had been secured by indirect elections to Provincial and Regional Councils; and when many more 'local people and above all Africans' had been brought into the higher echelons of public service. The fourth stage, following on rapidly from the third, would be reached when all government departments were under the control of ministers, the governor was no more than the King's representative, and 'internal self-government could be granted'. Clearly, each territory would develop at its own pace, more rapid in West Africa, less so in those territories of Central and East Africa where Africans had not yet 'developed to a stage where they can play their full part with the immigrant communities'. No clear timetable could therefore be established, though the report alluded to the 'adjustments which future policy will demand for twenty or thirty years or indeed longer' (ibid.: 204).

This bold planning has no particular value as a guide to the subsequent course of British decolonization in Africa, although grand claims have sometimes been made for a supposed 'Durham Report of the African Empire'.[2] As Hargreaves (1996: 106) suggests, it was 'something less than a blueprint for something less than universal independence'. Rather, it shows a British 'official mind' seeking to refashion completely the structures of its rule in Africa, literally from the bottom up, and within a would-be realistic timeframe. The 'official mind' did not think as one, however, and although many of the proposals coming from the CO 'mandarins' were accepted in principle, 'discussions revealed . . . a good deal of difference between the Colonial Office and governors, and between East Africa and West Africa' (G.B. Cartland, in Hyam 1992: xxxiii). Much of this disagreement crystallized around the figure of Sir Philip Mitchell, Governor of Kenya, whose arguments ranged from the particularist view that East Africa was more 'backward' than West, to the more general argument that the political reform was anyway hopelessly premature. Mitchell's counterblasts aimed one barrel at ill-informed metropolitan opinion, especially CO opinion, and one at any African nationalist who might come into range:

> The Government of Kenya . . . considers itself morally bound to resist processes which might be called 'political progress' by the misinformed or opinionated but would in fact be no more than progress towards the abdication of its trust in favour of . . . professional politicians . . . It may be difficult but will, for a very long time, be necessary to dispose of the moral courage and political integrity to say no to proposals for apparent progress of that kind, especially when the saying of it is held up to obloquy as 'British imperialism' and the rest of the current rubbish.[3]

By the time of the third stage of Cohen's consultation process, the 1948 Conference of officials and unofficials, intended as a showcase for the new policy, internal opposition had, to some extent, 'driven it underground' (Pearce 1982: 181). However, there are strong reasons for considering the 1947 discussions in terms of balanced institutional outcomes. On the one hand, although Mitchell's arguments met with a considerable degree of sympathy amongst his peers, this was far less the case amongst younger officials. Indeed, the proposals may be said to have achieved their 'instrumental or purely functional purpose', which was to motivate junior colonial administrators, including those whom the CO was even then recruiting (Porter & Stockwell 1989: 68). Moreover, the extent of conservative opposition may be overstated, and considerable common ground remained on the substance of policy, if not on its ideological underpinning. In particular, reformers and conservatives, CO officials and governors from across Africa, all shared what would turn out to be a basic misconception, which was that they expected to retain the initiative as planning was applied to the realities of late colonial politics.

The Urgency of African Politics: Gold Coast and Nigeria, 1945–51

By 1945, British official thinking favoured a model of local government, gradually evolving over at least a generation from the local base upwards towards eventual self-government. Notwithstanding the divergence between liberal and conservative positions on this, in practice, officials tended to err on the side of caution. This can be seen in the Gold Coast and Nigeria, which both entered the post-war period with new constitutions, ostensibly designed to mark the first phase of political development, but which were effectively obsolete from the outset. These two cases also show how, within a few years after 1945, the British framework for gradual change came to be stretched to breaking-point, as long-term timescales for reform succumbed to political pressures; or, as Rathbone puts it (1992: xlvi), policy was 'exposed to the urgency of politics'. Within a few years, officials had surrendered their self-appointed role as beneficent *deus ex machina* to ever-increasing political accountability; and future political developments were thus exposed to the influence that could be exerted by an able political leader such as Nkrumah or Azikiwe.

Both Gold Coast and Nigerian constitutions reflected British officials' aim of rationalizing colonial institutions and setting the terms of African participation within them. Both reflect the dominance of liberal thinking in the Colonial Office, but also the limits of reform as conceived at the time. Indeed, the governors responsible for the two constitutions, Sir Alan Burns for the Gold Coast, and Sir Arthur Richards in Nigeria, represent the liberal–conservative divide in the British official mind, but whereas Burns largely achieved his liberal objectives, Richards's initial proposals, if implemented, would have reversed Nigerian policy going back twenty years (Rathbone 1992: xxxvi–ix; Lynn 2001: xlix–li). Both constitutions left the basic structure of rule in place, with an all-powerful governor chairing an appointed Executive Council. Though still largely composed of officials, both Executive Councils had seen the wartime appointment of African 'unofficials'. In a major shift, Legislative Councils in both dependencies were now to contain unofficial majorities. However, the Gold Coast Constitution provided for only five directly elected councillors out of 18, representing Accra and three other towns, the others being indirectly elected representatives of traditional authorities. For Nigeria, the elective principle was restricted to three members only, representing Lagos and Calabar, thus retaining a provision in place since 1922 (which Richards sought to abolish). In both, the influence of 'unrepresentative' urban or western-educated nationalist opinion was supposedly contained.

Both constitutions reflected the legacy of Indirect Rule, with significant implications for the further development of territorial politics. Under Indirect Rule, extensive parts of both Gold Coast and Nigeria had been excluded from the Legislative Council's remit. Now Northern Nigeria, the *locus classicus* of Indirect Rule, comprising more than half the Nigerian population and territory, was to elect Legislative Councillors. Of three new Regional Councils, one represented the North, while the South had two, following the 1939 creation of a Western Region, whose ethnic composition was predominantly Yoruba, and an Igbo-dominated Eastern Region. The new Constitution embodied traditional Northern predominance, and an essentially conservative British view – forcefully advocated by Governor Richards – that the pace of political change should be slowed, or halted, to accommodate Northern rulers' concerns (Lynn 2001: xlix). The structural tensions generated by this Nigerian proto-federalism contrasted with the Gold Coast's unitary structure, where regional tensions only surfaced after the Gold Coast had moved closer to self-government. Here too, neither the confederation of Asante kingdoms contained within Ashanti province, nor the Muslim-dominated Northern Territories were subject to direct rule. Following wartime representations from bodies representing Asante chiefly authority, Ashanti now took four of 13 indirectly elected Legislative Council seats, although the Northern Territories remained unrepresented for the moment, according to the Indirect Rule model.

Complex new constitutional arrangements sat uneasily with the management of strikes and disorder associated with the post-war 'radical moment'. In Nigeria, Governor Richards published the proposals against the backdrop of unrest culminating in the five-week general strike that broke out in June 1945. Both the proposals and the strike offered a platform for the National Council for Nigeria and the Cameroons (NCNC), formed in 1944. The NCNC's leader, journalist and newspaper proprietor, Nnamdi Azikiwe, was a touchstone for British attitudes towards African nationalism: Richards's predecessor, Sir Bernard Bourdillon, admired and supported him, read his writings, and fed his ideas into British reformist planning (Flint 1999); Richards, on the other hand, condemned him as 'an irresponsible and dangerous figure' (Lynn), with alleged Communist sympathies. Expressing solidarity with the strikers, and condemning the constitutional proposals, the NCNC strengthened its credentials as a genuinely national party, notwithstanding the dominance of Igbos, including Azikiwe, within its ranks. Richards, meanwhile, responded by banning Azikiwe's newspapers, and, when further strike action threatened in November 1945, asked for a navy frigate to be sent to Lagos. For the moment, the wind was blowing with Azikiwe, and against Richards, who retired shortly after 'his' constitution came into force, but continued to champion the Northern Native Authorities in the House of Lords (as Lord Milverton of Lagos and Clifton). In August 1948, as the NCNC and others became more strident, and as tension mounted between groups representing Igbo and Yoruba interests, the new governor, Sir John Macpherson, initiated a three-year consultative process of 'constitution mongering' leading to a radically revised, and even more short-lived constitutional text (Chapter 7).

The preferred British policy of gradualism from the base up was broken most decisively in the Gold Coast. Burns's constitutional proposals were broadly welcomed by African opinion in 1944, but by the time the Constitution was implemented two years later, the Gold Coast was deep in crisis. Burns's departure in August 1947 coincided with the formation of a new political party, the United Gold Coast Convention (UGCC), demanding 'Self-government in the shortest possible time' (Rathbone 1992: xlii). Key strikes by railwaymen and by gold miners in late 1947 were resolved – in the former case, largely through groundbreaking mediation from African Legislative Councillors – but the issues raised 'would not stay in the workplace' (Cooper 1996: 250–2). Meanwhile, townspeople responded to harsh inflation with a consumer boycott, while rural producers protested, sometimes violently, at the 'cutting-out' policy implemented to control the 'swollen shoot' virus in the cocoa plantations, the social impact of which apparently concerned officials less than the threat to cocoa production (Rathbone 1992: loc.cit.). Against this background, police fired on a demonstration by ex-serviceman in Accra, on 28 February 1948, killing two. The riots and looting that followed in Accra and other towns, and the reaction of overstretched security forces, left 29 dead and 271 injured (Cooper 1996: 253). Governor Sir Gerald Creasy declared an emergency and detained without charge the UGCC's leader,

Dr J.B. Danquah (lawyer, kinsman of the Asante paramount king, the Asantehene, and general thorn in the colonial side), its secretary-general, Kwame Nkrumah, and four others. Creasy, apparently with 'cutting-out' on his mind, likened these detentions with 'the quarantine which is imposed on people who have caught a dangerous infectious disease' (in ibid.: 254).

The Watson Commission of Inquiry, speedily appointed by the Colonial Office, acted with equal speed: the three commissioners, 'Scottish Fabians of limited African experience', spent a bare month in the Gold Coast, reporting a month later, in June 1948 (Hargreaves 1996: 124). Their report was radical in its impact, less so in its content, representing a partial retreat from the thrust of Cohen's reforms, by reiterating Britain's 'moral duty to remain' until the Gold Coast could satisfy stringent criteria of 'cultural, political and economic achievement'. The report's recommendations on labour, agriculture and education fitted unremarkably within an official framework, and its constitutional reforms reflected a 'generalized developmentalism, a measuring of progress around European institutions and categories' (ibid.; Cooper 1996: 256). The report was hostile towards the UGCC, but also condemned traditional chiefly authority. This elicited a vigorous response from officials, suggesting that the commissioners, in their haste, had not sufficiently canvassed rural opinion, and contesting their 'prejudice . . . against Chiefs' (Andrew Cohen, Minute, 29 June 1948, in Rathbone 2000: 19–20).

The Colonial Office had little choice but to accept the Watson Commission's headline recommendation, which was that the 1946 Constitution, 'outmoded at birth', be redrafted. Its response, bolder even than Watson recommended, was to appoint a committee chaired by the Ghanaian judge, Sir Henley Coussey, and composed of forty African notables. Of the six detained UGCC leaders (released when the panic died down), five were 'moderate' enough to be included on the Committee; the sixth, Nkrumah, was thus left free to criticize the Committee's eventual findings, and to mobilize radical political opinion in the meantime. Also on the Committee were several senior chiefs, ensuring its treatment of traditional rulers would be gentler and 'more "African"' than Watson's (ibid.).

The following three years saw parallel political processes unfolding, together spelling irreversible change in the Gold Coast and beyond. The first was the emergence of the new constitution, following Coussey's recommendations in August 1949, taken further by the Accra government in consultation with the CO. This represented a highpoint of late colonial state-building, as British officials engaged, with sometimes palpable excitement, in the 'novelty of building an entirely new kind of colonial state' (Rathbone 1992: l). The 1951 Constitution provided for only three official seats in the Legislative Council; and three in the Executive Council, alongside eight African ministers, although officials held vital portfolios (finance, external affairs, defence), and the governor retained ultimate reserve powers, including the power to withdraw the Constitution (Hargreaves 1996: 125; Rathbone 1992: lii–liii). Ministers were backed, and hence restrained, by a still overwhelmingly European-staffed civil service. Coussey's conservative proposal was dropped for an upper chamber guaranteeing chiefly influence. However, indirect election through Provincial Councils ensured representation of chiefly constituencies, including the Northern Territories; in all only five seats (out of 56), all urban, were to be filled by direct adult male suffrage. The constitution provided what both 'moderates' and British officials hoped were sufficient checks and balances to ensure that further reform was gradual and contained. Crucially, this was meant as a definitive settlement rather than as a temporary staging post towards independence.

A parallel political process, flowing from Nkrumah's campaign to mobilize mass, national support, transformed much of the constitution's intended impact. In June 1949, Nkrumah split from the UGCC to form the Convention People's Party (CPP), which condemned the 'bogus and fraudulent' constitutional proposals, and launched a campaign of Positive Action to secure 'Self-Government NOW'.[4] Nkrumah's support came from the constituency most feared or despised, whether by officials, chiefs or the old coastal elite represented by the UGCC. 'Youth' in post-war Gold Coast could be glossed variously as the 'malcontents' of official reports, as 'socialist realist' icons in an age when Stalinism was the height of political fashion and a focus for official alarm, or as shiftless urban 'hooligans' or 'verandah boys' (the UGCC's preferred designation, verandahs being where such men were supposed to sleep). Most specifically, it signified 'youngmen', a concept embracing those men, not necessarily young, without kinship ties to royalty, and therefore excluded from its privileges, some religious, others more mundanely secular (Rathbone 2000: 23–4). The labour movement was instrumental in backing Positive Action, though Creech Jones was exaggerating wildly when he told the incoming governor in late 1949, Sir Charles Arden-Clarke, that the Gold Coast was 'on the edge of revolution' (in Rathbone 1992: xlviii). Despite a mounting toll of strikes through 1948 and 1949, the Trades Union Council's (TUC) did not wholeheartedly support Positive Action, with splits in key sectors such as mining between support for the CPP and local struggles over labour issues: officials fearing a paralysing general strike underestimated their own success in encouraging trades unions as 'autonomous bodies devoted to "industrial" issues' (Cooper 1996: 258). The planned general strike lasted two weeks in January 1950, and did not spread much beyond the major towns. Vigorous security measures worked, and Nkrumah and the top CPP leadership were charged with fomenting an illegal strike and imprisoned.

The two parallel processes came together in the elections of February 1951. Although Positive Action was a relative failure, prison enhanced Nkrumah's reputation (amongst both officials and his supporters, but in different ways). It did little to dent the CPP's discipline, or indeed Nkrumah's organizational flair: he kept control of the CPP by smuggling out instructions on lavatory paper traded with other prisoners (Nkrumah 1957: 106–7). The elections returned a 'famous victory' for the CPP, which, as expected, won all five directly elected seats, including the Accra Central seat which Nkrumah won from his prison cell, but also a further 29 indirectly elected seats. This upset complacent official predictions of the CPP's level of support in the countryside, the extent of chiefly authority, and the capacity of the UGCC to steal the limelight from the hobbled CPP. More seriously still, the results overturned the assumption underpinning Coussey's recommendations, of a Legislative Council representing all shades of opinion and regional interests, with a similarly balanced Executive Council. Instead, the Legislative Council had a CPP majority, and, although the governor faced down demands for an all-CPP Executive Council, he was obliged to release Nkrumah and to invite him to become Leader of Government Business (according to Coussey's quaint title) (Rathbone 1992: lvi–lvii).

French Colonial Planning and its Limits: Brazzaville and After

Extensive Gaullist colonial planning began with the establishment of de Gaulle's French Committee of National Liberation (CFLN), a provisional government in all but name, at Algiers in July 1943. Preparations for the Brazzaville Conference of January–February 1944 were therefore bound up with the gathering momentum of the Gaullist campaign. French officials displayed a talent for overlaying, and perhaps even wilfully confusing, the content of policy proposals with their propaganda value. As a propaganda 'event', the Conference seems to have achieved the desired effect, by presenting a clear message that the French empire was in capable, and possibly also liberal, hands under de Gaulle's leadership, and that no challenge to French sovereignty would be countenanced. Any remaining doubts on this score seem to have been allayed by the time of de Gaulle's visit to New York in July 1944. Brazzaville was thus de Gaulle's equivalent of Churchill's 'King's First Minister' speech.

Brazzaville was primarily intended as a forum for senior colonial officials in French sub-Saharan Africa, newly united under Gaullist authority, to discuss colonial policy and doctrine. Loyalty to de Gaulle was no guarantee of a liberal outlook on colonial policy any more than in other areas of public policy, and the Brazzaville Conference broadly underlined the continuities in the French 'official mind' (Institut Charles-de-Gaulle & IHTP 1988). Much of the debate centred on the reiteration of a 'colonial humanist' agenda which was certainly liberal, but hardly innovative, building on precedents going back to the 1930s, or simply rehearsed quintessential assimilationist doctrine. Recommending French as the exclusive medium of education sounded like a ringing endorsement of French Republican principles applied to the colonies, but in fact reflected general practice in sub-Saharan Africa (but not in Indochina, Madagascar or North Africa, all exempted from the principle) (Gardinier 1988). Economic policy was de-emphasized at the Conference, on the grounds that previous policy had tended to place too much importance on economics, and the largely hypothetical debate on this subject was more cautious in scope, for example on the subject of colonial industrialization, than some policy discussions by the Vichy regime (Marseille 1984: 344–6; 1988). The Conference's boldest recommendations were those proposing the abolition of forced labour and of the *indigénat*, that is, the code of 'native' justice exercised, often arbitrarily, by administrators. Even these were hedged around with caution: notwithstanding the strong case presented by Governor André Latrille of Côte d'Ivoire, whose report was compiled with the aid of the young Félix Houphouët-Boigny, the proposed ban on forced labour was to be delayed for five years after the war, so as not to interfere with the colonial war effort.

This mismatch between propaganda and substance left a certain gap in credibility, especially as no Africans were present at Brazzaville, and indeed only a few French politicians attended, as observers from the (unelected) Consultative Assembly at Algiers. Although the ineptitude of the ban on eventual 'self governments' was most marked when applied to Indochina (Chapter 4), it suggested that the proclaimed generous 'spirit' of Brazzaville was at odds with the letter of the governors' recommendations. However, although the tradition of a unitary imperial structure was apparently confirmed, thus locking the African Federations and Madagascar into the

French Republican embrace, an important corollary to French tradition opened a back door to political progress. This was the recommendation made at Brazzaville for African representation in an eventual Constituent Assembly. The Republic had long allowed parliamentary representation for the citizens of Overseas France, including assimilated 'natives'; indeed, this was implied in a colony's constitutional status (as opposed to a protectorate, etc.). Amongst French colonies in this strict sense were the 'Four Communes' of coastal Senegal (of which the most important was Dakar).[5] The so-called *originaires* ('original' citizens) of Dakar had thus been represented by a black African *député* since 1914. This quirk of colonial history now became a general principle extended to the whole of AOF, AEF, Madagascar and Djibouti, which all sent elected representatives to the two Constituent Assemblies (1945–6) and to both Chambers of the National Assembly of the Fourth Republic.

The drawing of political battle-lines for the debate ahead became apparent in the meetings of the commission, chaired by the Guyanese parliamentarian, Gaston Monnerville, appointed in early 1945 to devise a scheme for colonial elections. With an uncomfortable membership of official, political and semi-official 'expert' representatives, the Monnerville Commission amounted to a late colonial microcosm in which misunderstandings between nationalist politicians and the French 'official mind' were rehearsed. The Commission's fate was also indicative of things to come, in that the Minister of Colonies, Paul Giacobbi, overturned its bold but coherent recommendations, despite their backing by his senior civil servant, Governor Henri Laurentie. The Commission recommended a single electoral college, with no distinction between 'citizens' and 'non-citizens', and universal suffrage. Every territorial unit would comprise at least one constituency, but the size of a constituency would be approximately 800,000 inhabitants (i.e. about ten times bigger than in metropolitan France). On the advice of the African governors and governors-general, Giacobbi imposed separate colleges for citizens and non-citizens, in order to ensure representation of often tiny settler communities, and maintained limited suffrage for the non-citizens' college, based on criteria such as military service, literacy or post-holding (e.g. French-appointed village chiefs). African constituencies were initially composed of two neighbouring (but otherwise disparate) territories, although separate territorial constituencies were introduced after the October 1945 elections – in outline the future independent states of francophone Africa.

Although compromised from the start, the presence of African and other colonial *députés* in the two Constituent Assemblies, and in the National Assembly that followed, provided a veritable nursery of statesmen. Amongst the handful of Africans elected in the October 1945 Constituent Assembly elections were the future presidents of Senegal, Senghor, and of Côte d'Ivoire, Félix Houphouët-Boigny, and the president of the Provisional Government of the Algerian Republic from 1958, Ferhat Abbas. The first Constituent Assembly passed a number of laws which fleshed out key Brazzaville recommendations, notably the Law of 11 April 1946, presented by Houphouët-Boigny, which abolished forced labour, well ahead of the deadline set at Brazzaville. A further milestone law passed on 12 March 1946, presented by the Communist *député* and recently elected mayor of Fort-de-France (Martinique), Aimé Césaire, conferred the status of Overseas Departments (*Départements d'Outre-Mer*, DOM) on the Old Colonies of Martinique, Guadeloupe, Guyane and Réunion, which were thus incorporated, at least notionally, into the Republic (Hintjens 1995). In principle, DOM status squared with the federal scheme underpinning the French Union, as one of two possible end goals of political evolution within the Union (see Chapter 4). In practice, the March 1946 Law's implementation was delayed by two years, and the DOMs were exempted from the automatic application of metropolitan legislation by Article 73 of the Constitution, which allowed for laws to be adapted to suit their 'particular conditions and requirements'. Until the end of the Fourth Republic in 1958, the DOMs continued to be governed by decree in much the same way as they had been as colonies (ibid.). It was also in this brief window of reformist opportunity that the Law of 30 April 1946 was passed, introducing the principle of FIDES.

Although a distinctive feature of the French Union, African parliamentary representation was marked by some glaring inequities, not all of which could ever be ironed out of the system. First to go were the rotten boroughs created by the citizens' college, which in October 1945 elected three Europeans as the strident representatives of 8,000 voters in French West Africa. (The veteran Socialist mayor of Dakar, Lamine Guèye, won the fourth citizens' constituency.) The Law of 7 May 1946, presented by Lamine Guèye, was passed unanimously in the dying days of the first Constituent Assembly, creating a citizenship of the French Union, which, although only vaguely defined, nonetheless provided 'a reference point for future campaigns for equality between Africans and Europeans' (Chafer 2002: 63–4). It also made the retention of the double-college system untenable, in French West Africa at least, though it was retained in AEF and Cameroun, and in local assemblies, notably in the Algerian Assembly created by the 1947 Algerian Statute (Chapter 6). But although the numbers of Algerian, African and Malagasy *députés* increased from their October 1945 base, they were never more than a small minority in the Assembly, for if the number of overseas *députés* were ever allowed to reflect the demographic balance of '*la plus grande France*' (Greater France), France would simply become, as the veteran Radical *député* Édouard Herriot put it to the second Constituent Assembly, 'the colony of her former colonies'. Although Senghor condemned this pronouncement at the time as 'racism', Herriot was merely stating the obvious limits of French assimilation (27 August 1946, in Shipway 1996a: 107). So for the duration of the Fourth Republic, one metropolitan French citizen would continue to equate with approximately ten Africans.

Fear of a Communist-dominated Assembly, rather than popular disapproval of the French Union articles, led to the rejection of the constitutional draft in the referendum of 5 May 1946. The so-called 'Senghor Constitution' contained in the aborted May 1946 constitutional draft has rightly been seen as a blueprint for radical reform, but less plausibly as a 'missed opportunity' for decolonization (Lewis 1995). Even without considering what might have happened had the May 1946 constitutional draft been accepted (a French People's Republic? civil war? Anglo-American intervention?), it was always likely that the administration would seek to overturn or undermine what was seen as a communist spoiling tactic. Moreover, official objections to the draft stemmed not only from growing, and very slightly hysterical, anti-communism, but were also of an organizational nature: as the elections had demonstrated, the political and administrative infrastructure of the African Federations was still fragile, and would scarcely sustain the kind of demands that would thus be placed upon it. Conversely, the scheme was inextricably tied to communist support, and yet the Party apparently saw the foreseeable future of French Africa in continuing control by a properly democratic France (that is, one dominated by its biggest party, the PCF). The Party's chief colonial specialist, Henri Lozeray, stated the reasoning for this in 1945:

> 1. Because it is the aim of the French nation, in its fight against the trusts, which betray us at the same time as they plunder the colonies, to install a true democracy; this aim cannot fail to bring democracy to the colonial populations;
> 2. Because the lands occupied by these populations are threatened by covetous external forces, at a time when they are not in a position to ensure for themselves a truly independent existence. (in Moneta 1971: 150–2)

This stance was not far removed from that of the French political establishment as a whole, and suspicion of – presumably transatlantic – 'covetous external forces' was certainly shared by, say, the Gaullists. In effect, the PCF subscribed just as surely as its antagonists to the French 'myth' underpinning continuing colonial control (Marshall 1973; Lewis 1998; Chafer 2002).

The atmosphere was very different in the second Constituent Assembly, now led by the Christian Democrats in the new Popular Republican Movement (MRP). In June, Charles de Gaulle, having resigned as president of the Provisional Government in January, broke his silence to denounce the French Union. Following some stormy debates in the Chamber, and the decisive intervention of Laurentie and his colleagues from the Ministry of Overseas France, the draft presented for popular approval in the October 1946 referendum was much less radical in its implications both for the Republic and for the French Union (Lewis 1995). Although the legislative advances of the first Assembly were retained, 'Overseas Territories' in the new constitution effectively differed from colonies in name only. In particular, and in contrast to the British 'bottom-up' approach, priority was given to the carapace of French Union institutions, rather than to the softer internal organs of local representation; indeed, African territorial assemblies retained a 'provisional' status until 1952, and only took their final (and short-lived) form under the 1956 Framework Law (Chapter 7). A few months later, French repression of the Malagasy insurrection from the end of March 1947 (Chapter 6) demonstrated what could happen when nationalist high expectations came up against the obduracy and propensity for violence of the French system.

Paris in Africa, Africa in Paris, 1946–50

Given the intractability of France's other colonial problems, sub-Saharan Africa was a primary test bed for France's claims as a liberal colonial power. These claims rested on the integration of colonial dependencies in the constitutional structures of a new French Union; and on its investment of French public monies in African social and economic development. It is doubtful whether French officials and politicians were ever collectively committed to assimilating French Africa in a properly realized 'Greater

France', particularly given metropolitan France's own pressing need for post-war economic and political reconstruction. Strikingly, however, African politicians and trades unionists took up French claims, transforming French policy makers' rather dubious ideas of 'assimilation' into increasingly effective African campaigns for equality with metropolitan French voters and workers. In contrast with anglophone African nationalists, the initial goals francophone African politicians set themselves were thus not those of national self-determination, but were determined by a pointedly literal reading of French Republican concepts of citizenship: Africans would first seek their liberation *within* the French political fold.

The October 1946 referendum, which approved the second Constitutional draft, and the first National Assembly elections of the Fourth Republic, brought a sense of anticlimax after two hectic years going back to the Liberation of France. The ensuing period has been seen as one of 'policy sclerosis' (Chafer 2002: 83–4), as officials sought to stabilize colonial structures in Africa, even as violent conflict erupted and deepened in Indochina and Madagascar. However, the genie of African political mobilization could not simply be forced back into the bottle. The decade after 1946 in francophone Africa may be viewed rather as one of 'politics as normal', where *députés* and political activists, trades unionists and workers, officials in Africa and in Paris, sought to work effectively within the new structures. However, it was unclear what *was* normal, and in the circumstances of post-war reconstruction and an intensifying Cold War, politics could never be as normal as all that.

The most obvious beneficiaries of the new system were the elite group of African *députés*, who proved resilient in the multiple arenas of this late colonial politics: those of the colonial state, centring on the federal capitals of Dakar and Brazzaville, but also the more prestigious setting of the imperial capital's chambers and corridors of power. The key to the *députés*' success on the latter stage was their ability to exercise disproportionate influence to their number and 'colonial' status. As experience of the Constituent Assemblies already demonstrated, however ultimately disappointing, the African *députés* had much to gain from 'playing the system' in the new parliamentary regime, whose shifting system of multi-party coalitions favoured small groups prepared to take asymmetric advantage of alliances with larger parties. The Overseas *députés* thus 'naturally took a detached view of much French parliamentary business', and 'behaved, with growing effect, like territorial spokesmen in a federal senate' (Williams 1964: 181).

In their own territorial fiefdoms, the *députés* derived prestige and power from past legislative successes and the promise of future ones, but also simply from their status as African representatives in Paris. (The same applied to the Overseas members of the Council of the Republic and of the French Union Assembly.) The point may be illustrated by the case of Félix Houphouët-Boigny, French-appointed canton chief, auxiliary doctor, Catholic and cocoa-planter in Côte d'Ivoire, whose political career was launched in the wake of Gaullist takeover in AOF in 1943. Houphouët-Boigny mobilized a syndicate of fellow African cocoa-planters, with support from Governor Latrille, against the preferment given to the larger-scale European plantations in the colony. His campaign against forced labour – which directly benefited European plantations – culminated in the April 1946 law abolishing the practice. The issue was scarcely debated in the Assembly, as 'merely reminding the world that a system akin to slavery existed in French Africa rendered it indefensible' (Cooper 2002: 42). None-theless, the Houphouët-Boigny Law bolstered several careers, not only Houphouët's, as *députés* were able to demonstrate their achievements to constituents. The cocoa-planters' syndicate was also the core of Houphouët-Boigny's party, the Democratic Party of Côte d'Ivoire (PDCI), a key component of the federal party grouping, the African Democratic Assembly (RDA).

The RDA laid claim to pan-African nationalist credentials, and aspired to Federation-wide unity. Formed at a Congress at Bamako in the French Soudan (present-day Mali) in October 1946, it built on the overseas *députés'* solidarity in supporting the failed 'Senghor' Constitution. In principle, the RDA federated parties in each territory of AOF and AEF, along with the UN Trusteeship territories of Togo and Cameroun. Solidarity was compromised from the start, however, when the Socialist Minister of Overseas France, Marius Moutet, failing to secure his party's control of the move-ment, persuaded SFIO members, notably Guèye and Senghor, to boycott the Bamako Congress (Mortimer 1969: 105–7). Although hobbled from the start, both by internal disagreements, and by the absence of key political figures belonging to what was soon understood to be a rival SFIO camp, the RDA nonetheless enjoyed communist sup-port, and accepted a parliamentary alliance (*apparentement*) with the PCF. While the RDA achieved near-hegemonic dominance in Côte d'Ivoire and, eventually, Guinée, in Senegal it was restricted to a small urban base, in opposition to the SFIO. The RDA performed well in the November 1946 elections, gaining ten of 18 seats in AOF, AEF and Cameroun, but in indirect elections to the Council for the Republic (the Fourth Republic's upper house), with a double-college system in place, the SFIO's reliance on 'backstairs manoeuvre and administrative pressure' returned twelve of twenty second-college senators, including Moutet himself for the Soudan, as opposed to the RDA's seven.[6]

While the Communist–Socialist alliance held in France, Federation-wide African unity remained viable. The 'Tripartite' coalition, including the MRP, was built on obviously shaky ideological foundations, however, and did not long survive the advent of the Fourth Republic. In May 1947, the Socialist Prime Minister, Paul Ramadier, excluded Communist ministers from the government, and thus launched France's domestic Cold War. This irrevocable step increased the influence of each of these parties on the politics of the French Union, but the reciprocal importance of African politics for the parties was also considerable.

Party loyalties in Paris also loosely corresponded to official fiefdoms, as senior officials maintained party affiliations, and were often appointed (or transferred) on the basis of party ties. Of the 'Tripartite' parties, the SFIO traditionally had the strongest ties to the Overseas Territories, in particular to the Senegalese 'Four Communes' at the heart of the AOF Federation. Moreover, from January 1946 to October 1947, with a Socialist Minister of Overseas France (so renamed when Moutet took office), the party exercised strong control over the levers of patronage. A key colonial 'expert', having held the post in the Popular Front governments, Moutet's image as a revered party grandee was severely tarnished in African eyes by his role in the second Con-stituent Assembly debates. One of Moutet's last actions, before giving way in October 1947 to the new MRP minister, Paul Coste-Floret, was to nominate a fellow Socialist, Paul Béchard, to the Government-General at Dakar.

Machinations did not stem the SFIO's decline in Senegal, which was associated with the rise of an improbable anti-colonial outsider, Léopold Senghor. Unlike the SFIO party bosses in Dakar, notably Lamine Guèye, Senghor was a non-citizen from outside the Four Communes. He thus established a rival power base in the country-side, and allied, somewhat surprisingly for a Catholic modernizer, with the *grands marabouts* of the Muslim brotherhoods, the Muridiyya and Tijaniyya, who controlled the peanut-growing areas of Senegal (Hargreaves 1996: 152; Cooper 2002: 45). Tensions between Guèye and Senghor thus reflected those between the assimilated elite of the resource-rich, politically well-organized federal capital, Dakar, and the economically productive but more traditionally organized hinterland, whose 'big men' now saw their chance to secure political advantage from the new structures. Senghor's successful coalition building across Senegal led to his departure from the SFIO in 1948, to form his own *Bloc Démocratique Sénégalais* (BDS, Senegalese Democratic Bloc), and in turn to a prolonged battle between the BDS and the Socialist-led administration. This battle, with its dreary record of official favouritism, intimidation and ballot-fixing, was at least 'never racialized', since Senghor's adversary, the Socialist governor of Senegal, Laurent Wiltord (with backing from Béchard), was of Antillean origin, and was related to Guèye by marriage (Kras 1999: 91–113). The check to Senghor's career was only lifted in 1950, when a new minister, François Mitterrand, responded to Senghor's pleas by recalling Wiltord and Béchard.

The other Tripartite coalition member, and mainstay of the 'Third Force' which replaced it, the MRP, was a new political force with no claim to traditional colonial ties. Indeed, its lack of political tradition, aside from its association with the Resistance, led its leaders to project an image as forthright patriots, in whose hands France's territorial (and hence imperial) integrity was safe (Thomas 2003; Lewis 1998). More closely implicated than the SFIO in the backlash of 1946, which occurred under the premiership of its leader Georges Bidault, the MRP's hardline reputation in colonial policy was reinforced by the perceived ruthlessness of its man as High Commissioner in Madagascar during the 1947 Insurrection, Pierre de Chévigné.[7] Christian Democracy was still fluid as an ideology in France, and the party could appeal to two separate, and partially opposed constituencies in Africa: first, to the Catholic missions, representing the paternalist, 'welfare' end of the civilizing mission; and secondly, to the tiny but vociferous settler lobby (Thomas 2003). It was the former which provided it with an African following in several territories and with second-college *députés* in Oubangui-Chari and Cameroun.[8] Moreover, Christian Democracy found a sympathetic hearing amongst a number of senior officials, most notably the Rue Oudinot's Director of Political Affairs from 1947 to 1952, the tactful and impeccably liberal Robert Delavignette.

The largest group of African politicians remained associated with the party with the most dynamic approach to French Union politics. The PCF's *entrée* to Africa, substituting for the SFIO's machine politics, came via tried-and-tested methods of political education. While British officials often worried about communist influence on allegedly impressionable Africans, French officials were daily confronted with the real thing. Following the Gaullist takeover in AOF in July 1943, Communist Study Groups (GEC) sprang up in several cities, and party members amongst junior civil servants, including schoolteachers, assisted party formation and unionization. The party had its sympathizers too amongst senior officials, most notably Governor Latrille, who brushed off settlers' accusations that his palace in Abidjan was a 'nest of Stalinists' (in Shipway 1996a: 108). Although the PCF's organizational methods and its rhetoric of colonial liberation were well suited to mobilizing Africans, it is worth reiterating that it stopped short of advocating independence for African territories even after the party's break with the French mainstream in May 1947.

Two related questions hung over the RDA in the first legislature of the Fourth Republic: what benefit derived from communist support? And how did official perceptions of that support impact on the way the party was treated? Both questions may be addressed with reference to AOF's richest and most populous territory, Côte d'Ivoire, and to its political boss, and *de facto* leader of the RDA, Houphouët-Boigny, whose answer to the first question above, given in March 1948, is worth quoting for its frank admission of tactical pragmatism, both with regard to communist values and to French metropolitan political concerns:

> We have good relations with the PCF, it is true. But our alliance does not mean in the least that we are Communists. Houphouët, a Communist? How could a traditional chief, doctor, landowner, and Catholic like myself be a Communist? But our alliance with the PCF has been of great value to us, in that we have found parties who have welcomed us, when others were paying us no attention, and with these friends on our side we have achieved some success in our cause. . . . This is how we have got our point across. And if, in return, we have put our voting papers at the disposal of the Communist parliamentary group in votes on other issues, why should that matter to us? (in Chaffard 1965: vol. 1, 102–3)

By this time, however, the evidence was growing for a pessimistic answer to the second question. Already in early 1947, Ivorian settlers had their revenge on Latrille, who was recalled to Paris. His hardline successor, Péchoux, encouraged secession from the PDCI of a pro-MRP 'Progressist' wing, and favoured moves towards the recreation of a separate territory of Haute-Volta.

In 1932, Haute-Volta had been absorbed into Côte d'Ivoire, in order to facilitate recruitment of Mossi migrant labour to the coastal plantations – the Mossi chiefs had thus been natural allies in Houphouët's stand against forced labour. Now that alliance was broken, as officials offered the greater prize of a separate Haute-Volta, which was delivered in March 1948. All three *députés* elected to the National Assembly for Haute-Volta were affiliated to the MRP, to which the new Governor also belonged. The MRP thus acquired a comfortable fiefdom, but still had to learn to respect the voting weight of African *députés*. In September 1948, the three Haute-Volta *députés* joined a new group, the Overseas Independents (IOM), whose seven-strong membership also included Senghor. A newly appointed prime minister, Robert Schuman, solicited the IOM's support for his parliamentary investiture. No doubt with his mind on weighty European matters, Schuman omitted to respond to their questions about colonial policy. Already sensitive about the 'pro-government' tag applied to them from the Left, the IOM cast their seven votes against Schuman, who lost by six (and never regained the premiership, though as Foreign Minister he retained his grip on European affairs) (Mortimer 1969: 128–31).

At times over the following two years, it looked as if a new front in the Cold War might be opened in AOF, as Côte d'Ivoire hovered on the brink of insurrectionary violence. 1948 was after all the year of the show-trial of the Malagasy *députés* for allegedly instigating Insurrection, and France experienced a violent wave of strikes, and their violent repression on the orders of a Socialist Interior Minister, Jules Moch, as the CGT sought to apply the Cominform 'two camps' policy. In the wider world, events as varied as the Czechoslovak coup of February, the launching of the Malayan insurgency and even the Accra riots in Côte d'Ivoire's anglophone neighbour, the Gold Coast, could all be interpreted as signs of impending Communist aggression against the western 'camp'.

Initially, the RDA held firm to its troublesome *apparentement* with the PCF: as Gabriel d'Arboussier, RDA senator for Côte d'Ivoire, argued to the RDA's Coordinating Committee, 'Our militants are not persecuted because of our *apparentement*, but because of the RDA's fundamental position of struggle against colonialism' (Mortimer 1969: 143). The status quo was thus reaffirmed at the RDA Congress outside Abidjan, in January 1949, the first since Bamako. Despite the IOM's defections, causing the RDA's disappearance from Togo and Dahomey, the RDA remained strong across much of AOF and AEF, although nowhere as strong as in Côte d'Ivoire. Indeed, the PDCI at home was coming to resemble a (proto-national) state within a (late colonial) state, and the existence of parallel systems of justice, law enforcement and identity cards partly provoked the ensuing trial of strength. In February 1949, Governor Péchoux moved to crush the RDA, promoting break-away factions from the party, arresting its supporters, removing sympathetic chiefs from office, and using rivals to provoke violent incidents, which were then broken up by police and troops; RDA supporters responded with rioting and looting. The parliamentary immunity of *députés*, senators and territorial councillors alone spared the party leadership from arrest, although this had not worked for the Malagasy *députés* in 1947, and at one point, backed by large crowds of supporters in his home village (and future capital), Yamoussoukro, Houphouët managed to persuade troops not to carry out a warrant for his arrest (ibid.: 147).

In the end, the government and Houphouët-Boigny pulled back from the brink, and Côte d'Ivoire was spared its fate as 'the next Madagascar'.[9] Houphouët-Boigny's political salvation, however, came from a different source, as a new Minister of Overseas France in September 1950, François Mitterrand, in his first major office, engineered a less troublesome *apparentement* for Houphouët-Boigny with his own party, the UDSR (Social and Democratic Union of the Resistance), which was able to punch well above its insubstantial weight within the 'Third Force' coalition. Although the Left of the RDA never forgave him his alleged treachery, Houphouët maintained his grip at home, and was eventually rewarded in Paris, from 1956, with a string of ministerial posts in the regime's ever-changing governments.

The Central African Federation

The Federation of Rhodesia and Nyasaland, or Central African Federation (CAF), represented Britain's biggest effort to reconcile the progressive terms of late colonial rule with a long-term future for white settlers in Africa. This may readily be seen as indicative of an imperial power seeking to 'set the clock back', ignoring the realities of resurgent African nationalism elsewhere on the continent, and it is certainly striking how little heed was paid to the interests and outlook of Africans in this period, as articulated by local nationalist movements in all three territories concerned. In another way, too, Federation continued an older strain in British imperialism, in which CAF was viewed as a potential new White Dominion, while the settlers emulated their predecessors in the 13 American colonies, preparing a new 'Boston Tea Party' if their demands were not met. The modern twist to this strand of the tale was the possibility that, if left to drift away from British influence, white Rhodesians might be pulled into the orbit of a newly confident and strident Afrikaner nationalism (Hyam 1987). The apparent contradictions in the British position may be partly resolved if the Federation is seen as yet another attempt by British policy makers to identify, appease and collaborate with the most powerful set of local nationalists. It just so happened, in this case, for the moment at least, that those nationalists were white.

The three territories that formed the Federation – Southern and Northern Rhodesia and Nyasaland – tended to be drawn together and held apart in almost equal measure. Although settled later and more sparsely by Europeans than the South, and only unified as a territory in 1911, Northern Rhodesia was 'ideologically no more than an extension of the commercially controlled colonial system of Southern Rhodesia' (Rotberg 1966: 26). The axis of this extension was the railway that struck north from the Zambezi towards Belgian Katanga. Northern Rhodesia's main commercial interest lay west of the 'line of rail', in the rich deposits of the Copperbelt. The urge to 'marry' the two Rhodesias increased after Southern Rhodesia achieved self-government in 1923. However, the settlers' aim was not federation, but amalgamation of North and South. Nyasaland, with few settlers, and more densely populated by Africans, was not included in these plans; rather, an amalgamation of the two 'trans-Zambezian' protectorates alone was considered by officials, if not by settlers; this new entity might then join Tanganyika and Southern Rhodesia in an eventual East African Federation (ibid.: 97–101). Although settler numbers grew rapidly in the two Rhodesias, especially after 1945, there were still 15 times more Africans than Europeans even in Southern Rhodesia, while in Northern Rhodesia Africans outnumbered settlers by more than fifty to one, and settler numbers remained negligible in Nyasaland.[10]

British policy makers' dilemma was articulated by a 1939 Royal Commission: while 'identity of interests' pointed to 'political unity', immediate amalgamation was ruled out by the 'fear that the balance between the races is not fairly held in Southern Rhodesia; the avowed policy of segregation, under the name of "Parallel Development", and the institution of the colour bar stand in the way'; these conclusions were broadly endorsed by Lord Hailey in 1941 (Rotberg 1966: 111–14). In order to sidestep amalgamation, an advisory Central African Council (CAC) was created in 1944, composed of officials and European unofficials, which served as a forum for identifying the three territories' shared interests. However, settler leaders participated in this forum on the understanding that it was potentially a step towards their goal (Murphy 2005a: 56). Despite these reservations, the CAC's agenda over several years constituted a veritable prospectus for a modernizing late colonial state, including: the projected Kariba dam across the Zambezi, transport, customs union, currency union, soil conservation, tsetse fly clearance, healthcare provision, broadcasting, the running of the new Central African Airlines (Rotberg 1966: 216–17).

Proposals for Federation started to emerge in 1948, as settler leaders came to recognize that amalgamation would never be accepted in London. From the imperial perspective, a key factor here was the Nationalist Party's victory in the May 1948 South African elections, which suggested the need, as Andrew Cohen put it, to 'strengthen Southern Rhodesia's hand in dealing with the Union [of South Africa]' (in Murphy 2005a: 59). Nonetheless, arguably, the CO's change of heart, with Cohen emerging as one of Federation's most influential advocates, mostly reflected shifts in settler politics at this time, as Southern Rhodesian elections in September 1948 gave a working majority to the pro-amalgamationist Prime Minister, Sir Godfrey Huggins (ibid.). A pattern now developed, as Rhodesian leaders forced the pace by a mixture of 'government by blackmail' and unilateral constitutional discussions (notably at the 1949 Victoria Falls Conference). Meanwhile, CO officials and their counterparts at the Commonwealth Relations Office (CRO, responsible for Southern Rhodesia) sought to offset Labour ministers' concerns about Federation by playing up fears of South African influence in the two Rhodesias. In particular, Afrikaner settlement in Northern Rhodesia, usually exaggerated, was a convenient tool for both officials and settlers, to the extent that officials headed off any 'piecemeal tinkering' that might make it appear that the 'danger' had abated (ibid.: 63). On a separate question, Nyasaland was included in the proposed federal structure from the start, although the fiscal and economic case for this was never entirely persuasive, either in terms of Nyasaland's interests or those of the Federation. Politically, however, Nyasaland was essential to CAF, as Cohen put it, 'in order to justify its setting up'; in other words, to dress Federation as something more than simple Rhodesian amalgamation (ibid.: 67–71).

The Labour government accepted Federation's merits as a state-building exercise, but remained unconvinced by the official view that 'Africans might well come to realize the very substantial advantages of closer association' (in Rotberg 1966: 232). While existing African land rights and 'native administration' were to be maintained in the protectorates, the settlers' preferred approach was reflected at the 1949 Conference, where Africans were granted only token representation at federal level, in an electoral formula which equated one European with 100 Africans, a proportion even the Algerian *pieds noirs* might have envied (Rotberg 1966: 222; and see next Chapter). At the heart of Federation was the 'partnership' of Africans and Europeans, but settlers and nationalists agreed – from diametrically opposed perspectives – that this vague formula did not rule out 'senior' and 'junior' partners or, as Huggins put it, unconsciously echoing Lenin, the partnership of horse and rider (ibid.: 228–30; Hargreaves 1996: 146). By September 1951, when a further conference convened at the Victoria Falls, the Colonial Secretary, James Griffiths, and Commonwealth Secretary, Patrick Gordon Walker, were edging closer to accepting the federal case, despite strenuous objections expressed at the Conference by African Legislative Councillors for the two Northern territories – present for the first time at such a meeting, against vehement settler protests (Mulford 1967: 28; Hyam 1992: docs 433–5, 444). Two weeks before the British general election, Griffiths and Gordon Walker signed their names to a memorandum urging the government after the election to endorse the principle of federation.

The debate over Federation catalysed African mobilization in the two protectorates, though rather less in Southern Rhodesia, where Africans arguably had few rights left to lose. A Nyasaland African Congress (NAC) formed in 1944, but before Federation provided a focus for its activities, it had not 'found a modern political voice' (Rotberg 1966: 195). Its influential 'overseas representative' was Dr Hastings Kamuzu Banda, Malawi's future president, then in medical practice in London, who attended the Pan-African Congress in Manchester in 1945, lobbied MPs and the Fabian Colonial Bureau, and sent funding to NAC. The Northern Rhodesian Congress formed only in 1948 from a loose-knit Federation of African Societies, and at first opposed Federation with loyalism, arguing that Northern Rhodesia should be renamed 'Queen Victoria's Protectorate' to distinguish itself from the South (ibid.: 211). It became the African National Congress, in August 1951, led by a former teacher, Harry Nkumbula, who had collaborated with Banda during several years of study in London, returning to Northern Rhodesia in 1950 (Mulford 1967: 20–2). Congress politics radicalized in both Northern territories over the following two years, with Nkumbula diagnosing a 'cold war between the British government and the indigenous peoples of Africa', and arguing for effective African self-government as the only alternative to Federation (Rotberg 1966: 238).

The decisive factor for rapid progress was the fall of the Labour government following the October 1951 elections. Urged on by CO and CRO officials, the new Conservative Colonial Secretary, Oliver Lyttleton, announced, only a month after taking office, that his government unequivocally supported Federation (Murphy 2005a: 65). Over the following two years, officials failed to halt a stream of further concessions to settler leaders. This was partly because it was becoming plain that nothing could be done to reconcile African nationalists to Federation, so in effect it became less crucial to appease African opinion. Moreover, Conservative leaders, at least in private, were dismissive of African objections, agreeing perhaps with the new Commonwealth Secretary, Lord Ismay, that 'the average Northern Rhodesian African is of the mental calibre of a British child of ten', and hence that 'we have got to give him better food and better education before we even think of full political emancipation' (in ibid.: 66). Conversely, the prospect of a Southern Rhodesian referendum, promised by Huggins in 1948, enforced an effective ban on any official statement that might reassure Africans, but which might thereby 'cause alarm' amongst settlers and jeopardize the referendum; the success of this strategy came with a 65 per cent vote in favour of federation, in April 1953 (ibid.: 66–7). Thus the Federation of Rhodesia and Nyasaland came into existence in October 1953, with the provision that a review, after a maximum of seven years, would make Federation permanent. Ironically enough, it was this mechanism that would set in motion the Federation's dissolution into its three constituent parts, and that would confirm that Britain had after all chosen the wrong set of nationalist collaborators in its most ambitious late colonial project.

Notes

1   For the 'bottom-up' stages, see O.G.R. Williams's five stages for West African political development, in ibid.: liv and doc. 70; for the 'top-down' stages, Agenda Report, Appendix III, 'Constitutional development in Africa', ibid.: doc. 59.

2 Robinson (1980) was writing both as historian and as participant, since at the time of the African Governors' Conference he was a member of Cohen's staff.

3 30 May 1947, in ibid.: doc. 45. See also the entertaining 'Extracts from the Diary of Sir Philip Mitchell', in Porter & Stockwell 1989: 276–7.

4 Hargreaves (1996: 127n.) suggests a possible 'tactical withdrawal' here in relation to Nkrumah's earlier calls for 'complete and absolute independence'.

5 The other colonies represented in the National Assembly of the Third Republic (1875–1940) included the Antilles, Réunion, the Indian city-colonies (*Etablissements*), New Caledonia, Polynesia, and Cochinchina.

6 Ibid.: 111–12, 116–17. Together with four first-college senators, almost half of the SFIO's 37 senators represented overseas territories. The traditional title 'Senator' quickly replaced the official 'Councillor of the Republic'.

7 See Chapter 6. Chévigné's predecessor, who set the tone for the repression of the Malagasy insurgency, was the Socialist, Marcel de Coppet.

8 The Catholic *Abbé* Barthélémy Boganda (Oubangui-Chari); and Prince Douala Manga Bell (Cameroun, non-citizen's college), son of a chief killed in revolt against German rule. A third MRP *député*, Dr Louis Aujoulat, a liberal European mission doctor, represented the Cameroun first college.

9 In his March 1948 speech, already quoted, Houphouët had cited the example of the Malagasy *députés* in support of the *apparentement*, from which the MDRM had not benefited.

10 Hargreaves 1996: 83:

		S. Rhodesia	N. Rhodesia	Nyasaland
European population:	1938	61,000	13,000	1,900
	1946	83,000	22,000	2,000
	1950	129,000	36,000	4,000
African population:	1950	1,960,000	1,849,000	2,330,000

6

The Late Colonial State at War:
Insurgency, Emergency and Terror

– Mr Ben M'Hidi, do you not think it cowardly to use women to plant bombs carried in baskets to kill civilians?
– Give us your machineguns and planes, and we'll give you our bombs and baskets.[1]

No, torture is not indispensable in wartime, you could do without it very well. When I think about Algeria, I am very sorry, because torture was part of a certain ambiance. We could have done things differently.[2]

I must admit I don't like going on [record] saying such things but I think honestly if people said hearts and minds to me I simply said yuck.[3]

The black *askaris* were the ones doing the beatings, but they were being directed by the *Wazungu*.[4]

War in a variety of novel forms was a defining experience of the post-1945 crisis which eventually shook the colonial empires apart. This seems an unproblematic assertion where the French or Portuguese empires are concerned. In particular, France fought sustained wars in Vietnam and Algeria, and coverage of France's 'wars of decolonization' can embrace all of France's decolonization outside sub-Saharan Africa and the smaller island colonies of the Caribbean, the Indian Ocean and the Pacific (Clayton 1994). British decolonization reflects rather less the primacy of armed conflict, although British troops were engaged in action in every 'peacetime' year from 1945 to 1968, mostly in circumstances of colonial 'Emergency'.

The theme of war has often been displaced from the centre of accounts of decolonization. Regional studies of decolonization in, say, 1950s sub-Saharan Africa can give the impression of a process either embraced by more or less peaceful politics, or within an enduring 'steel frame' of colonial control. Moreover, as has been suggested, what is often meant by 'decolonization' is 'End of Empire', and taken as a whole, from the perspective of Westminster, Whitehall or Fleet Street, British decolonization was a largely peaceful process marred by occasional 'local difficulties', barely touching the lives of British constituents, taxpayers or newspaper readers in ways which may be compared with the French or Portuguese experience. It would have seemed absurd to suggest that British rulers might somehow be forced to leave by beleaguered Chinese communists in the forests of Malaya, poorly equipped and uncertainly motivated Mau Mau 'savages' or rioting Greek Cypriot teenagers intoxicated by dreams of *Enosis* (Union) with Greece.

More generally, coming so soon after the 'Total War' of 1939–1945, these typically small-scale, local conflicts could all too easily be buried under the 'greater' concerns of post-war reconstruction and the Cold War. Even France's larger-scale colonial wars swiftly followed its own Liberation from enemy occupation, so that war in Indochina and Algeria became inextricably bound up with still unreconciled memories of defeat and occupation, collaboration and resistance. This may help explain why the term 'war' was not officially used in France to designate the Algerian conflict, officially referred as 'operations for the maintenance of order in North Africa', until a French National Assembly vote in June 1999, 37 years after Algerian independence.[5]

Colonial wars were thus readily subsumed under official formulae for controlling disorder: Emergencies, police actions, Special Powers, and so on. This 'normalization' of colonial disorder was also abetted by the more misleading euphemisms of politicians and the media, such as 'events' (too bland), 'tragedy' (too preordained) or 'pacification' (too much the opposite of the truth).[6] Some of this imprecision arose initially from permissible confusion or vagueness. When do such wars begin, in the absence of a recognized declaration of war, or even of a clearly discernible set of combatants? Many colonial wars began well before colonial authorities recognized them as such – after all, rebellion and its repression were a deceptively 'normal' part of the life of the colonial state going all the way back to conquest. British Emergencies, by their very nature, were only declared in response to an already escalating conflict, and thus marked the highpoint of repression by colonial authorities, rather than its origin (Füredi 1994a: 149). Even the Algerian War followed this pattern, since full Special Powers, the equivalent of Emergency regulations, were passed by the Mollet government in March 1956, some 15 months after the FLN launched its insurrection on 1 November 1954; before then a 'state of emergency' was limited to designated zones (Branche 2001: 36–7). Conversely, for many historians, the Algerian War effectively began with the insurrections which broke out at Sétif and Guelma in Eastern Algeria on 8 May 1945, the very day of Victory in Europe (Jauffret 1990, 1994).

Neither was victory ever a foregone conclusion on either side. Thus, although Mau Mau was effectively militarily defeated within approximately two years of the declaration of Emergency in October 1952, the Emergency remained in force until 1959, and Mau Mau fighters remained in the forests until amnestied in 1961. Arguably the focus of battle had simply switched to the detention camps of the so-called 'Pipeline', Britain's own African Gulag (Elkins 2005; Anderson 2005), where consistently brutal and intermittently murderous efforts continued to 'rehabilitate' Mau Mau detainees. These efforts remained largely invisible to the outside world – that is, until the death of 11 'hard core' detainees at Hola Camp in March 1959 precipitated a major moral turning point in Britain's and Kenya's decolonization. The Algerian FLN also stared military defeat in the face in 1959–60, but the focus of the Algerian revolution had switched to the international stage and to negotiations with the French government, from which a settlement emerged far more favourable to the Algerian cause than the situation 'on the ground' might have suggested. Similarly, in only one of three Portuguese wars, in Guiné-Bissau, did insurgents come close to defeating the Portuguese colonial army. The military norm for these conflicts was stalemate, even if the political and diplomatic consequences of stalemate could be far more decisive. Mau Mau and Malayan communists alike continued to fight long after their cause was lost, in the latter case until the insurgent leader, Chin Peng, formally laid down his arms in 1989. Even so clear a victory as General Vo Nguyen Giap's, in the pitched battle of Dien Bien Phu in 1954, did not necessarily conclude France's long-drawn-out war in Vietnam: mercifully, Pierre Mendès-France's settlement at Geneva annulled his threat to resign, and to commit the conscript army to war before doing so.

This chapter will focus on two contrasting pairs of cases: Madagascar and Kenya; Algeria and Cyprus. In the background, a further pair which we have already considered, Malaya and Indochina, provided crucial experience of counter-insurgency and offered important lessons, although not necessarily the right ones. The match is perhaps closest between the first pair, where the colonial power found itself confronted with insurrections that could all too readily, but misleadingly, be characterized as 'primitive', in Madagascar and Kenya. The second pair, the Algerian War and the Emergency in Cyprus, have perhaps relatively little in common, except timing, but juxtaposition nonetheless reveals some striking parallels in the tactics and methods deployed on either side. Nowhere more than in these late colonial war zones do we need to maintain the idea of 'separate stories' leading to decolonization. And yet parallels may readily be drawn, and various common themes identified. Later in the chapter we draw some threads together by considering the conduct of these variously 'dirty' wars, and their impact on eventual decolonization.

Background and Origins of War

Why did these violent challenges to colonial order emerge when and where they did? As with earlier colonial revolts, disorder could be sparked by circumstances of particular material hardship, such as obtained across the colonized world towards the end of the Second World War. Famine was, as we have seen, a crucial factor in determining events in parts of India and in Northern Vietnam, and there were acute food shortages in 1944–5 in many parts of Africa, which thus form an important part of the background to the abortive Algerian insurrections in May 1945 and to the Malagasy insurrection. However, in neither of these latter cases was violence simply spontaneous. Rather, although insurgents escaped the control and direction of an overarching nationalist movement, violence was geared to a degree of political preparation and to heightened expectations of colonial concessions. In these cases of unplanned or, in the Malagasy case, nationally uncoordinated revolt, colonial armed forces seized the opportunity for wholesale repression, enthusiastically assisted, in Algeria, by vengeful settlers falling into the role they made all their own. The French general commanding operations in Algeria warned the government – as it turned out, quite accurately – that he had created 'peace for ten years', a breathing space which the colonial regime comprehensively wasted (Horne 1996: 28; Jauffret 1994). In Madagascar, repression cost the lives of tens of thousands of Malagasy, destroyed the principal nationalist party, the MDRM (Movement for the Democratic Renovation of Madagascar), and thus set back nationalist organization for the remainder of the colonial period and beyond.

A strong *prima facie* argument can be made linking disorder and violence to particularly acute contradictions in colonial social structures. Although, as has been argued, the late colonial 'official mind' sought to remake and rationalize aspects of colonial rule, colonial administrations faced particular problems arising from the presence of substantial ethnic minorities, or from a preponderance of European settlers. However, a distinction needs to be made between the background to violence and its immediate causes. As we have seen, for example, the Malayan Union policy, directed precisely to achieving a 'multi-racial' political solution for Malaya, had not excited much enthusiasm on the part of the Chinese and Indian communities who stood to gain from it, and the Malayan Communist Party's departure from its strategy of trades union entryism and radical industrial action was a direct response to the British *volte-face* (Chapter 4). On the other hand, as will be further argued below, the MCP's overwhelmingly predominant Chinese membership informed the course of the insurgency and its ultimate defeat. A similar distinction may also be made for Cyprus, where communal differences between the majority Greek population and the Turkish minority (constituting approximately 20 per cent of the total) formed an essential part of the landscape of British colonial rule, and where the eventual *casus belli*, constituted by the Greek Cypriot desire for *Enosis* with the Hellenic motherland, very obviously excluded Turkish minority rights. Even here, however, inter-communal relations were an eventual casualty of Greek violence rather than a proximate cause – indeed, Turkish communities and police officers were not initially targeted by Greek insurgents, and a violent Turkish response to the Greek campaign, in the form of riots and terrorism, only emerged almost three years into the Emergency, in 1958 (Anderson 1994).

Settlers presented colonial authorities with their most complex problems, and consistently forced the contradictions in the late colonial state to breaking point. Where a significant community of settlers existed, their interests formed the primary focus for policy making, out of all proportion to their number, even under 'peaceful' circumstances. Not only was the protection of settler interests a *sine qua non* in any proposed reformist programme, but settlers were also the most likely obstacle to its implementation. Where violent disorder erupted, insurgents often targeted settlers, their farms and plantations, clubs and businesses, sometimes their families. This was not usually the primary form of violence – and the victims of all these wars were overwhelmingly on the side of the colonized. For instance, more Europeans died in traffic accidents in Nairobi during the Emergency than the 32 killed by Mau Mau (Atieno Odhiambo & Lonsdale 2003: 3). Even so, settlers constituted a 'front line', as combatants or vigilantes, but also in arguing for a tough colonial response and in blocking compromise. Of the cases considered here, settler interests were a decisive factor affecting the course, duration and outcome of conflict everywhere except Cyprus (and, amongst the three main Portuguese dependencies, Guiné-Bissau), and to the list might also be added the conflicts in Morocco and Tunisia, and, of course, Rhodesia. In Algeria and Kenya, settler interests constituted a primary cause of insurrectionary violence, not only because of their presence, but also because they were able to block reforms under the terms of late colonial state building.

Post-war colonial reform or the lack of it was crucial in creating the conditions for the outbreak of colonial disorder, but this was far from the whole story. Many institutional factors led to that bloodiest of late colonial wars, in Algeria, such that conflict could only have been avoided with great difficulty; but this would leave out of account the political agency, the strategic genius, and a considerable measure of good fortune, of a small but determined vanguard, the 'nine historic' leaders of a new-minted organization, the FLN, which emerged from, and largely opposed, the main-stream nationalist movement. Conversely, we might ask why conflicts on the scale of those under consideration did not erupt elsewhere: why were there not *more* Mau Maus? There were certainly many instances, even amongst Kenyan ethnic groups other than the Kikuyu or, for example, in Southern Rhodesia, where insurrection was averted in ostensibly similar circumstances (Ogot 2003; Ranger 1985). Moderate nationalist politicians more or less consciously eschewed the all too likely bloodbath that would ensue from insurgency. Thus, as we have seen, Houphouët-Boigny helped steer Côte d'Ivoire away from the escalation of the violent 'events' of 1949. Similarly, Julius Nyerere felt obliged to promise that his Tanganyikan African National Union (TANU) would not commit 'things of the forest' – thus recognising British fears about Mau Mau, as well as the British savagery which such 'things' elicited (Iliffe 1979: 520).

Moreover, while colonial authorities used Emergencies as a robust means of polit-ical control, what was often missing was any fundamental intelligence of the precise nature of the challenges they faced, and violence was either unexpected or came from an unexpected quarter. And yet colonial authorities typically prepared for just such a challenge. Thus, British colonial administrations defined the scope of Emergency regulations – allowing a range of measures from the prolonged detention of suspects to the use of military force 'in support of the civil power' – well in advance of their being needed. Although the initiative for such pre-emptive measures lay with indi-vidual colonial governments, rather than with London, a profound sense of urgency may be detected on the part of officials in London in the wake of the series of crises which marked 1948 (Malaya, the Accra riots, but also the intensification of the Euro-pean Cold War); following this, officials in London and in the field agreed on the need to control, and perhaps even to pre-empt, disorder (Füredi 1994b). Indeed, colonial officials quite naturally regarded Emergency as the continuation of late colo-nial politics by other means. Parallels may thus be drawn between the cases considered here, and those where relations between officials and nationalists broke down almost completely, or where an Emergency was declared, for example British Guiana, but where insurgency was not on the cards (ibid.). More inchoately, the British feared 'another Mau Mau' in, for example, the Nyasaland Emergency of 1958, but were also perhaps frustrated when a similar movement could not be identified, and thereby easily repressed (ibid.; Darwin 1994; Chapter 8).

The Malagasy Insurrection

The 1947 Insurrection in Madagascar has sometimes been compared with that of Mau Mau (Cooper 1988), and that comparison will be developed here. Yet in one

significant respect the two insurgencies are very different, namely that, while Mau
Mau has become one of the most widely studied of anti-colonial movements, the
Malagasy insurgency remains one of the most obscure and mysterious, and in many
ways France's forgotten colonial war.

Two profound differences between the Malagasy and Mau Mau movements
become apparent immediately. First, much more than Mau Mau, the Malagasy insurgents placed themselves in a long line of resistance to colonial rule, going back fifty
years to the French conquest and annexation of 1895–6 (an anniversary marked in
August 1946 by a 'day of national mourning'), and defined their goal as national
liberation and restoration of national sovereignty. Fighting under the red-and-white
flag of the Malagasy monarchy, emblazoned with 18 stars representing the united
'peoples' of Madagascar, they would have had no difficulty in conceiving their struggle
in terms of a national 'imagined community'. The insurrection thus followed in the
footsteps of the 1896 rebellion of the Menalamba, or 'Red Shawls', but also of the
shadowy VVS revolt of 1915 (*vy vato sakelika*, or fire, stone, branching), whose members included two of the three Malagasy *députés* in 1946–7 (Ellis 1986; Tronchon
1986). A legacy of more immediate importance was that of the somewhat unorthodox
PCRM (Communist Party of the Region of Madagascar) of the interwar period, which
formed the networks of support for the nationalist party founded in February 1946,
the MDRM (Shipway 1996b). The PCRM also supplied the personnel and organizational principle for the secret societies which spearheaded the insurrection,
principally the PA.NA.MA. (Malagasy National Party) which before 1947 fused
with Jina, whose name evokes the sacred nature of the oath of loyalty – immediately
conjuring up parallels with Mau Mau (Tronchon 1986: 159).

Although post-war liberal officials initially kept an open mind on Madagascar,
which was sometimes identified as one country which might be considered as having
acquired the 'political personality' necessary for eventual autonomous status within
the French Union (Chapter 4), the thesis of national unity was discounted in favour
of an official version of Malagasy history, in which France had liberated the oppressed
Malagasy 'coastal peoples' from the 'imperialism' of the Merina kingdom; this found
political expression, against the background of worsening political disorder in
Madagascar up to March 1947, in official encouragement (to put it no more strongly
than that) given to a new Party of the Malagasy Disinherited (PA.DES.M.), whose
candidates split the nationalist vote in territorial elections held in early 1947,
and whose members were often targeted by insurgents (Shipway 1996b; Delval 1986;
Chapter 2).

The second fundamental point of difference with Mau Mau arose from the
fact that the Malagasy Insurrection was meticulously planned *as* an insurrection in
support of a national cause. The launch of simultaneous attacks island-wide across
Madagascar, during the night of 29–30 March 1947, developed to full-blown insurrection only as planned on the forested Eastern side of the island, for insurgents
lacked arms and men, and, as in 1896, only the East offered suitable terrain. At its
greatest extent at the end of July 1947, the insurrection under its two commanders,
'Marshal of the Malagasy Armies' Victor Razafindrabe and 'Inspector-General of
Armies' Michel Radaoroson, covered most of the south-east, controlling a population
of 1.6 million composed of ten different ethnic groups, and had cut off the capital,

Tananarive (Tronchon 1986; Clayton 1994: 83). Insurrection thus provoked a French military response in a far clearer causal chain than was, as we shall see, the case for Mau Mau.

The relationship between insurgents and the 'legitimate' nationalist movement is also crucial, but ambiguous. The lifting of the parliamentary immunity of the three Malagasy *députés*, and their condemnation as instigators of the insurrection after a virtual show trial in Tananarive, was based on no less self-serving a case than the British arrest and prosecution of Kenyatta and other KAU leaders for implication in Mau Mau. Indeed, the French case rested on the evidence of a telegram sent on 27 March by two of the three, Joseph Ravoahangy and Jacques Rabemananjara, signing for the third, Joseph Raseta (who was in France), to MDRM political bureaux across the island, warning against precipitate action: although they had got wind of the planned attacks, the telegram was almost certainly not, as the French authorities alleged, a coded message launching the insurrection (unless 'no' meant 'yes'). Rather, the three men were highly critical of the insurrection, just as Kenyatta was consistently critical of Mau Mau for criminal irresponsibility. The truth was no doubt more complex than the French allowed, and the *députés* were arguably 'guilty', but not as charged. Quite apart from perhaps justifiable French suspicion that MDRM leaders 'protested too much', and the fact that the MDRM, quickly banned, was heavily infiltrated by the secret societies (which were also banned), the three *députés*, two of whom, Raseta and Ravoahangy, were veterans of the national cause enjoying immense prestige at home, could be seen as playing a risky double political game. As *députés* in the French National Assembly, they were elected representatives of the 'One and Indivisible Republic' participating in the already somewhat tarnished imperial project of the French Union. However, by regarding themselves, and portraying themselves to their electorates, as ambassadors, consorting with 'heads of state', notably Ho Chi Minh, during his sojourn in Paris over the Summer 1946 (Tronchon 1986: 335–7), and pleading the self-evident justice of the Malagasy national cause, they not only quickly exhausted the limited reserves of French official liberalism, but also risked raising unrealistic political expectations at home. The thinking behind the insurrection may be seen in this light as partly encouragement for the *députés*' Parisian campaign, partly the articulation of disappointment that they were achieving so little. Here, as elsewhere, violent subaltern revolt was thus the expression of profound disillusion with the caution of revered elders.

One final point of comparison between the Malagasy and Mau Mau insurgencies is that, while both presented the colonial forces ranged against them with a prolonged military challenge, in neither case was the outcome, in purely military terms, ever in doubt. By the end of 1947, the French army had tripled military forces on Madagascar to 18,000 men, including detachments of the Foreign Legion and substantial numbers of *tirailleurs sénégalais*, whose reputed ruthlessness (just like that of other colonial levies) gave colonial authorities an unspoken alibi against charges of brutality.[7] Outgunned and overwhelmed, and starved of the Anglo-American intervention on which insurgents pinned their hopes with almost millennial fervour, the insurrection was crushed almost completely by the end of 1948.[8] The cost of this 'pacification' may be counted in the tens of thousands of Malagasy who lost their lives, many of them women and children, driven from rebel villages by soldiers, who perished from 'physiological wretchedness' (Tronchon 1986: 71–4).[9] Thus, swift and brutal military action in effect closed the chapter of Malagasy Insurrection, and Madagascar became in many ways the docile member of the French Union that France expected.

Mau Mau

Unlike 'poor white' Algerian *pieds noirs*, Kenyan white farmers cultivating the fertile, so-called White Highlands conformed closely to the archetypal vision of European settlerdom – indeed they were largely the begetters of the archetype, although it is their socio-economic role which interests us here, rather than the associated myths of gin-soaked expatriate aristocrats indulging in adulterous 'white mischief'. As farmers, they were close to one source of tension which led to Mau Mau amongst Kenya's dominant ethnic group, the Kikuyu (constituting some 20 per cent of the Kenyan population). Although only a tiny part of European-farmed land in central Kenya was taken from ancestral Kikuyu lands, by the mid-1940s the Highlands had long been home to large numbers of Kikuyu 'squatters' who had moved onto land left uncultivated by under-resourced Europeans. These tenants provided a reservoir of casual labour on white farms, in return for which they gained grazing rights and the sense of a new homeland, which Kikuyu pioneers felt belonged to them more fully than it had to the 'wasteful' Maasai from whom the land had been taken (Lonsdale 1990: 407n.). However, this informal *quid pro quo* rapidly turned into an exercise in colonial control, as interwar legislation curbed Kikuyu grazing and introduced onerous contour-terracing (courtesy of African labour) designed to promote soil conservation (Anderson 1984). What for squatters in the 1930s was the 'sweeping of a broom' had by the mid-1940s become a whirlwind of change (Cooper 1988: 318). As settlers sought to extend their farms on the back of wartime profits, squatters were forced into demeaning contracts as wage-labourers, or expelled from their land, whence they drifted either to the crowded Kikuyu reserves, to Nairobi, or to a marginal existence between the two. This harsh campaign, which contributed directly to Kikuyu radicalization, was driven by the interests of newly confident settlers, backed by the robustly conservative Governor Philip Mitchell. However, settlers' efforts squared readily with the 'fantasies' of rational, ordered economic and social development emanating from London in this period. In short, this was the 'second colonial occupation' writ large, and indeed the prototype of the concept (Low & Lonsdale 1976).

In Kenya, as in Algeria, the alliance of settlers and a conservative administration also served to block effective political reform. In 1944, the first African, Eliud Mathu, a witchdoctor's son who had studied at Fort Hare in South Africa and Balliol College, Oxford, was nominated to the Legislative Council, but the Kenyan African Union, which was formed around him, was left in the cold, and when Jomo Kenyatta returned to Kenya from London in 1946, he was denied a political role in the colony: keeping the settlers on side meant that Governor Mitchell could ill afford to 'associate too closely with African populists' (Hargreaves 1996: 141). The Kikuyu Central Association (KCA), which might have constituted a legitimate outlet for Kikuyu grievances, had been banned in 1940, and its subsequent clandestine operations included the spread of the oathing which was to be such a central feature of Mau Mau's

activities, and a focus for the repulsed fascination of Europeans. When Kenyatta
arrived in Nairobi, he was briefed by KCA members on the organization's readiness,
but riposted that what was now at stake was a struggle, not for Kikuyu rights but for
national independence. However, over the few years to the declaration of the Emergency, with Kenyatta's energies effectively contained by the growing crisis amongst
the Kikuyu, KAU's national project made little headway, failing in its dual objectives
of developing KAU into 'an effective constitutional instrument', and uniting Kenyans
(Ogot 2003: 18). There were nonetheless signs that its influence was spreading outside
Kikuyuland, and after the arrest of KAU's Kikuyu leaders following the declaration of
the Emergency in October 1952, the party was able to struggle on with a new executive
led by a brave Legislative Councillor for the Nyanza province of Western Kenya, Odede
Rachilo. Odede too was arrested in March 1953, and on 8 June 1953, KAU was finally
banned as an alleged front for a terrorist organization (ibid.: 20–1). Indeed, by extending the ban to all political organizations, the Kenya government had effectively reset
Kenyan national politics to zero, and when the ban was partially rescinded two years
later, only parties with a strictly regional focus were allowed registration.

It is easier to define categories to which Mau Mau did *not* belong than to explain
what it was. As already suggested, it was *not* a planned insurrection in support of a
national cause; indeed it was *not* in any clear sense a nationalist movement, as it did
not – at least not yet – have a 'national' following within Kenya. Mau Mau did not
have the monopoly within post-war Kenya of determined and even violent resistance
to colonial pressures. Nonetheless, many other groups had found a tolerable *modus
vivendi* within Kenya's political geography at this period (Lonsdale 2003: 52–5). Conversely, Mau Mau was not as exclusively Kikuyu-centred as the British might have
liked to believe: there were many non-Kikuyu amongst Mau Mau gangs, particularly
those recruited from Nairobi; significantly, of the 11 who died at Hola camp, one
was a Turkana (Anderson 2003; Atieno Odhiambo 1995: 40). Nor did Mau Mau seek
at first to overthrow the colonial state, and it never developed the momentum to do
so. And it was *not*, as the British alleged, the brainchild of the 'leader to darkness and
death' (so described by one British governor as late as 1960), Jomo Kenyatta, Kikuyu
elder and 'African intellectual', whose anthropological training at the London School
of Economics might have inspired (but did not) the various oathing ceremonies
which bound Kikuyu to the cause. It was certainly *not* the atavistic return to tribal
barbarism portrayed by the settlers and the British media. It was not even called Mau
Mau, except by its opponents, although what they meant by it remains a matter of
conjecture: was it simply 'something larger than' KAU (the Kenyan African Union),
since *ma* in Swahili is an amplifying prefix, *ka* a diminutive, or were Mau Mau the
'greedy eaters', warriors who raided their own neighbourhoods in times of hunger
(Lonsdale 1990: 393n.; 2003: 60)? The latter explanation expresses disapproval,
but also the recognition that Mau Mau were not solely to blame. The rebels' name
for themselves, the Land and Freedom Army, is more helpful still: '*ithaka na wiathi*'
may be translated as 'land and freedom', but this should be understood as '"land
and moral responsibility" or "freedom through land", the highest civic virtue of
Kikuyu elderhood' (Lonsdale 1990: 416n.). Thus Mau Mau was the attempt – or
rather several overlapping and sometimes contradictory attempts – to work out a
profound crisis in Kikuyu society, as various groups within that society, such as

dispossessed squatters, land-hungry migrant workers and the 'Forty Group' in Nairobi (that is, the borderline-criminal gangs of young Kikuyu men initiated in 1940, or who claimed to have been so), found that they were excluded from the carefully bounded religious and moral order which determined land ownership, marriage and hence personal self-determination. The Mau Mau oaths were a transgression of this order, since they were taken by juniors in defiance of their elders, or by men and women together, but transgression had been forced upon the oath-takers by the upheavals of colonial society, and indeed the oaths typically expressed longing for a return to order (Peterson 2003). It was an increasingly widespread transgression: at an early stage of the Emergency, British officials estimated that as many as 90 per cent of the 1.5 million Kikuyu had taken at least one Mau Mau oath (Elkins 2003: 192).

British actions following the Declaration of Emergency shaped the Mau Mau insurgency more decisively than was the case in other late colonial wars. Before then, Mau Mau was 'the partisan sector of a crowded arena' (Lonsdale 2003: 60). Although many Kikuyu oath-takers eschewed violence, the movement was developing into one of widespread political protest and disorder, cattle-maiming and attacks on property, as well as the murder of 'loyalist' chiefs, informers, police and the occasional European. At a mass meeting in July 1952, Jomo Kenyatta warned against 'criminality', and Senior Chief Nderi reassured his jeering listeners that 'Our Government knows that you are hungry and it will feed you'. Three months later, Nderi was murdered by Mau Mau (ibid.: 59). The murder of another loyalist, Senior Chief Waruhiu, pushed a new governor, Sir Evelyn Baring, to respond to settler pressure by declaring an Emergency on 20 October 1952, and by rounding up Kenyatta and other KAU and 'known' Mau Mau leaders. Far from decapitating Mau Mau, these arrests apparently persuaded many Kikuyu that violence was now respectable, while the indiscriminate and often brutal 'screening' of suspected Mau Mau drove many to take the oath. Kikuyu squatters were now expelled *en masse* from the White Highlands, and migrant workers were 'repatriated' to the Kikuyu reserves from all over Kenya and East Africa, via unsanitary 'transit camps' (Elkins 2003). As Kenya turned into an increasingly totalitarian state, more and more young Kikuyu, men and women, took to the forests of Mount Kenya and the Aberdares, where the Land and Freedom Army, some 20,000 strong at its height, took the Mau Mau war into a new phase.

Although it took British forces some time to marshal resources, poorly equipped Mau Mau fighters in the forest, like the Malagasy insurgents before them, were no match for search-and-destroy missions and air raids on their forest strongholds. In the reserves, meanwhile, the war was transformed into a civil war, as a Home Guard was recruited from Kikuyu 'loyalists', and a radical 'villagization' programme implemented, by which, within the space of 18 months from June 1954, more than a million Kikuyu were resettled in 800 or so new villages, brutally policed by the Home Guard, fortified and defended against Mau Mau insurgents, who could thus neither raid villages nor take supplies from their fellow Kikuyu (Elkins 2005: 233–65 & passim). Thus, the Mau Mau war was not simply 'over' when the forest war was considered won, and the military effort scaled down, in early 1956. The remaining Mau Mau gangs, numbering perhaps 1,500, continued to fight beyond the end of the Emergency in January 1960, until they were amnestied in 1961. After all, part of the problem of 'terrorism' is precisely the challenge it offers to the state's 'monopoly of legitimate violence': arguably, the problem posed by *any* resistance to colonial rule was made more acute under the conditions of 'late colonial' rule. Moreover, it was now that many of Mau Mau's myths became entrenched, and an engaging picture emerges of a utopian counter-society. This was partly to compensate for the lost world left behind, since a landless young Kikuyu was even further from marriage and elder status in the depths of the forest; but partly it constituted a kind of nationalist utopia, appealing to other peoples across Kenya, mirroring the institutions of the colonial state, sometimes playfully. When Field Marshal Dedan Kimathi, Knight Commander of the East African Empire, and Prime Minister of the Kenya African Government which he created in the Aberdares in 1955, corresponded with the colonial administration, he gave a forest 'post office' as his return address (Peterson 2003: 88–93; Lonsdale 2003: 60f.). Learning that the security forces did not have a photograph of him, Kimathi had one hand-delivered to a British camp (Anderson 2005: facing 279).[10] Secondly, and more significantly for the future of the late colonial state in Kenya, the focus of the war simply switched from the military to the civil sphere, particularly after Operation 'Anvil', in April–May 1954. Arguably the single most decisive action of the whole war, this was the round-up of all young Kikuyu men in Nairobi – or, rather, of the entire male population of Nairobi, from whom the Kikuyu were identified via the hated pass system (*kipande*), and, apart from a minority with secure employment or lodging, either detained as potential Mau Mau, or 'deported' back to the already crowded Kikuyu reserves (ibid.: 200–12; Elkins 2005: 121–5). This was less a triumph of late colonial control than an implicit admission of the limits of that control, since an entire group was thus effectively criminalized on the basis of their ethnic affiliation. Operation Anvil drained the reservoir of recruits to the forest forces, but also massively multiplied the scale of the task facing the British. For, whereas the insurgency numbered perhaps 20,000, from this point on the Kenya civil administration confronted a potential enemy composed of tens of thousands of detainees destined for 'rehabilitation' (that is, brutalization within the camp system of the Pipeline), and, more widely, of the estimated 90 per cent of 1.5 million Kikuyu who had taken at least one Mau Mau oath. This was indeed a battle for 'hearts and minds', and a savage one, conducted behind the barbed wire of the detention camps and the watchtowers of the villagization programme, to which we return in the final section of this chapter.

The Algerian War to 1958

When the FLN launched its insurrection on 1 November 1954, accompanied by a grandiose Proclamation promising to restore 'the sovereign, democratic and social Algerian state within the framework of Islamic principles', it was as if a brand-new national movement had leapt fully formed into the Algerian arena ('Proclamation du FLN', 1 November 1954, Eveno & Planchais 1989: 83–6). Overnight, about thirty attacks were launched across Algeria, concentrated in the same Eastern region that had seen the 1945 Sétif and Guelma risings, and in the remote Aurès mountains.[11] French authorities were caught unawares, since police had largely discounted rumours of impending violence; a recent tour by François Mitterrand, Pierre Mendès-France's

Interior Minister, had not identified immediate security concerns. The bold message of a 'national Movement reach[ing] its final phase of realization', and of international solidarity, with neighbouring Morocco and Tunisia poised to achieve independence, barely outweighed the frustration of a nationalist cause 'floored by years of immobilism and routine, badly oriented, deprived of the indispensable backing of public opinion, overtaken by events, crumbling . . .'. This was a clean break, but also a culmination point of political engagement and of struggle for its leaders. All of the 'nine historic' FLN leaders, average age 32, were seasoned players in the tortuous politics of Messali Hadj's MTLD (Movement for the Triumph of Democratic Freedoms, so called since 1946), all were outlaws or former inmates of French gaols, or both. What started as a poorly equipped insurgency – largely dependent on mountain *maquisard* forces toting hunting rifles – needed time, organization, and, not least, good fortune, to bring its limited means into alignment with its stated end-goal of national liberation.

The FLN's rise needs placing in the context of, first, French post-1945 policy and, secondly, the Algerian nationalist movement. Reformism in Algeria aimed, as else-where, to rationalize French rule, in the face of wartime shortages, rising popular unrest and the harassment of nationalists, including even the moderate, urbane, middle-class and francophone (in a word, 'safe') Ferhat Abbas. The wartime Gaullist regime, based in Algiers from 1943 until after the Liberation of Paris, had made a promising start with a bold set of reforms proposed in 1944, in response to Abbas's 1943 'Manifesto of the Algerian People', which called for an autonomous Algeria within a federal imperial structure (Pervillé 1986). However, tracing the same trajectory as the French Union articles in the constitution-making process of 1945–6 (Chapter 5), the Algerian reformist programme was compromised by the drift to the Right in French politics. The 1947 Algerian Statute, opposed even by moderate Algerian *députés*, was thus unremarkably ambitious, proposing a uniform system of local administration to replace the *communes mixtes* (under direct administration, outside areas of European settlement); recognition of Arabic as an official language alongside French; the separation of Islam and the state on the Republican model of '*laïcité*'; the extension of civilian administration to the Saharan territories; and suffrage for Algerian women (two years after Frenchwomen had first voted) (Droz & Lever 1991: 33–5; Horne 1996: 69–70). The problem lay not so much in the Statute's text as in its application. Overseeing this proposed legislative programme was a new Algerian Assembly, whose double electoral college ensured numerically equal representation of both communities; effectively, one European vote was worth eight Algerian.[12] Not content with this balance, the new Socialist Governor-General, Marcel-Edmond Naegelen – who equated Algerian nationalism with wartime separatism in his native Alsace – sought to delay elections. When the first round, in April 1948, indicated 95 per cent second-college support for the MTLD, officials stepped in with a wide repertoire of election-rigging techniques. The staggering final result was nine seats for the MTLD, eight for Ferhat Abbas's moderate UDMA (Democratic Union of the Algerian Manifesto), two for the SFIO, and 41 for 'official' candidates, dismissed by nationalists as '*beni-oui-oui*' (yes-men). Consequently, by 1954, virtually none of the Statute's proposed reforms had been enacted (Chenntouf 1986). Its terms were largely reproduced in the 1957 Framework Law (thrown out as dangerously liberal) and in a watered-down version in early 1958, quickly rendered obsolete by de Gaulle's return to power in May 1958. The Algerian Assembly further lost legitimacy when it was boycotted from the outset by the MTLD, and eventually, from late 1955, by the UDMA. The Statute's failure did not make insurrection inevitable, nor did persistent harassment of both major parties, but it deprived Algerian nationalist aspirations of any conceivable legal outlet.

The roots of insurrection were firmly in the MTLD, and yet in many ways the FLN was the opposite of its parent organization, tracing its origins to the clandestine Special Organization (OS), formed in early 1947 within the MTLD, in order to prepare insurrection. The OS, masterminded by Ahmed Ben Bella and Hocine Aït Ahmed, set to work forming *maquis* and raising funds through armed robbery (Oran's main post office was raided in 1950). It was broken up by effective French intelligence in 1950, and those OS members who eluded capture, or who escaped from gaol, either fled the country or took to the mountains. While the MTLD enjoyed its leader's immense prestige, particularly amongst migrant Algerian workers in France, younger, middle-class militants criticized Messali's autocratic but directionless leadership. With Messali under house arrest in France, in early 1953, 'Messalistes' split from a new central committee, inclined to ally with the rival UDMA. In March 1954, former OS leaders, with some disgruntled 'centralistes', formed the CRUA (Revolutionary Committee for Unity and Action), which prepared the insurrection and negotiated inconclusively with President Nasser of Egypt. The CRUA dissolved to form the FLN immediately prior to the insurrection (Droz & Lever 1991: 49–54; Horne 1996: 74–9). Unlike the MTLD, the FLN insisted on collective leadership, initially of the 'nine', backed by a 'committee of twenty-two', thus improving the party's chance of survival in case of an individual's capture or death.[13] The 'nine' also represented all possible tendencies: francophone middle-class townsmen and peasants from the Aurès; representatives from most Algerian regions; and, crucially, both Arabs and Berbers, although this fault line had already caused fractures within the MTLD, and would do so in the FLN, and for that matter in independent Algeria. Over time, collective leadership also accommodated the ever-widening split, exacerbated by the French Army, between the military leaders of the ALN (National Liberation Army) and an 'external' leadership operating in Tunis, Cairo and New York.

In its first ten months or so, the insurrection could easily have become one of so many localized, inconclusive and defeated colonial revolts in Algeria and beyond. The first night was dismal indeed – eight dead, including (against standing orders and ostensibly by accident) the first French civilian, four wounded, various damage – but the coordinated attacks and the appearance of tracts bearing the Proclamation impressed French officials. Over the winter, the insurrection stayed largely contained within the Aurès, spreading in early 1955 to Kabylie, the poor mountainous home of the Berber Kabyles and principal source of Algerian migrant labour. Starved of aid promised by Nasser, the insurrection's survival was assisted by clumsy French tactics. These included banning the MTLD and arresting its leaders, many of whom joined the FLN on their release; armoured patrols and laborious sweeps of the mountains which failed to locate, much less to destroy, small bands of hungry, ill-equipped ALN; and aerial bombardment of 'suspect' villages, including the unauthorized use of napalm. The first reports of torture in Algeria date from this period; so too do the first protests by French intellectuals (Bourdet 1955; Mauriac 1955; Branche 2001: 32–3).

The ALN's own terror tactics, such as the theatrical murder and horrific mutilation of *caïds* and village policemen, and other 'collaborators', played into the hands of colonial propaganda just as surely as did Mau Mau oaths and massacres. Meanwhile, through early 1955, contacts were maintained between the FLN and Mendès-France's Governor-General, Jacques Soustelle, an anthropologist specializing in pre-Columbian Mexico, chosen as a dynamic 'outsider' with impeccable liberal credentials.

One event crystallized the revolution into something new and irreversible. On 20–1 August 1955, in a re-run of the events at Sétif and Guelma ten years before, but this time coordinated by a national leadership, raids by uniformed ALN detachments on police stations and other public property were combined with widespread and savage violence by a 'mobilized' peasant *jacquerie*, which left 123 dead, including 71 Europeans. The Army's swift intervention curbed the insurrection's momentum, but, as in 1945, the *colons*' retaliation was massively disproportionate, and was only alleviated by Army protection of non-combatant Algerians. Officially, 1,273 were killed in reprisals, but according to the FLN's own enquiry, never seriously discredited, the number was nearer 12,000 (Droz & Lever 1991: 77). Although the Governor-General's floral tributes to the European dead were trampled by enraged *pieds noirs* in the Philippeville cemetery, Soustelle's own personal conversion now began, from promoter of Algerian 'integration' to die-hard champion of '*Algérie Française*'. In February 1956, replaced by Guy Mollet's incoming Socialist-led government, he was accorded a farewell 'Roman triumph' through the streets of Algiers (ibid.: 80).

The August 1955 insurrection demonstrated the FLN's capacity to mobilize mass support, but at terrible cost in lives and in its credibility as a 'rational' nationalist movement. With the gulf that now widened between Algerians and *pieds noirs*, this was perhaps the 'point of no return' in this most absolute of colonial struggles. It also comprised a calculated message to a major nationalist rival, since the Constantinois was the UDMA's stronghold and Ferhat Abbas's home region; indeed, in a calculated outrage, his nephew was murdered, '*pour encourager les autres*', in the family pharmacy in Constantine. This odious gesture was probably redundant, since Ferhat Abbas was already discussing a mooted alliance with the FLN; this came into effect in early 1956, after UDMA representatives resigned from the Algerian Assembly. January 1956 also saw agreement between the FLN and the Association of the Ulemas, which published a manifesto calling for Algerian national independence. Meanwhile, the Algerian Communist Party (PCA), run like its 'big sister' the PCF by working class and intellectual Europeans, had made common cause with the FLN, and had thus been dissolved by Soustelle in September 1955. PCA militants formed independent *maquis* groups, but in June 1956 the FLN refused a common front organization (emulating the wartime French Resistance) and PCA members were absorbed into FLN structures, largely sidelined and sometimes betrayed (ibid.: 83, 106).

With the path to national unity thus mapped out, there remained only the problem of Messali's party, banned in November 1954, and reconstituted as the hubristically named Algerian National Movement (MNA) in December. By 1956, rivalry between MNA and FLN was turning into civil war, as the MNA pushed out of Algiers to establish guerrilla groups in Kabylie, challenging Belkacem Krim's grip on this region. Gradually, MNA forces were pushed further south towards the Sahara, where the French army tolerated them as a sign of fracture in the national movement. It was here, on the southern borders of Kabylie, that the FLN committed one of its most infamous atrocities, the massacre of almost 400 male villagers in the Melouza district, who had refused to declare for the FLN, on 28 May 1957 (ibid.: 107). The self-styled 'general' of a 'National Army of the Algerian People', Mohamed Bellounis, regrouped his remaining forces in the Southern Territories, which attracted FLN interest following the discovery of Saharan crude oil in 1957. Bizarrely, Bellounis received French military aid, and some interest from the French media,[14] in return for vigorous resistance of FLN incursions; but Bellounis became an uncomfortable ally, and he and his troops were liquidated by French paratroops in July 1958 (Droz & Lever 1991: 108). In Paris and other French cities, where Algerian workers and shopkeepers, traditionally loyal to Messali, were lucrative sources of FLN 'taxation', the battle for influence was just beginning in 1956; once underway, this vicious urban civil war-cum-gang war continued almost until the bitter end, overseen by police and the thuggish paramilitary CRS (Republican Security Brigades). As late as October 1961, when the Paris police massacred several dozen Algerians who were demonstrating peacefully against a police-imposed curfew, it was still just about plausible that the dead bodies found floating in the Seine were the result of a fratricidal 'settling of accounts', as claimed by the then Prefect of Police, Maurice Papon.[15]

With national coordination came internal consolidation. In August 1956, FLN leaders held a twenty-day conference in the Soummam Valley in Kabylie, under the noses of the French army. This was the brainchild of an increasingly dominant leader, Abbane Ramdane, a Kabyle PPA/MTLD veteran, gaoled and tortured in 1950, who had joined the FLN on leaving prison in January 1955. The conference reaffirmed the FLN's collective leadership, while asserting two fundamental principles: the primacy of political over military action; and that of the interior over the exterior. The first of these was designed to dissuade military commanders from acting as independent warlords (a tendency reflected in the Constantinois insurrection). Conversely, privileging the interior undermined the 'nine', most of whom were now based abroad; indeed, Ben Bella and other external leaders were 'accidentally on purpose' prevented from attending. The conference reorganized the six *wilayas* (districts) covering Algerian territory, subdividing them into zones, regions and sectors, and established an Algiers Autonomous Zone (ZAA), commanded by Larbi Ben M'Hidi. It also created a new command structure, with a five-man Committee of Coordination and Execution (CCE), based in Algiers, answering to a National Council of the Algerian Revolution (CNRA) of 34 members, in whom Algerian sovereignty was vested pending independence from France. In effect, the FLN's revolutionary project was that of a 'counter-state', ready to replace the colonial state, rather than the usual anti-colonial nationalist strategy of the 'counter-society', designed to take over an existing state (Harbi 1980: 178; Droz & Lever 1991: 116–22, Horne 1996: 143–6).

French Algerian policy also shifted radically during 1956, although the direction of this shift was not necessarily predictable from the formation of a left-wing government, led by the Socialist Guy Mollet and including Mendès-France, following legislative elections in January. Mollet was committed to negotiation, and his government included a new Minister-Resident for Algeria, General Georges Catroux, a distinguished Gaullist 'proconsul' (Governor-General of Indochina in 1940) who had played a key role in negotiating Morocco's independence. However, when Mollet visited Algiers on 6 February, although he withstood the *pieds noirs*' orchestrated fury, he apparently distinguished the egg- and tomato-throwers from the *colons* of socialist stereotype. This epiphany led to his requesting Catroux's resignation, a striking success for *pied noir* street politics which was to be re-enacted with diminishing returns over the following six years. Catroux's replacement, Robert Lacoste, a technocrat with no Algerian baggage, rapidly devised a bill granting the government wide-ranging Special Powers, which was approved in March by almost all political parties, including the communists. Although the bill included a far-reaching programme of economic, administrative and military reform, the core of Mollet's Algerian policy was his deployment of the conscript army. By calling up recent year-classes of reservists (who had completed national service) and extending conscription to 27 months, the army quintupled its strength in Algeria to 450,000 by end 1957, a figure which remained constant until 1962. This transformed the war on the ground, but also – literally – brought home its significance to ordinary French citizens, many of whom protested as their sons' troop trains left for embarkation at Marseille. Mendès-France resigned in May when he felt that the balance of ministerial opinion had tipped against negotiation. Although desultory contacts were maintained with the FLN over the summer, this route was definitively barred by a reckless act of piracy. On 22 October, the French pilot of a Moroccan DC3 airliner flying from Rabat to Tunis, carrying four of the 'nine' historic leaders under the Sultan of Morocco's protection, was persuaded to land at Algiers, where its passengers were arrested. Although Mollet was not party to the plot, he acquiesced in it in the face of widespread French public approval (Droz & Lever 1991: 86–95, 101–2).

Mollet was, however, wholeheartedly involved in the Franco-Anglo-Israeli collusion which led to the ill-fated Suez expedition. This too was the work of an inner clique of ministers and generals, bypassing the niceties of cabinet government and parliamentary approval (Thomas 2000a: 120–1). Whereas for the British, the attack on Suez may be viewed as a misbegotten bid to stem imperial decline or to shore up Britain's regional presence, for the French the expedition's priority was 'Algeria, Algeria and Algeria' (ibid.: 125; Shlaim 1997: 514). The generals' motto, '*Algérie 1956 Capitale Suez*' (in Thomas 2000a: 211), held a grain of truth, as the ALN were being armed by Nasser, and the FLN had been appealing to Nasser's pan-Arabism since 1954. The miscalculation was to suppose that the FLN depended on this material and ideological support, and that a bold 'strike at the head' would bring the FLN's collapse; meanwhile France would exorcize the ghosts associated with a 'Munich syndrome' (which had some kinship with the demons haunting British Prime Minister, Anthony Eden). Furthermore, just as Algeria determined Suez, so also the expedition's failure impacted on the French military outlook in Algeria: the paratroops who spearheaded the French attack had been stationed in Algeria and returned there embittered and convinced of their government's spinelessness (ibid.: 124, 127–9). Their next mission, also under the command of Colonel Jacques Massu was in the grimier policing role forced upon them in the Battle of Algiers.

In different ways, therefore, the Soummam Conference and the Suez expedition set the stage for the war's next phase. The focus now shifted from the countryside, where it went unappreciated by international opinion, to the capital, where the FLN could visibly assert itself as sole representative of the Algerian people. Algiers was not

Stalingrad, and the battle fought there was hardly warlike (Droz & Lever 1991: 126–7). Rather, it consisted of an ever more random series of terrorist bombings and murders, countered by *pied noir* reprisals, and by an effective exercise in intelligence gathering by Massu's paras – also morally abhorrent given its reliance on torture. Pontecorvo (1965) renders all of this grippingly, including the *pied noir* extremists' bombing of the Casbah on 10 August 1956, and the first bombings of European civilian targets, on 30 September, carried out by women activists, Djamila Bouhired, Samia Lakhdi and Zohra Drif (Eveno & Planchais 1989: 113–16). Portrayed as a heroic defeat by Pontecorvo (and by his co-producer, Saadi Yacef, playing himself under his *nom de guerre*, Djafaar), the Battle of Algiers was a largely unmitigated disaster for the FLN. At the heart of the new strategy, the general strike, in January 1957, was successfully broken by tactics which the British had never dared use against Indian *hartals*: forcing Algerian shopkeepers to do business by tearing down their shutters, driving dockers to work at gunpoint, and so on. Within three months of Massu's assumption of police powers, on 7 January 1957, the Casbah was encircled, its inhabitants screened, most of the ZAA's 5,000 or so militants killed, captured, tortured, 'turned' as informers, or fled, its weapons and explosives mostly captured, its network largely destroyed. With the number of attacks reduced from 112 in January to 29 in March, the first phase of the battle was over. Ben M'Hidi's accidental capture, on 17 February, deprived the FLN of a capable leader, the eighth of the 'nine' to be eliminated, but also persuaded the CCE to flee the capital to Tunis. Saadi, who assumed command of the ZAA, evaded capture until June 1957, and survived captivity, his death sentence commuted by de Gaulle to life imprisonment. The definitive end of the battle came with the death of Saadi's formidable lieutenant, Ali-la-Pointe, betrayed by an informer, blown up when French charges designed to expose his hideout detonated cached explosives, on 8 October 1957 (Droz & Lever 1991: 127–32; Horne 1996: 183–218). One additional victim of the battle was Abbane, whose grip on FLN strategy was broken at a CNRA meeting in Cairo, in August 1957. In December, after an acrimonious fight back, Abbane was lured into a trap in Morocco, and strangled, perhaps personally, by one of the *wilaya* commanders (Droz & Lever 1991: 122–4).

By the end of 1957, the FLN leadership had been driven from Algeria, while the ALN was pinned down by an extensive grid system, or *quadrillage*, garrisoned by conscripts. With the bulk of ALN forces stationed in Tunisia, and the internal ALN dependent on arms shipments, the French army poured huge resources into two electrified barbed-wire barriers running parallel to the Moroccan and Tunisian borders; the Morice Line in the East (built over Summer 1957 and named after the then Defence Minister) stretched some three hundred kilometres from the desert to the coast. The barriers served not simply to deter enemy incursions, but rather signalled the point where ALN groups had broken the wire. Once a break was detected, troops from the five para regiments stationed along the line were sent in pursuit; fighters circumventing the barrier to the South were tracked across the desert by camel patrols. The barriers were highly effective in starving the ALN of arms and men, and, indirectly, in widening the split between the FLN's 'interior' and 'exterior' leadership. Villagers living in the 20–30-kilometre-wide zone between the wire and the frontier were driven into refugee camps in Tunisia (Droz & Lever 1991: 132–3; Connelly 2002: 140–1).

This 'barrier war' led by a chain of events to the fall of the French Fourth Republic. On 8 February 1958, asserting an officially defended but legally dubious right of 'hot pursuit', French B26 bombers raided an ALN base near the Tunisian village of Sakhiet Sidi Youssef, but hit the village as well, killing seventy villagers; a Red Cross aid mission, also hit, was in Sakhiet that day supplying Algerian refugees. The ensuing diplomatic storm brought to a head the efforts of Tunisian president, Habib Bourguiba, to reconcile necessary support for the FLN with his essentially pro-French orientation. Bourguiba insisted on an Anglo-American mission of 'good offices', to address the whole range of Franco-Tunisian questions. This in turn generated heavy-handed American efforts to internationalize the conflict, if necessary at the expense of Félix Gaillard's embattled government (Connelly 2002: 160–8). Faced with a 'diplomatic Dien Bien Phu' (in ibid.: 169), Gaillard duly fell on 15 April, following a confidence debate chiefly characterized by anti-American sentiments.

The last government of the regime, the twenty-fifth since 1946, was not installed until June, although a new prime minister, Pierre Pflimlin, was named in early May. However, Pflimlin's apparent willingness to treat with the FLN counted against him in Algiers, where, on the day of his investiture, 13 May, *pieds noirs* in open revolt combined with senior Army officers in a Committee of Public Safety under Massu's leadership. Two days later, the commander in Algeria, General Raoul Salan, to whom the government in Paris had granted full civil and military authority (thus effectively sanctioning the Algiers *coup*), spoke to the crowd from the balcony of the Government-General building in Algiers. Prompted by a Gaullist go-between, Salan's concluding cry of '*Vive de Gaulle!*' pointed towards the revolt's unanticipated outcome. The crisis still had more than two weeks to run, and brought France to the brink of civil war: on 24 May, Committees of Public Safety took control of Corsica in emulation of the Algiers movement, and the Interior Minister, Jules Moch, contemplated meeting the threat of parachute drops on Paris with hastily formed militias. It was against this background that the 68-year-old de Gaulle came out of retirement, distanced himself from the rebels, and accepted President René Coty's nomination as Prime Minister on 1 June. His two conditions were that he be granted 'full powers' in Algeria, and that France's Fifth Republican Constitution be prepared. Although it was not immediately apparent, the Algerian War was moving towards its endgame (Chapter 8). And yet it is a measure of the scale of the conflict and the stakes invested on all sides, that France under de Gaulle would spend more time at war in Algeria than it had under the Fourth Republic.

The Cyprus Emergency

Points of comparison between Cyprus and Algeria are ostensibly slight, whether in terms of the scale of conflict, or of Cyprus's importance from an imperial perspective. Nonetheless, both conflicts represented 'Decolonization-by-Trauma', where there was minimal common ground between the opposing sides (Holland 1995: 37–46). Indeed, in some ways the lines were more starkly drawn in Cyprus even than in Algeria, since there was little doubt where Greek Cypriots stood on the central demand of *Enosis*, no nationalists with whom the British felt they could 'do business', and no identifiable group of Greek Cypriot 'loyalists' to whom the British could turn. The communal lines were also more clearly drawn between the four-fifths majority Greek population and the Turks, lines which became more entrenched as the conflict continued, with profound consequences for an independent Cyprus. Similarities between the two theatres also extend to the brutal methods employed on all sides in a bitter and uncompromising 'dirty war'.

Enosis was hardly a new demand after 1945, given that the British had confronted it since taking over the island from Turkish rule in 1878; in the 1931 riots, its supporters had burned down Government House in Nicosia, since when the island's self-governing constitution had been suspended. It was thus difficult to imagine, let alone implement, the usual colonial 'half-way house' reconciling Greek Cypriot demands and British interests. In terms of British priorities, protection of the Turkish community, some 20 per cent of the population, rated second place to British strategic interests in the Eastern Mediterranean. From this imperial perspective, Cyprus's role was enhanced after 1945 by the 'loss' of Palestine and uncertainties over the Suez Canal Base's future; it was from Cyprus that the Soviet Union's Southern flank might eventually be attacked, and it was from Cyprus that the Anglo-French attack on Suez was launched. Moreover, it was Cyprus that led a Colonial Office minister, Henry Hopkinson, in the House of Commons on 28 July 1954, to formulate the impromptu principle that 'there are certain territories in the Commonwealth which, owing to their particular circumstances, can never expect to be fully independent'. While those 'particular circumstances' might conventionally refer to political or economic readiness for independence, this 'wholly novel' argument suggested that Cypriot self-determination was ruled out by British strategic interests (Holland 1994b: 168–9).

The defeat of the Communist insurgency in Greece in 1949 gave fresh impetus to Greek nationalism, and hence to calls for *Enosis*. In late 1949, a plebiscite organized by the Greek Orthodox Church in Cyprus showed 96.5 per cent in favour of *Enosis*. Ironically, Britain's closest potential ally was the Communist Party of Cyprus, AKEL, an eclectic group of leftists, some of whom might have been 'perfectly comfortable inside the British Labour Party'. AKEL had good reason to fear *Enosis*, given the Greek state's record on dealing with Communism, but the Cyprus government persisted in seeing the party as the principal target for eventual repression (ibid.: 149, 159). The island's economic backwardness was also a factor, measurable both in rural poverty and in undeveloped state infrastructure; here there was no 'second colonial occupation', only post-colonial tourist invasions. Rapid urbanization and the soaring cost of living, which saw food prices rise fourfold between 1939 and 1951, boosted leftist politics, giving AKEL control of most towns during the 1940s (Anderson 1994: 180). This in turn enhanced the value of *Enosis* to an increasingly militant Orthodox Church, led by Archbishop Makarios III, as a tool for recapturing political control. At a different level, for Lawrence Durrell (1957), in his celebrated account of life in Cyprus in the mid-1950s, it might have helped appease European-oriented, urban middle-class youth, key players in the subsequent insurgency, if the Cyprus government had provided so much as a municipal swimming pool in Nicosia.[16]

British policy in the five years leading up to the Emergency was one of resistance to further constitutional initiatives, such as the implementation of a constitutional text drafted in 1948, combined with measures more or less designed to provoke disorder, so that the government could 'clear the ground': press freedoms were curbed, Greek Cypriot councillors were jailed for provocatively renaming streets in Limassol, an attempt was made to curb Church influence in schools, the Church youth organization was banned, and a raft of sometimes absurd restrictions included banning blue pencils in schools, with which pupils might draw the Greek flag. In short, the government did all within its power to exercise what one official saw as 'the use of emergency powers without an emergency'. As the Labour politician, Richard Crossman, suggested, following a visit to the island, Cyprus was run as an 'amiable police state' (Holland 1994b: 154–6). The barriers to progress in Cyprus seemed all the more galling when contrasted with constitutional reform elsewhere in the empire. Indeed, the Governor from late 1951, Sir Robert Armitage, previously Chief Secretary in Accra, had watched Nkrumah's rise to power, and kept his photo on his desk. At bottom, the British attitude was based on a belief that Greek Cypriots 'could not possibly be serious about *enosis* because they never did anything concrete to bring it about' (ibid.: 163). While attempts at violent subversion of the colonial status quo might therefore (and did) come from Greece, it was complacently believed that such efforts would never enjoy active Greek Cypriot support.

By the end of 1954, both British and Greek Cypriots had drawn a line, as Makarios concluded (persuaded by Hopkinson's 'never') that negotiated reform would only come with the threat of violent disorder. The agent of violence was EOKA (National Organization of Cypriot Fighters), led by Colonel George Grivas, a Cypriot hero of the Greek army, who saw *Enosis* through the prism of an 'authoritarian, militarist romanticism', as a means of renewing Greek nationhood (Holland 1985: 253). Although British forces intercepted a major arms shipment in January 1955, other caïques followed the captured *Aghios Georghios* to the many remote bays on Cyprus's West coast. EOKA's campaign began on 1 April 1955 with a wave of bomb attacks on radio transmitters, government buildings, military installations and isolated police stations, paralleling the Algerian FLN's early attacks a few months before. From the outset, EOKA targeted the police, murdering and intimidating Greek Cypriot officers, but also infiltrating police structures and particularly police intelligence. Another favoured EOKA tactic deployed youngsters, Durrell's sixth-formers amongst them, in rowdy street demonstrations as a means of tying down police and, with luck, provoking them into violence against 'mere schoolchildren' (Anderson 1994: 185–6). In time, these teenagers might be recruited to the terrorist gangs.[17] Widespread Greek support for *Enosis* did not necessarily equate with approval of EOKA tactics, but usually translated into tacit acquiescence.

The British responded by appointing a new military governor, Field Marshal Sir John Harding, in September 1955. British actions had already been stepped up, with the first curfews and collective punishments, the banning of EOKA, and the creation of a Police Mobile Reserve to police urban riots, recruiting entirely from the Turkish community. By the end of October 1955, soldiers had been granted the same legal status as police, and on 26 November 1955, an Emergency was declared. British experience in counter-insurgency was now brought decisively to bear, with visits to Cyprus by General Templer amongst other experts on colonial policing (ibid.: 187–9; Mockaitis 1990: 180–9). Three distinctive elements may be identified in the British response to EOKA, first of which was a progressive shift from Greek to Turkish officers across the police force: whereas in 1954, 60 per cent of Cypriot police were Greek (already proportionately less than the Greek population), by 1957 they were out-numbered five to two. Secondly, British officers were drafted in, from colonial forces but also from British county constabularies. Harding hoped that the 'British bobby's' sterling qualities might ensure effective policing but also rub off on Cypriot officers. In fact, recruits to the UK Police Unit acquired an unsavoury reputation for brutality. Expatriate units constituted 20 per cent of police forces at the height of communal violence in 1958. Thirdly, British military and police intelligence were overhauled, and though EOKA's fragmented structure presented particular challenges, a reformed Special Branch, necessarily staffed by expatriates, made spectacular progress in track-ing down EOKA units, particularly following the June 1956 capture of Grivas's diaries during a mountain offensive (Anderson 1994: 189–200). EOKA was never defeated by these means, however, and the February 1959 amnesty allowed the elusive Grivas to return to Greece a national hero. (He returned a decade later to lead EOKA B in a renewed effort to secure *Enosis*.) As elsewhere, more tangible progress was to come in the political domain.

Archbishop Makarios constituted the third point of a triangle, distancing himself from EOKA violence while resisting the lure of British proposals for some compromise short of *Enosis*. During negotiations in early 1956 with Harding and the Colonial Secretary, Alan Lennox-Boyd, Makarios refused an emerging formula allowing Greek predominance within a self-governing Cyprus. At this point, EOKA's influence still weighed too heavily, as its actions throughout these negotiations seemed designed to indicate. In order to weaken EOKA's point of the triangle, on 9 March 1956, Makarios was simply removed from the equation, not by the judicial means deployed against Kenyatta, since Makarios carried too much spiritual weight for that, but by the elegant solution of exile to the Seychelles. With Makarios silenced, the most active phase of counter-insurgency began, partly boosted by troop build-ups on the island in pre-paration for Suez. Meanwhile, the forging of a constitutional solution was entrusted to Lord Radcliffe, who had earlier drawn the lines of Indian Partition. By December 1956, Radcliffe presented constitutional proposals which closely foreshadowed the terms agreed in the eventual settlement more than two years later: Greek Cypriots were to dominate within a unitary state, rather than federation (much less partition), with strong safeguards for the Turkish minority. However, several things had to happen before this solution could be implemented, the first of which was Greek Cypriot acquiescence, and possibly even the renunciation of *Enosis*, a delicate process initiated by the release of Makarios in March 1957.

The next unavoidable step in resolving the Cyprus problem involved squaring up to its Turkish dimensions, embracing both Cyprus's near neighbour some forty miles north of Kyrenia, and the Turkish minority, whose relative quiescence was coming to an end. In August 1955, Britain brought Turkey into play alongside Greece, in a tripartite conference in London. This was a hazardous move, and Turkish domestic volatility induced Ankara's consistently tough stance over the years to come. This much was clear when the tripartite conference failed, following riots directed against Turkey's sub-stantial Greek minority (Holland 1985). Moreover, by raising the spectre of partition as an extreme alternative to *Enosis*, Turkey's involvement polarized community rela-tions on the island, though the Cyprus government's increasing reliance on Turkish recruits to the police was already having this effect. Although EOKA was under orders (as captured documents revealed) not to target Turkish policemen as it did Greek, consistently more Turkish police than either Greek or British were killed or injured. Turkish casualties typically prompted demonstrations or retaliations, and from 1955 an underground organization called Volkan (later TMT) exacted reprisals against Greek Cypriots and their property. At least tacitly, the British welcomed TMT as a 'counter-foil to EOKA', indirectly protecting the police and deflecting EOKA resources (Anderson 1994: 192). The first more generally motivated communal rioting occurred as EOKA intensified its activities following Makarios's exile in March 1956; more followed, and from June to August 1958, inter-communal violence killed 56 Greek and 51 Turkish civilians. By this stage, police officers from both communities were considered unreliable, thus increasing reliance on British troops and police (ibid.: 192–3).

Finally, the British had to relinquish the view of Cyprus implied by Hopkinson's 'never'. This formed part of a wider reappraisal of British imperial interests in the wake of the Suez debacle (Chapter 8). The potential for such a change of heart was signalled in London, where a new prime minister, Harold Macmillan, took office in January 1957. Makarios's return from exile was Macmillan's prime ministerial opening gambit on Cyprus, one moreover which was bitterly contested by many within the governing Conservative Party, prompting the only post-war British cabinet resignation on an imperial question, that of Lord Salisbury. Over the summer of 1958, as Cyprus became ungovernable except by British force of arms, London determined to resolve Cyprus's strategic role through the securing of the sovereign military bases of Akrotiri and Dhikelia (and rights over some other areas), rather than through control of the whole island. Archbishop Makarios too feared that partition was becoming more likely as international opinion turned against *Enosis* in the face of communal violence and the continuing EOKA campaign, which by late 1958 was targeting British civilians in the streets of Nicosia. In December 1958, Makarios asked Grivas to suspend EOKA activities, and on 19 February 1959, the agreement was reached by which Cyprus became independent in August 1960 (Holland 1998, 1985: 254–6; Anderson 1994: 200–2).

'Dirty Wars', Winnable Wars? The Impact of Terror and Counter-insurgency

Of all the colonial wars fought after 1945, only in Indochina were the forces of anti-colonial nationalism transformed into an army capable of inflicting battlefield defeat, at Dien Bien Phu, on a well-armed colonial expeditionary force. Straightforward military action was only ever part of counter-insurgency and, reversing Clausewitz's maxim, politics was the continuation of colonial war by other means. In the rest of this chapter, we therefore examine various common threads in insurgent and counter-insurgent strategies. First we address the question of whether these wars were in fact winnable, as well as the price paid in the moral currency of 'atrocities', whether in the shape of insurgent 'terror', or that of torture.

Much depends on how 'terror' is defined, and the late colonial wars treated here were still a generation away from the practices and outlook of the early twenty-first century. The broad label of terror may be understood in two distinct ways, though both are matters of method rather than moral or partisan considerations. In other words, it is not simply the case that one person's terrorist is another's freedom-fighter – an insurgent could be both, or neither. First, terror assumed the form of terrorist attacks, whether on military and police personnel and bases or on 'civilian', usually European, persons or property, typically the 'banditry' of the MRLA or the urban bombing campaigns of Algeria and Cyprus. There was a clear political calculus to the deployment of terror and counter-terror tactics which cannot be accounted for simply by a conception of 'excesses'; conversely, it goes almost without saying that the awful rationality of those acts does not excuse them.

Secondly, terror was 'the insurgents' form of justice in the absence of a judiciary and prisons' (Hack 1995: 95n.). It is almost impossible to look beyond the brutal means by which this rough justice was exercised, and typically colonial propaganda precisely did not look beyond those means, which contributed heavily to the demonization of Mau Mau and the FLN.[18] On the insurgent side, however, these were above all political wars for the control of people, not territory, even if they often shaded off into personal, family or 'tribal' conflicts, or 'village wars' (Antlöv 1995). The Viet Minh's level of organization and doctrine was sufficient in itself to allow something like a system of community justice. By contrast, the FLN were rarely allowed enough of a breathing space to pay more than lip-service to the local democracy of village councils, or *djemaa*, which figured in the Soummam manifesto (Ageron 1995). The FLN's proclaimed objective of 'political cleansing' in the Proclamation of 1 November 1954 heralded a repertoire of cruel punishments designed to purge the nation of colonialism's corrupting influence, in the form of tobacco, alcohol, *kif*, prostitution, organized crime; thus Ali-la-Pointe, a former pimp, forged his legendary reputation in Algiers by purging the Casbah (Eveno & Planchais 1989). These practices are comparable with the exemplary punishments and summary executions meted out to collaborators, also in the absence of judges and prisons, in the 'wild' purges which swept parts of France at the Liberation in 1944, although these often focused disturbingly on the humiliation of women (Vergili 2002). More generally, in all these wars, casualties always included those endured by the colonized at the hands of insurgents, whether 'collaborating' chiefs and their entourage, or Kikuyu Guard; or the innumerable Algerian *caïds* or village policemen killed and left mutilated at the entrance to their villages; or Greek Cypriot policemen targeted by EOKA. Often, as in the case of the Lari massacre in Kenya in March 1953, violence reflected deep-seated conflicts over settlement going back a generation or more (Anderson 2005: 119–80).

An economy of permissible levels of violence was clearly exercised by movements as diverse as the Algerian FLN and the Malayan Races Liberation Army. Thus, at the 1956 Soummam Conference, it was held that the indiscriminate violence of a rampaging Algerian mob in the August 1955 Constantinois insurrection should be avoided within a properly coordinated national strategy. Later, the backlash of horrified, if far from disinterested, press coverage of the Melouza massacre in 1957 was such that the FLN tried to blame the killings on French paratroopers – showing a curious delicacy, given that it coincided with an increasingly desperate bombing campaign in Algiers (Ihaddaden 2001: 375–8). The MRLA also pulled back from its campaign of violence against British economic targets in 1950, a decision that was known and acted upon by British counter-insurgent forces, and was a crucial factor in the turning of the military tide in Malaya (Hack 1995).

The challenge for colonial armies and police was thus to confront terror without deploying reciprocal tactics that were at least as condemnable as those of the enemy. All too frequently, the challenge was failed or ducked. It is axiomatic that, whether facing extreme provocation or in the 'fog of war', or whether as part of a tacitly sanctioned policy, none of the various colonial combatants in these quintessentially 'dirty wars' – no colonial army, professional or conscript, no police force or gendarmerie, no group of 'loyalist' Home Guard or levied troops, *askaris*, *tirailleurs*, *harkis* or Gurkhas, no settler community or armed militia defending an invisible front line – was untouched by the stain of abusive and transgressive violence. Some campaigns were 'cleaner' than others, and yet, while the scale of violent atrocities and systematized brutality was doubtless greater in Algeria than elsewhere, recent research on Kenya in particular surely undermines the sometimes complacent view that British officials and soldiers were somehow immune. Once the euphemisms and evasions are stripped away, indiscriminate collective punishments, massacre, torture and other 'excesses' were common to all of the conflicts studies here. It can have been no consolation, say, to two dozen Chinese villagers of Batang Kali in December 1948, that they were not killed in some remote corner of the Algerian *bled*, but shot by panicky, inexperienced Scots Guardsmen; or to 'hardcore' Mau Mau detainees that 'only' 11 of their number died at Hola camp that day in March 1959; and few Greek Cypriot insurgents would have concurred with the Governor of Cyprus, General Harding, that they should be 'thankful that it was British troops with whom they had to deal', following allegations of British abuse after a bombing incident at a football match (in Mockaitis 1990: 52).

'Excesses' may have been the result of panic, poor training and discipline or inadequate troop numbers in the face of an uncertainly 'rational' enemy. In a report on alleged French atrocities in Algeria, in late 1955, the British Military Attaché in Paris felt:

> . . . that it would be too much to expect continued restraint by the young men in the French army in North Africa. It has been said that British troops would not have behaved in this manner, but it is difficult to find a case since the Indian mutiny, when British troops have been so tested as were these young Frenchmen. (in Thomas 2000a: 155)

As he continued, there were 'at least four' proven cases of atrocities in Kenya, and they 'did not make pretty reading', while Algeria was perhaps fifty times bigger than the area of Mau Mau, with ten times the number of troops deployed. What remains shocking was the apparent propensity of ordinary 'young men' (the repetition of this motif bears underlining) to commit such atrocities, and although he meant British and French soldiers, no less a sense of shock attaches to the ordinary Algerians, Cypriots, Malayan Chinese, Kikuyu and others who committed 'outrages'. Indeed, the phenomenon of ordinary soldierly bloodthirstiness has only now found its historian, whose work bears on one conflict germane to those under discussion here, namely the American war in Vietnam (Bourke 2000). Thus it was typically the instances of apparently blithe acceptance of brutality – the 19-year-old junior officer or jaded police inspector, drafted in from London, let loose on Mau Mau or EOKA suspects, the Gurkhas or Royal Marines photographed cheerfully displaying the severed heads or hands of dead Chinese insurgents, the reports of sporting 'tallies' and rewards for dead insurgents – which caused scandals in the British press (Mockaitis 1990).

A further distinction may be made between actual incidents, the extent of which has often remained hidden, and the atmosphere of fear, recrimination, rumour and psychotic fantasy which enveloped colonial conflict. In Madagascar, for example, where the use of torture is reliably documented, it was also the case that wild rumours spread amongst the small, but hysterically disposed settler population, concerning not only the alleged atrocities committed by 'treacherous' Malagasy, but also a fantastical torture chamber run by a notorious police inspector: both sets of rumours were discounted by Colonial Under-Secretary Gaston Defferre, sent on mission to the island after the outbreak of insurrection, whose Report was in other respects a whitewash (Tronchon 1986: 77–8, 273–6). In Cyprus, also, the truth probably lies somewhere between British denials of all but isolated, unauthorized incidents and Greek Cypriot allegations of widespread official brutality, tempered by disdainful acknowledgement of British 'politeness' (Holland 1995: 42–3). In truth, even exaggerated or invented rumours of atrocities, or the open advocacy or exercise of violence by enraged settlers in Kenya or Algeria, helped to undermine the colonial state's imagined future.

While there can be little doubt that torture – taken in a broad sense to cover all forms of corporal or psychological mistreatment of detainees – was endemic to all these conflicts, and to all sides, more precision is clearly needed. An analytical distinction might therefore be made between the often brutal interrogation or 'screening' of captured insurgents or suspects on a raggedly defined battlefield, and the institutionalization of torture designed to extract intelligence or simply to establish 'guilt', such as we find in Algeria and, in a different way in the detention system in Kenya – indeed, in both cases, colonial authorities arguably lost sight or control of any initial, 'rational' purpose.

It may never be possible to explain or understand how the widespread practice of torture in Algeria developed into an invasive 'gangrene' (Stora 1991), from the taint of which France, the cradle of human rights, has still not fully recovered to this day. Long before the start of the insurrection, beatings and other forms of 'muscled interrogation' were commonplace in police cells, and were unavailingly prohibited by Governor-General Naegelen, in 1949. After 1 November 1954, a hard-pressed, inadequately commanded professional army, many of whose officers and men were veterans of Indochina and Madagascar, was unlikely to exercise restraint against suspected 'rebels', far from the eyes of journalists and intellectuals. This was improvised torture, requiring only a tub of water, a rifle-stock or the infamous '*gégène*', that is, a portable signals magneto (*gé-génératrice*), from which cables could be attached to a detainee's body, usually to mouth or genitals. Liberal politicians such as Mendès-France, Mitterrand and Soustelle called in vain for an end to all 'excesses'. In March 1955, Roger Wuillaume, a senior civil servant unassociated with police or army, was appointed to investigate the prevalence of torture in Algeria. He recommended that, where there was reckoned to be minimal 'risk to the health of the victim', certain techniques, including the use of water or electricity, should be 'recognized' and 'covered with authority'. This ultra-pragmatic 'reason of state' went unheeded and un-published, as did a further report by Jean Mairey the following year (Horne 1996: 196–7).

With the onset of the Battle of Algiers, the French army faced a challenge that had already defeated the British in Palestine, and confronted them again in Cyprus: a campaign of urban terrorism where the aggressors could melt away into the urban environment, and where the need for intelligence became paramount. Torture became more refined, less 'artisanal', and moved to the centre of French strategy, as Massu's paras offset their soldierly distaste for an urban policing role with the vigour of their intelligence gathering. Massu (1972) claimed the *gégène* was safe, having tried it on himself and his staff, although presumably without adopting the detainee's mindset: after all, he could stop it at will, and was unlikely to be shot 'trying to escape', or to be sent on one of the 'firewood details' (*corvées de bois*) from which none returned. By now, the army had trained interrogation units, the heavily euphemized *Dispositifs Opérationnels de Protection* (DOP), and suburban villas and farms were given over to interrogation. When the DOP were overwhelmed with work, as frequently was the case in 1957, the paras stepped in (Droz & Lever 1991: 140–2).

The Battle of Algiers has become a test case for assaying the necessity of torture and the moral poison it generates. The campaign's success, leading to the FLN's near-elimination from Algiers and the dispersal of its leadership, may be contrasted with the British near-farcical failure to capture Colonel Grivas in his suburban hideout in Limassol (Mockaitis 1990). Conversely, commentators, including the nonagenarian Massu, quoted at the outset of this chapter, have questioned how efficiently it generated accurate information, as opposed to the mass of false information thrown up by desperate victims, or how its benefits weighed against the support for the FLN generated by French abuses. Other methods were arguably more effective, such as the use of double agents (although many of these were 'turned' under torture), pioneered by Captain Paul-Alain Léger, which led to the capture of FLN leaders including Saadi Yacef (Léger 2002). Léger's elaboration of the technique of '*bleuite*' ('blue-itis', after the agents' capacious blue work overalls) was reminiscent of the 'pseudo-gangs' deployed by Captain Frank Kitson against Mau Mau, or the shadowy 'Q groups' in Cyprus (Anderson 2005: 284–6; Kitson 1960; Mockaitis 1990: 173). Gangs of *bleus* were used to devastating effect to infiltrate Wilayas 3 (Kabylie) and 4 (Algérois), which in 1958–9 tore themselves apart in a murderous search for traitors – it is perhaps no coincidence that Wilaya 4's desperate commander, Mohamed Si Salah, contemplated a negotiated peace in 1960 (Horne 1996: 260–1, 322–3; Sellam 2001).

Torture generated toothless reports and committees, provoked high-profile resig-nations, and spawned a mass of articles in the intellectual journals, pamphlets and manifestos, and a string of *causes célèbres* (Le Sueur 2001: 197–205). There can be little doubt that it was a major contributory factor in turning the French people and their leaders against the war in Algeria. And yet it continued to the bitter end, and the DOPs' victims by 1961–2 included OAS terrorists from the settler com-munity. But military logic had long evaporated from a perverted hidden world, where torturers' discourse obscenely mimicked the 1950s consumerist obsession with cleanliness and domesticity; or, where male and female detainees lived alongside their torturers for weeks as enforced servants or concubines, an experience which left torturer and tortured alike little chance of return to 'normal' humanity (Ross 1995: 112–13; Anon. 2000).

'Hearts and Minds'

In the end, what mattered to the colonial state was winning, not simply in terms of policing and control, but also politically, in ways which could be reconciled as closely as possible with the aims of the late colonial state. As the prevailing discourse of the time would have it, this was a battle for the 'hearts and minds of the population', although it may be doubted that victory was ever assured on this most difficult of terrains.

The purely military record of these campaigns was ultimately quite creditable, although colonial armies necessarily traced a rapid 'learning curve'. The British lessons of counter-insurgency had already been learnt, sometimes painfully, in Ireland after the First World War, the Arab Revolt in Palestine, 1936–9, in the 1930–2 Burmese revolt or in policing the North-West Frontier. Although this experience had been dissipated by the more conventional orthodoxies of the Second World War, the commanders in Malaya (Briggs, Templer), Kenya (Erskine) and Cyprus (Harding) all had pre-war experience of irregular warfare (Mockaitis 1990). Similarly, the French army's traditions revolved around North Africa, while very different experience was derived from the Resistance careers of many French commanders. Indeed, given this vast experience of counter-insurgency, the campaigns' early stages sometimes seemed remarkably inept. In the Tonkin delta, for example, forts and blockhouses protected roads and intersections, but left untouched the villages and paddy fields in between (Droz & Lever 1991; Clayton 1994). Laborious cordon-and-search operations, with massive 'sweeps' through the Malayan or Kenyan forest, merely drove insurgents through the gaps in a thinly spread cordon (Mockaitis 1990: 163). Similarly, 'NATO-style' armoured patrols followed the few roads of the Aurès mountains, in *ratissage* ('raking') operations as ineffective as they were picturesquely named ('Violette', 'Véronique', etc.) (Horne 1996; Droz & Lever 1991). However, it took time, and lobbying in metropolitan capitals, to build up the troop numbers needed for more sophisticated tactics. The painstaking establishment of an intelligence picture also took time. According to one British report in Malaya: 'It is little exaggeration to say that the security forces have every advantage except information whereas the bandits have only got information' (Mockaitis 1990: 164). Meanwhile, static defence and cumbersome sweeps of unsuitable terrain at least prevented insurgent troop concentrations.

If it was tricky to locate insurgents in jungle or open country, it was more difficult to distinguish insurgents from 'innocent' villagers, or to separate active guerrillas from their 'passive' wing. Early efforts tended towards the somewhat counter-productive solution of collective punishment. Indeed, it was such a punishment that was inflicted on the 24 villagers of Batang Kali shot in December 1948. Even as late as 1952, soon after his arrival as British 'supremo' in Malaya, General (later Sir)

Gerald Templer's authoritarian reflexes were demonstrated in the strict 22-hour curfew he imposed on the town of Tanjong Malim, as punishment for a nearby ambush – this was far from the 'hearts and minds' policy with which Templer's name is indelibly associated (ibid.: 53, 122; Hack 1995). Curfews, closures of public amenities and other punishments were also applied as almost completely ineffectual punishments for terrorist attacks in Cyprus (Mockaitis 1990: 135–6; Anderson 1994). An improvised doctrine of 'collective responsibility' in Algeria resembled German practice against Resistance movements in occupied Europe, and with similarly negative results: Kabyle peasants were forced to repair the sabotage which the ALN had coerced them into undertaking the previous night; less fortunate 'suspects' were summarily beaten or shot (Horne 1996: 113–15).

Some punishments were more elemental: in Madagascar, newspaper reports that prisoners were thrown from aircraft over rebel villages were denied, of course, but the official explanation was less than convincing (especially as the first aircraft mentioned, the Junkers Ju52, had been the mainstay of wartime German paratroop drops):

> Prisoners are only exceptionally transported by aircraft. Air force has JUNKERS, ANSON, GOËLAND and DOMINIE aircraft. Windows do not open wide enough for human body to pass. Personnel and equipment may be parachuted through door if this is removed in advance. Moreover, any attempt of this kind could cause damage to delicate parts of the aeroplane.[19]

The British in Iraq and the Sudan had long pioneered the use of aircraft to quell colonial revolt, albeit hedged around with restrictions to meet the 'minimum force' requirements of imperial policing (Omissi 1990). The Italian air force was notably less restrained, using poison gas in the invasion of Ethiopia. Now British-made Spitfires, armed with rockets, were used against rebels at Sétif in 1945 (despite protests from the British Consulate-General in Algiers),[20] while Lincoln heavy bombers and adapted Harvard trainers attacked Mau Mau camps in the forest, and B26 bombers were used to bomb 'rebel' villages in Algeria, sometimes with napalm. Although it may seem an absurd strategy, bombing the forests of Mount Kenya or the Aberdares drove Mau Mau onto higher, less hospitable ground, and further away from the targets of their raiding parties (Anderson 2005: 263).

Once the early part of the counter-insurgent learning curve was passed, the battle for military control was within the grasp of colonial armies. In Malaya, so-called 'white areas' cleared of rebels started to appear from 1953, suggesting that the military tide was turned even before Templer's arrival (Hack 1995: 89–92). In Kenya, the Mau Mau forest forces were reduced to a containable nuisance within two years or so of the declaration of Emergency. British deployment of 'minimum force' may be contrasted with French (and American) traditions derived from the existence of a large standing army (Mockaitis 1990: 173ff.). But those traditions could be equally effective, if sufficient resources were deployed. Even in Indochina, the expeditionary force at Dien Bien Phu was not beaten by rag-tag irregulars, but outgunned by a conventionally equipped national army, superbly commanded by General Giap. In Algeria, by contrast, the military tide seemed to be turning in France's favour, perhaps by early 1958, when the system of *quadrillage* and the 'barrier war' started to pay off.

Indeed, the army's sense of betrayal from late 1959 onwards may be attributed in part to its commanders' not unrealistic sense that victory was around the corner, although the political terrain was less plausibly grasped by the French military mindset.

However, military strategies were always coupled with political solutions, to which we now turn. The most far-reaching solution to the problem of separating insurgents from their supporters, at the core of British counter-insurgency doctrine in Malaya, was resettlement, subsequently transmuted into 'villagization' in Kenya, mirrored in the 'regrouping centres' in Algeria, and eventually translated into American 'strategic hamlets' in South Vietnam. This was the counter-insurgency response to Mao Zedong's oft-cited insurgent operating like 'a fish in water', although General Harold Briggs, Director of Operations in Malaya from 1950 to 1952, preferred an epidemiological analogy:

> The problem of clearing Communist bandits from Malaya was similar to that of eradi-
> cating malaria from a country. Flit guns and mosquito nets, in the form of military
> and police, though giving some very local security if continuously maintained, effected
> no permanent cure. Such a permanent cure entailed the closing of all the breeding areas.
> (in Mockaitis 1990: 115)

This was signally successful in Malaya, leading to the resettlement in 'New Villages' of some 350,000 Chinese squatters, with the regrouping of a further 600,000 plantation workers. Now the Min Yuen were isolated from insurgents in specially constructed compounds. Issued with identity cards and subjected to food rationing, they could supply insurgents only at expense to themselves and their families, and at the risk of denunciation. Inevitably, the provision of sanitation, education and healthcare fac-ilities followed some considerable way behind the security arrangements, although it was this aspect of the scheme which subsequently attracted most attention for its contribution to winning 'hearts and minds'.

The military effect of resettlement was more immediate than its social impact. In October 1951, the MCP switched from armed struggle to subversion, partly, as British intelligence committees thought, in recognition of its dwindling access to the Min Yuen. This was obscured at the time by the continuing scale of attacks, and, not least, by the assassination of the High Commissioner, Sir Henry Gurney, on 6 October 1951 (Hack 1995: 88–9). British intelligence was also enormously improved by direct access to Chinese villagers, many of whom proved susceptible to rewards, allowing relocation to Hong Kong or Bangkok. For those identified as harbouring communist sympathies, detention camps beckoned. Although these filled rapidly from the start of the Emergency, the situation of the Chinese in Malaya suggested a dual solution to overcrowding and to communist organization in the camps. First, from 1949, a programme of rehabilitation was instituted, which aimed, as a March 1953 Malayan Government White Paper put it, 'to balance these repressive measures by something constructive and at once more humane and intelligent'. By 1953, the first rehabilita-tion centre had returned 1,280 Chinese to their community, of whom only eight 'relapsed' (Mockaitis 1990: 114). However, secondly, this relatively small number was far outweighed by the flow of detainees deported to China as, technically, illegal aliens; although halted by Mao's victory in late 1949, the flow resumed the following

September, as Beijing welcomed 'victims of imperial persecution' (Elkins 2003: 199, 221n.).

Military priorities were uppermost in the parallel French 'regroupment centres'. These came about following the creation, from March 1956, of 'forbidden zones' in the mountains, from which local peasants were expelled, and where any remaining man or beast could be shot. The 'protection' of these displaced persons was improvised subsequently, as was the usually inadequate provision of food, hygiene and work for the camps' growing numbers (Ageron 2001; Cornaton 1998). Although the camps welcomed those allegedly fleeing FLN exactions, the policy was probably as good a recruiting tool as any for the rebellion. No systematic census of the camps was made, but 900 existed by the end of 1958, 'home' to more than a million regroupees by June 1959, and perhaps more than two million lived in the camps by mid-1961, representing between 12 and 45 per cent of the population in any given area (Ageron 2001: 359–62). Many more drifted from the countryside to the urban shanty-towns, thus accelerating a 'rural exodus' and leaving a poignant legacy (which some saw as the 'army's revenge') for independent Algeria.

Rehabilitation had no direct equivalent in French thinking, but an appeal to 'hearts and minds' was nonetheless made. Civil authorities never succeeded in wresting control of regroupment policy from the army, although the camps inspired the largely rhetorical 'Thousand Villages' policy, which fed into de Gaulle's 1959 Constantine Plan (Chapter 8). However, the camps became the focus for one of the French army's few redeeming institutions in Algeria. The Specialized Administrative Sections (SAS) were small, under-resourced units, often composed of reservist officers, whose role was part administrator, part social worker, part intelligence officer. The former 'Native Affairs' Bureaux in Morocco provided a model for the SAS, and many officers transferred from one to the other. A cognate policy had also been essayed in the latter stages of the Indochina war, where GAMOs (Mobile Operational Administrative Groups), staffed by Vietnamese officers, operated alongside conventional army units (Zervoudakis 2002: 51–3; Omouri 2001). The SAS' role was riven with both external and internal ambiguities. They were extremely vulnerable to FLN attack in the remote outposts they initially established; but even within the camps, uncertainty as to whether they were spies or administrators counted against them. Ironically, the army command was also dismissive of the SAS' quasi-civilian functions, to which 'tactical imperatives' were always to be preferred, even in 'pacified' zones. SAS officers were thus disdained by the more traditional army intelligence chiefs (2e Bureau), and the recently created, more prestigious, but arguably far less effective, 'psychological warfare' units (5e Bureau) (Ageron 2001: 341; Villatoux & Villatoux 2001; Aggoun 2002).

From a military perspective, applying the resettlement scheme to Kenya had much to recommend it. Villagization forced the Kikuyu to abandon their scattered farmsteads, which were burned to prevent their return, and grouped them into heavily guarded compounds, enclosed by barbed wire and spiked trenches, which they themselves were forced to construct. As in Malaya and Algeria, the policy deprived insurgents of ready food supplies, and, coupled with Operation Anvil, cut them off from potential recruits. The forests were declared 'forbidden zones', where Erskine's troops could shoot on sight. However, villagization touched cruelly on the raw nerves of Mau Mau's quarrel with their fellow Kikuyu. If Mau Mau were fighting a war for 'Land

and Freedom', then the new villages deprived them of both, and indeed pointed the way towards land redistribution to Kikuyu loyalists. With Mau Mau fighting in the forest, and many thousands of suspects detained even before Operation Anvil, those left behind were the women, the old and the vulnerable. Moreover, the villages were controlled by precisely those elements within Kikuyu society whom Mau Mau opposed, the loyalists who had been recruited into the Kikuyu Home Guard. These were overseen by dubiously motivated officers of the Kenya Regiment, recruited from the settler community. We enter here into one of the darkest episodes of the Mau Mau war, an almost unbearable catalogue of forced labour, abuse, torture, rape and murder, partially recoverable through oral testimony, but finding little echo in official records (Elkins 2005: 238–65; Anderson 2005: 297–307). Although rehabilitation of these 'Mau Mau-infected' villagers, as in Malaya, was an essential part of the villagization programme, it was barely applied, partly for lack of resources, partly because of official sidelining of the rehabilitation programme (Elkins 2005: 236–7).

Malayan lessons were quite naturally, and directly, applied in the detention camps of the Kenyan 'Pipeline'. Indeed, a Kenyan official, Thomas Askwith, was seconded to Malaya, and subsequently appointed Commissioner for Community Development and Rehabilitation (ibid.: 104). Malayan parallels quickly broke down, however. Askwith borrowed the classification of detainees as either 'white', 'grey' or 'black', according to their level of indoctrination and commitment; the system later encompassed many shades of grey, in one of late colonialism's more extreme attempts to impose order on troublesome colonial subjects (ibid.: 317–18). Whereas in Malaya, irreconcilable – 'black' – detainees could simply be deported, this option was unavailable to the Kenyan government, which thus envisaged permanent detention for 'hardcore' Mau Mau. This helps explain the extensive nature of the camp system, ultimately numbering more than a hundred camps, including holding camps, works camps, special detention camps (for example, Kapenguria in the Northern desert, where Kenyatta and other KAU leaders were held), camps for different ethnic groups, for women and juveniles, and exile camps (including, most infamously, Hola) (ibid.: 369).

Rehabilitation in Kenya went to the heart of what it meant to be Mau Mau, and of British officials' understanding of the African 'primitive mind'. Whereas, presumably, no one in Malaya needed to ponder what it meant to adhere to communist beliefs, in Kenya a committee was formed, chaired by Askwith, to 'Enquire into the Sociological Causes and Remedies for Mau Mau (Elkins 2003: 137–9; Anderson 2005: 281f.). The key participants were eminent anthropologist and initiated Kikuyu elder, Louis Leakey, and a self-taught psychiatrist, Dr J.C. Carothers.[21] Between them, they concocted a 'cure' comprising manual labour, literacy classes, Christian witness if appropriate, but, crucially, the forced confession of the Mau Mau oath, which, in Leakey's view, would thus be broken. This, then, became the basis for the rehabilitation regime instituted in the camps of the 'Pipeline', along which perhaps 70,000 detainees passed in all, in one direction or the other, depending on whether they co-operated, or conversely became hardened by their experience in the camps.

Rehabilitation by force did not work, and by early 1957, with perhaps 30,000 Kikuyu men, women, and even children, still detained, policy shifted towards an accelerated release of prisoners, to be achieved not through relaxation of the brutal techniques of rehabilitation, but through their intensification, with the aim of reducing detainees to a few thousand 'hard core'. It was in pursuit of a new, more efficient, 'dilution technique', masterminded by Terence Gavaghan (quoted at the outset of this chapter), on 3 March 1959, that 11 detainees were beaten to death at a new exile camp at Hola, in Eastern Kenya. Although it was initially reported that the men died 'after they had drunk water from a water cart', the attempted cover-up was exposed by Barbara Castle, MP, the culmination of a long campaign on her part to expose the horrors of the camps, but also the marking of a moral turning point in British's post-war empire (Elkins 2005: 344f.). This was arguably the point when Britain, having 'won' its war against Mau Mau, lost its battle to determine Kenya's future, and marked the transition to a more accelerated process of decolonization. A few months later, President de Gaulle's offer of Algerian self-determination in September 1959 confirmed that the African decolonizing endgame had begun.

Notes

1 Imagined exchange between a French journalist and the recently captured Larbi Ben M'Hidi, in Pontecorvo (1965). Ben M'Hidi was military commander in Algiers of the Algerian National Liberation Front (FLN), captured in February 1957, then 'found hanged' in his cell; General Paul Aussaresses claimed responsibility for his murder in his blood-curdling memoirs (2001).

2 General Jacques Massu, French commander in the Battle of Algiers, 1957, speaking in 2000, in Beaugé 2000.

3 Terence Gavaghan, former District Officer in Kenya, introduced new methods for breaking Mau Mau oaths in British detention camps from 1956, speaking in 1998, in Elkins 2003: 214.

4 Oral testimony of Mau Mau suspect, in ibid.: 195. *Askaris* = African levied troops; *Wazungu* = Europeans (in Swahili).

5 The vote also approved the term 'combats in Morocco and Tunisia'. The complete formula now appears on a plaque beneath the Arc de Triomphe in Paris, alongside those for the dead of 1870, 1914–18, 1940 and the Resistance.

6 The latter term was singled out as an example of language misuse, by two such different writers as George Orwell (1946) and Roland Barthes (1957).

7 Malagasy traumatic memories of 'Senegalese' brutality were real enough: see Mannoni (1970). The title track of the Malagasy band Tarika's album, *Son Egal* (Green Linnet Records, 1997) urges its Malagasy listeners, fifty years on, to forgive the Senegalese (*Sonegaly*) who were, after all, equally victims of colonial oppression.

8 Tronchon (1986: 45n.) lists estimates of insurgents' weaponry by the end of April 1947: 3 automatic rifles, 24 rifles, 70 muskets (. . . ?), 3 machine-guns, 1 Sten machine-pistol (and six magazines), 9 revolvers, 18 hunting rifles, 1 semi-automatic carbine, 4 anti-tank weapons. Insurgents relied on spears and knives, home-made small arms and, as rumour insisted, the power of magic suggestion. For the latter, see Mannoni's crudely Freudian interpretation of the chants of 'water, water' (1970, 59), supposed to liquefy bullets, and Fanon's statement of the slightly obvious, that the *tirailleurs'* rifles were in fact rifles and not phallic symbols (Fanon 1952: 86).

9 Fremigacci (2004) has scaled down the long-accepted, but largely unfounded, official estimate of 89,000 deaths, suggesting perhaps 10,000 deaths in combat and a further 20–30,000 deaths of refugees – a still appalling record for a relatively localized conflict.

10   The slender evidence provided by Tronchon (1986) points to a parallel Malagasy insurgent culture, with its counter-state and playful reversal of polarities and values, its secret signs and passwords, for example, wearing the traditional Malagasy straw hat 'like a panama' to show membership of PA.NA.MA; or viz the adoption of *noms de guerre* lifted, via a non-conformist education, from John Bunyan's *Pilgrim's Progress* (Ellis 1986).

11   The traditional figure of seventy attacks has been revised downwards by Jauffret (1998); and see Branche 2001: 36.

12   The first college comprised some 500,000 European voters and 58,000 Algerian 'full' citizens, the second, 1.3 million Muslim electors, out of a population of 860,000 Europeans, 7.7 million Algerians in 1948 (Droz & Lever 1991: 34n.).

13   Only one of the nine, Belkacem Krim, survived without capture to negotiate independence with the French. Two were killed in action, one, Ben M'Hidi, was murdered in French captivity, and five survived captivity; four of these, Ben Bella, Aït Ahmed, Mohamed Khider and Mohamed Boudiaf, were captured in the infamous 'skyjacking' of October 1956 (see below). This latter event not least demonstrated the strength of the collective principle.

14   A photographic essay on Bellounis in *Paris-Match*, June 1957, was one of very few Algerian stories, including Saadi Yacef's capture in the Battle of Algiers, to set alongside the birth of Princess Caroline of Monaco in that year.

15   Papon's responsibility for the massacre became a burning side-issue in his 1997 trial for war crimes during the German Occupation: Golsan 2000.

16   Durrell taught English in a Nicosia high school before becoming Government Information Officer for two years at the start of the Emergency.

17   By Grivas's own estimates for February 1956, EOKA numbered 1,033 men, comprising seven mountain gangs, 75 village groups and 47 town units: cited in Anderson 1994: 198.

18   Commentators noted the 'primitive' signification of this propaganda. Thus, Graham Greene pointed out that a Bren Gun inflicted wounds just as savagely as a *panga* (farm knife): in a letter to the *Times*, in Lonsdale 1990: 398.

19   Archives Defferre, Archives Communales de Marseille, Tel. No. 595. API, Moutet à Haut Commissaire Tananarive, & Tel. no. 1006, Cab.Mil., 5 juin 1947.

20   PRO, FO371/49275.

21   A parallel might be drawn between Carothers and Mannoni, amateur psychiatrists both, cf. Mannoni's disarmingly titled 'decolonization of myself' (1966).

7

Towards Self-Government:
Patterns of Late Colonial African
Politics, 1951–1957

For many years successive Governments in the United Kingdom have pursued, with a broad measure of public support, a Colonial policy of assisting dependent peoples to reach a stage of development at which they can assume responsibility for managing their own affairs. As a result, constitutional development is proceeding steadily in many parts of the Colonial Empire. This process cannot now be halted or reversed, and it is only to a limited extent that its pace can be controlled by the United Kingdom Government . . . In the main, the pace of constitutional change will be determined by the strength of nationalist feeling and the development of political consciousness within the territory concerned. Political leaders who have obtained assurances of independence for their people normally expect that the promised independence will be attained within their own political lifetime; and if they cannot satisfy their followers that satisfactory progress is being maintained towards that goal, their influence may be usurped by less responsible elements.[1]

. . . when you speak of assimilation to our compatriots in the overseas territories, they understand it, first and foremost, as economic and social assimilation and assimilation in relation to standard of living. And if you say to them that France wants to realize assimilation overseas, they reply: Well, give us immediately equality in wages, equality in labour legislation, in social security benefits, equality in family allowances, in brief, equality in standard of living.[2]

Kwame Nkrumah's 'famous victory' in the Gold Coast elections of February 1951 marked a new phase in late colonial politics. This was for two broad reasons. First, just as the Gold Coast offers a historical paradigm for the narrative of African national liberation, so too Nkrumah was widely seen at the time, and indeed conceived of himself, as an inspirational example, influencing events variously in Nigeria, in French Africa, or in British East Africa. For officials too, events in the Gold Coast represented a kind of Rubicon, which, once crossed, made it less likely that officials would seek to 'hold the line' elsewhere, and though the British policy of advance towards self-government had not ostensibly changed, it made a huge difference to recognize that the timing of this advance might be rapidly foreshortened. French officials too had perhaps crossed a lesser Rubicon of their own in their handling of Houphouët-Boigny and the RDA, but in any case could ill afford to resist the logic of further reform when their policy was compared with that in neighbouring British colonies.

Secondly, however, the Gold Coast was perhaps the foremost example of a wider shift in the late colonial state in Africa, from colonial administration by official *fiat* to African political agency. Post-war reforms – however cautious and sometimes half-baked – had certainly contributed to this shift, by encouraging the formation and rapid spread of political parties and trades unions, and by legislating gradual change in the status of ordinary Africans from colonial subjects to voters and citizens. What officials had not anticipated, however, whether in British and French Africa, was the emergence of an autonomous, expanding and vibrant 'civil society' as a largely unintended consequence of top-down official reform; indeed, this period has been characterized by Crawford Young as a 'golden age' in the associational life of African colonial societies:

> For a brief moment in history – which passed totally unperceived at the time – a swiftly congealing civil society basked in the sun of relative autonomy. The weakening will and authority of the terminal colonial state opened hitherto closely guarded social space. (Young 1994: 237)

In this chapter, therefore, we will examine in more detail the *forms* of this late colonial African politics, but we need also to consider its *content*. Gallagher (1982: 148) attributed the absence of 'freedom-fighters' in West Africa to there being 'nothing to fight over except a time-table'. Of course, even in the Gold Coast and Nigeria, the timetable still represented quite a significant struggle (though not the heroic 'struggle' implied by nationalist rhetoric or decried by a disbelieving Gallagher). However, there were many other things over which African politicians fought. Even Nkrumah's oft-quoted injunction, 'Seek ye first the political kingdom', implied a broader agenda than the quest for self-government. Rather, as Rathbone (2000: 7) argues, African nationalist politics combined two agendas, the first of which, much studied, was the 'forced expulsion of colonial overrule'; but the second, overlapping, and largely neglected, agenda was a 'commitment to ushering in a new kind of state, freed not only of alien rule but also of what nationalists conceived of as the unprogressive elements of the past'. With the first agenda on its way to being realized, Nkrumah gave more emphasis after February 1951 to the ambitious goals which comprised the second. Framed more generally, seeking to take over the colonial state was not enough; African politicians had also to determine the nature of the state over which they wished to assume power. This second, broader political agenda embraced a variety of goals, some congruent with those of an earlier, more confident colonial state – particularly the development agenda – but many also pointing forward to the solidarities and the divisions of the eventual post-colonial state.

The chapter is divided loosely into three sets of case studies. The first set comprises three British dependencies which moved definitively towards self-government in the early 1950s. In both the Gold Coast and Nigeria, officials and their moderate African allies at the end of the 1940s had steered the constitution-making process towards a carefully balanced outcome, ensuring representation of a wide range of political constituencies, while maintaining official control. Self-government may have been the aim, but it was understood as self-government by a national polity designed with British interests in mind. In the Gold Coast, these careful calibrations had been swept aside by the 1951 election results; while in Nigeria, it was not so much the election results as their subsequent political ramifications which upset British calculations. In this section we also consider a third case, the Sudan, which reached independence in 1956, a year before Ghana and four years before Nigeria, although it was not as politically 'advanced' as either, but where the impetus for change was generated by Britain's worsening relations with Egypt.

In the second part of the chapter, we turn to French Africa, including a separate focus on Cameroun, whose distinctive political destiny reflected its status as a United Nations Trusteeship territory. This same status applies to our last, separate case, Tanganyika, whose distinctiveness has more to do with the rapid emergence of a singularly successful nationalist movement, thus providing a possible model for other, more 'difficult' decolonizations.

The Gold Coast

As political theatre, the Gold Coast elections of February 1951 could not be faulted: a sweeping victory by a party whose leader went straight from prison to form what was in effect a nationalist government. Even Gandhi and Nehru had not managed better in their time. In fact, although the step was unpalatable to many officials, including at first the Governor, Charles Arden-Clarke, it had become clear that Nkrumah's Convention People's Party (CPP) was not the dangerous force for irresponsible extremism that officials had supposed. The party's role in encouraging voter registration boosted its victory, but also persuaded officials that party leaders were prepared to 'play the game'. Although Nkrumah, once elected, maintained a militant stance of 'Tactical Action', replacing the earlier campaign of Positive Action (Chapter 5), this implied cooperation with officials, however grudging, and largely boiled down to 'token boycotts of imperial rituals' (Rathbone 1992: lvii).

Nkrumah's relationship with Arden-Clarke is central to the process which led to independence for Ghana six years later. Arden-Clarke and his officials were breaking radically new ground, where even the interwar precedent of Indian 'dyarchy' was only partially helpful, since Indian executive responsibilities had remained at provincial level. Arden-Clarke held his officials to the line of accepting Nkrumah as 'moderate' and responsible, and to a programme of political education which sometimes flew in the face of political realities – '*He* is being educated by *us*', carped one official in 1953 (in Hargreaves 1996: 129). Arden-Clarke pursued the 'constitutional road' despite fellow governors' not unfounded misgivings that uncomfortable precedents were being set for their territories. An incoming Conservative government in late 1951 also shared those misgivings. Indeed, Nkrumah's promotion to prime minister, in March 1952, was a milestone not least because the new Colonial Secretary, Oliver Lyttlelton, acquiesced in it. Thus began more than 12 years of British decolonization presided over by the traditional party of empire. Nkrumah's elevation was largely a question of nomenclature, if a highly symbolic one, but Arden-Clarke and Nkrumah were soon contemplating further, substantial constitutional revision, and the 1954 elections were planned as the last before independence.

Nkrumah too was steered steadily along the 'constitutional road', while maintaining the momentum of a genuinely popular movement. Nkrumah had much to gain from appropriating core elements of British policy, notably the development portfolio, for which he assumed personal responsibility until Arden-Clarke persuaded him to devolve it to a cabinet committee. Of special interest to Nkrumah was the prestigious project to dam the Volta River in order to power an aluminium smelter, under the terms of a ten-year development plan overhauled in 1952 (Rathbone 1992: lvii). An ambitious programme of infrastructural development was subsidized from colonial development funds and from rising cocoa prices, which saw government revenues increase by 50 per cent over the six years from 1951 (Hargreaves 1996: 129). Here too Nkrumah adopted settled British policy of controlling cocoa receipts through a Cocoa Marketing Board, fuelling suspicions that he was developing the South at the expense of the cocoa-growing Ashanti region; this grievance was soon taken up by the Asante federalist movement (see below). Nkrumah and his ministers were reined in by the business of government, and isolated from the radical popular support which had buoyed their electoral success. As Alan Lennox-Boyd, Lyttleton's successor as Colonial Secretary, argued in September 1955:

> Many criticisms can be made against Dr Nkrumah and his Party, but they have behind them a solid record of good administration. Their willingness to learn . . . gives good grounds for hoping that they will continue to rise to the responsibilities of their position even when the wisdom of the present Governor is no longer available to them and they have to face their more extreme supporters on their own. (in Füredi 1994a: 254)

It has been suggested that British officials cynically sought to 'capture' moderate nationalists such as Nkrumah by splitting them off from their popular base; and by setting them a series of 'tests' to prove their loyalty – for example, the CPP was induced to purge radical ministers, and to pass measures designed to prevent the spread of communist influence in the Gold Coast (ibid.: 258–9). A somewhat different complexion is given to the matter if the steps taken to expel ministers found guilty of corruption are added to the list of official 'tests' (Hargreaves 1996: 129–30). The prize for acquiescence was in any case substantial as the 'constitutional road' neared its end, and here the principal obstacle lay in reaction to a quite different aspect of Nkrumah's radicalism.

By early 1954, acting in concert with British officials, with a wide national following, and with the scheduled June 1954 elections virtually a foregone conclusion, the CPP-led Cabinet could be forgiven for thinking that the 'struggle' was over. As Accra's *Daily Graphic* put it: 'Self government for the Gold Coast is no longer a political issue but an administrative and constitutional exercise. Our problems are more of an internal nature rather than an external one' (2 February 1954, in Rathbone 2000: 59).

However, internal problems weighed heavily during the three years to independence. At stake was the proposed unitary nature, and indeed the political culture, of the emerging national state. Though the 1951 Constitution was designed to allow

representation of diverse regional and chiefly interests, the CPP's victory had channelled support from a wide range of constituencies into something approaching a
'national' consensus. Moreover, the CPP's impetus was largely attributable to the
success of its self-consciously modernizing campaign directed against the chiefs,
particularly in its appeal to a class of 'youngmen' (*nkwankwaa*) whose 'youth' was
defined by an absence of kinship ties to royalty (Chapter 5; Rathbone 2000: 23–4).
Officials, meanwhile, were torn between their traditional support for chiefly interests,
and the consonance of the CPP's ideological position with their own modernizing
agenda (ibid.: 20ff.). Notwithstanding lingering nostalgia for the older certainties of
Indirect Rule, British policy was fully consistent with Nkrumah's local government
reforms, creating directly elected local councils and reducing Native Authorities'
remit to questions of tradition and custom: these reforms were incorporated in
the 1954 Constitution, which also introduced a single system of direct elections to the
Legislative Assembly.

The June 1954 elections returned the expected substantial CPP majority, thus
crystallizing opposition to the centralizing, modernizing programme espoused by
Nkrumah and the British. At its most straightforward, this opposition was expressed
by the chiefs of the Northern Territories, now fully incorporated into Gold Coast
representative structures; the newly mobilized Northern People's Party (NPP) captured 12 of 17 Northern Territories seats (Rathbone 1992: lxi). The position in the
Ashanti region was more complex, as the Asante kingdoms had been heavily involved
in earlier nationalist politics, albeit in the older-style 'moderate' politics of the United
Gold Coast Convention (UGCC), whose leader Dr J.B. Danquah was a kinsman of
the Asantehene, the Asante paramount king. Moreover, Ashanti was at the heart
of Gold Coast cocoa production (especially since it was less affected by 'swollen-
shoot' than the coastal plantations), and Nkrumah's manipulation of farmgate prices
was, as already mentioned, a source of bitter resentment. The National Liberation
Movement (NLM), formed in late 1954, was not simply a force for conservative
reaction, as Nkrumah portrayed it, not least because it mobilized CPP dissidents
drawn from the ranks of the 'youngmen' who had flocked to the CPP in the first place
(Allman 1993, 2003). However, the NLM was ideologically extremely vulnerable, as
it could ill afford to be seen to oppose momentum towards independence, and had
left it dangerously late to make an impression: with no presence in the Legislative
Assembly until a by-election in 1955 secured one seat, it pursued a twin-pronged
approach of lobbying the CPP government and the British while engaging in sometimes violent extra-parliamentary activities.

The NLM's campaign for a federalist constitution led nowhere, although it placed
significant obstacles in the 'constitutional road': talks in the Gold Coast and London,
mediation by a former Indian governor, a select committee and, not least, further
elections in July 1956, which provided the NLM with seats, but not outside their core
region of support. The option existed to meet the NLM's violence with state repression, but the changed parameters of politics meant that this could be contemplated
neither by Nkrumah, who would thus confirm the NLM's portrayal of his government as 'despotic', nor by Arden-Clarke. Nkrumah pursued the assault on chiefly
authority in matters of local government and justice, which continued until he was
ousted in 1966 (Rathbone 2000). He even played the regionalist card, splitting off a

new Brong-Ahafo region by 1958, where chiefs had historically resisted Asante para-mountcy and consequently supported the CPP (ibid.: 34–5). Meanwhile, the NPP's proposal that the Northern Territories maintain their status as a British Protectorate after independence was firmly rebutted by Lennox-Boyd (Rathbone 1992: lxv).

A third strand of regionalist opposition had to be handled with more delicacy, since the Togoland Congress's campaign for a separate Ewe homeland pertained to the Western part of the former German colony of Togo, administered from Accra as a United Nations Trusteeship Territory. Here, too, Nkrumah and Arden-Clarke saw eye to eye in resisting Ewe claims, as settled British policy opposed the possibility of the Ewe drifting into the French political orbit within a united Togo. Indeed, one-third of the Ewe lived in territory that had not formed part of the German colony, one-third in French Togo, and one-third in British Togoland. The Togoland Congress thus allied with the NLM, although its separatism was incompatible with NLM proposals for a federal Ghana. In a plebiscite held on 9 May 1956, the people of the Trust Territory voted by 93,095 to 67,492 for integration into Ghana – not an overwhelming defeat for the separatist movement, but sufficient for the UN Trusteeship Council to recommend the termination of the Trust at independence (ibid.: lxi, lxv; Michel 1986).

Independence followed, rescheduled because of the unplanned 1956 elections, and on 6 March 1957, Ghana became the first Black African member of the Commonwealth. The maintenance of the Queen as Head of State, a substantial expatriate presence in the civil service and a British commander of the armed forces, all appeared to signify that Britain had managed to bring off the trick of maintaining post-colonial influence. More obviously, these were symptoms of the rush to independence, as were a series of unresolved questions, notably concerning the extent to which Britain would continue to fund Ghana's development (Rathbone 1992: lxix). Nkrumah was the acclaimed champion of a new African nationalism, who in 1958 hosted the prestigious All-African People's Congress at Accra (Hargreaves 1996: 174, 180). By 1960, Ghana was a republic (although still within the Commonwealth), and it was clear to everyone that the break with the colonial past was terminal.

Nigeria

In Nigeria, British officials approached the new decade confident that they could manage reform, keep ahead of nationalist demands for self-government, and contain nationalism within a carefully constructed federal constitution. When the new constitution came into effect, in November 1951, its architect, Governor Sir John Macpherson, believed that British rule in Nigeria still had at least thirty years to run (Lynn 2001: lx). The constitution resulted from a wide-ranging consultation process, and though it reproduced the arithmetic of the 1947 text, whereby Northern representation within the federal House of Representatives equalled that of the Western and Eastern regions together, it now granted legislative powers to three Regional Assemblies, created regional Executive Councils, and established a federal Council of Ministers on which sat six officials and four unofficials from each region.

Elections to the new Assemblies did not overturn official calculations as in the Gold Coast, but they underlined unanticipated aspects of the system's political logic, leading to the constitution's failure within two years. First, with three decades of gradual evolution stretching before his mind's eye, Macpherson vetoed ministerial responsibility for the Council of Ministers, who, though collectively responsible to the House or Representatives, had no clear-cut powers to instruct officials, and no prime minister. This suited the Northern People's Congress (NPC), for whom any progress towards federal self-government was inherently problematic, but frustrated the Action Group (AG), which dominated the Western Region, and the National Congress of Nigeria and the Cameroons (NCNC), representing the Eastern Region but with Western support as well. This shortcoming was felt acutely when, in March 1952, Nkrumah became prime minister in Accra, a step that Macpherson thought might 'save the Gold Coast for the Empire' but lose Nigeria (ibid.: doc. 152, lxi–lxii). However, by the time a new constitutional text came into operation in October 1954, the emphasis had shifted even further away from central government.

Furthermore, the 1951 Constitution tipped the balance between representing regional interests and exacerbating regional tensions. The problem arose because each Regional Assembly elected members of the federal House of Representatives by simple majority, thus further identifying the three parties with their respective regions. The one exception to the inevitable 'winner-takes-all' effect was the capital, Lagos, which elected NCNC members to all five of its seats in the Western Regional Assembly. Nnamdi Azikiwe, one of the five, then failed to be nominated to the federal House of Representatives, with the paradoxical result that the principal advocate of Nigerian self-government found himself Leader of the Opposition within the Western Regional Assembly, without a national role, or an official role in his party's Eastern stronghold. The further irony, however, was that Azikiwe resolved this paradox by his election to the Eastern Regional Assembly in June 1953, thus undermining the campaign for national unity which he had personally championed (ibid.: lxi, lxiv).

Nigeria's 'constitutional road' over the coming years was thus shaped by the seismic friction resulting from a constantly shifting overlap between party politics, ethnic and regional tensions, and competing visions of Nigeria's future. The NCNC remained most closely associated with the cause of national unity, and was the only party operating effectively outside its 'home' region, but Azikiwe's difficulties, and the party's relatively disappointing performance in the Western Region, accentuated by NCNC defections to the AG, tended to pull the party back to its Eastern, and specifically Igbo, roots. However, when, in 1953, Azikiwe sought to impose party discipline by calling for the resignation of rebellious NCNC members of the Eastern Executive Council, six (of nine) quit the party, forcing the NCNC into opposition in its home region (ibid.: lxiv–lxv).

The Action Group had its origins as a Yoruba cultural movement, the *Egbe Omo Oduduwa*, resisting the perceived threat of Igbo penetration of the West. This threat was encapsulated in the possibility of a centralized Nigerian state, since Igbos, whose average educational attainment was higher than other Nigerian groups, were more likely to take up state employment. Though the AG rivalled the NCNC in favouring self-government, it did so on a strongly regional basis. Thus, it pushed for greater ministerial responsibility, sought to extend local government reform in the West, and politicized Western appointments to marketing boards – a key institution of continuing British control here as in the Gold Coast (ibid.: lxiv). Rivalry with the NCNC also took territorial form: when the NCNC moved to split off Lagos from the West as a separate region (thus playing to Yoruba anxieties), the AG proposed realigning the boundary between the Western and Northern regions, in order to incorporate Yoruba Muslims in the West. The move was ruled out of order, but worried Northern rulers represented by the NPC.

With more than half the Nigerian population, three-quarters of Nigerian territory, and a strong tradition of localized rule encapsulated in the Native Authorities, the ethnically and religiously diverse Northern Region was vulnerable to incursions by Southern parties trying to capture local electorates, while local rulers' authority was threatened by the thrust of post-war local government reform. The NPC thus fought off AG and NCNC attempts to ally with a rival Northern Elements Progressive Union (NEPU), and opposed moves to break the Northern Region into smaller units, such as a region for the so-called Middle Belt. However, the NPC's biggest threat came from moves towards self-government on AG or NCNC terms, since a Nigerianized civil service would almost inevitably recruit mostly Southerners of any stripe (ibid.: lviii). Parity with the South was thus a bulwark against too rapid change. So too was the threat of Northern secession, already wielded in the consultation period for the 1951 Constitution, and repeated in the NPC's response to an AG motion in 1953 calling for 'self-government by 1956'. The motion was amended by the NPC leader, the Sardauna of Sokoto, to read 'as soon as practicable'; but the Sardauna also referred somewhat ominously in debate to 'the mistake of 1914' (the date on which Nigeria was united) (ibid.: lxv–vi).

Northern leaders could rely on the instinctual support of British officials from the governor down, while Northern secession threatened the overriding British priority to maintain a united Nigeria. However, officials' gradualist approach to Nigerian self-government was clearly dissipating, and a shift may be detected in the run-up to the 1954 constitution, from a policy of 'managing colonial reform in order to pre-empt the demand for self-government' (Lynn 2001: xlix) to one acknowledging, as Macpherson put it to the three regional leaders in June 1953, that 'the clear political objective for Nigeria . . . was self-government' (ibid.: lxviii). This shift, however, did not preclude British attempts to even out differences between North and South, and to secure as favourable a settlement as possible, and 'dilatory tactics' were a key part of British policy until 1958, when a firm date for independence was set (ibid.: loc.cit.).

Meanwhile, Macpherson sought to balance Southern demands against Northern caution by accentuating the pull of regional government in the 1954 Constitution, and by conceding that individual regions could attain self-government by 1956 if they so wished. Ironically, in the elections that followed, the NCNC achieved perhaps its biggest political *coup* in its rivalry with the AG, winning a surprise majority in the West by attacking the AG's record in regional government. This upset British calculations, forced the AG into opposition in its home region, and excluded it from central government, which now comprised three officials, three NPC and six NCNC ministers. The result was reversed after two years, when fresh House of Assembly elections in the West produced an AG majority, but by then the dominant trend was towards consolidation of power in all three Regions (ibid.: lxxiv).

The trend was clearest, and most threatening to British policy, in the Eastern region where, in early 1955, the Assembly docked expatriation allowances to senior

British officials, thus effectively Nigerianizing regional government, since demoralized British officials were expected to go home within the year. Although the governor rescinded the measure under his reserve powers, it joined a list of grievances which had been building for some considerable time between Azikiwe and the governor; these included a succession of budget crises and pending corruption charges against Azikiwe and his ministers. The 'Eastern crisis' which simmered over the summer of 1955 was the last occasion when officials 'seriously contemplated halting the progress to Nigerian self-government': this would have involved suspending the Constitution, in turn requiring military backing, with the deployment of British troops as 'a precaution and a stiffener'. In the end, officials concluded that Azikiwe was unlikely to risk chaos in the East before achieving self-government, and the crisis was resolved following a private 'talking to' which a headmasterly Lennox-Boyd administered to Azikiwe in London, in November 1955 (ibid.: lxxv–vi). Poor relations continued between Azikiwe and British officials for more than a year, as Azikiwe was investigated on corruption charges involving his interest in the African Continental Bank. A commission of enquiry reported in January 1957, finding Azikiwe 'guilty of misconduct as a Minister'. However, Azikiwe refused to resign, and his position was endorsed by elections in the East, which increased the NCNC's majority (ibid.: lxxvi–vii). Further British attempts to bring pressure on Azikiwe now seemed all the more likely to backfire.

The case against Azikiwe also delayed a planned conference on regional self-government until May 1957. By this time, following Ghana's independence in March, an AG motion in the House of Representatives, calling for Nigerian independence in 1959, was carried unanimously, supported even by the NPC. The main issue for the May 1957 Conference was thus the date of independence (ibid.: lxxviii). While the CO sought to postpone a decision, Lennox-Boyd was forced to concede that a date would be fixed following House of Representatives elections in late 1959. This pointed to a date in 1960, although the decision was only finalized at the last of Nigeria's major constitutional conferences, which opened in London in September 1958. By this time, the essentials of Nigeria's independent statehood were settled. In particular, the North retained a slight majority in the federal House of Representatives, 174 out of 320 seats, but survived intact: proposals for a Middle Belt region, backed by the AG, were shelved, and replaced by the weaker idea of minority rights. British policy may be summarized in the view, expressed in 1957, that 'it is not worthwhile risking the forfeiture of Nigeria's goodwill . . . for the sake of hanging on for . . . a further three or four years' (in ibid.). This was the authentic official voice of the imperial endgame, articulating an approach that runs through the decolonization process from this point on.

The Sudan

Historians have usually treated the decolonization of Africa's second largest country as a by-product of Anglo-Egyptian relations (Holland 1985: 103; Darwin 1988: 208–9; Louis 1999: 340–1; Springhall 2001: 88–9). This is all the more surprising given the Sudan's importance during the Scramble for Africa, and the Sudanese origins of some of late Victorian imperialism's great myths: the relief of Omdurman and the Anglo-French stand-off at Fashoda, and not least the Mahdiya, the rising against Egyptian rule led by Muhammad Ahmad al-Mahdi, an iconic embodiment of Britain's imperial enemies. Little more than a half-century after the establishment of British rule, this was also one of the great failures of decolonization, leaving a decades-long post-colonial legacy of civil war.

The Sudan's constitutional status from 1899 to the 1950s was the highly anomalous one of an Anglo-Egyptian Condominium, in which British officials governed while Egypt retained sovereignty. The Sudan's former existence at the heart of a Turco-Egyptian empire stretching far into the African continent also explains the territorial divide between a predominantly Arab, Muslim North and a more ethnically mixed, part-Christian, Black African South. This divide was reinforced by the focusing of British resources and administrative energies in the North, while the more quiescent Southern provinces were relatively neglected and were 'massaged into the structures of local administration' only in the 1930s (Johnson 1998: xliii). British rule was also anomalous in that a self-contained, sometimes parochial Sudan Political Service (SPS) was recruited and run by the Foreign Office; or rather, mostly not run, since Khartoum's communications followed the chain of command through Cairo, and a separate Sudan desk was created in the FO's African (formerly Egyptian) Department only in the 1950s. The Sudan's isolation from developments in British colonial policy extended even to its ineligibility for Colonial Welfare and Development funds; when in 1946, the Governor-General, Sir Hubert Huddleston, made a direct appeal for Treasury funds to endow the Gordon Memorial College in Khartoum, he was refused (ibid.: xlvii).

Sudanese political history under colonial rule was dominated by, and articulated with, Britain's relations with Egypt. Although the question of Egyptian sovereignty was moot until Britain's unilateral grant of Egyptian independence in 1922, it became a central issue for more than thirty years thereafter, both in the negotiation of the 1936 Anglo-Egyptian treaty and in the protracted renegotiation of that treaty after 1945. Although the Sudan was discussed more often at British Cabinet level than many other colonial topics, it was almost invariably as an issue of secondary importance to the defence of the Suez Canal Zone (ibid.: xxxvi; Kent 1998: vol. 1, xxxvi). A further long-running issue concerned the waters of the Nile, a question which coloured the Khartoum government's relations with Egypt, but also with Ethiopia and with British colonial governments in Uganda and Kenya; the Nile also provided an opening for Egyptian agents in the Southern Sudan, in the shape of the Egyptian Irrigation Department.

Anglo-Egyptian relations tended to push the Sudan towards self-government from the 1920s, when 'Sudanization' evolved as a way of supplanting Egyptian influence, and eventually of replacing Egyptian administrators and soldiers with Sudanese. Following the Atlantic Charter, British and Egyptian negotiators both championed Sudanese self-determination, although the more usual Egyptian complaint was that self-government eroded Egypt's sovereign rights over the Sudan (Johnson 1998: lx, lxv). Conversely, the British could be accused of applying the usual gradualist arguments in order to hang on, particularly in the undeveloped South. Hence, British proposals for Sudanese political reform tended to be in advance of the rest of Africa;

a discomfited CO thus objected to the system of direct elections devised for the 1948 Legislative Assembly, and to the 'most awkward imaginable' statement to the House of Commons by the Foreign Secretary, Anthony Eden, in October 1952, welcoming progress to 'government by an all-Sudanese Cabinet, responsible through an all-Sudanese parliament to the Sudanese people' (ibid.: lxxiii).

Sudanese political leaders in the North were more than equal to the task of ensuring that their political role was never reduced to that of a 'pawn in [British] Egyptian policy', as Margery Perham feared it was in 1953 (in Louis 1999: 340). The pattern of British collaborative relations with local notables was indeed structured around the Egyptian question. Thus, from the early 1920s, the government shifted its support from one religious brotherhood, the Khatmiya, whose leader, sayyid Ali al-Mirghani, had supported Egypt during the Mahdiya, to the Ansar, followers of sayyid Abd al-Rahman al-Mahdi, son of the Mahdi (Robinson 1972: 135–7). These religious notables exerted influence over an emerging class of educated '*effendia*' who filled the lower ranks of the civil service – *effendi* being a respectful term which British official-dom characteristically turned into an insult, as with '*babu*' or 'intellectual'. Many were graduates of the elite Gordon Memorial College, modelled on the British 'Public Schools', which, 'in its capacity as an *effendi* machine . . . also propelled nationalism' (Sharkey 2003: 65). Many *effendia* backed the White Flag League in the 1920s, modelled on the Egyptian *Wafd*, whose uprising in 1924 was swiftly repressed. Nationalist aspirations were eventually channelled into a broad-based Graduates' Congress, formed in 1938. In 1942, the Congress presented a memorandum to Sir Stafford Cripps, calling for the Sudanese application of the Atlantic Charter. When this was – predict-ably – rebuffed by the Sudan government, the Congress split into divers factions, plundering the Arabic political lexicon to advocate autonomy, union or federation with Egypt, or outright independence. The post-1945 pattern of Northern Sudanese politics was shaped by this factionalism, but also by a more clear-cut divide. While Congress, dominated by the pro-Egyptian Khatmiya and by the Ashiqqa ('blood broth-ers') Party, mostly boycotted official institutions, a new Umma ('Nation') Party, backed by Abd al-Rahman, stood in elections to the Advisory Council, formed in 1943, and to the later Legislative Assembly (Johnson 1998: xlviii).

By the early 1950s, Britain and Egypt were moving almost imperceptibly closer to an agreement weighing Egyptian sovereignty against Sudanese self-determination, when, on 8 October 1951, Egypt abrogated both the 1936 treaty and the 1899 co-dominion agreement. A formula was agreed in April 1952, but was thrown into question along with all other aspects of Anglo-Egyptian relations, by the Free Officers' Coup of 23 July 1952, which overthrew the Egyptian monarchy. The fundamental issue re-mained unchanged, but initiative for resolving it shifted, as Cairo outflanked London and Khartoum by negotiating agreements with all Sudanese parties, most notably with the Umma Party in October 1952. Although agreements differed from party to party, the essential deal was self-government, followed by the suspension of the con-dominium to create a 'free and neutral atmosphere' for Sudanese self-determination, for which Egypt, not Britain, now effectively stood as guarantor (ibid.: lxx).

From here an inexorable, if still tortuous line may be traced through to inde-pendence. The Anglo-Egyptian agreement on Sudanese self-government and self-determination, signed on 12 February 1953, led to elections in November 1953, in which the Umma Party was beaten by an alliance between the pro-Egyptian Khatmiya and a National Union Party (NUP) formed from the Ashiqqa, whose founder, the former mathematics teacher Ismail al-Azhari, became prime minister. An accelerated process of Sudanization was completed by August 1955, by when only two hundred British officials remained, a sixth of the previous total (ibid.: lxxx, docs 375, 291). This opened the way to curtailing the process of self-determination, although fittingly, it was a twist in the Egyptian tale – Nasser's 1955 Czech arms deal, which led to Suez – which released the British government from its fear of offending Egypt. At this point, the Governor-General was instructed to inform al-Azhari of British willingness to recognize Sudanese independence. The timing of the declaration of independence was decided and executed by al-Azhari, almost anticlimactically, on 1 January 1956 – while the Governor-General, Sir Knox Helm, was in England on Christmas leave (ibid.: lxxxvi–vii).

The fundamental issue on which successive governors-general failed to make a stand was the fate of the South under Northern dominance. British policy towards the South was more like that prevailing elsewhere in British Africa, in that officials sought to control gradual political and administrative modernization – which was all the more necessary given pre-war neglect of Southern administration. The official view inverted the usual colonial theme, emphasizing the artificiality of Sudanese boundaries – which, for once, were the result of something other than European colonial expansion – and the historical, or 'natural', divide existing between North and South. For the Northern Sudanese, by contrast, Sudanese unity was based on 'bonds of religion, language, blood, education and the Nile', as al-Azhari put it in 1945; he also admitted 'above all, the economic need of the North for the South' (ibid.: l, docs 26, 35). According to this version of Sudanese history, an Arab *mission civilisatrice* had been halted by the arrival of the British; it was perhaps unfortunate that the factors listed by al-Azhari were all 'based on the institution of slavery' (ibid.; Sharkey 2003: 132–3). One British option was therefore Southern secession, but this quickly ran into the insuperable obstacle of Egyptian sovereignty claims, and was ruled out early in the post-war period. The 1947 Sudan Administration Conference thus recommended the South's full incorporation into Sudanese administrative and legislative structures. Since no Southerners were present at this conference, a separate meeting of interested parties was held at Juba to present its findings (Johnson 1998: lxi). The alternative for the British was the familiar one of playing for time, urging delays in the implementation of self-government, seeking to extend the process of Sudanization to allow the training and recruitment of Southern Sudanese, claiming special reserve powers for the Governor-General in the South, even offering Commonwealth membership as a means of extending British official influence: in short, measures that were all too readily dismissed as 'colonialist'.

During this period, Southern Sudanese opinion was largely taken for granted by British officials, partly because there were relatively few Southerners to consult, since the Christians who formed the Southern equivalent of the *effendia* were few in number.[3] Political crisis in the South built slowly, and by early 1955, with Sudanization under way, Southern politicians, even those belonging to the majority NUP, argued more urgently in favour of federation, at conferences held in the South in late 1954 and 1955. Ironically, they received Egyptian backing, as Cairo turned to the South as a way of offsetting Northern enthusiasm for independence. A dramatic eleventh-hour demonstration of Southern anxieties came in August 1955, when Southern troops of the Equatorial Corps mutinied at Torit, in Equatoria province. Although Egyptian influence was no doubt a factor, officials were worried by the extent of popular support for this rising. The RAF flew Northern troops south to enforce surrender, but most mutineers fled to neighbouring Uganda, alongside large numbers of civilians, missionaries and others, thus generating the first of many such refugee crises in this region of Africa. In this and other respects, the endgame of Sudanese decolonization, which the Torit mutiny served to accelerate further, offered gloomy portents for the post-colonial Sudanese state's likely development (Johnson 1998: lxxxii–v).

French Africa: the End of Assimilation

The new decade also promised a fresh start in French Africa, where elections to the National Assembly in Paris stabilized French African politics following a period of turbulence. However, the initiative now increasingly lay with African politicians, and not least with African trades unionists, as they realized a major legislative goal, the 1952 African Labour Code. Ironically, both for French officials and for African leaders, the moral of this period might be inscribed: 'be careful what you wish for'. For African leaders, equality within the French system was becoming less attractive, not only compared with anglophone nationalist achievements, but also when offset by the gravitational pull of territorial politics. For officials, conversely, assimilationist logic within the federal frameworks of AOF and AEF was proving politically costly, as representation in Paris bestowed political influence without concomitant responsibility; it also pointed towards spiralling financial costs for the French state, as the hard-won entitlements of African workers translated into hard cash. Although 'self-government' remained an alien concept in 1951, officials and politicians, albeit for contrasting reasons, thus started to converge on a strategy of 'territorialization' – or, as its critics had it, 'balkanization' – which, as implemented in the 1956 Framework Law, aligned late colonial French rule in Africa more closely with its British equivalents.

The June 1951 National Assembly election results reflected earlier confrontations. Many officials were unconvinced by Houphouët-Boigny's accommodation with François Mitterrand's party, the small, centrist UDSR (Chapter 5). Officials had not changed their ways either, and deployed various electoral 'dirty tricks', withholding voting cards from supporters of 'anti-government' candidates, stuffing ballot boxes, only distributing ballot papers for favoured candidates, and so on: Senghor complained that the nineteenth-century colonizer of Senegal, Governor Faidherbe, still voted in elections in St-Louis, usually three or four times (Mortimer 1969: 164). RDA strength was thus reduced to three *députés*, including the unassailable Houphouët-Boigny. The winners were the less cohesive Overseas Independents (IOM), with nine seats out of twenty in AOF, AEF and Cameroun. These included Senghor and a colleague in Senegal (confirming the SFIO's decline in its former stronghold), and several *députés* allied with the Christian Democrat MRP (Mortimer 1969: 170–2). In France, this was the election in which a beleaguered 'Third Force' coalition sought to exclude Communists to its left and the Gaullist RPF (Rally of the French People) to its right, with a blatantly manipulated form of proportional representation. In Africa, conversely, officials secured the election of several RPF *députés*, either because of wartime Gaullist loyalties, as in Tchad and Oubangui-Chari (though the colourful Abbé Barthélémy Boganda survived in the latter territory), or simply to favour a candidate representing conservative chiefs, as in Mauritania and the second Côte d'Ivoire seat. In Cameroun and AEF, where the two-college system was retained, settlers on the RPF ticket held all three first-college seats; the two AEF *députés*, Malbrant and Bayrou, both veterinary surgeons, were already a byword for resistance to reform. By contrast, the European IOM *député* and future minister, Dr Louis Aujoulat, a mission doctor, transferred from the first to the second college in Cameroun, and was duly elected.

This was the start of an electoral cycle: new territorial assemblies were elected in March 1952, which in turn elected the federal Grand Councils in Dakar and Brazzaville; elections followed to the Council of the Republic (the Fourth Republic's upper chamber), to the largely toothless Assembly of the French Union, then municipal elections, before the cycle restarted with National Assembly elections in January 1956. Each offered an opportunity to rethink the terms of African participation in French institutions, and to reflect those terms in a revised electoral law. However, in 1951, although the franchise was extended to include heads of household and mothers of two children 'living or dead for France', the double college was retained in AEF and Cameroun. In early 1952, the territorial assemblies were granted proper legal status, but a law granting them budgetary powers ran out of parliamentary time; here, too, the double-college system persisted. The pattern was repeated in November 1955, when a law passed introducing universal suffrage and abolishing the double-college system. However, the Prime Minister, Edgar Faure, defeated in a confidence vote, dissolved the Assembly before the law could be enacted; the January 1956 elections were therefore held under the old rules (Mortimer 1969).

This familiar narrative of missed opportunities, official obstruction and intermittent Parisian attention to African affairs was starting to impact on African leaders' strategy. Two strategies could be pursued, conceivably in tandem: seeking closer involvement with the Parisian government, and pursuing the logic of territorial politics. In shifting political sands (mostly shifting rightwards after 1951), both the RDA and the IOM tended to vote for any prime minister seeking investiture unless there was good reason not to; this tactic made it less likely that colonial reforms would be buried; it could also be rewarded by liberal appointments at the Rue Oudinot or even ministerial posts (ibid.: 174). Senghor and Aujoulat thus served in various governments up to 1956, at which point Houphouët-Boigny took up the baton. The alternative, territorial strategy was one for which the IOM, although ostensibly the 'winners' of the 1951 elections, were less favourably positioned than the RDA. In February 1953, the IOM sought to overcome their institutional weakness by forming a co-ordinated, inter-territorial 'Movement of the Overseas Independents', the name itself a contradiction in terms. Efforts to revive the 1946 spirit of unity, along with the federalist theses which had underpinned that unity, could not disguise the fact that, in contrast with the RDA, the parties at the Movement's founding congress were regionalist groupings or 'one-man shows' (ibid.: 190–1; Morgenthau 1964: 417ff.).

While the IOM thus remained a 'parliamentary group which failed to achieve an effective grass-roots organization', the defeated RDA was better placed to build on the 1951 results (Mortimer 1969: 197–8). Ostensibly, Houphouët-Boigny had little to show for his alignment with the UDSR, also outflanked from the right; Mitterrand was kept away from the Rue Oudinot, though more senior ministerial posts beckoned. The March 1952 territorial elections largely mirrored the 1951 results, with strong showings for the RDA in Côte d'Ivoire, Soudan and Moyen-Congo outweighed by near-annihilation elsewhere (ibid.: 174–5). With some exceptions, notably the Camerounian UPC (see below), RDA-affiliated parties eschewed the pro-Communist orientation still championed by its secretary-general, Gabriel d'Arboussier. Rather, over a parliamentary term, the RDA capitalized on two underlying trends. The first was the softening of the administration's hard line, as officials learned to accept RDA strategy, and Houphouët-Boigny's rejection of communism, at face value (see Messmer 1992: 211–12). The spectacle of Nkrumah's political progress was perhaps a factor in the official change of heart.[4] Secondly, more fundamentally, electoral behaviour was changing as reforms filtered through. Even a modestly extended franchise in 1951 was enough to shift the electoral balance away from the assimilated, urban elite and the narrow categories of rural post-holders to something approximating to a mass electorate. The full extent of this shift became apparent in 1956, when officials had largely released their stranglehold of electoral registration. Indeed, the biggest increases in registered voters from 1951 to 1956 – that is, even without universal suffrage – occurred in those territories where the RDA and other 'rebel' parties were hard-pressed in 1951: 371 per cent in Côte d'Ivoire, 147 per cent in Guinea, 142 per cent in Oubangui-Chari, and a staggering 634 per cent in Niger, but only 26 per cent in Senegal and 15 per cent in Soudan (ibid.: 168–9).

Other factors reinforced the pull of territorial politics, not least the basic fact that *députés* were responsible to territorial electorates. When a seat in Paris translated into a substantial majority in a post-1952 territorial assembly, it started to feel like real political power. Thus, Houphouët-Boigny's consolidation of power translated into a massive 28 out of 32 second-college seats for the PDCI in the territorial assembly; in a spirit of comprehensiveness, the RDA list included five Europeans and some 'ex-RDA-RDA' who had deserted the party during the repression (ibid.: 175; Morgenthau 1964: 204–5). For the Oubangui-Chari *député* Boganda – having left the MRP and the Church after marrying his French secretary – a lonely political existence in Paris was converted into 17 of 26 second-college seats in Bangui; his Movement for the Social Evolution of Black Africa (MESAN) thus trounced the RDA, to which he felt no need to affiliate, since he was already 'the unquestioned leader of his territory' (Mortimer 1969: 175).

Splendid isolation in Paris counted for less than support 'back home'. Despite the territorial assemblies' still limited powers, they provided greater potential for cultivating mass support, for both the victors and the also-rans of 1951–2. Many of the next generation of leaders nourished their careers from a local base, criticizing the self-interest or detachment of their 'Parisian' rivals. Léon M'Ba of Gabon, whose moment came with his election as mayor of Libreville in November 1956, and then as victor in the territorial elections of 1957, pursued a steady campaign of vituperation against Jean-Hilaire Aubame, the 'bread-eater' who spurned the humble manioc of his constituents (Bernault 1996: 223–4). The Guinean leader, Ahmed Sékou Touré, better known as a pro-Communist trades unionist, ran (and lost) in the 1951 elections on a very different basis, as descendant of the nineteenth-century warrior, Samory Touré. In August 1953, even while Sékou Touré was preparing a two-month strike in support of the African labour code (see below), a by-election to the territorial assembly in his home region of Upper Guinea allowed him to prove his credentials amongst his Malinké kinsfolk, as he beat the sitting *député* to win the seat (Mortimer 1969: 200). Although he again lost the bigger prize in a National Assembly by-election a year later, Sékou Touré came second with 36 per cent of the vote, and was credited with being 'the real *député*', beaten by official fraudulent tactics (Mortimer 1969: 205–6). In 1956, he led his party to victory; this was the Guinean branch of the RDA, the Democratic Party of Guinea (PDG), whose near-hegemonic status in Guinea rivalled the PDCI's in Côte d'Ivoire. In this way, the ground was already being prepared for the post-Framework Law regime of autonomous territories.

Meanwhile, an oceanic shift was occurring in the assimilationism which had informed French African policy since the war. After an arduous legislative process stretching back to late 1947, the African Labour Code was passed in November 1952 – even then only under the pressure of impressively coordinated strike action across French Africa (Cooper 1996a: 292–305). In the meantime, a further, symbolic piece of legislation, the 'second' Lamine Guèye Law of June 1950, passed unanimously, had established the key principle of equality of wages and benefits for African civil servants (ibid.: 282 & n; for the 'first' Lamine Guèye Law, see Chapter 5). This was now extended to all African wage labourers, including the private sector, although it still excluded most African workers, particularly agricultural workers, whose status as 'customary' labour was left unregulated. Before the Labour Code could be implemented, two further battles remained to be fought, the first of which concerned the Code's forty-hour working week, which for Africans – but not officials – implied no loss of earnings in relation to the earlier 48-hour week, in other words, a 20 per cent rise in the minimum wage. It was on this issue that Sékou Touré led his two-month strike in Conakry, the longest of a wave of strikes which forced a climbdown: on 28 November 1953, the government accepted the 20 per cent rise (ibid.: 310). The second battle was over family allowances, demanded by African civil service unions since 1946. On this issue, strike action in 1954–55 was less effective because of increasing tensions between rival unions. However, official surveys portrayed 'a young labour force, with a high percentage of bachelors, a low incidence of polygamy, and small families', suggesting that a carefully modulated system of family allowances was affordable (ibid.: 316). This was introduced on 1 January 1956 in AOF, six months later in AEF. This was the high-water mark of French assimilationism, and of the late colonial state's modernity; the tide was about to turn.

Even as the campaign for equal rights with French metropolitan workers reached its climax, African trades union leaders were kicking away that campaign's institutional supports, and moving towards African autonomy. African trades union branches resented the overweening control exercised by the metropolitan *centrales* of the great French unions, principally the Communist-led CGT (General Confederation of Labour). For officials applying Cold War logic, an African CGT split from its *centrale* was clearly desirable, and as early as October 1951, officials unavailingly pushed the rising CGT 'star', Sékou Touré, to provoke a split (ibid.: 409–10). In 1952, Houphouët-Boigny encouraged a breakaway union, but only in Côte d'Ivoire (Mortimer 1969: 180). Not until November 1955 was the first substantial autonomist trades union formed, in Senegal, the CGT-Autonome (CGTA – some said 'A' stood for 'administrative'). Joined in May 1956 by Sékou Touré's Guinean movement, by the end of 1956, it rivalled the CGT's membership (Cooper 1996a: 414). In January 1957, after more than a year of damaging disunity, CGT and CGTA merged into a single General Union of the Workers of Black Africa (UGTAN); although CGT bosses assumed leadership of the new union, Sékou Touré soon outmanoeuvred them. By this time, however, the greater cohesion which came from a dominant African *centrale* was offset by the very different conception of autonomy enshrined in the Loi-Cadre.

The Loi-Cadre (Framework Law) passed on 19 June 1956 was an idea whose time had come, although *prima facie* it corresponded more to French reformist rationales than to African aspirations. French officials' growing sense that the limits of social assimilation had been reached was recognized by the Governor-General of AOF, Bernard Cornut-Gentille, in September 1954, confidentially warning of a potential protest movement amongst African civil servants (Cooper 1996a: 413). French politicians and journalists too were starting to count the escalating costs of assimilation and of French development projects. In the National Assembly debate on the proposed Law, quoted at the outset of this chapter, Pierre-Henri Teitgen (MRP), who, as Minister for Overseas France in the 1955 Faure government, had had a hand in its preparation, spelled out the likely costs to the French taxpayer of a continued policy of assimilation: 'Attaining this goal would require that the totality of French people accept a decrease of their standard of living by 25 to 30 per cent for the benefit of their compatriots of the overseas territories' (ibid.: 425). Raymond Cartier subsequently articulated the more general argument, in the glossy magazine he edited, *Paris-Match*:

> Perhaps an Office de la Loire would have been better than an Office du Niger. It might have been better to build a super-hospital in Nevers rather than Lomé, and Bobo-Dioulasso's High School in Tarbes. Where did France's interest lie? The billions spent by FIDES in Black Africa, not to mention the 1,400 billion francs invested overseas since 1946, might have been enough to modernize the French economy and make it competitive in international markets. (1 September 1956, in Marseille 1984: 11; Cooper 1996a: 392)[5]

The 'Cartiériste' argument – that formal empire was simply becoming too burdensome – was to be central, in one form or another, to the colonial powers' recalibration of power which accompanied eventual decolonization.

Meanwhile, momentum in favour of political reform had been building since 1954–5. Charged with *not* pursuing constitutional reform for fear of overloading an already extensive 'overseas' agenda, Mendès-France's Minister of Overseas France, Robert Buron (ex-MRP), confined himself to preparing largely technical reforms of 'decentralization and deconcentration' (Mortimer 1969: 202). He pressed ahead in one area, however, pushing through a new Statute for Togo. As a UN Trusteeship territory, Togo was separate from AOF's institutional structures. Moreover, expeditious reform was a response to UN pressures, but also a desirable way of beating the British at their own game over Eweland (see above). Togo offered a precedent, not only for

France's other Trusteeship territory in Cameroun, but also for AOF and AEF. However, the Statute, passed on 16 April 1955, compared unfavourably with parallel British examples, since the appointed 'council of government' presided over by the Governor (renamed Commissioner of the Republic) had no real executive powers. It also failed to satisfy the pro-independence Committee for Togolese Unity (CUT), whose policy had shifted from pan-Ewe irredentism to Togolese nationalism. However, pro-French parties won a substantial victory on a healthy turnout in territorial elections held in June 1955, albeit with a strong official 'helping hand'. None of this convinced the UN mission which toured in August and September, and recommended against ending the Trusteeship in either the British or French halves of Togo without a plebiscite: in the British case, this took place in June 1956 (ibid.: 203–4; & see above).

If the Togo Statute represented one model for change, the existing federal system was ostensibly more likely to form the basis for reform. Thus a National Assembly committee, chaired by Senghor, reported in July 1955 on revision of the Constitution's French Union articles (ibid.: 235). This represented the culmination of Senghor's campaigning going back to the ill-fated 'Constitution Senghor' defeated in the May 1946 referendum (Chapter 5). However, the political conjuncture worked against painstaking constitutional revision. The January 1956 elections were won by a left-centre coalition of Socialists, Radicals and UDSR, led by Guy Mollet (SFIO). In Africa, the fortunes of IOM and RDA were reversed, with the RDA tripling its representation to nine (dominating the UDSR, which now renamed itself UDSR-RDA), and the IOM halved in strength to seven. Paradoxically, the IOM, part of a defeated right-wing coalition, now shifted to the left; while the RDA, whose leader, Houphouët-Boigny, was a junior minister in a Socialist-led coalition, shifted rightwards (ibid.: 227–32). For the new Minister of Overseas France, Gaston Defferre, Socialist mayor of Marseille from 1953 until his death in 1986 and a formidable political operator, the moment called for swift reform, in order to head off unrest in Black Africa to add to the escalating conflict in Algeria. Although the law's preamble alluded to Senghor's proposals, in fact it reversed the thrust of the French Union's development since 1945, although in a cunning move designed to attract Gaullist support, the idea was put about that this was the continuation of de Gaulle's so-called *politique de Brazzaville* (Messmer 1998: 139–40). The device of the Loi-Cadre (framework law or enabling law) secured parliamentary consent for a series of ministerial decrees, thus initiating sweeping institutional reform far more effectively than the cumbersome legislative process which had obstructed the Labour Code for five years.[6] Indeed, the law was probably unconstitutional, since the Constitution required prior consultation of the territorial assemblies and the Assembly of the French Union before any amendment of French Union membership status (ibid.: 235; Chafer 2002: 165). The government was granted until 1 March 1957 to pass its decrees.

The Loi-Cadre shifted powers to the territories, away from Dakar and Brazzaville, and away from Paris. Reforms were presented as of primarily administrative import, notably the distinction drawn between 'state services', controlled by the Republic, and 'territorial services', funded from territorial budgets. In practice, this pointed towards the occlusion of the intermediate, federal level. Other measures acquired political weight as the decrees were debated in the Assembly. Notably, although the Law did not specify whether new territorial executive councils were to be appointed, as in the Togo Statute, or elected, the latter idea soon took hold. Similarly, although it was initially unclear whether the territorial assemblies had law-making powers, rather than simply applying laws passed in Paris, this was ultimately clarified to territorial advantage. By early 1957, a radically new system of autonomous colonial states had emerged, subject to legislation by territorial assemblies elected by a single college and universal suffrage, and governed by an executive council chaired by a High Commissioner (i.e. the Governor) but with a Vice-President and members elected from the Assembly. The Governments-General became mere 'organs of co-ordination' between Paris and the territories. Although a federal executive was not ruled out, and was favoured both by the Senghorian federal model, and by the Governor-General of AEF (but not his colleague at Dakar), it was left for the territorial assemblies to decide, and a successor to the old Grand Councils never emerged before independence – the palace built to house the institution at Dakar, with lavish FIDES funding, thus sat empty (Mortimer 1969: 236–40).

Elections to the territorial assemblies confirmed the shift to territorial politics. Senghor, who suspected French officials of promoting the new system as a means to 'divide and rule', quickly made the charge of 'balkanization'. In the short term, the rapid dismantling of the Federations suggests French miscalculation rather than conspiracy, although the more 'territorialist' African leaders, particularly Houphouët-Boigny and M'Ba, favoured the move. Indeed, the strongest opposition to the federal system (familiar to students of the present-day European Union) had always come from the biggest contributors to the federal budget, especially Côte d'Ivoire, which, under the old system of *ristournes*, received back from Dakar less than it contributed in tax and customs revenues, whereas the poorer territories benefited handsomely. Senegal had also been a net contributor, but benefited from the advantages of hosting federal services in Dakar (Chafer 2002: 155; Benoist 1982: 198–202). Conversely, at the September 1957 Bamako Congress, most leaders, including those with more power at home, such as Sékou Touré and Boganda (who saw himself as a future president of the AEF Federation), lobbied hard, but in vain, for the rapid creation of a federal executive, which was now reinterpreted, somewhat ambitiously, as a shield between Paris and the territories, guaranteeing the autonomy of the latter. This was a period of rapid political change, and by early 1958, when Defferre's successor Gérard Jacquet toured French Africa, the still largely untried system was already straining under the demands made of it (Messmer 1998: 144). However, few could have predicted the transformation of sub-Saharan Africa that would result from General de Gaulle's return to power in May–June 1958, and from the approaching climax of the Algerian endgame.

Cameroun

Cameroun was always likely to test the rules of French African politics, and break many of them. Like Togo, it was formed from the bulk of a former German colony held by France, first as a League of Nations Mandated territory, and since 1946 as a UN Trusteeship Territory. Like Togo, German Kamerun had been split between French and British rule, but unlike Togo, reunification was partially achieved in 1961. Whereas for practical purposes Togo was viewed as part of AOF, Cameroun remained a distinct

entity, larger, richer, more handsomely funded by FIDES, and a rich prize coveted by
local settlers (12,000 strong by 1954) who, as in AEF, retained a separate electoral
college until 1956; Cameroun had been the seat of the so-called Estates-General of
French Colonization, which had briefly mobilized settler interests in 1945–6. By end
1956, Cameroun was also the setting for French sub-Saharan Africa's only post-
1945 insurgency, a conflict that would drag on even after independence.

Many exceptional aspects of Cameroun's post-war political life revolved around
the Union of the Camerounian Populations (UPC). Led by a civil servant and radical
trades unionist, Ruben Um Nyobé, the UPC formed in 1948 alongside the CGT-
affiliated Union of Confederated Camerounian Trades Unions (USCC), and made its
name in the labour campaigns of Cameroun's lively post-1945 'radical moment'. As
a branch of the RDA, the UPC was the target of persistent official hostility, and failed
to win seats in either the 1951 legislative elections or the 1952 territorial elections.
The Cameroun Territorial Assembly (ATCAM) was thus dominated by the Camerounian Democratic Bloc (BDC), led by Louis Aujoulat, and by Northern Muslim
chiefs and their protégés. Aujoulat, the only European occupying a second-college
seat, was elected leader of ATCAM; by 1954, the BDC had ceded its majority to a
Socialist faction backed by a Socialist High Commissioner, prefiguring Aujoulat's
defeat in the January 1956 elections (Mortimer 1969: 213–15).

Since Um Nyobé was in the minority of RDA leaders resisting Houphouët-Boigny's
moderate line, and the UPC stayed aloof from official territorial politics, two parallel
political worlds emerged in Cameroun. Unlike the Ivorian and Guinean hegemonic
mass parties, the UPC was organized on the classic pyramidal model of the communist 'vanguard' party, with a Political Bureau at its summit and a series of 'comités de
base' at village level. By early 1955, French officials counted 450 committees, drawing
inevitable parallels with the Viet Minh, with Um Nyobé as the 'Camerounian Ho Chi
Minh'. In its southwestern heartlands neighbouring Nigeria, the UPC's counter-
administration outperformed official local government structures, while a thriving
semi-clandestine press indoctrinated a highly literate population (Joseph 1977: 228–
31; Chaffard 1967: vol. 2). Although UPC leaders and militants mostly belonged to
the local Bassa and Bamiléké peoples, it refused ethnic affiliations, claiming members
drawn from many ethnic groups across Cameroun, and an even wider base of sympathizers amongst social groups, particularly African civil servants, who could not
risk joining such a disfavoured if not yet proscribed organization.

Notwithstanding the influence of communist analytical tools and organizational
models, the UPC was primarily driven by anti-colonialism. Unfettered by participation in French institutions, the UPC developed a radical political and social agenda,
but, following the pre-1950 RDA line, this was more nationalist than communist
(Joseph 1977: 210–13, 218–22). The UPC's nationalism determined perhaps its most
irksome feature to French officials: challenging France's Trusteeship, it called for
immediate reunification and independence for 'Kamerun' (a name reflecting the claim
to pre-1919 borders). In December 1952, Um Nyobé made his first appearance before
the UN General Assembly in New York. Annual Visiting Missions from the UN
Trusteeship Council were consistently critical of France's tendentious interpretation
of the 1946 Trusteeship Agreement, and of the insufficiencies of reforms, for example
the limited powers of ATCAM. However, the UN rejected demands for reunification,

dismissing petitions from the UPC and from groups in the British Cameroons. This reflected the complications of the Ewe question in Togo, where reunification, arguably based on a stronger case for self-determination, was nonetheless headed off (Gardinier 1963: 64). A flaw in the UPC's claim was that its core support came from ethnic groups who had been split by partition. The idea took root despite UN scepticism and French opposition, however, and in 1961 British-held Southern Cameroons opted by plebiscite for reunification, while the Northern Cameroons fused with Northern Nigeria (Joseph 1977: 204–8).

By early 1955, a new High Commissioner, Roland Pré, was apparently moving towards a showdown, clamping down on UPC activities in a tense situation increasingly resembling Côte d'Ivoire in 1949. In late May, a week-long wave of violent riots in Douala, Yaoundé and across UPC heartlands, led to at least 26 deaths, hundreds wounded, and the wholesale arrest of known party militants. Unlike PDCI leaders in 1949, Um Nyobé and his lieutenants had no parliamentary immunity, and were forced into hiding to avoid arrest (Joseph 1977: 265ff., 360–1). The riots were officially glossed as an abortive Viet Minh-style insurrection urged on by more radical party elements, while the UPC evoked 'vast military operations'. Privately, some French officials were dismayed by Pré's inflexibility, though not perhaps by his aims (ibid.: 357). It is likely that the UPC leadership, hemmed in by Pré's strong-arm tactics, felt compelled to follow the advice of hardliners. However, the scale of the rioting also reflected socio-economic deprivation in the big towns and Southern provinces (ibid.: 270–4, 288). In July, the UPC was banned, at Pré's insistence, under the 1936 law banning French fascist leagues. It was also expelled from the RDA for rejecting the party line since 1950; two senior RDA politicians had already visited Cameroun in early May, seeking to establish a rival, orthodox RDA branch (Mortimer 1969: 217). These public moves accompanied continuing police action against the UPC, while Pré, in a bid for local 'hearts and minds', pursued local government reform and infrastructural development in affected areas (Joseph 1977: 289–93).

At times over the following 18 months, Cameroun's two parallel political worlds seemed about to converge, as politics shifted leftwards to embrace a moderate version of the UPC's platform. The growing nationalist mood, partly attributable to the vacuum left by the UPC, also reflected a worsening economic crisis as cocoa prices slumped: cocoa production had been the motor of Camerounian growth since 1945, contributing over 54 per cent of Cameroun's export earnings in 1952–4, but dropped by almost half by 1956 (ibid.: 298–9). Pré's replacement by Pierre Messmer in April 1956 heralded a more concessive approach including the release of UPC detainees, and tacitly allowed UPC leaders to circulate freely, although the ban remained in place until after independence. In June, the Socialist president of ATCAM since 1954, Paul Soppo Priso, placed himself at the head of the Movement of National Union, a broad front united on a 'minimum programme' embracing Aujoulat's BDC as well as the UPC. Apparently Um Nyobé's brainchild, the Movement enjoyed logistical support offered by the UPC's clandestine structures (ibid.: 313). Over a few months, it won significant concessions from Paris, including a revised Cameroun statute (in preference to the unsatisfactory 'Togolese model'); and the promise of elections so that ATCAM could debate the statute with proper authority. Crucially, an amnesty law was promised that would allow the UPC to field candidates. Meanwhile, a new pro-French 'third force' emerged in the strongly Catholic regions of central Cameroun, whose leader, André-Marie Mbida, declared himself 'the foremost *interlocuteur valable* in Cameroun'. Combined with the conservative, predominantly Muslim population of Northern Cameroun (some forty percent of the electorate), this ensured the defeat or containment of any nationalist coalition (ibid.: 322–5). The National Union was in any case inherently vulnerable, and crumbled between the French government's apparent wish for Um Nyobé to perform an Houphouët-like *volte-face*, and the UPC's refusal to abandon its primary objectives of independence and reunification. The amnesty law was delayed until after the deadline had passed for submitting candidatures, by which time the National Union had voted, against the UPC, to stand in the elections, come what may. In these circumstances, even an election boycott might seem, as one UPC militant put it, a 'striking victory for the colonialists and their lackeys' (ibid.: 329–31). A week before the elections, the UPC began its insurrection, sabotaging communications in the Sanaga Maritime region, and harassing and murdering election candidates.

The elections on 23 December 1956 reflected Cameroun's increasingly regionalized politics: Mbida's self-styled Democrats won twenty seats, 38 went to the Camerounian Union, led by Ahmadou Ahidjo, son-in-law of a powerful Northern ruler, and Soppo Priso's Group for Camerounian National Action won only eight seats. A new Cameroun statute was passed by decree in April 1957, and the Prime Minister, Mbida, proudly proclaimed his country's 'three-quarters independence'. By the end of 1957, a new High Commissioner, Jean Ramadier, in a move of dubious legality which cost Ramadier his job, forced Mbida out of office in favour of Ahidjo, who in 1960 would lead Cameroun to independence under an increasingly authoritarian regime (Messmer 1998: 131, 143; Mortimer 1969: 245). Cameroun's parallel worlds now diverged more widely than ever. Like the Malagasy and Mau Mau before them, UPC *maquisards* were well organized but poorly armed and geographically isolated, and their insurrection never stood a chance. Um Nyobé apparently aimed to re-open negotiations with the French and with the autonomous Camerounian government (Joseph 1977: 346–7). Attempts at mediation failed, however, and in December 1957, substantial French reinforcements moved in to Sanaga Maritime, deploying by now familiar counter-insurgency tactics. Faced with France's apparent willingness to concede quasi-independence to Ahidjo, UPC morale crumbled, and in September 1958, Um Nyobé was killed by a French patrol, possibly betrayed by rivals in an increasingly fissiparous movement. The insurrection in Sanaga Maritime was wound up, and an amnesty encouraged 3,000 insurgents to lay down their arms; it even allowed UPC moderates to fight Legislative Assembly by-elections. However, a more extensive phase of the insurrection began in the Bamiléké region, and continued sporadically past independence, occasioning the first deployment of French troops in de Gaulle's post-colonial African *chasse gardée* (Clayton 1994; Chipman 1989).

Tanganyika

The Trusteeship Territory of Tanganyika was a Cinderella amongst British colonies in Africa. Cinderella-like virtues came with Tanganyika's status as a poor, 'backward' and overlooked dependency, and these virtues helped it to become the first colony in British East and Central Africa to gain independence, in 1961. Some Tanganyikan virtues were negative ones. One of the reasons the Groundnuts Scheme was such a disaster (Chapter 5) was because it failed to take into account Tanganyika's fragile ecology. This also explained why Tanganyika was sparsely populated, and for that matter relatively unattractive to settlers, except for the sisal-growing and coffee-planting areas (and coffee-planting was as much an African as a European enterprise). European settlers were far fewer than in Kenya – 20,000 in 1957 compared with almost 70,000 in Kenya by 1960 – and outnumbered by some four hundred Africans to one. The settlers themselves, many of Greek or German stock, were less united, and exercised less influence on the British Conservative Party.[7] As in Kenya and Uganda, a substantial Asian community (some 76,000 in 1957) competed for status with Europeans and Africans. Tanganyika had no counterpart to the Kenyan White Highlands, and no equivalent of the overcrowded Kikuyu 'reserves'. Indeed, not the least of Tanganyika's virtues was that there was no Mau Mau, although officials sometimes feared there might be. Rather, Tanganyika's ethnic diversity made it unlikely that any single ethnic group might act alone, much less dominate an eventual territory-wide nationalist movement. Tanganyika in the 1950s also possessed significant positive virtues, many of them associated with the nationalist movement formed in 1954, the Tanganyika African National Union (TANU), and with the skills of its leader, Julius Nyerere.

TANU marked a new departure, but its origins lay in an African Association formed in 1929, which became the Tanganyikan African Association (TAA) in 1948, when it 'possessed all the elements of nationalism except the determination, the techniques, and the popular support to seize power' (ibid.: 434). In the early 1950s, it was operating effectively in local disputes thrown up by Tanganyika's 'second colonial occupation', and was developing a cohesive structure in the capital, Dar es Salaam. As with Cameroun and Togo, Trusteeship status gave TAA politicians the added impetus of appeals to the UN Trusteeship Council's periodic visiting missions. In 1953, the Governor, Edward Twining, back-handedly conferred nationalist credibility on the TAA by prohibiting civil servants from membership, extending the ban to the equivalent European and Asian associations and to the more radical regional movements (ibid.: 505). TANU was the brainchild of the 32-year-old Nyerere, son of a government chief and a Catholic convert, who, returning from Edinburgh University in 1952, was elected TAA president in April 1953. The immediate aim was to head off regional revolt which might trigger official repression; but the longer-term strategy was to create a centralized, well-organized, law-abiding movement. Its constitution, agreed in July 1954, followed the British Labour Party and Nkrumah's CPP: Africans (only) could join by paying a modest subscription, trades unions and tribal unions could affiliate, TAA branches could simply change their name to TANU, though some more militant branches resisted; policy was made by a national executive committee elected by annual conference. TANU espoused pan-African ideals, and identified with illustrious nationalist models, such as the CPP. And yet its declared aim, 'to prepare the people of Tanganyika for self-Government and Independence', fell short of Nkrumah's 'self-government NOW' (ibid.: 511–12). Rather, Nyerere emphasized the need for the 'educational and economic development of our people'. Pressed by a sympathetic

UN visiting mission in August 1954, he foresaw independence in 25 years (ibid.: 516–17). Party membership soared, on a convincingly territory-wide basis, swelling party coffers. For the moment, however, TANU was prevented from engaging in one defining activity of politics, as there were no elections to contest.

Otherwise 'intrinsically unimportant' to the reforming CO, aside from its interest to the UN, Tanganyika was seen as a multi-racial half way house between white-dominated Kenya and black-dominated Uganda. Governor Twining's mission was thus to institute reform, to which end he convened a Committee for Constitutional Development comprising the Legislative Council's unofficial membership: seven Europeans, four Africans and three Asians (ibid.: 475–6). The proposals that emerged from this committee enshrined the principle of multi-racialism as Tanganyika's 'official creed'. Its aim, as Twining saw it, was 'to build up a community where merit is the criterion, not colour', although no doubt European criteria of 'merit' applied (ibid.: 481). The Legislative Council (Legco) appointed in March 1955 was to retain its official majority (thus preventing settler domination), but with racial parity determining the appointment (not election) of ten unofficial members for each of the three communities. A new, multi-racial, local government tier of county councils was created, midway between Legco and the purely African 'native administrations' (NAs). Yet again the late colonial state was seeking to penetrate deeper into African society; 'a racial issue on which Africans could unite' (ibid.: 484), it was vigorously opposed by the more dynamic chiefdoms. When county councils proved unviable, Twining deepened African opposition by extending multi-racialism to district level, where it impinged on the NAs' autonomy, bringing Sukumaland, on the shores of Lake Victoria, to the verge of open rebellion.

Multi-racialism rapidly became a stick with which to beat TANU. As Twining later recalled: 'I read [TANU's] Manifesto very carefully. It demanded that Africa should be for the Africans, Tanganyika for the black Tanganyikans. We Europeans were not even allowed to join. This policy of black racialism was contrary to the principles of the Trusteeship Agreement and to the policy of the British Government' (in ibid.: 521). To promote multi-racialism and counter TANU, a United Tanganyika Party (UTP) was established in February 1956, led by a liberal white farmer, Ivor Bayldon. UTP appealed to the Asian community, and even drew African support, including half the African Legislative Councillors and, eventually, two-thirds of the party's membership. This allowed Twining to contemplate the next stage: in April 1956, only a year after establishing the new Legco structure, Twining announced elections in two stages in 1958–9, in which each voter would choose candidates from each community. Voter lists, drawn up on the usual criteria of property, education and office holding, already pointed to multi-racialism's inescapable contradictions. Even after revision by a Legco committee, the proposed qualifications were the most restrictive of any British colony – just as French Africa was embracing universal suffrage. Conversely, electoral arithmetic still pointed to a crushing African majority. By late 1957, with Nyerere urging voter registration, Twining even suggested rescinding tripartite voting but the CO needed multi-racialism to work in Kenya and thus it could not be abandoned in Tanganyika (ibid.: 555–6).

Much turned therefore on whether Africans accepted multi-racialism, but UTP and Twining were losing this argument before TANU's persuasive advocacy of a democratic, primarily African, Tanganyika – a principle also endorsed by the UN. Twining briefly considered more robust tactics, banning Nyerere from public speaking in January 1957. However, with a UN mission imminent, this ban was rescinded in July. Nyerere accepted a place on Legco, but rejected a position as 'assistant minister' on the Executive Council. In January 1958, TANU voted for responsible government by the end of 1959, failing which it vowed to adopt Positive Action. The biggest obstacle to TANU's eventual electoral victory was now a TANU boycott, but Nyerere won the argument on this, suggesting that TANU needed to dirty its feet to get beyond multi-racialism, and that a boycott would entrench UTP in power and might lead to TANU's proscription (ibid.: 556–7). Meanwhile, a fading UTP radicalized its programme in order to stay in the ring, but lost conservative support in consequence. In June 1958, UTP representatives even offered an electoral pact, but Nyerere refused to unite 'with a thing that is utterly dead' (ibid.: 561). The elections were in two stages, with five provinces contested in September 1958, five in February 1959. In September, TANU won 13 of fifteen seats, having decided late in the day to back Asian and European candidates as well as African; two seats went to unopposed, non-UTP Europeans. UTP fielded only two candidates, including their leader, Bayldon, and withdrew from the February 1959 elections, in which TANU won all 15 seats. Nyerere was thus hardly exaggerating when he wrote, in September 1958, that the 'atmosphere has been suddenly revolutionized . . . There is now more than a chance that we may work our democratic revolution here in a manner that might revolutionize the whole trend of events in East and Central Africa' (in ibid.: 562).

In January 1959, East African governors restated the CO's strategy of 'gradualness' (originating in Cohen's reform programme of the 1940s). For Tanganyika, an unofficial majority would be elected to Legco in 1965, and a 'substantial measure of self-government' would be attained after 1969 (10 April 1959, Hyam & Louis 2000: doc. 116). By early 1960, Tanganyika was committed to independence by 1961. What had changed in the meantime? Part of the answer lies in Tanganyikan politics. Following Twining's retirement, his successor, Richard Turnbull, with experience of Mau Mau, was less committed to multi-racialism than to keeping order; Nyerere's comment was that 'if a Colonial Governor is not an Arden-Clarke, then the more embedded he is in the 19th century the better' (Iliffe 1979: 563). After the Governors' meeting, faced with TANU supporters clamouring for 'responsible government', Turnbull argued, in extensive correspondence with London, for a far more rapid timetable. But for Tanganyika's 'democratic revolution' to take hold, and indeed to spread, a substantial shift was needed in the British stance; how that came about forms the starting point for our final chapter.

Notes

1 'The Future of Commonwealth Membership', January 1955, in Boyce 1999: 119.
2 Pierre-Henri Teitgen, ex-Minister of Overseas France, debating the 1956 Loi-Cadre, 20 March 1956, in Cooper 1996a: 424–5.
3 But see Sharkey (2003) for Southern arguments that Sudanese identity was a 'hybrid identity, to which Arab and African cultures have equally contributed'; also Warburg 1992.

4   Cf. Houphouët-Boigny's riposte to d'Arboussier's public criticism: 'Did Kwame [i.e. Nkrumah] refuse to collaborate with the Conservatives who replaced Labour in power? He raised no battle cry against the British in Malaya, the Atlantic Pact, English constituencies or German rearmament. Kwame acts. He has his feet on the ground. He does not dream.' 24 July 1952, in Mortimer 1969: 178.

5   The Loire is France's longest river; Nevers and Tarbes are quintessentially provincial, medium-sized towns; Lomé and Bobo-Dioulasso are in present-day Togo and Burkina Faso respectively.

6   Gaston Defferre, as Interior Minister in the first government of François Mitterrand's presidency from 1981, would similarly use a Framework Law to push through his decentralization reforms.

7   Unlike many other settler colonies, Tanganyika settler numbers did not increase after 1945, except temporarily for the 'groundnutters'. The African population was 8,788,466 in the 1957 census. By January 1960 some 1m of these were TANU members: Iliffe 1979: 567, 574.

8

Wind of Change: Endgame in Colonial Policy, 1958–1964

The wind of change is blowing through this continent and, whether we like it or not, this growth of national consciousness is a political fact. We must all accept it as a fact, and our national policies must take account of it. (Harold Macmillan, 3 February 1960, in Hyam & Louis 2000: doc. 32)

Algeria costs us more than she brings us. France's responsibilities constitute a military and diplomatic mortgage. It is a fact, decolonization is our interest, and is therefore our policy. (Charles de Gaulle, 11 April 1961, in de Gaulle 1970b: vol. 3, 288)

Independence can only be conceived under the following conditions: institutions must be solid and well-balanced; experienced administrative cadres must be in place; social, economic and financial order must be well-established, and in the hands of tested agents; the population must have attained a level of intellectual and moral education without which any democratic regime is derisory, deceitful and tyrannous. (King Baudouin of the Belgians, 13 January 1959, in Stengers 1995: 313)

When the former Colonial Secretary [Lennox-Boyd] was questioned about universal suffrage, we could never pin him down to a statement of final aim. But without that final statement we will never win the confidence of Africans. Democracy is not merely a wonderful moral idea which we grant people. It is not a luxury. It is a practical necessity. All of us on this side of the House are subversive. We all believe that this Government are a really crummy lot. But the reason we do not take to the hills with a sub-machine gun is because we know that the opportunity for change will come and will come peacefully. (Anthony Wedgwood Benn, MP, 2 November 1959, in Porter & Stockwell 1989: doc. 76, 518)

On 3 February 1960, at the end of his African tour, the British Prime Minister, Harold Macmillan, addressed both houses of the South African Parliament in Cape Town. The nub of his speech, quoted above, has come to encapsulate the European colonial powers' acquiescence in decolonization at the start of a new decade. In 1960 alone, 17 states gained their independence, 16 of them African. In the British general election of October 1959, Africa had, unusually, featured in the manifestos of both major parties. With an increased Conservative majority, Macmillan's dynamic new Colonial Secretary, Iain Macleod, had the authority to pursue a more urgent African policy. This did not escape Macmillan's Cape Town audience, who received his address in hostile silence – particularly his carefully pitched criticisms of South African *apartheid*. A response of a kind came a few weeks later, on 21 March, with the shooting of 67 demonstrators by the South African police at Sharpeville; a year later, South Africa declined to renew its Commonwealth membership, causing Macmillan to reflect that the 'the wind of change has blown us away' (in Hyam & Louis 2000: xl). Macmillan was not perhaps an instinctive decolonizer, he headed the traditional party of empire, and it had taken him three years to reach this point, since he became prime minister in the wake of the Suez crisis. Although the imagery was deliberately vague, the 'wind of change' was not thought likely to blow down imperial flagpoles or uproot British assets. In particular, Macmillan still assumed clement weather for settler minorities with a controlling interest in much of Eastern and Central Africa. Change came with a momentum which Macmillan had thus scarcely envisaged, and by the time he stepped down as prime minister in 1963, Southern Rhodesia was the last bastion of English-speaking white minority rule outside South Africa.

Five days before Macmillan's speech, President Charles de Gaulle had made a very different address on French television, dressed in a brigadier-general's uniform (the rank to which he had been promoted in June 1940). The speech was a stirring appeal for loyalty, addressed to the army and to the French people, facing insurrectionary violence by Africa's most demanding European minority, the *pieds noirs* of Algeria (29 January 1960, de Gaulle 1970b: vol. 3, 166). De Gaulle's return to power, in May–June 1958, in response to an earlier revolt by *pieds noirs* and fractious army officers, marks a turning point in decolonization, and a momentous step in twentieth-century France's history. De Gaulle had insisted on a new constitution, France's Fifth Republic, and its third new regime since the 'abyss' of 1940. His election as President of the Republic, with 85 per cent of the vote in an indirect ballot, heralded a new era of presidential primacy, political stability, and executive decision making. (The Fifth Republic's characteristic system of direct presidential elections was introduced only after the war ended in Algeria, in October 1962.) In no area of policy were decisions more urgently needed than in Algeria, already at war for almost four years. De Gaulle was to prove an effective decolonizer: 14 of 16 new African states in 1960 were former French dependencies. In September 1959, de Gaulle made his most far-reaching decision to date, recognising Algeria's right to self-determination, to be exercised within four years of the end of hostilities. And yet, not even the most sweeping French vision of Algerian self-determination *circa* 1960 envisaged that close to a million *pieds noirs* might simply flee Algeria, as was to happen in 1962, when the choice presented to them was between 'the suitcase or the coffin'. Suspicion that de Gaulle might sacrifice settlers' interests, and defy the army's vision of French national interests, only started to crystallize after January 1960, and was apparently confirmed at a press conference on 11 April 1961, quoted above, where de Gaulle redefined French interests in terms of decolonization, and in so doing prompted the Army's final, abortive revolt over Algeria.

In early 1960, the transformative power of the 'wind of change' was perhaps most clearly discernible in the Belgian Congo, whose future was being settled in Brussels even as Macmillan and de Gaulle spoke. At a Round Table Conference of Belgian and Congolese political parties, convened in January 1960, the starting point for discussions, imposed by an unexpected Congolese 'common front', was an agreed date for independence set at 30 June 1960. Startlingly, independence had been on the Congolese agenda for only 12 months, having been promised, somewhat in panic, following riots in the capital, Léopoldville, in January 1959. King Baudouin, quoted above, had cautiously defined independence according to a gradual and extensive 'Belgian model' of amicable decolonization. Even in early 1960, Belgians still believed in a comfortable Belgian-Congolese Community, whose constitution was modelled on that of Belgium, supported by the European-dominated pillars of administration and armed forces. In fact, those pillars rapidly crumbled as Congolese troops mutinied against their officers, and European officials fled. Congolese independence almost instantly became a by-word for the 'anarchy', violence and international meddling that could follow an ill-planned retreat from colonial responsibilities.

This chapter focuses on the French, Belgian and British colonial endgames in Africa, as represented by four principal cases: Algeria, and before it French sub-Saharan Africa; the Belgian Congo and the Federation of Rhodesia and Nyasaland. Each case will be considered in some detail, although it should be recognized that the policy of the departing colonial power was set in a wider context, embracing the rapid decolonization of Tanganyika (soon to become Tanzania, with the addition of the island sultanate of Zanzibar), Uganda and Kenya; the Belgian departure from Rwanda and Burundi (the Trusteeship territory of Ruanda-Urundi); and the beginnings of Portugal's retarded retreat from its African empire.

Aside from timing, and notwithstanding some striking contrasts, what all these cases share is the sense of shift, at some point in the late 1950s, as policy makers' search for a definitive solution to the problems of late colonial rule in Africa was transformed into a far more urgent push to bring about – or acquiesce in – radical change within an immediate timeframe. Although previously, as we have seen, officials had sought to rationalize and reform colonial rule, in Africa this had been coupled with a sense that time was on the side of the colonial powers. To be sure, in specific cases, most notably that of Ghana, political events had driven the timetable towards independence far more rapidly than planned, and this in turn had a decisive influence on developments in other countries, most obviously Nigeria. And yet imperial capitals had so far held the line, with the British drawing clear distinctions between West Africa and East, where protracted timetables were still envisaged for the realization of self-government (to say nothing of independence). Even the Suez crisis, the impact of which is treated as self-evidently profound in studies of British imperial decline, had a largely intangible influence on African colonial policy. Within three weeks of taking office, to be sure, Macmillan had requested 'something like a profit and loss account', in which financial and economic gains and losses from the departure of 'each of our Colonial possessions' might be weighed against 'political and strategic considerations' (28 January 1957, Hyam & Louis 2000: doc. 1). However, following a strong steer from the Colonial Secretary, Alan Lennox-Boyd, the eventual report did not allow individual colonies to be 'written off', and various arguments were deployed in defence of existing imperial commitments (ibid.: docs 2–3, 28–37). Thus Macmillan had no call yet to forecast any but the mildest 'wind of change', though at the very least the explicit stock-taking required in the 1957 exercise served as a baseline against which subsequent policy could be measured (ibid.: xxiv–v).

A parallel French pragmatic approach to the French Union has already been traced in the rationale underpinning the 1956 Framework Law, as well as the unofficial but nonetheless influential 'Cartiériste' argument, that French development funds would be better spent at home (Chapter 7). But before the advent of de Gaulle, the 1956 Law looked like a mechanism for ensuring stability rather than further rapid change. Algeria was a different proposition altogether, where obstreperous settlers and their metropolitan sympathizers had consistently blocked even the most tentative reforms, diffidently proposed by successive unstable French governments; here surely the more likely scenario was some explosive military catastrophe, or perhaps a humiliating 'diplomatic Dien Bien Phu'. It would take all of de Gaulle's authority to impose a solution in France's most problematic colonial dependency. Indeed, it was difficult enough to determine what the terms of such a solution might be, but a large part of de Gaulle's achievement stemmed from the clear-sightedness that may be discerned already in his first, famous speech at Algiers, on 4 June 1958.

In the French and British cases, therefore, a change of heart was in part determined by a change of metropolitan political fortunes, markedly so in the French case, where in May–June 1958 Algeria had effectively brought down the unloved regime of the Fourth Republic. But even in Britain, although the October 1959 elections brought no great surprise or upset, public and political opinion had recently navigated a moral turning point in the wake of revelations about the murder of 11 detainees at Hola camp in Northern Kenya, which coincided with the declaration of Emergency in Nyasaland (Chapter 6 and below). These events were crucial to Macleod's calculations as Macmillan's new Colonial Secretary, although Macleod brought to the office a change of personality and mindset perhaps more than a shift in policy (Hyam & Louis 2000: xlvii–viii). The 1959 scandals also reinvigorated the Labour opposition's campaigning for the application of 'one man one vote' in Africa, thus further reducing the government's room for political manoeuvre (Goldsworthy 1971: 279–316); this much was clear from the debate on the Queen's speech following the elections (A. Wedgwood Benn, quoted above).

These shifts in the balance of political opinion need to be set alongside the sense of diminishing options as British governments responded to the contraction of British power, and to the costly burden of British defence. The overall aim of the 1957 Defence Review, also undertaken by Macmillan's post-Suez cabinet, was thus to reduce defence expenditure from 10 to 7 per cent, while maintaining a British world role (Hyam & Louis 2000: xli–ii). The February 1957 Defence White Paper gave enhanced priority to the development of the British nuclear deterrent, while phasing out National Service over the following five years. This latter measure was largely driven by economic considerations, since the training and rapid turnover of short-term National Servicemen were prohibitively expensive, but the move also squared with Britain's 'long and honourable tradition of voluntary military service'. Crucially, the new 'emphasis on highly trained mobile forces' would clearly reduce Britain's capacity to conduct lengthy counter-insurgency operations (Porter & Stockwell 1989: doc. 71, 452–64). And as Wedgwood Benn also reminded the House of Commons:

'It will be British boys who will be sent to Central Africa if blood begins to flow there' (in Porter & Stockwell 1989: 520).

British responses to decolonization were as nothing compared with the rising tide of indignation and protest, violence and counter-violence, with a powerful undertow of profound lassitude, that increasingly characterized the French public response to the Algerian question. Here the question of conscription was raised rather differently, since French conscripts and reservists had been fighting in massive numbers in Algeria since the passing of Special Powers in 1956 (see Chapter 6). However, this too represented the infringement of tradition, since the Republican 'citizens' army' was intended for defence of the '*Mère-Patrie*', which, all constitutional niceties notwithstanding, did *not* include fighting colonial wars across the Mediterranean. This, therefore, was a further weak point in France's ideological armour, and a focus for dissent, ranging from Communist campaigns to encourage and shelter deserters, to the Manifesto published by 121 intellectuals in *Le Monde* on 4 September 1960, which argued the 'right of insubordination' (Le Sueur 2001: 209–10). A further contrast may be made in respect of the nuclear option, which for the British 'official mind' could be presented as a cheaper alternative to a costly standing army. For de Gaulle, whose instincts as a military modernizer can be traced back to the 1930s (when he unavailingly advocated professionalization and mechanization of the French army), the concept of a French *force de frappe* became an alternative to the deeply old-fashioned conduct of colonial campaigns to defend an '*Algérie de papa*', for which he barely disguised his disdain. The implicit view of nuclear strategy displacing colonialism in France's worldview was only temporarily confused by the perceived need to retain a French Sahara, in part for nuclear testing, an issue which absorbed a disproportionate and ultimately fruitless amount of negotiating time in 1961–2.

More intangibly, it is perhaps in this period that public and political opinion in general, on both sides of the Channel, started to perceive the maintenance of empire as an obstacle to the growing prosperity of post-war society. When Macmillan argued, in July 1957, that 'most of our people have never had it so good', he did not refer directly to the likely impact on decolonization of defence spending cuts, although as his speech marked 25 years' service by Alan Lennox-Boyd (then Colonial Secretary), the thought may have been on his mind. The theme was central to the Conservative message, however, and Macmillan was keen to attract the floating votes of a 'new middle class' potentially resentful of 'any diversion of resources for colonial purposes' (Holland 1985: 208–9). A similar case may be made for France, fast approaching the climax of the so-called '*trente glorieuses*', the thirty 'glorious' years of economic expansion from 1945 (Fourastié 1979), and engaged in a heady love affair with the cars and 'white goods', indoor WCs and fitted bathrooms of an American-derived consumerist culture (Ross 1995).

Although Ross critiques the way in which, since 1962, French culture has tended to separate out the 'two stories' of decolonization and modernization, the problem for many seemed rather to be one of too close an involvement in the traditionally remote affairs of empire, as ordinary French young men were implicated in the horrors of the Algerian war, and as the war started to spill over onto metropolitan territory. At first, as we have seen (Chapter 6), the conflict at home was largely contained within deprived 'ghettos' in Paris and other French cities, whose heavy concentration of Algerian migrant workers had not yet been displaced to the still unbuilt concrete tower blocks of the surrounding *banlieues*. Before the war was finally brought to an end, however, ordinary Parisians were to become witnesses and victims of murderous violence, as the Paris police lashed out at Algerian and Leftist demonstrators in October 1961 and February 1962 (see below), and as the settler terrorists of the OAS started to pick metropolitan targets from the president on down. The clash with domestic 'normality' could be underlined in trivial, but nonetheless telling ways: though the signatures of 121 intellectuals and artists arguably had little effect on people beyond *Le Monde*'s elite readership, the banning of blacklisted signatories from France's single, state-owned television channel, and also from radio and public events, told a different story.

Finally, in the period of African endgame, it becomes even more important to consider our cases from an international perspective. The comparative and competitive aspects of late colonialism have been noted throughout this study, and indeed late colonial rule may in part be characterized by official self-consciousness, as colonial states emerged from the protective isolation of earlier times. As already noted, British divergent approaches to, say, West and East Africa were now largely redundant, while an unofficial principle of 'no immunity from neighbouring trends' ensured that developments in, say, Tanganyika would necessarily be followed in neighbouring Kenya (Hyam & Louis 2000: lii). Between empires there now emerged a sometimes rather circular, official preoccupation to avoid 'another Algeria' or 'another Congo': indeed, while Belgian officials were keen to avoid the all-out conflict and bloodshed of Algeria (and while, more directly, the Léopoldville riots of January 1959 were inspired by events across the river in Brazzaville), de Gaulle sought to avoid, amongst other things, the sudden collapse of colonial rule witnessed in the Congo. Part of the reason for the 1959 shift in policy towards Tanganyika entailed official recognition of the risk that, without extensive British concessions, the relatively attractive figure of Nyerere might be embroiled by TANU's 'wild men' into the kind of disorder already developing in neighbouring Congo and Rwanda, although the precedents of Mau Mau and the 1905 Maji Maji rebellion were even closer to hand (Hyam & Louis 2000: li–ii). Territorial contiguity heightened awareness of these comparisons: Northern Rhodesia shared a thousand-mile frontier with the Congo, and at various moments it was feared that settlers might break with the Central African Federation to merge with the secessionist regime in Katanga (Hyam & Louis 2000: doc. 392 & lxxii).

Decolonization had been on the international agenda at least since the signing of the Atlantic Charter in 1941, but it was perhaps only now that avenues started to be closed off, or at least partially occluded, for the colonial powers as a consequence of coordinated action by anti-colonial nationalists. The April 1955 Bandung Conference suggested the onset of a kind of snowball effect in this regard: its impact was limited by its restricted membership of sovereign states only, along with a few privileged nationalist invitees such as Archbishop Makarios of Cyprus and an FLN delegation including Hocine Aït Ahmed; a vague but generous 'spirit of Bandung' was summed up by Jawaharlal Nehru, who declared that 'Asia wants to help Africa' (Holland 1985: 254; Connelly 2002: 81). Kwame Nkrumah extended the principle of solidarity in two conferences he hosted at Accra in 1958, the first for eight independent African governments, while to the second, All-African People's Conference, in December, he invited radical nationalists from across Africa, to whom he offered encouragement and support (Hargreaves 1996: 174). With the explosion of UN membership in 1960, the focus shifted to the UN General Assembly, which on 14 December 1960 passed its momentous Resolution 1514(XV) on the Granting of Independence to Colonial Countries and Peoples (in Chamberlain 1998: 26–7). In particular, this advanced the novel principle that 'Inadequacy of political, economic, social or educational preparedness should never serve as a pretext for delaying independence'. However, the provision that 'immediate steps' should be taken to transfer power to non-self-governing territories never resolved into a firm timetable, and the British official view by 1963 was that this 'Soviet-inspired' Resolution did not amend the colonial powers' obligations under Article 73 of the UN Charter to provide information on colonial development, with which they had happily complied since 1945 (Hyam & Louis 2000: lxx–lxxi & doc. 46).

Shifts in metropolitan social and economic priorities, and symbolic gestures in the international sphere, provide an essential context to what follows. However, the one cast-iron principle in the endgames of the African colonial empires in this period was that, however rapidly and radically imperial policy makers shifted to the mode of rapid colonial disengagement, and however detailed the tactics and negotiations, even the most robust imperial stance was pushed further and faster than originally envisaged.

'France will Decide': Algeria and sub-Saharan Africa

De Gaulle's enigmatic and sometimes self-contradictory utterances on France, Algeria and the empire, before and after the 1958 watershed, have generated their own distinct sub-branch of historiography (Touchard 1978: 147–52; Connelly 2002: 178). His earlier record as a colonial policy maker was, as we have seen, only marginally more conclusive, notwithstanding the constant decolonizing vision implied by his war memoirs (de Gaulle 1970a). But the world had changed since January 1946, when he left office, and de Gaulle was changing with it. Indeed, the one constant in de Gaulle's policy was his ability to interpret its every shift, often despite the evidence, as French initiative pursued in France's sole interest. This lofty single-mindedness, and the breathtaking ruthlessness it generated, allowed de Gaulle to move from seeking to win the war and to determine the future of an eventual Franco-Algerian state, to advocating Algerian self-determination on French terms, to pushing for a French withdrawal at (almost) any cost. De Gaulle's decisive action was not restricted to Algeria, however, and before considering France's ultimately tragic withdrawal from North Africa, we turn first to the prior, more precipitate, and in some ways even more unexpected, withdrawal from French territories south of the Sahara, which provided the context for an Algerian solution, and a first test of de Gaulle's vision for France's future overseas.

Sub-Saharan Africa, 1958–1960

Unlike Algeria, the territories of AOF, AEF and Madagascar, though still finding their way within the structures established following the 1956 Framework Law, arguably did not need fixing in 1958. Nonetheless, the promise of a new Constitution, quite apart from the return of the 'man of Brazzaville' (a near-mythical personage revived two years before in order to bolster Gaullist support for the Framework Law), pointed inexorably towards a further wave of change. One significant step towards political autonomy was implemented immediately, as the elected Vice-Presidents of the Territorial Councils were promoted to President (in place of the High Commissioner). Pierre Messmer's first task as High Commissioner-General of AOF, appointed in July 1958, was to prepare de Gaulle's first official African visit since the Brazzaville Conference. De Gaulle's mission, simply put, was to 'explain to the Africans why they should vote yes in the forthcoming [constitutional] referendum' (Messmer 1998: 145). In doing so, de Gaulle would set down the choices which confronted the African territories, and which would be transformed into independence within less than two years.

De Gaulle's African tour did not ultimately go as planned, although he was welcomed warmly in Tananarive and, especially, in Brazzaville, where he talked up his own myth, claiming that it was here that 'France, through my voice, opened the road which has taken the African territories towards self-determination' (in Institut Charles-de-Gaulle & IHTP 1988: 252).[1] In Abidjan, too, Félix Houphouët-Boigny, Minister of State in de Gaulle's government, ensured the crowd's rapturous acclaim. De Gaulle's substantive message at each stop was that, in the forthcoming referendum, on a constitutional text not yet finalized, the people of Overseas France would be voting, not for or against the new constitution like their metropolitan *concitoyens*, but for or against membership of a new Community – this discrimination was purely a matter of interpretation, but since the interpreter was de Gaulle, it counted, despite some official and African misgivings (Sanmarco 1983: 212). A 'no' vote would thus be interpreted as a vote for independence, and France would 'draw all the necessary conclusions', although, as de Gaulle put it, this warning was 'for form's sake' (Tananarive, 22 Aug. 1958, in de Gaulle 1970b: vol. 3, 32–3). Further, each territory would then elect to become either a Territory or a State, according to a distinction that can be traced back to the federal idea first mooted in 1944–5 (see Chapter 4). Constitutional revision would also allow a subsequent decision by a territory to seek independence, which France would not oppose.

It was at the next stop that de Gaulle's expectations were challenged decisively. Ironically, Conakry, the capital of Ahmed Sékou Touré's Guinée, had been included in the itinerary as the new Minister for Overseas France (and former Governor-General), Bernard Cornut-Gentille, hoped that personal contact with the General would dissuade Sékou Touré from a 'no' vote (Messmer 1998: 146). This tactic backfired disastrously, as Sékou Touré broadcast to the crowds of party loyalists his defiant message that 'There is no dignity without freedom. We prefer poverty in freedom to wealth in slavery', and proclaimed Guinée's 'legitimate right to independence' (Chafer 2002: 174–5). De Gaulle, visibly angered, warned Sékou Touré privately that he was up against a Republic that no longer 'preferred scheming to decision making', and that 'France lived for a long time without Guinée' and could continue to do so in future (Messmer 1998: 150); he had already resumed his wartime conviction that he spoke for France and the Republic. If Sékou Touré's stage-managed intransigence was merely a clumsy gambit to challenge de Gaulle's terms, he had badly miscalculated. But he was not alone in so doing, and in Dakar, too, where Senghor and the Council President, Mamadou Dia, had made themselves scarce, de Gaulle addressed hostile 'placard carriers' with a no longer *pro forma* warning of what a 'no' vote would entail.

In the event, Sékou Touré secured an overwhelming 95.22 per cent 'no' in the referendum of 28 September 1958, while Côte d'Ivoire's 'yes' was even closer to unanimity, with a 99.98 per cent vote (224 brave souls voted no!) on a registered turnout of 98 per cent. These were the territories where a single party (PDG, PDCI) most obviously held sway under a charismatic leader, and in some territories the turnout was substantially lower (Chafer 2002: 178-9). The only real doubt arose in Niger, with a 37 per cent turnout, where the Council President, Djibo Bakary, had campaigned for a 'no'; but he secured only 21.57 per cent (some 8 per cent of the electorate), defeated by a tacit alliance between conservative chiefs and the High Commissioner, Colombani. Bakary subsequently went into resentful exile after fresh territorial elections forced him out of office (Messmer 1992: 243-4). Guinée's independence followed swiftly, despite Sékou Touré's protests that 'we wish to remain within the French and Western orbit, in every possible way', and High Commissioner-General Messmer was called on to execute one of the most abrupt and absolute of decolonizations (Messmer 1992: 240-3). The political logic behind this 'dreadful wrecking operation' (Johnson 1972: 246) was clear enough: as Houphouët-Boigny put it, in October 1958, the Guinean example would spread if France were seen to 'show preferment to those choosing secession over those choosing the Community' (in Messmer 1992: 242n.). Within two months, all French personnel had withdrawn, taking anything portable with them. Sékou Touré's championing of the pan-African cause, and his subsequent flirtations with Soviet, Chinese and American emissaries, however ultimately unproductive, showed by counter-example what France had to preserve in the rest of her African domains.

The truncated Community would prove even less durable than the post-1956 system it replaced. Guinée's departure dealt the deathblow to an already moribund Federation of AOF. Although AOF could have applied for membership of the Community *en bloc*, French officials were sceptical of its viability. Moreover, the leaders of the richest territories in both AOF and AEF, Houphouët-Boigny and the Gabonese leader, Léon M'Ba, were actively hostile to the idea. Indeed, although both opted for statehood within the Community, both leaders saw their national interests served by close alignment with France. M'Ba even requested for Gabon the status of Overseas Department (DOM, on the model of the Antilles and Réunion, Chapter 5); the proposal was rejected out of hand in Paris, to the disappointment of the High Commissioner, Louis Sanmarco (Sanmarco 1983: 210-11). Conversely, Paris's advocacy of strong, authoritarian presidential rule – following the Gaullist example – was more enthusiastically received, since it corresponded to emerging realities, not least in Gabon and Côte d'Ivoire (ibid.: 218).

The French endgame south of the Sahara thus took the form of an abstruse political battle between rival visions of the region's future, none of which was eventually realized. By January 1959, the arch-federalist Senghor had corralled four states – Senegal, Soudan, Haute-Volta and Dahomey – into a new Mali Federation (named after a pre-colonial West African empire). At this point, Niger's future was still undecided following Bakary's difficulties, and Mauritanian leaders preferred to look northwards to their Arab kin in the Maghreb (Chafer 2002: 181–2). Within three months, anti-federalists in Haute-Volta and Dahomey, no doubt backed by the administration despite official 'strict neutrality' (Messmer 1992: 245), had forced their withdrawal from the embryonic federation. Sealing this defeat for the federal principle, in July 1959, Houphouët-Boigny convened a new Council of Entente, intended as a customs union within the Community, backed by a 'solidarity fund' derived in part from Ivorian cocoa receipts, and comprising Côte d'Ivoire, Niger, Haute-Volta and Dahomey. When the two-state Mali Federation announced its intention to seek independence, in December, Houphouët-Boigny picturesquely acknowledged the implications for his initiative: 'I have been waiting in vain on the church steps with my bouquet of faded flowers' (in Chafer 2002: 183–4). Confronted with Malian independence, and that of the two French Trusteeship territories of Cameroun and Togo (see Chapter 7), the Entente states moved rapidly to full independence in 1960. The Council itself limped on into the 1960s, but was powerless to resist the shocks of post-colonial *coups d'état* (e.g. in Benin (ex-Dahomey), 1963), or of divergent approaches to the 1967 Biafran secession crisis (Messmer 1998: 90–1). The Mali Federation's declaration of independence in June 1960 precipitated fundamental differences between the two states' leaders, Senghor and Modibo Keïta, the latter favouring a more authoritarian political culture within a unitary state; he and Senghor, who resented Keïta's meddling in Senegalese power structures, also disagreed over which of them should be president. By the end of 1960, Senegal was independent in its own right, while the name Mali was retained by the culturally rich but economically wretched former territory of French Soudan (ibid.: 184).

In AEF, the High Commissioner-General, Yvon Bourges, backed a federal entity within the Community, based on a stronger tradition of federal cohesion which only Gabon resisted. A new Council of Prime Ministers (CPM) pursued the proposed Union of Central African Republics (URAC) throughout 1959. However, de Gaulle's acknowledgement of Mali's right to independence in December 1959 (in de Gaulle 1970: 148–54) deadened the impetus for URAC, and increased M'Ba's hostility to any federation including the Gabonese 'milch cow'. Despite efforts to keep URAC going with only three states, bound by treaty to Gabon, the initiative had all but collapsed by mid-1960 (Lanne 1995). As elsewhere in French Africa, independence was granted separately to the four states of Gabon, Congo-Brazzaville, the Central African Republic (former Oubangui-Chari) and Tchad. Madagascar also readily embraced the interim status of 'sovereign state' that it had demanded since 1945 (and indeed since French annexation in 1896), and duly gained independence in 1960.

Apart from the potent symbolism of the '*Année de l'Afrique*', what had fundamentally changed as a consequence of these political manoeuvrings? Though France had certainly secured its own interests in the region, it had hardly done so by its own achievements or planning, even aside from the Guinean debacle. Nonetheless, French 'neo-colonialism' in the region initially seemed mostly the continuation of policy going back to 1956 and beyond. At the extreme, Houphouët-Boigny's first government included five former French officials. More generally the new states were the recipients of French financial and military aid, while technical aid was dispensed by eager *coopérants* sent by a Ministry of Cooperation still recognizable as the former Ministry of Overseas France. The first generation of independent leaders were mostly those elected or re-elected in the 1957 elections, though Niger had changed hands, as we have seen, and in Brazzaville a half-baked *coup d'état* had brought to power the Abbé Fulbert Youlou in early 1958; here, as in Gabon, ending the double electoral college had the paradoxical effect of strengthening the hand of local settlers, who backed both Youlou and M'Ba (Bernault 1996). The lively opposition of trades unionists and student 'nationalist' radicals in many West African states was also unchanged, as was the likelihood that in due course that opposition would be stifled by the new regimes' prevailing authoritarianism (Cooper 1997; Chafer 2002: 193ff.).

For the moment, however, de Gaulle's attention was elsewhere, as may be illustrated by pursuing one thread in the preceding narrative. On 22 December 1959, his mission at an end, Pierre Messmer left the Government-General's palace in Dakar (now the site of Senegal's National Archives), made his way on foot past guards of honour and curiously silent crowds, 'neither shouting nor clapping nor whistling', and sailed for Marseille (Messmer 1992: 246–7). Two months later, having proved his worth as a servant of the Gaullist state (and of the Fourth Republic before it), Messmer became Minister of Armies, a post he was to retain throughout de Gaulle's presidency (to 1969), and thus applied his considerable skills to the war in Algeria. We follow him there, though first we must we must return to June 1958.

Algeria, 1958–1962

Few in the four years from May 1958 would have disagreed with de Gaulle that 'Algeria blocks everything'. Indeed, it was unclear what room for manoeuvre even de Gaulle could create, confronted as he was by the mounting belligerence of *pieds noirs* and the army who had brought him to power, the impasse of the military situation, despite (and partly because of) the huge reserves of manpower and resources deployed, the insufficiency of previous French policy, and the threat of a 'diplomatic Dien Bien Phu' (Connelly 2002: 169–70), as the FLN offset military stalemate with an effective campaign to internationalize the conflict.

The first steps of de Gaulle's Algerian policy came within three days of his taking office. From the balcony of the Government-General building in Algiers (where, a few weeks before, General Raoul Salan's cry of '*Vive de Gaulle!*' had set events in motion), de Gaulle told an expectant crowd of *pieds noirs*, a few 'fraternizing' Algerians visible in their midst, what they thought they wanted to hear. If they listened carefully above the sound of their own voices, *pieds noirs* might not have acknowledged de Gaulle's professed empathy ('*Je vous ai compris!*'), grasp of events ('I know what happened here') or vision of 'renewal and fraternity' which they 'wanted' to bring about. Even less might they have accepted de Gaulle's proposed single category of Algerian French citizens, all ten million sharing the same rights and duties, protected by a 'coherent, ardent, disciplined' – and obedient – French army (4 June 1958, de Gaulle 1970: 15–17). Adding to the ambiguity a few days later at Mostaganem, de Gaulle allowed himself a single call of '*Vive l'Algérie Française!*' This was enough – and vague enough – for the moment, and it was on this basis that Algerians voted in the September 1958 referendum. Just to make sure, the army stepped up its harassment of the FLN, spread rumours that those not voting would be arrested, or lose state benefits, and a cartoon strip instructed voters which voting slip to use – white for 'yes', unlucky purple for 'no' (sometimes only the first of these was distributed). Ninety-six per cent of those voting, some 76 per cent of Algerian registered voters, got the message (Droz & Lever 1991: 196).

Detailed policy now started to emerge. A week after the referendum, at Constantine, de Gaulle announced an ambitious five-year plan for the construction of a new, modern, industrialized and democratized (but French) Algeria. The Constantine Plan promised to use Saharan oil and gas revenues to fund 'great metallurgical and chemical complexes', land redistribution to Algerian farmers, new homes for a million people, 400,000 jobs, salaries equalling those of metropolitan France, education for two-thirds of Algerian children (and for all within three years). This was the last and most spectacularly utopian project for engineering the late colonial state. It rebutted 'Cartiériste' cost-cutting arguments for imperial retreat, while also providing rich meat for French propaganda efforts, at home and abroad. Its provisions fed into later negotiations, and its legacy can be traced in post-colonial Franco-Algerian relations (3 October 1958, de Gaulle 1970: 48–51; Connelly 2002: 282–3). Paul Delouvrier, appointed in December 1958 as Delegate-General in Algeria, was a civilian with a reputation for liberalism, and a new-style technocrat recruited from the European Coal and Steel Community. Delouvrier was a 'new man', but a prudent one: even before moving to implement the Plan, he announced that 'France will remain' (Droz & Lever 1991: 202–3).[2] In any case, Delouvrier was there to do de Gaulle's bidding. On one issue, the Constantine Plan was quickly shown to be a failure. At least ten years too late, de Gaulle offered a single college for the forthcoming legislative elections. With the FLN hardly needing to call a boycott, the turnout was miserable, and failed to return plausible Algerian '*interlocuteurs valables*'.

In effect, the Constantine Plan was the civilian, 'hearts and minds', component of a two-pronged strategy, whose more immediate aim was the reinvigorated prosecution of the war. Three weeks after Constantine, encouraged by initial contacts with the FLN suggesting their readiness to parley, de Gaulle offered a '*paix des braves*', an Arcadian 'warriors' peace' allowing combatants, as he put it, 'without humiliation to return to their families and to work'. In reality, the FLN were being invited to capitulate: as he privately made clear to Salan, any FLN emissary would be despatched to 'some corner of France' to discuss ceasefire terms with low-ranking military officials (Droz & Lever 1991: 199–200). The army, it seemed, was to get what it wanted, but at a price: Delouvrier replaced the unreliable Salan (whose disobedience in a 'higher' cause was habit-forming over the following three years), and military command passed to Salan's recently appointed second-in-command, Maurice Challe, an airforce general with no prior colonial experience. Challe, however, was soon converted to the cause, and the Challe Plan represented an extension of earlier strategy. '*Quadrillage*' would continue to protect the 'useful' parts of Algeria, but the squalid 'regroupment camps' were to be transformed into permanent villages. The 'barrier war' was to be intensified, with more crack troops stationed along the Morice Line to pursue attempted ALN incursions. However, a highly mobile war was to be launched against the ALN's mountain strongholds, with small commando groups rapidly deployed by the innovative use of American-supplied helicopters. Facing a dip in conscript numbers as military service hit the 'hollow years' of those born in 1939–45, Challe promoted the use of North African troops, the 'best hunters of *fellaghas*' (ibid.: 203–4). Although Challe's highly successful operations in 1959 did not destroy the ALN, they did paralyse it fairly effectively. However, the plan created political as well as military expectations: two years later, when a discredited Challe was invited to head the 1961 putsch, the generals' wildly ambitious plotting turned on swift execution of the Challe Plan to its limits, in order to present Paris with the *fait accompli* of the FLN's annihilation (Connelly 2002: 238). Meanwhile, the brave new world of the Constantine Plan morphed into a dystopian Algeria bounded by electrified wire, divided up into a garrisoned grid, overflown by helicopters, its peasants corralled into concrete villages, brainwashed by the leaflets and loudspeaker vans of the army's psychological warfare units.

The FLN was playing its own game of political 'make believe', but one which meshed more closely with international anti-colonial opinion. The FLN's defeat in the 1957 Battle of Algiers had undermined the strategy agreed at the 1956 Soummam Conference (Chapter 6). With the FLN leadership driven abroad, the French stranglehold on Algeria reinforced the trend to ideological diversity and strategic disunity between the six *wilayas* (military districts), and exacerbated tensions between 'internal' and 'external' leaders which erupted into crisis as independence approached. The FLN leadership now sought to address this structural problem, while meeting the challenge posed by de Gaulle's renewal of French resolve. On 19 September 1958, in Cairo, just nine days before de Gaulle's referendum, a Provisional Government of the Algerian Republic (GPRA) was declared, with Ferhat Abbas as President. Hocine Aït Ahmed, one of the 'historic' leaders skyjacked by the French in 1956, had first mooted the idea in March 1957 from captivity. FLN reports collated over the summer of 1958 ascribed every possible benefit to the proposal: it would help to rally Algerians to the cause, boost the morale of ALN fighters, counteract regionalist tendencies or ethnic tensions within the movement, perhaps even force the rival MNA to 'see reason' (Harbi 1981: 183–226; Connelly 2002: 183–5; Meynier 2002: 209–13).

The FLN was declaring Algerian independence before a single hectare of Algerian territory had been liberated, transcending its 'outlaw, rebel, underground' status, and commanding the respect of the international community. It gave the FLN equal status with the governments of Algeria's newly independent Maghrebine neighbours, who had hitherto tended to regard the FLN as 'a minor and an incompetent', excluded from the top table of independent states, and existing on sufferance on Tunisian soil (Connelly 2002: 182–3). Tunisian President, Habib Bourguiba was being courted by France over base rights and a proposed oil pipeline bypassing the FLN's zone of influence, while Morocco, with claims to Algerian territory in the Western Sahara, was actively hostile to the ALN. Building on the FLN's guest-starring role as non-state actor at the 1955 Bandung Conference, the GPRA would project itself even more effectively in the United Nations, and, whereas hitherto French diplomacy had only to contend with an annual General Assembly debate, now it faced a war of attrition as state after state recognized the GPRA, or was offered inducements not to do so. Aït Ahmed had also pointed up the 'magical' aspects of a government that would be 'everywhere and nowhere', its ministers popping up in Cairo, Tunis, New York or Belgrade (the Non-Aligned Movement's home under Marshall Tito's aegis) – everywhere, in short, but Algeria (in ibid.: 184–5).

The GPRA thus broadened the international front in the Algerian war. Within ten days of its creation, 13 states had recognized the GPRA, including all Arab states except Lebanon (which followed soon after), while many others, including China, Yugoslavia, and the new African radicals, Ghana and Guinée, offered *de facto* recognition by inviting official visits from GPRA ministers. The FLN had information bureaux in twenty capitals, including London, Berne, Tokyo and Bonn, though New York eclipsed them all, site of UN headquarters but also home of American advertising agencies, which acted for both the FLN and the French government (ibid.: 194–5). The Franco-Algerian cold war also took more heated forms, as FLN agents, enforcers and gun-runners were targeted for assassination and bombing by French secret services, particularly in the Federal Republic of Germany, whose staunch support of France was often sorely tested (ibid.: 202–3).

The Constantine Plan constituted an atlas for French integration policy, but in the next, crucial stage of his Algerian policy, de Gaulle moved into uncharted territory. Although de Gaulle haughtily refused to accept 'that Ghana dictate French policy', and much less would he bow to American wishes, he was inclining to the force of international opinion. With a General Assembly debate on Algeria looming in the Autumn 1959, de Gaulle met the UN Secretary-General, Dag Hammarskjöld, in July, and apparently proposed a 'state of self-determination' for Algeria (ibid.: 205). Bracing the Army for change was more delicate: in an ostensibly routine tour of officers' messes in the Algerian battle zones, de Gaulle dropped heavy hints, telling Challe's men that the 'era of European administration was past . . . We can only act in Algeria on Algeria's behalf and with Algeria's help in a way that the rest of the world understands' (in Droz & Lever 1991: 221). At a press conference on 16 September 1959, broadcast on primetime television, de Gaulle proclaimed Algeria's right to self-determination, to be exercised not more than four years after the end of combat, which was defined as a drop in the number of the FLN's victims below two hundred in a year (de Gaulle 1970: vol. 3, 117–23; Lacouture 1986: vol. 3, 73–6). At this point, Algerians 'in their twelve départements' (i.e. excluding the Sahara) would choose between three solutions. In effect, de Gaulle's rhetoric made the choice for them. The first option was secession from France – the option chosen by Sékou Touré a year before – which de Gaulle warned would lead to 'political chaos, bloodletting and before long a war-mongering communist dictatorship'. Secondly, 'Francization', Algeria's full inclusion in a France stretching 'from Dunkirk to Tamanrasset', was an extreme form of integration appealing only to settlers. The preferred option was 'the government of the Algerians by the Algerians, assisted by, and in close union with, France for economic affairs, education, defence, foreign relations'. Although the comparison was unthinkable, de Gaulle was placing policy on the same footing as Britain's, but just as the latter was about to shift to a more rapid embrace of self-government. Nonetheless, decolonization was at last acknowledged, even if deferred to a moment of 'readiness' decided by France, and on terms protecting essential imperial interests.

Over the following year or more, all sides prepared for a seismic shift while still clinging to landmarks in a familiar political landscape. Algerian policy remained fairly constant with only incremental shifts in emphasis, with de Gaulle reassuring the army of the need for victory even while taking further steps. Thus, 'Francization' gradually slipped from view, while the theme of 'Algerian Algeria', first explored in public in March 1960, found definitive expression in a press conference on 4 November 1960, when de Gaulle predicted that 'an Algerian Republic will exist one day' (Connelly 2002: 228). This left open the question of whether, or rather when, de Gaulle would recognize the GPRA as sole negotiating partner. In September 1959, de Gaulle still shied from naming the FLN, merely reiterating the offer of a *'paix des braves'*. De Gaulle repeated the offer on 10 November, but now he invited the GPRA to discuss the 'conditions of the end of hostilities'. Sensing that de Gaulle might sway UN opinion, the GPRA's adept, if rather graceless, counter-proposal named the imprisoned historic leaders as its negotiating team (Droz & Lever 1991: 225–7). Discreet contacts continued through 1960, culminating in the first official talks between the FLN and the French government, at Melun in June 1960. These stalled on the question of whether a ceasefire should precede negotiations, as the French insisted, whereas for the FLN a ceasefire was part of any settlement (ibid.: 255). Even now, de Gaulle was prepared to consider other options: on 10 June, at the Elysée Palace, the president secretly met Si Salah, hard-pressed commander of the fourth *wilaya* (based in the Algiers hinterland), who was prepared to defy the GPRA and to accept a ceasefire, if he could bring other commanders with him. The initiative foundered following Salah's return to Algeria, where he and his men were violently purged; Si Salah was killed a year later, in a French ambush *en route* to an FLN trial in Tunis (Meynier 2002: 425–9). De Gaulle's acknowledgement of the need for a negotiated withdrawal prompted a further referendum, on 8 January 1961, in which three-quarters of French metropolitan voters approved self-determination, as did all major political parties apart from the PCF; in Algeria, 39 per cent voted 'yes' and 42 per cent stayed away (Droz & Lever 1991: 264). The end was now in sight.

The January 1961 referendum vote reflected the opinion of ordinary French people sick of the war, but also recognition that an 'Algerian Algeria' was never going to be agreed by Algeria's European population or supported by a – non-existent – 'third force'. Pro-French Algerians were expendable in this equation: when an Algerian parliamentary delegation protested that they would suffer, de Gaulle replied frostily, 'Then you will suffer!' (ibid.: 234). Triumphant in May 1958, already sensing betrayal in September 1959, *pied noir* extremists ('*ultras*'), the army and their metropolitan sympathizers constituted a more formidable obstacle to progress. Their plotting, street violence and subsequent terrorism provided a jagged counterpoint to France's withdrawal from Algeria, although they perversely helped de Gaulle's case by demonstrating the opposition he faced. In the climactic 'week of the barricades' in January 1960, *ultra* leaders in Algiers, who controlled the uniformed settler militias formed to fight FLN terrorism, prepared for insurrection, barricading themselves into the university, where the militiamen stockpiled arms (including automatic weapons and bazookas) and medical supplies. Gendarmes advancing on the barricades, with unloaded weapons, were met with a fusillade which killed fourteen officers and wounded 123. The army's refusal to storm the barricades reflected insurgents' understanding with many middle-ranking army officers; but this understanding did not spread much beyond Algiers, and the hoped-for Algerian 'fraternization' never materialized. After a week of revolutionary theatre, most insurgents melted away, and the ringleaders surrendered, or escaped to exile in Spain; die-hards enlisted in the 1st Parachute Regiment of the Foreign Legion (1er REP) in lieu of prison (ibid.: 232–46). Challe was dismissed after a decent interval, his resolve having been found wanting, and Jacques Soustelle, gravitating towards dissidence, resigned as Minister of Information. By end 1960, a Front of French Algeria (FAF), spearheaded by the *ultras*' Parisian lawyers, joined in a clandestine alliance to form the Secret Army Organization (*Organisation Armée Secrète*, OAS), which, led by Soustelle, Salan, ex-Resistance leader Georges Bidault and others who should have known better, conducted a vicious two-year campaign of bombing and assassination in France and Algeria, designed to remove the 'traitor' de Gaulle and his allies, to protect French Algeria, and, failing that, to reduce Algeria to the 'state in which France found it in 1830'.

In his dramatic television speech on 29 January 1960, de Gaulle claimed to be the living embodiment of national legitimacy (in de Gaulle 1970b: vol. 3, 166). This was difficult to gainsay, especially when de Gaulle reassured the army that he still intended to crush the rebellion. By April 1961, a new challenge was being prepared by a 'clique of retired generals' (as de Gaulle called them), headed by Challe and including Salan, backed by many officers posted away from Algeria after the previous year's debacle. The trigger for action was de Gaulle's press conference of 11 April 1961, quoted at the outset of this chapter, when he all but declared his intention of withdrawing from Algeria. Asked whether an independent Algeria might become the cockpit of Cold War conflict between Soviets and Americans, de Gaulle's dismissive retort, 'May it bring them much pleasure!', showed his disdain for the army's conviction that French Algeria was the last bastion of the Christian West (Lacouture 1986: vol. 3, 155). At midnight on 21 April, the 1er REP marched on Algiers, and the putschists quickly took control of the capital, to *pied noir* acclaim. But Parisians watched the dawn skies for a parachute invasion that never materialized, the ageing Sherman tanks and half-tracks that ringed the National Assembly were never put to the test, and the ill-prepared generals had neither the momentum nor the supplies to defeat either de Gaulle or the FLN: as de Gaulle put it, 'the most serious thing about them . . . is that they are not serious'. The tacit support of many officers failed to translate into action, the navy stayed loyal and the airforce flew its planes beyond the generals' reach. Crucially, the mass of conscripts refused to follow orders, preferring to tune in to de Gaulle's higher authority on their transistor radios – a timely irruption of consumerist modernity into a dying colonialism. After the putsch's ignominious collapse, and the subsequent purge of the army, Salan and his fellow putschist Jouhaud assumed command of the OAS, which recruited many dissident officers, and sought to harness their extravagant theories of 'psychological warfare' to generate a proto-national *pied noir* revolution through terrorist violence, while drawing egregious parallels between de Gaulle and Pétain, French officials and the Gestapo, and hence between OAS and the wartime Resistance (Droz & Lever 1991: 301–15, 322–5).

It was thus against the background rumble of the OAS's 'festival of plastic explosive' and the FLN's renewed violence (suspended to allow the putsch to work to Algerian advantage) that, on 20 May 1961, Franco-Algerian negotiations finally opened at Evian, on the French shore of Lake Geneva. What did the two sides bring to the table? The starting point for the French team, led by Louis Joxe, a career diplomat who had replaced Delouvrier as Delegate-General the year before, was essentially unchanged since September 1959: French recognition of Algeria's right to choose between association with France and secession, the latter requiring partition to secure French interests. Joxe announced a unilateral French ceasefire, the release of 6,000 prisoners, and greater freedoms, including contacts with the GPRA, for Ben Bella and his fellow detainees. For the FLN negotiating team, headed by Belkacem Krim, Foreign Minister and Vice-President of the GPRA, last of the nine 'historic' leaders still alive and at liberty, the position was also straightforward, having remained unchanged since the Soummam Conference: no ceasefire without prior recognition of an indivisible, independent and sovereign Algeria (ibid.: 317).

While the GPRA refused a ceasefire until the Evian Accords were signed ten months later, the negotiations turned on two substantive questions: the Sahara and the fate of the *pieds noirs*. Insofar as French officials had discussed these issues, most extensively in a highly secretive Working Group on the Future Structures of Algeria, their proposals usually resolved them 'at the expense of Algerian sovereignty' (Connelly 2002: 219, 236). The Sahara's separate status was self-evident to French officials: mapped by French cartographers, administered separately by the French army (until two Saharan *départements* were created in 1957), its inhabitants had few ties to the North, while its economic and strategic value was entirely a matter of French enterprise, not only oil and gas, but also the nuclear testing grounds at Reggane, where the first French nuclear test was conducted in February 1960. Now at Evian, French negotiators argued for a separate plebiscite of the Saharan peoples – but then, if Saharan self-determination was separate, why not also that of the Kabyles? Also explored were fanciful and, at bottom, unattractive possibilities of co-sovereignty or multi-national pooling of resources, but such creativity with regard to international norms perhaps merely reflected a weak negotiating position (ibid.: 245). De Gaulle settled the issue, conceding on 5 September that 'there is not a single Algerian who does not think that the Sahara ought to be part of Algeria' (in ibid.: 255); the spectre of partition, which had haunted the FLN, now receded. Resources were another matter: exploitation of oil and gas remained a joint Franco-Algerian enterprise until nationalized in the 1970s, while nuclear testing rights were agreed for five years, alongside 15 years' extra-territorial rights for the naval base of Mers-el-Kebir (in fact abandoned after six years).

Stakes in the European minority's future were far higher, although, until late in the day, the almost universal assumption was that European settlers *had* a future in Algeria. The French at Evian argued a special case for the *pieds noirs*, more numerous and more permanently established than other settler communities, and who should thus be accorded special protections within the Algerian state. The FLN team countered with Moroccan and Tunisian precedents, where no deal had been struck for the hundreds of thousands of European settlers – although, in fact, settlers had been leaving both countries in droves since independence, harried by property seizures and attacks (ibid.: 243). French special pleading ran strictly counter to principles that would be applied within the 'One and Indivisible' French Republic. Discussions at Evian led to the intriguing communitarian proposal that European rights in Algeria might be balanced by minority status for Algerian immigrants in France, but this was at best a debating point. This was perhaps the one issue over which talks might have broken down as negotiations proceeded. In the end, the best deal that could be secured for the *pieds noirs*, alongside flimsy guarantees of representation in Algerian institutions, was that three years after independence they would have to accept Algerian citizenship or be considered resident aliens. In reality, the *pieds noirs'* future was probably settled well before the OAS's apocalyptic violence ruled out peace between the European and Algerian communities. Although the *pieds noirs'* eventual stark choice between 'the suitcase or the coffin' was not realized until early 1962, it was already clear that there was little room for other more generous futures.

The first phase of Franco-Algerian negotiations at Evian came to an inconclusive close on 13 June, and further talks in July came to nothing; secret talks from October led to an exchange of notes in December (Droz & Lever 1991: 318–22). However, this period was principally characterized by the OAS's escalating violence, and by its hugely successful campaign to win *pied noir* 'hearts and minds'. The battle was also taken to France, where bombing targets included government ministers, communists and intellectuals. Serial attempts on de Gaulle's life culminated in his most spectacular escape: six weeks after Algerian independence, at Petit-Clamart, OAS machine-gunners hit his official Citroën DS with 150 bullets, without so much as grazing the President.[3] Two further outrages on French soil were not the OAS's work, though it may have directly influenced them. The first was the Paris Police's savage repression of an FLN-led (but peaceful) demonstration of Algerians on 17 October 1961, which resulted in several hundred Algerian casualties, dozens bludgeoned to death and thrown in the Seine. The second occurred during a march led by the PCF and trades unions, on 8 February 1962, when a police baton charge caused the deaths of nine demonstrators, who were crushed in the entrance to the Charonne metro station (ibid.: 324, 326–7).

The decisive shift in France's negotiating stance came in further talks commencing on 11 February 1962. The French and Algerian teams met, far from the spotlight of media (and OAS) attention, in the remote, state-owned Chalet du Yéti, at Les Rousses near the Swiss frontier. De Gaulle's instructions were simple: 'Succeed or fail but above all do not let negotiations drag on indefinitely'. After eight long days of inconclusive parleying, de Gaulle, in daily telephone contact with Joxe, insisted on agreement 'today', and agreement was duly reached at 5 a.m. the following morning, 19 February 1962. The basic terms – ceasefire followed by self-determination – could have been agreed nine months before at Evian, but the detail covered not only base rights and the fate of the European minority, but also the terms of the ceasefire and the remit of the joint Provisional Executive that would oversee the transition to independence (ibid.: 327–8; Connelly 2002: 260–2). A further tense week of negotiations followed at Evian, culminating in the signature of the Accords on 18 March 1962; the long-awaited ceasefire began the following day.

In the ensuing chaos of the three-month interim period preceding independence, three threads may be identified in the skein of events. The first of these was the climax and ultimate political failure of the OAS's campaign. In a fresh wave of murderous terror, Operation 'Rock and Roll', coinciding with the resumption of talks at Evian, Algerian intellectuals and professionals were targeted. Amongst the former was Mouloud Feraoun, gunned down by an OAS hit squad, whose posthumous *Journal* ([1962]2000) provides one of the most telling testimonies of the war. The list of targeted 'professionals' soon extended from doctors and pharmacists to flower-sellers and domestics. 'Monsieur de Gaulle's ceasefire is not the OAS's': the organization now moved to the next revolutionary phase, calling a general strike, and fortifying the Algiers working-class district of Bab-el-Oued for an insurrectionary last stand. The murder of six conscripts provoked a massive counter-attack by the army, but in the ensuing 'battle', OAS fighters retreated, leaving the local population to bear the brunt of repression. Then, on 26 March, Algerian *tirailleurs* policing a banned *pied noir* demonstration in the Rue d'Isly, responded to shots from surrounding rooftops by firing into the crowd, killing 46 and leaving hundreds wounded (Lever 1993). Hereafter, the OAS's campaign became ever more randomly violent. Even before Salan's arrest on 20 April, its strategic options were reduced to an abortive effort to secure a partitioned zone around Oran ('Israelization', according to Salan's replacement, Susini); and its increasingly horrific 'scorched earth' policy.

Secondly, betrayed by the OAS, *pieds noirs* in turn deserted the OAS: Mao's insurgent 'fish' now found the sustaining medium of popular support draining away, as the trickle of European exodus turned to a flood. The OAS responded with spiteful, bathetic terror, threatening the families and friends of those who left, even resorting to destroying their luggage at the quayside (Lever 1993). Officials had imagined various scenarios, including a maximal exodus, but French negotiation and planning were, perhaps naïvely, based on an assumption that *pieds noirs* would remain. At Les Rousses, Robert Buron envisaged the departure of '2 or 300,000 Europeans, maybe more' (in Connelly 2002: 262), but the guarantees agreed for the *pieds noirs* became progressively meaningless beyond this threshold, as their numbers shrank to irrelevance alongside the Algerian population. Thus a substantial tranche of the Evian Accords was rendered null and void by the *pieds noirs*' departure. Over the three months leading up to independence, almost all the 800,000-plus European population left, with minimal possessions, mostly for France (which many had never seen), Spain or Israel. Given France's prosperity, all soon 'occupied the place they deserved given their hard work and dynamism' (Messmer 1998: 170). Whether they could have remained without the OAS's campaign remains moot, though few on the French side from de Gaulle on down retained much faith that the FLN would honour the Evian Accords.

Thirdly, a less happy fate awaited many tens of thousands of Algerians who had fought on the French side, collectively known as the *harkis*. Their number had declined from a peak of some 200,000 in early 1961; as we have seen, they played a key role in the Challe plan, and the army seems to have conceived Algerian troops as a vague 'party of France', who might engage in an eventual Algerian civil war (Messmer 1998: 171).[4] Before the Evian Accords were signed, flexible rules allowed Algerian troops to remain in the army, and irregulars to enlist, and stipulated that 'repatriation' (i.e. to France) should not be refused where individuals or their families were threatened (ibid.: 173). In the chaos of the interim period, the number of requests for repatriation rocketed as the FLN reneged on the protections offered by the Accords, and the French army was increasingly powerless to act. The numbers of those massacred then and later cannot be determined, but the lowest estimates of around 10,000 might conservatively be multiplied by at least five (Messmer 1998: 174–5; Pervillé 1993). In May, Louis Joxe, now Minister of Algerian Affairs, forbade French assistance to Algerians seeking to reach France. This order was widely disregarded by army officers loyal to 'their' troops, so Joxe shamefully ordered the punishment of those responsible;

Pierre Messmer, as Minister of Armies, countermanded this order, but the political damage had been done (Messmer 1998: 176). The 100,000 or so Algerians who took refuge in France (*harkis* and their families) were housed in spartan and overcrowded military camps and ex-Vichy detention camps, the last of which were emptied only in the 1970s. The *harkis* faced an uncertain future, shunned by their homeland (and nonsensically blamed much later by the FLN for the rise of militant Islamism), and yet not fully accepted by a France eager to 'turn the page': more than a generation on, the '*enfants de harkis*' still occupy a distinct and uneasy niche amidst France's 'immigrant' communities.

Belgian Congo: Demise of a 'Platonic' Ideal

Nowhere in Africa was the late colonial state more efficiently, more intensively, and more profitably run than in the Belgian Congo. Nowhere were healthcare and primary education more handsomely provided for (but not secondary or higher education), nowhere did officials penetrate more extensively into the countryside and into African lives – and nowhere were fewer concessions made to political reform. Officials of rival empires looked on with some apprehension that this Belgian 'formula' might actually work, and it was 'a great relief' for British officials in the mid-1950s that Belgian territories could no more be isolated from nationalist political mobilization than elsewhere (Ronald Robinson, in Stengers 1995: 311). However, when the 'Platonic' paternalist colonialism of Belgium's 'philosopher-kings' (Hodgkin 1956: 52) was succeeded by an attempt to stage a 'model' decolonization, the Congo acquired exemplarity of a different kind, as Belgian policy collapsed in the face of the new political realities. Indeed, nowhere else did more remain undecided until *after* the declaration of independence, including the future of officials, soldiers and settlers, and the political and territorial unity of the post-colonial state.

Belgium's 'philosopher-kings' were more ubiquitous than officials elsewhere in colonial Africa: with 10,000 Belgian civil servants in the Congo at the time of independence, 'no Congolese, rural or urban, could have failed to perceive he was being administered' (Young 1965: 11). This was particularly noticeable in the countryside, where agricultural officers monitored an extensive compulsory labour regime almost to the end. The administration improved on Plato in its generous provision of healthcare, providing medical examinations for $6^{1}/_{2}$ million Congolese in 1955 (of a total population of some 15 million). The administration constituted only one part of an interlocking 'trinity' alongside the Church and big business. The Church's reach in the Congo was as extensive as the administration's, with nearly 6,000 European missionaries, mostly Belgian, 200 Congolese priests and several hundred Congolese religious ministering in 1958 to more than five million declared Christians, 80 per cent of them Catholics (ibid.: 12–14; Soumille 1995: 395). Economic interests were also extensive, and companies enjoyed privileged access to officials contemplating a profitable second career on the board of one of the mining, cotton or railway companies (Young 1965: 14–18). Lucrative mining interests were concentrated in the South-Eastern provinces of Kasai (diamonds) and Katanga (copper and tin). The system was remarkably self-contained, with little interference from Belgian political parties or public opinion. The largely toothless Colonial Council in Brussels comprised six members elected by parliament, representing all three main Belgian political parties, and eight members nominated by the King, representing a carefully balanced set of official, regional and commercial interests (ibid.: 24).

'The days of colonialism are past', declared the wartime Governor-General, Pierre Ryckmans in 1946. However, change was to be managed under strict official control, with an emphasis on gradualism, even more marked than in British doctrine, reinforced by a vision of Belgian history in which civic, regional (Flemish and Walloon) and eventually national identities were built from the ground up. A further key concept was the Belgian-Congolese Community, corresponding to the French Union, but also echoing British multi-racialism, since the Community embodied parity of representation for Europeans and Africans. Timescales remained vague, although the centenary of the Congo Free State's foundation in 1885 seemed a fitting date for eventual 'emancipation', whatever that meant. A thirty-year plan proposed in 1955 was treated in colonial circles as either naïve or dangerous, or both, although its largely comparative approach avoided analysis of perceived Congolese demands (ibid.: 36–7; Stengers 1995: 312; Van Bilsen 1958). A more concrete plan followed in July 1958, when the Colonial Minister, Léo Pétillon, announced a Working Group composed of parliamentarians and senior officials, but no Congolese. This Working Group took evidence from several hundred Congolese and Belgians, and reported in December 1958 on the steps needed for 'an autonomous State benefiting from a democratic regime, with respect for the rights of men and African values' (Stengers 1995; Young 1965: 163). The proposed regime comprised an elaborately tiered structure of directly elected communal and district councils, in turn electing provincial councils. At the highest tier, a legislative council including indirectly elected Congolese and settler representatives would advise an appointed government council (Young 1965: 166–8). There was no mention of eventual independence. Thus the Belgian 'official mind' reached the starting gate for colonial political reform, through which the British and French had passed more than a decade before.

In this version of Aesop, the tortoise metamorphosed into a hare. Before Pétillon's proposals could be announced, the Congo's situation was transformed by several days of rioting in the capital, Léopoldville, in early January 1959; the conservative official death toll was 49. Until this point, Belgian reformism flowed from an exclusively internal debate. Now, almost literally overnight, a Congolese nationalism had apparently burst fully formed onto the political stage. Belgian recognition of this came on 13 January 1959, when Pétillon and the King made separate speeches (the latter quoted at this chapter's outset), amplifying the Working Group's proposals with a hastily improvised, and slightly panicked, promise of independence, hedged around with qualifications. Although no timetable was suggested, and it seemed reasonable to imagine it stretching into an indefinite future, the Congo's 18-month dash to independence had begun.

Aside from over-reaction to largely leaderless violence, the Belgians' palpable shock in January 1959 forced an awakening to the emergent realities of Congolese politics. Surprise was understandable, given the Belgian colonial state's prior effectiveness in setting the political agenda. Indeed, the Congo offers a baseline against which late colonial political developments elsewhere can be measured: the Congolese had extremely limited access to secondary education, thus inhibiting the development of an intelligentsia; there was no political process, and political parties had no legal existence; trades union organization, legalized in 1946, was barely tolerated; and an African press only appeared in the late 1950s. Crucially, the colonial state had isolated its subjects from the outside world, controlling the issue of passports and limiting travel opportunities even to Belgium. By 1958, only a few Congolese had been accepted in Belgian universities, and the visit of several hundred Congolese to the 1958 Brussels Exhibition provided novel contact with European and African political and intellectual currents (ibid.: 277–81, 291).

Although Congolese political activism was thus extremely limited, a plethora of associations pre-dated the political parties that entered the ring in 1958–9. These included alumni associations or mission-sponsored *cercles des évolués*, and countless ethnic associations offering mutual aid amongst a migrant urban membership. They had little political resonance, but offered valuable organizational training for potential leaders: in 1953, the future Prime Minister, Patrice Lumumba, mission-educated *évolué* and postal worker, was either president or secretary of seven associations in Stanleyville (ibid.: 295). The nationalist movement's subsequent fragmentation along ethnic and regional fracture lines is suggested already by the strength of the ethnic associations, many dating back to the 1920s. Of these, the closest in outlook to a nationalist party was ABAKO, formed in 1950 to represent the Bakongo (80 per cent of the population of the Léopoldville region). ABAKO's president from 1954, Joseph Kasavubu, drew prestige from the messianic Kimbanguiste cult, which venerated Simon Kimbangu, a former Protestant preacher-turned-prophet who died in 1951 after thirty years in prison (Hargreaves 1996: 192–3). When in 1956 *évolués*, including Lumumba, published a manifesto appealing for loyal Congolese participation in the thirty-year plan, ABAKO riposted with calls for 'immediate emancipation' (Young 1965: 276–7). The banning of an ABAKO meeting precipitated the January 1959 riots, and ABAKO was subsequently scapegoated. The expulsion of its members from the capital had the paradoxical effect of radicalizing the surrounding countryside.

The Working Group's hearings in 1958 prompted the formation of two further major nationalist players: the National Congolese Movement (MNC) and the Confederation of Tribal Associations of Katanga (CONAKAT, constituted as a party in 1959). Between January 1959 and the date of independence, more than a hundred parties were formed. Even amongst the bigger parties, there was a low premium on unity, and parties tended to organize around individuals, or to form strong ethnic affiliations. The MNC split into three factions, two with strong regional bases grouped around individual leaders, Lumumba in Stanleyville (MNC/L), and Albert Kalonji in Elisabethville (MNC/K); MNC/K developed into an exclusive Baluba movement, while MNC/L almost uniquely developed the potential for national organization. Few other parties had a substantial following, or developed a rural presence. By mid-1959, ABAKO's grip on the Léopoldville region effectively supplanted the administration, raising the spectre of armed Belgian intervention. The Algerian example helped dissuade Belgian public opinion from supporting the deployment of conscripts, especially as the Belgian Socialist Party was vigorously campaigning against conscription (Young 1965: 154–5, 297–301; Stengers 1995: 315). The breakdown of order was thus a significant factor in inducing Belgium to favour rapid withdrawal come what may.

The January 1959 Declaration offered a Belgian 'model' of decolonization, based on a programme of political reforms culminating in independence, and dependent upon Congolese cooperation (Stengers 1995: 313). However, in a volatile political situation, the measured process implied by the King's speech, even with the promise of independence, seemed to radicalized Congolese at best nebulous, at worst a lure. As a liberal Colonial Minister, Van Hemelryck, toured the country through 1959, contacting 'all who could be considered as public opinion in the Congo of today', Belgian endeavours gradually crystallized around the elections called for December 1959, as a means of electing *interlocuteurs valables*, or, as Congolese opinion saw it, as a colonial ploy to designate biddable stooges. From mid-1959 ABAKO and its allies campaigned for a Round Table conference, to be held preferably in Brussels, at which Belgian and Congolese parties would negotiate *before* elections took place. The government eventually conceded the Round Table, and announced that independence would be granted in 1960, but it insisted on the December elections. These showed a substantial victory for 'moderate' political forces, but were undermined by ABAKO's boycott in Léopoldville province (Young 1995: 158–60, 170).

What emerged from the Round Table conference, which met in Brussels in January–February 1960, was diametrically opposed to the Belgian gradualist model. A decisive factor was the last-minute formation of a 'common front' of all the Congolese parties, who thus imposed their will on a divided Belgian parliamentary delegation. In particular, the Congolese insisted on setting 30 June 1960 as the date for independence. Much flowed from this decision, since there was little time to resolve the major differences still separating the Congolese parties, and only a properly united nationalist movement might have been strong enough to exercise moderation in such a fraught colonial endgame (ibid.: 161). Sheer momentum also helps explain why a Fundamental Law was adopted so closely resembling the Belgian bicameral constitution. This postponed the settlement of major issues until after independence, including whether the Congo would be a unitary or a federal state and also the relationship between Head of State and Prime Minister, since it was long assumed, even by many Congolese, that the King would remain Head of State of an independent Congo (ibid.: 175–8). Belgian reserved powers in foreign affairs, defence and finance was also abandoned in the face of Congolese pressure. Although Belgium was thus induced into conceding a more 'generous' settlement than it wished, it retained an apparently cast-iron guarantee of continuity and order, in that the army, the *Force Publique*, had an exclusively European officer corps, and the administration was staffed by Europeans at all but the lowest echelons (ibid.: 172–5). Conversely, the non-Africanization of these two institutions was a powerful source of discontent for two powerful groups expecting to benefit directly from independence: clerks and soldiers.

Independence thus brought with it all the stability of a decelerating spinning-top. Elections in May had further confirmed the fragmentation of the Congolese parties, with three parties – MNC/L, ABAKO and the National Party of Progress (PNP) – commanding between them a bare majority of 69 in the 137-seat Chamber of Deputies, and nine others holding seven or more seats. Only in one of six provincial assemblies did a single party hold a majority: the MNC/L in Lumumba's Eastern stronghold around Stanleyville (ibid.: 302–3). A difficult compromise in June led to Kasavubu's appointment as President, with Lumumba as Prime Minister of a deeply divided coalition government. The *Force Publique* broke first: equally unimpressed by Lumumba's blandishments and by their Belgian commander's formula, 'After Independence – Before Independence', Congolese soldiers mutinied in a movement which quickly spread to garrisons across the country (ibid.: 316). The mutiny started a chain of events, rapidly unravelling the independence settlement. After Kasavubu and Lumumba agreed to Belgian troops keeping order, Belgian naval forces pointlessly bombarded the port city of Matadi, killing 19, provoking the mutineers to violence, and widening the Belgian–Congolese split. Although the European death toll in this early period was perhaps less than two dozen, acts of violence, rape and public humiliation directed against missionaries and settlers were more widespread. Following a Belgian announcement on 12 July that civil servants, in all of the Congo outside Katanga, were deemed unable to carry out their functions, and could thus be integrated into the metropolitan civil service, the administration was Africanized by the massive flight of almost all 10,000 European officials. Settlers, too, whose numbers had reached 110,000 before 1959, since dropping to 80,000, left *en masse*, although some 20,000 remained behind, mostly in Katanga (ibid.: 317–21). Along with the *Force Publique*'s transformation into a Congolese National Army (ANC), this effected a swift, almost total and so far relatively bloodless decolonization.

Now Katanga declared its 'independence' led by the CONAKAT President, Moïse Tshombe, and, with support from Belgian troops and former *Force Publique* officers, expelled all Congolese troops who were not from pro-CONAKAT areas. The secession of the Southern half of neighbouring Kasai province followed in August. In both provinces, mineral wealth reinforced a strong sense of ethnic identification, further intensified in Kasai by the discrimination suffered by the Baluba, a mobile group of traders and clerks, across the Congo. In both provinces, mining gave settlers a vested interest in secession; the *Union Minière du Haut-Katanga*, notably, saw Katanga's future as lying in the neighbouring Northern Rhodesian Copperbelt. Katangan secession prompted Lumumba's appeal for United Nations intervention, and thus started the internationalization of Congolese decolonization, with the arrival of the first UN troops on 15 July. However, Lumumba's aim of re-imposing Congolese unity, if necessary by force, did not square with the UN's priority of preventing a wider international conflict (ibid.: 322–3; Hargreaves 1996: 196). Lumumba also appealed to fellow African leaders, who responded without enthusiasm, and to President Khrushchev, who in August sent ten aircraft and sixty trucks, packaged with a 'pro-Soviet' label which stayed round Lumumba's neck for the limited remainder of his days.

Congolese disintegration continued with the collapse of the parliamentary regime, triggered by Lumumba's downfall. Lumumba's was the biggest single party in the Chamber of Deputies, and he had even stronger support in Stanleyville, hundreds of miles eastwards. In Léopoldville, Lumumba's enemies included five major ethnic groups, the Church, trades unions and most of the press. His judgement was called into question following his appeal to the Soviet Union, but also after a brief, bloody campaign against South Kasai, which turned into an anti-Baluba pogrom (Young 1965: 324–5). On 5 September, Kasavubu, suspecting that Lumumba wanted his job, invoked a measure copied from the Belgian Constitution – but which no Belgian sovereign since Léopold II has dared apply – allowing the Head of State to dismiss the Prime Minister. Although of questionable legality, this move was accepted at face value by the UN. An inquorate parliamentary session on 13 September accorded extraordinary powers to Lumumba, but effective power in Léopoldville had already passed to a duumvirate of Kasavubu and newly promoted General Joseph (Sésé Séko) Mobutu, kick-starting his epic political career at the head of a 'college of commissioners'. Parliament did not reconvene until the formation of a national government in August 1961. Meanwhile, Lumumba's supporters decamped to Stanleyville where a rival legitimist government was established in November under Vice-Premier Gizenga. On 27 November, Lumumba escaped from the double cordon of Congolese and UN guards around his residence (one detaining him, the other protecting him), but on 2 December his convoy was captured by Baluba troops a few miles short of friendly territory, and in January he was transferred to Elisabethville and assassinated, almost certainly with CIA connivance, although he did not apparently 'fall into a river full of crocodiles', as Macmillan and Eisenhower had suggested he might (ibid.: 325–31; Hyam & Louis 2000: lxxii).

The consequence of a decolonization compressed into 18 months was thus to leave substantial business still unfinished after independence, including the precipitate 'Africanization' of army and administration, and the splits in national unity that were not repaired until more than four years after independence. The moment of greatest disarray was marked by Lumumba's assassination, at which point Congolese political authority was split between four rival capitals, two, Léopoldville and Stanleyville, the seats of legitimist governments, and two, Bakwanga and Elisabethville, heading secessionist statelets. Each had its own army, and all except Bakwanga had powerful international backing. Remarkably, after an initial period of complete political flux, all four managed to function reasonably efficiently as political and administrative units, and services such as education, transport and road maintenance were largely kept up through the good offices of the missions and provincial governments. The outside world's received idea of Congolese 'anarchy' and 'chaos' was thus slightly misleading, although perception mattered when it came to colonial governments and settler opinion, not least in the neighbouring Central African Federation. Military action too was largely kept in check by UN peacekeeping troops, drawn mostly from non-European states, notably from India, although they could not prevent violence against the civilian populations of the marches between rival territories.

From early 1961, the process of restitching the fabric of national unity began, as a series of Round Tables culminated in the 'Lovanium' reconciliation between Léopoldville and Stanleyville in August 1961. This created a national government led by the conciliatory figure of Cyrille Adoula, but Stanleyville under Gizenga soon re-entered into 'dissidence', isolated by Léopoldville's blockade, and by the closing of the Sudanese border, which restricted the possibilities for material Soviet support. The resistance of a National Committee of Liberation created in October 1963 was eradicated in late 1964, partly by Belgian paratroops airlifted by the US Air Force. South Kasai was reintegrated in early 1962, but the Katangan secession was terminated only in January 1963, after UN troops failed to expel the many Belgian 'military advisers' and international mercenaries sustaining the Tshombe regime. The Léopoldville regime thus emerged triumphant, but it bore little resemblance to the abortive parliamentary democracy of 1960, especially after Mobutu established a military dictatorship in 1965, at the outset of his protracted transformation into the 'walking bank account with a leopard-skin hat' of the 1990s.[5]

Central African Federation

The Federation of Rhodesia and Nyasaland, or Central African Federation (CAF), was formed in 1953, in spite of total opposition from nascent nationalist movements in all three federated territories. However, its ultimate success or failure would depend on the reconciliation of competing African and settler nationalisms, as Africans mobilized with increasing effectiveness against ebullient settlers' ambitions to transform the Federation into an independent white-dominated Dominion. Within ten years, it had been reduced to its constituent parts, as two independent African states, Zambia and Malawi, emerged from the crumpled framework, while the stronghold of white supremacy in Southern Rhodesia would endure almost two decades more of pariah status and armed conflict before the achievement of African majority rule and Zimbabwe's independence in 1980. The principal focus here is on Northern Rhodesia, which constituted the lynchpin of the Federation.

The birth of the Federation heralded a period of limbo for the Northern Rhodesian ANC, which had lost its initial *raison d'être*: fighting Federation. It maintained visibility with various campaigns, and its militant credentials were enhanced in January 1955, when Harry Nkumbula and the party's secretary-general and rising star, Kenneth Kaunda, were imprisoned for possessing 'banned literature', mostly consisting of copies of an innocuous publication sent by the British Labour MP, Fenner Brockway (Rotberg 1966: 273). The party lost ground in the Copperbelt, where it was engaged in a power struggle with the African Mineworkers' Union (AMWU), led by the moderate Lawrence Katilungu. Even during the battle over Federation, in April 1953, Katilungu had refused support for two days of 'national prayer' called by Nkumbula. The AMWU now had even less reason to give ground to ANC militancy over an apparently lost political cause. Rather, the ANC's agenda intersected and worked against the AMWU's struggle for 'stabilization' of its members' status as workers. In this, the union found itself in competition with separate unions representing more privileged white miners and better-paid African clerks, and in conflict with the employers' ambitions to modernize their industry without conceding the profoundly un-colonial principle of 'equal work for equal pay' (Cooper 1996a: 336–48). This struggle briefly brought the AMWU closer to ANC in 1956, when the Copperbelt experienced its biggest wave of strike action, leading to a short-lived emergency in September 1956. Katilungu was abroad at the time, and industrial peace was restored quickly after his return (Mulford 1967: 26, 45–6).

The new Federal government, led by Northern Rhodesian former trades unionist, Sir Roy Welensky, was dissatisfied too, but in this instance with the Federation's provisional status, with Governors retaining significant responsibilities in the protectorates. British cabinet responsibilities for the Federation were also shared, sometimes uncomfortably, between the Colonial Office and the Commonwealth Relations Office (CRO). The CRO's sympathies for the Federal government became clear when, on 26 April 1957 (a month after Ghana's independence), the Secretary of State, Lord

Home, promised a review of the Federal constitution by October 1960. This was to consider a programme for attaining full Commonwealth membership, understood to mean independence (ibid.: 51–2; Hyam & Louis 2000: doc. 492). Federal legislation followed, enlarging the federal assembly, while limiting African representation through a new dual franchise, which divided voters into two classes, defined by education and income: 'ordinary' (almost all European or Asian) and 'special' (exclusively African) (Mulford 1967: 52, 57–8). In Northern Rhodesia, this system was refined in the 1958 constitution introduced by the Governor, Sir Arthur Benson, which created 'ordinary' (i.e. European-dominated, urban) and 'special' (African-dominated, rural) constituencies, with two reserved 'special' seats within settler-dominated areas (Lusaka and the Copperbelt), and *vice versa*. In the elections set for March 1959, as in the contemporaneous 'multi-racial' elections in Tanganyika (Chapter 7), candidates would receive votes from all racial communities. Everything depended on the extent of voter registration and the goodwill of the parties – it might cynically be said it was thereby set to fail from the outset.

By setting a deadline for fixing the Federation's status, Lord Home's declaration galvanized the Nyasaland African Congress (NAC) and Northern Rhodesian ANC. In July 1958, after many false starts and rumours, Hastings Banda returned to Nyasaland, after five years in Ghana, having left home some 42 years before. In August, he assumed leadership of NAC, and started a vigorous, though avowedly non-violent, campaign for 'freedom' and against the 'stupid so-called Federation' (Rotberg 1966: 287–8). In December 1958, he was back in Ghana for the All-African People's Conference, where he conferred – or, allegedly, plotted – with Nkumbula and Kaunda, by now the estranged leaders of rival parties. Nkumbula's increasingly moderate line was opposed by militants in the Copperbelt, in the remote northern Luapula province, and along the shores of the rising Lake Kariba, where many villagers faced resettlement. His authoritarian leadership also attracted increasing criticism, although his prestige as nationalist founding father made him almost unassailable (Mulford 1967: 67–76). Suspicion that Nkumbula was about to commit ANC to participating in the March 1959 elections added to Kaunda's growing conviction, strengthened by recent contacts with Nehru's Indian National Congress, that the forthcoming struggle required a highly disciplined movement, with a dedicated, self-sacrificing leadership, and that Nkumbula was no longer the man for the job (Rotberg 1966: 290–1). The split came in October 1958, after Kaunda and colleagues walked out of a turbulent national executive meeting, announced a rival Zambia African National Congress (ZANC), and proposed to reject the Benson constitution and to boycott the impending elections. (The name Zambia was a contraction of Zambezia, an earlier name for the general area of Northern Rhodesia.) After the Accra Conference, Kaunda stayed in Ghana, seeking to persuade Nkrumah of the wisdom of the split, and securing his support for the new movement (Mulford 1967: 75–81).

The scene was now set for the crisis of March 1959, as federal and territorial governments sought to consolidate Federation by crushing its opponents. The focus of their efforts was Nyasaland, where multi-racialism was least plausible, given the low numbers of settlers, and where Banda's campaign was taking off. In January, the NAC executive, in Banda's absence, voted to abandon non-violence, though the growing spate of violent incidents was as yet independent of political direction (Darwin 1994:

218–34). On 20 February, at a meeting of the federal and territorial governments, the Southern Rhodesian Prime Minister, Sir Edgar Whitehead, announced his intention to declare an Emergency, as a pre-emptive strike against the Southern Rhodesian ANC. By banning the party, and detaining some 400 activists, he freed up federal troops to be sent to Nyasaland (ibid.: 225). Welensky urged the Governor of Nyasaland, Sir Robert Armitage, to recover the 'initiative', but Armitage was anyway inclined to respond to mounting disorder, and to the sound and fury of settler opinion. He also chose to put faith in an intelligence dossier outlining an NAC 'murder plot', in which officials and settlers would be assassinated on an unspecified 'R-day'. On 3 March 1959 – by fateful coincidence, the same day as the infamous massacre at Hola camp a thousand miles to the North – 'Operation Sunrise' began with the declaration of an Emergency and the round-up of NAC leaders, including Banda. After more than two weeks of disturbances, 51 Africans were dead, including more than twenty shot at Nkata Bay on the first day. But the operation's scope had broadened into an attempt to 'eradicate Congress leadership and doctrines': by mid-May a thousand or more NAC members were in detention (ibid.: 226–8).

For the British government, the worst was yet to come. Facing extensive criticism from opposition Labour MPs, and wishing to postpone a broader enquiry, the government appointed a four-member commission of enquiry, headed by a senior barrister, Sir Patrick (later Lord) Devlin. The tactic backfired disastrously. Reporting in July, Devlin exonerated Armitage from bowing to federal pressure, and acknowledged that the level of disorder justified the Emergency, but he condemned the excessive use of force, dismissed the idea that Banda now favoured violence, and discounted the 'murder plot' as a groundless pretext for action. Devlin shook the imperial self-image to the core by suggesting that 'Nyasaland is – no doubt temporarily – a police state', where all opposition to Federation was repressed. The Cabinet's wild comparisons with Mau Mau and even the Indian Mutiny were not made public, but the deeper lesson had only started to sink in, that anti-Federation opinion, 'extremist' or otherwise, was only containable by the kind of detention policy which had underpinned the defeat of Mau Mau, but for which the British government – thankfully – no longer had an appetite (ibid.: 228–31; Hyam & Louis 2000: doc. 494).

Northern Rhodesian events took a less drastic turn, but the outcome was hardly less pregnant with doom for the Federation's future. Here a deadline was set by the elections scheduled for 20 March. ZANC's emergence confused the political picture in Northern Rhodesia, and the dividing line between ZANC supporters and the old Congress remained unclear (Mulford 1967: 76f., 85–6). It was thus impossible to determine the likely effectiveness of ZANC's boycott, or its responsibility for the disappointing electoral registration figures. In the rural 'special' constituencies, just over half the estimated number of eligible voters registered, but in the reserved 'special' constituencies, the key to Benson's multi-racial policy, only one-fifth of eligible voters registered. However, with or without ZANC's boycott, and whatever the turnout, this was still an overwhelmingly white election. Moreover, Benson failed to produce genuinely multi-racial voting, as African 'special' voters voted against the settlers' United Federal Party (UFP), while, conversely, European 'ordinary' votes overwhelmingly determined the election of Africans. Nkumbula won the ANC's only seat, while the UFP won both reserved 'special' seats (ibid.: 97–9).[6]

These dismal results were overshadowed by the Governor's ban on ZANC on 11 March, nine days before polling day. In contrast to the botched Emergency in Nyasaland, Benson had acted swiftly, arresting ZANC's leaders on 12 March and rusticating them to remote areas. Again unlike Nyasaland, there was only scattered violence in the towns and the more radical outlying provinces, and election day passed off peacefully. In a radio broadcast, Benson outlined an alleged three-stage plan across the Federation leading to outright revolution, a plan which in Nyasaland had 'gone off at half cock'. He conjured up a Mau Mau-like rural reign of terror, 'invoking witchcraft and unmentionable cursings', and colourfully compared ZANC to Murder Incorporated, the American gangster syndicate (ibid.: 95–6). Benson resisted pressure from Salisbury to declare a full-scale Emergency. However, London, Salisbury, Lusaka and Zomba apparently thought as one on the rationale for banning nationalist parties in order to shut down dangerous radicalism (Mulford 1967: 104–5). Conversely, Benson and Armitage suspected Federal government manipulation of the crisis with a view to transferring responsibility for security to federal troops, and hence accelerating federal independence (ibid.; Darwin 1994: 227–8). In this, the Emergencies across the three territories achieved the exact opposite of their intended objective.

By the start of 1960, Central Africa had reached a major turning point, although the degree of turn was at first apparently slight. Macmillan, passing through Salisbury *en route* for Cape Town, did not mention the 'wind of change' (which had passed unnoticed in a speech in Accra) (Hyam & Louis 2000). To do so might have upstaged the Monckton Commission, set up to advise on the forthcoming Federal review, which started work in February. In Nyasaland, the banned NAC reconstituted itself in September 1959 as the Malawi Congress Party (MCP); the name 'Malawi' was a possibly fanciful invention of the still imprisoned Banda (Rotberg 1966: 309). Nyasaland now trod a clear path towards federal secession and independence, though the process was not completed until 1964. The newly appointed Iain Macleod was as circumspect as the Prime Minister in public, but in Cabinet he argued vigorously for Banda's release on 1 April 1960, and for a Nyasaland conference, which took place in London in July 1960. This established a constitution allowing African majorities in both Legislative and Executive Councils, albeit with 'responsible government' under continuing control of a governor, and within the Federation. This effectively anticipated Monckton, since any African majority would demand secession (Hargreaves 1996: 215). In the August 1961 elections, the MCP won all twenty seats on the 'lower roll' (replacing the earlier 'special' electorates) and two of eight 'upper roll' seats, and five (later seven) MCP members were appointed to the ten-seat Executive Council (Rotberg 1966: 313). After more than a year of 'responsible government', a further London conference in November 1962 agreed self-government for early 1963, followed by full independence in March 1964. Nyasaland's secession from the Federation was confirmed in December 1962 (Hyam & Louis 2000: docs 510–12; Rotberg 1966: 312–14). Even before independence, Banda was manifesting the autocratic and puritanical tendencies which marked his long career as President into the 1990s.

In January 1960, Kaunda was released from detention and promptly assumed the presidency of a new United National Independence Party (UNIP), which had split away from ANC, and which developed rapidly into a disciplined mass party to match

Kaunda's ambitions. Its first campaign was a strident boycott of the Monckton Commission, which toured Northern Rhodesia in February–March 1960. Monckton acknowledged the 'remarkable degree of control' exercised by UNIP (and, after some hesitation, by ANC), and by MCP in Nyasaland, that had prevented witnesses from coming forward (Mulford 1967: 149). Monckton's terms of reference excluded secession, which explained the parties' hostility, but his report, a multi-faceted document including Notes of Reservation from 17 of 25 commissioners, highlighted Africans' 'almost pathological dislike' of Federation, noted Britain's right to consider requests for secession, and recommended African majorities in all three Legislative and Executive Councils. It concluded that, while 'Federation cannot, in our view be maintained in its present form', dismantling it would be 'an admission that there is no hope for survival for any multi-racial society on the African continent' (Hargreaves 1996: 215; Porter & Stockwell 1989: vol. II, 539–57).

These were high stakes indeed, and the sequence of conferences, talks, boycotts, walk-outs, and threatened and actual violence, suggest just what was required for multi-racialism to prosper in Central Africa. The long-awaited Federal Review conference opened in London in December 1960, but was rapidly shelved in favour of separate constitutional conferences, as urged by the three nationalist leaders, including Joshua Nkomo, leader of Southern Rhodesia's National Democratic Party (NDP). The Southern Rhodesian conference, concluding in February 1961, agreed a constitution which marginally advanced African representation, addressed some discriminatory practices, and substituted a Bill of Rights for the British government's residual right to intervene in Southern Rhodesian internal affairs (Hargreaves 1996: 216). By this time, with a sabre-rattling Welensky in Salisbury threatening to send federal troops across the Zambezi, the Northern Rhodesian conference was approaching deadlock. Three days after the conference's suspension on 17 February, Macleod announced the first attempt (of three) to draw up an acceptable constitutional proposal. As he explained in Cabinet, while no plan could 'meet in full the wishes of both the Africans and the Europeans', he hoped this one 'would not provoke violence from either side', but that a multi-racial solution was preferable to Monckton's racially based recommendations (i.e. for an African majority) (Hyam & Louis 2000: doc. 502). In a Legislative Council of 45 elected members, alongside six officials, 15 were to be elected by upper-roll voters, including more Africans, and 15 by an expanded lower roll for which an estimated 70,000 Africans were eligible. Crucially, 15 new National constituencies were to be elected by both rolls voting together. Everything hinged on complex rules for the National seats, which, in Macleod's proposals, marginally favoured African candidates, thus pointing to an overall African majority. This drew further wild threats from Welensky, and some UFP ministers resigned. But UNIP and ANC also rejected the proposals, fearing that the franchise and constituency boundaries would be settled over nationalists' heads. After several months of wrangling, Macleod presented a second set of proposals in late June (largely not his work), which virtually ruled out an African majority (Mulford 1967: 184–6, 193–7).

This time it was Kaunda's turn to condemn British 'betrayal' of Africans, and at a UNIP conference in early July, Kaunda was unanimously granted 'emergency powers' to implement a 'master plan' of non-violent direct action (ibid.: 198.). However, over two months, the UNIP leadership lost control of militant local branches particularly in Northern and Luapula Provinces. The ensuing violence resulted in perhaps 27 deaths, and the widespread destruction of schools, bridges and government property. More than 3,000 were arrested, mostly known UNIP militants, but many UNIP supporters' houses and villages were burned, and UNIP alleged atrocities by the security forces. In September, following talks with Kaunda, Macleod offered to reopen constitutional talks provided the disturbances ended. Kaunda's appeals for calm took effect almost immediately, amidst European grumbling that violence appeared to pay dividends (ibid.: 199–206). Macleod at this point had evidently strained his party's patience, and in October 1961, he was promoted out of harm's way, although he kept his Cabinet seat. However, his successor, Reginald Maudling, pursued his policy and pushed through a third set of proposals, in February 1962, which reset the rules for the National seats to something like their original form a year before – a year which, as Macmillan acknowledged, had 'achieved nothing' (Hyam & Louis 2000: lv). Macmillan now ended the ambiguity arising from shared Cabinet responsibility for the Federation, which tended to mirror tensions in the Salisbury–Lusaka axis: in March 1962, Macmillan's deputy, R.A.B. Butler, assumed overall responsibility for Central Africa, and steered Federation to its eventual dissolution on 31 December 1963.

When Maudling's constitutional proposals passed in March 1962, Northern Rhodesia was still two-and-a-half years, two constitutions and two general elections from independence. The first of these elections, in October 1962, amounted to a last-ditch test of multi-racialism and hence of Federation. It was also a formidable technical exercise, in which electoral registration was followed by the delimitation of three sets of constituencies (upper roll, lower roll and National), each set covering the whole territory. For UNIP, having accepted the constitutional settlement, the challenge was to move towards African majority rule from within the multi-racial framework. This entailed applying the lessons of the previous year's disturbances by imposing party discipline, reorganizing regional structures, and making the leadership more representative through an extended National Council (Mulford 1967: 234–5). Secondly, it meant maximizing African voter registration: in part thanks to UNIP's energetic campaigning, more than twice as many Africans as estimated were registered on the upper roll, while the lower roll exceeded estimates by more than 30 per cent. However, fewer than one-tenth of Africans of voting age were registered. Thirdly, the party tried to make itself acceptable to the European electorate, fielding politically innocent 'new men' as candidates rather than seasoned militants, but also campaigning vigorously for the National seats, which would determine the election (ibid.: 250–4, 259).

The imponderable factor as the election approached was the role played by other parties, none of which campaigned as did UNIP in all three parts of the election. ANC revival in this period brought the party much-needed funding, partly through links forged with Moïse Tshombe in Katanga. But ANC's inclination to European-friendly and even pro-Federal 'moderation', enhanced by association with Tshombe, was also attractive to the UFP, which needed to secure African electoral support. By mid-1962 a covert UFP–ANC alliance had been formed, a deeply cynical manoeuvre which compromised the election's multi-racialist credibility, and dented UNIP's chances of victory (ibid.: 240–4). On the upper roll, UFP won all but one seat, while UNIP gained one-fifth of the vote (and the remaining seat); this loosely corresponded to the proportion of Africans on the roll. On the lower roll, UNIP won 12 seats with almost four-fifths of the vote, while ANC, with two-thirds of its support localized in one province, won three. The ANC and UFP reaped the benefits of their alliance in the National seats, winning two each. By-elections were held two months later in the ten remaining seats, where criteria for winning the seats had not been satisfied, and a further two seats were filled by European ANC candidates, and one by UFP (ibid.: 284–7). (The fifteenth National seat, reserved for Asians, was won by a UNIP-backed independent.) Consequently, UFP won 16 seats to UNIP's 14, and Nkumbula filled the unlikely role of kingmaker, temporizing on the question of whether he would honour his electoral pact or his role as 'father' of Zambian nationalism. Nkumbula's nationalist conscience won out as it had to, and the hard-won deal gave UNIP and ANC three seats each in the Executive Council, with ANC supplying the two European Councillors required by the constitution (ibid.: 299–300). But even before Kaunda and Nkumbula took office, following a confused sequence of meetings in Lusaka, London, and even Elisabethville (where Kaunda agreed to meet Tshombe), they secured Butler's agreement in principle to a new constitution, allowing African majority rule and secession from the Federation.

The following year passed in uneasy politics and in the painstaking preparation of fresh elections under a new constitution. In the January 1964 elections, of 65 'main roll' constituencies, 55 were won by UNIP, almost half of them uncontested, while the other ten went to a still disorganized, but regionally strong ANC. And though UNIP failed to win a single one of ten 'reserved roll' constituencies, it nonetheless won 35 per cent of the European, Asian and mixed race vote on this roll, in a minor, tardy and unsung victory for multi-racialism (Mulford 1967: 323–8). Kaunda thus became Prime Minister, and on 24 October 1964, anniversary of the United Nations and of the short-lived ZANC, Zambia became an independent Republic within the Commonwealth.

The Federation of Rhodesia and Nyasaland passed into history at midnight on 31 December 1963, bringing to an end Britain's ten-year experiment in 'multi-racialism'. That it lasted so long points up the Macmillan government's reluctance to abandon its hopes of creating a durable settlement for Britain's European collaborators, but also the sheer arduous complexity of constitutional 'due process'. Southern Rhodesia's white minority now sought independence, its economic gains from federal structures over the years compensating its political losses. The federal assets it salvaged included Salisbury's University College, the switches controlling the Kariba power station, whose dam straddled the Zambezi dividing the two former Rhodesias, and, not least, an impressive army and modern air force (Hargreaves 1996: 218). Zimbabwean Africans would not escape as easily as their Northern neighbours from the grip of white minority rule, which passed its fortieth anniversary in 1963 with 15 years still to run. Nkomo's NDP soon rejected the insubstantial reforms promised in February 1961, and it was banned in December 1961. Its successor, the Zimbabwe African People's Union (ZAPU), was also outlawed in September 1962, as nationalists gradually progressed from non-violence to sabotage campaigns and onwards to guerrilla war. In August 1963, the movement split between ZAPU, whose rump support was concentrated amongst the Ndebele, and the Zimbabwe African National Party

(ZANU), led by the Reverend Ndabaningi Sithole, with support amongst Zimbabwe's two-thirds majority Shona. ZAPU and ZANU were both banned on 26 August 1964, and their leaders detained (Ranger 1998: 203–9). White Rhodesians too were slipping towards radicalism, as evidenced first by the electoral victory of the populist Rhodesian Front of Winston Field, in November 1962, and then, in April 1964, by the replacement of Field by the hardliner, Ian Smith, who, in a curious parody of decolonization, proclaimed Rhodesia's Unilateral Declaration of Independence on 11 November 1965. Its terms, like those of Ho Chi Minh's Declaration of Vietnamese Independence twenty years before, echoed those of 1776. Rhodesia's defiance could hardly be seen as resistance to imperial over-rule. Not only had Macmillan's successor as Prime Minister, Sir Alec Douglas-Home (formerly Lord Home), already proclaimed 'the virtual end of the process of decolonization' (11 February 1964, Hyam & Louis 2000: doc. 389). But Smith also took comfort from the apparent confirmation by Harold Wilson, Prime Minister since Labour's election victory of October 1964, of the outcome of British defence spending cuts since 1957: there would be no British military intervention in Rhodesia, and it was a delusion to expect a 'thunderbolt, hurtling through the sky and destroying the enemy, a thunderbolt in the shape of the Royal Air Force' (in Murphy 2005a: cvi). Independence for Zimbabwe under African majority rule would thus be secured by force of arms, but in nationalist hands, and the further substantive intervention of the former imperial power would be limited to the transition to full independence in 1980.

Notes

1   De Gaulle also inspired a widespread 'cult of power' across Moyen-Congo and Gabon, surrounding a big-nosed, warlike, dancing figure called *ngol*; however, the Gaullist RPF's efforts to harness this cult's popularity seem to have been uniformly unsuccessful (Bernault 1996: 187–95).

2   On the 'new man', personified by the *Express*-reading, Mendès-France-supporting young executive, see Ross 1995; Delouvrier was seen as a 'Mendésiste', though 'liberal' or 'communist' could hardly have packed more venom for most *pieds noirs*.

3   This event forms a prelude to the otherwise fictional narrative in Forsyth (1971) and Zinnemann (1973), relating a further near-miss assassination. The cast of the film wittily includes Jean Martin, 'Colonel Mathieu' in Pontecorvo (1965), now playing a minor, short-lived OAS operative. It was after Petit-Clamart that de Gaulle proposed the shift to direct presidential elections, in order to provide his eventual successor with greater legitimacy.

4   *Harkis* constituted one of several categories of irregular Algerian combatants (*harka* = detachment); the name has come to apply to all Algerian combatants on the French side, including regular troops. Messmer (1998: 170–2), citing the work of C.-R. Ageron and others in the archives, gives a total number in all categories combined of some 140,000 in early 1962; see also Pervillé 1993.

5   The phrase is Bernard Kouchner's, founder of Médecins sans Frontières and, at the time, French Secretary of State for Humanitarian Aid: in *Le Monde*, 29 September 1991.

6   The UFP won 11 of 14 seats held by Europeans, and two of six African seats. It was denied an overall majority in the Legislative Council by the presence of ten officials.

9

Conclusion: The Impact of Decolonization

The Vietnamese people's great victory at Dien Bien Phu is no longer, strictly speaking, a Vietnamese victory. Since July 1954, the problem that the colonial peoples have set themselves has been the following: 'What do we have to do to bring off a Dien Bien Phu? How do we go about it?' . . . This atmosphere of violence changes not only the colonized but also the colonialists as they become aware of multiple Dien Bien Phus. This is why colonialist governments are increasingly in the grip of ordered panic. Their aim is to stay one step ahead, to shift liberation movements to the Right, to disarm the people: quick, let's decolonize! Let's decolonize the Congo before it becomes another Algeria. Let's pass the Framework Law for Africa, create the Community, revise the Community, but please, please, let's decolonize, decolonize . . . So they decolonize so quickly that they impose independence on Houphouët-Boigny. (Fanon [1961]2002: 69)

Were the countries fully ready for Independence? Of course not. Nor was India, and the bloodshed that followed the grant of Independence there was incomparably worse than anything that has happened since to any country. Yet the decision of the Attlee Government was the only realistic one. Equally we could not possibly have held by force to our territories in Africa. We could not, with an enormous force engaged, even continue to hold the small island of Cyprus. General de Gaulle could not contain Algeria. The march of men towards their freedom can be guided, but not halted. Of course there were risks in moving quickly. But the risks of moving slowly were far greater. (Iain Macleod, *The Spectator*, 31 January 1964, in Porter & Stockwell 1989: vol. II, doc. 82, 571)

Aside from some predictable contrasts of tone and perspective, these two roughly contemporary analyses of the decolonizing endgame offer a perhaps surprising degree of consensus and complementarity. Intellectual honesty in both cases may reflect the fact that neither writer felt obliged to follow his respective 'party line'. We will never know how differently Frantz Fanon might have couched his polemic had he not been writing in haste in an effort to beat the leukaemia that killed him in December 1961 (Macey 2000: 454–5), had he lived to see the triumph of the Algerian cause which he had served for several years, or to experience the many causes of post-colonial disillusion which are prefigured in his text. Iain Macleod had been British Colonial Secretary at the time Fanon was writing, but by 1964 he was no longer in government, and was thus free to respond to criticisms of Britain's headlong imperial retreat by Lord Salisbury, a more orthodox Conservative defender of empire who had resigned from the Cabinet in 1957 over Macmillan's Cyprus policy. From both sides of the colonial divide, therefore, the view emerges that the events of the late 1950s and early 1960s, or more generally of the period from 1945, were driven by imperial efforts, impelled by imperial weakness and by the growing momentum of anti-colonial mobilization, to accelerate the end of colonial rule in Africa and elsewhere, even if this meant imposing independence on (for Fanon) objectively pro-colonial leaders, or on countries which (for Macleod) were not yet ready for independent statehood.

In concluding this study of decolonization, it may be worth asking just *what* it was that came to an end in this abrupt way, thus dissatisfying both the anti-colonial would-be revolutionary and the liberal colonial reformer (and his imperialist party colleagues). Several orders of answer might be given, corresponding loosely to Braudel's timescales for historical enquiry. First, then, this was the point at which the British empire stuttered to the end of its prolonged cycle of 'decline, revival and fall' (Gallagher 1982). That Britain had succeeded in stemming imperial decline over the *longue durée* has been ascribed to the canny pragmatism of an 'official mind' which preferred the sinews of informal empire to the cumbersome trappings of direct control. When the latter became necessary, it was sustained by the management of astutely cultivated collaborative relationships at the imperial periphery. This pragmatism had periodically allowed Britain to reconfigure its imperial holdings, and in the twentieth century had assisted its revival from the depredations of two world wars, but after 1945, the British 'official mind' had faltered in its attempts, either to recruit new collaborators in a radically changed geopolitical and ideological climate, or, for that matter, to entice the new American power into sharing in a grand imperial partnership, on something approximating to the old informal model (Louis & Robinson [1994]2003).

This by now largely unassailable 'peripheral' approach may help us to appreciate how the greatest of the colonial empires persisted for so long and why it finally dipped below the threshold of viability. However, Gallagher, Robinson et al. tell us little of other, lesser, modern empires (while the older Spanish and Portuguese empires had shrunk to shadows of their former greatness well before the twentieth century). Moreover, in the present context, it might seem perverse to favour an approach which thus places formal colonial rule in a kind of historical parenthesis as the less favoured mode of imperialism. Further, although the key concept of collaboration has been central to the present study (notwithstanding the extraneous moral connotations of the term itself), its explanatory power in the period of decolonization may be doubted, conveying, as Darwin (1991: 101) acknowledges, the idea of the colonial power somehow 'using up available collaborators like a film star running through spouses'. Crucially, also, the concept of collaboration, concentrating as it does on the functional aspects of colonialism, leaves little room for the ideological content or political purpose of particular collaborative choices in the later colonial context.

The present study has drawn at various points on Frederick Cooper's comparative work on British and French imperialism (e.g. 1996a, 1997, 2002). Cooper's vision too has drawn back to embrace the imperial *longue durée* (2005), but in its concerns with the workings of formal colonial rule, some of which are shared here, the primary perspective adopted is inevitably that of the Braudelian 'conjuncture'; that is, in this case, the period of perhaps eighty years within which the colonial empires were conquered or consolidated, institutionalized within their final borders, disrupted by the events of 1914–18 and especially 1940–5, and thus approached the final 'twenty years crisis' of decolonization. Cooper's recently formulated idea of the British or French (and perhaps also Belgian or Dutch) 'empire-state' may help us to understand, beyond the workings of an unwavering 'official mind', just what it meant to 'think like an empire', and moreover an empire which, 'far from being an anachronistic political form in the "modern era"', took its responsibilities as a modern state increasingly seriously (ibid.: 154, 200). To be sure, before the Second World War, there was typically a yawning gap between the rhetoric of 'trusteeship' or 'civilizing missions' and the realities of colonial rule on the ground, which, as suggested here, constituted a kind of improvised 'bricolage' whereby colonial conquests were sometimes crudely adapted to governmental or commercial purpose. British India, however, the largest and most complex of colonial states, was in the interwar period already being developed as a grandiose model for the future of modern colonialism, or so it no doubt seemed to the framers of the constitution which emerged from the 1935 Government of India Act. The fact that this Act was consequent upon nearly two decades of intermittently intense conflict between British officialdom and an assertive nationalist movement also prefigured subsequent developments elsewhere within what has been characterized as the 'late colonial state'. Across the colonized world, various political options were explored, ranging from nationalist mobilization to communist organization and agitation, to monarchical restoration, to 'moderate' political accommodation with colonial rule. However, and although violent resistance to colonialism manifested itself in various recurrent, but unfailingly abortive forms, it has been argued here that, even if colonialism showed signs of fatigue or self-contradiction, particularly in the wake of the economic crisis of the 1930s, there was as yet little evidence to suggest the imminent emergence of a viable alternative to colonial empire as a 'normal' feature of the international system. As its new constitution came into force in 1937, none could reasonably have predicted that even India was on course to break away from British over-rule within a decade, or that it would do so as two separate states.

The Second World War occupies a central position in any account of decolonization, but it must be recognized that its impact was necessarily multi-layered and pluridimensional, with some devastating immediate consequences and others that took time to work themselves out, whether in the manner of a time-delayed fuse or of a pack of dominoes. This time around, as was recognized early on by both Churchill and de Gaulle (in his Appeal of 18 June 1940), it truly was a world war in breadth and depth. The global reach of the war was far more extensive and more evenly spread than in 1914–18, the colonized fought, laboured and died in large numbers for 'their' empire-states, and colonized regions in Asia, Africa, the Middle East and the Pacific constituted central theatres of war, where empires changed hands (for example, between Vichy and de Gaulle), were fought over, occupied or, in the case of Southeast Asia, eclipsed and then, in 1945, fought over all over again. The war also brought challenges to the sustaining ideologies of the colonial powers, whether enshrined in the anti-colonialism professed by the two emerging Superpowers, or in the fact that the war was increasingly cast as a struggle for democracy and national self-determination and against fascism and racial discrimination. The colonial powers could derive little comfort from the argument that American anti-colonialism and Soviet anti-imperialism were both to some extent self-serving, given the contrast between British and French exhaustion, sapped morale and (in the British case) over-extension at war's end, and the dynamism of the Big Two (with Britain a poor Third and France a grudging Fifth behind Nationalist China). Indeed, from the perspectives of *longue durée* and political conjuncture, the Second World War effectively settled the matter of imperial statehood once and for all. Thus Niall Ferguson may be forgiven some rose-tinted hyperbole when he argues that Churchill's victory in 1945 'could only ever have been Pyrrhic', that 'the British sacrificed [their] Empire to stop the Germans, Italians and Japanese from keeping theirs', and asks rhetorically: 'Did not that sacrifice alone expunge all the Empire's other sins?' (2003: 363). Less forgivably, having thus talked up Britain's 'truly noble' shouldering of its imperial burden, Ferguson goes on to expunge almost the entire process of decolonization from the historical record . . .

In the present context, the Second World War may perhaps best be understood as an accelerator of imperial change, articulating a shift, in Braudelian terms, from the conjunctural perspective to that of event. It is at this level of enquiry that we may determine the nature of what ultimately collapsed over the 15 or 20 years from 1945. This *late colonial shift* not only quickened the pace of change along an apparently parabolic curve, but also transformed the way in which imperial futures were perceived, not only by colonial officials forced to relinquish the leisurely timescales of secular colonial evolution, but also by the colonized, for whom the deadening certainties of pre-war colonial rule had suddenly been lifted. Well before Dien Bien Phu, both colonizers and colonized acted on the presumption that empires *could* be lost after 1945, though it was far from certain that they *would* be, or how quickly. This perceptual shift was typically reflected in a qualitative change in colonial policy making, which has been variously characterized as an attempted 'second colonial occupation' or as the 'interventionist moment' (Cooper 2005: 188) in the life-cycle of colonial 'empire-states'. However, it was equally reflected in the ways in which colonial initiatives were taken up, transformed, or simply rejected, by an emerging generation of political and social actors within the forum of the late colonial state, and in the growth of a distinctive late colonial politics. The substantive shift was thus not so much on one side or other of the colonial dialectic, but in the nature of the interaction itself.

In a 'first wave' of decolonization, in South and Southeast Asia after 1945, circumstances were heavily weighted against the colonial powers, and change took place very rapidly indeed. Arguably, the concept of a late colonial shift is least applicable in the case which perhaps most colours our view of decolonization in the immediate post-war period, but which remained *sui generis* to the last. In India, just as 'lateness came early' (Darwin 1999), so too did imperial demission, as the war's aftermath brought British rule dangerously close to the 'edge of the volcano'. Here the alternative to a humiliating, staged military and administrative withdrawal, mooted by the penultimate Viceroy, was the accelerated imperial endgame promoted by his successor. This allowed Britain to retain some measure of dignity in retreat, as did arguably the resilience of the state structures reinforced a decade before. However, while the creation of separate, communally divided successor states was probably inevitable by this stage, the 'moth-eaten' form of the partition, the haste with which it was implemented, and the scale of the violence that resulted, were by-products of British weakness, as Macleod acknowledged in 1964, but also of British face-saving expediency. While the formula of an amicable Transfer of Power to newly self-governing Dominions accorded well with British sensibilities, and reasonably reflected short-term realities in post-imperial India and Pakistan, as also in Ceylon, it represented a poor euphemism for events in Burma, where British control was never recovered in the wake of Japanese retreat. Burma set a precedent followed only by the Republic of Ireland and, later, South Africa, by rejecting membership of a British Commonwealth of Nations which all too quickly lost relevance as the husk of shrinking British imperial power and reach.

Explicit policies of imperial retreat were the exception rather than the rule in the immediate post-war period. Aside from the Philippines, already promised independence by the United States (a deceptively reluctant colonial power), Southeast Asia was the object of determined efforts by the British, French and Dutch to recover colonial positions lost to wartime Japanese expansion. These efforts can seem self-deluding attempts to restore an imperial *status quo ante*, or taken to illustrate 'the dangers of failing to accommodate political movements in the colonies' (Cooper 2005: 188). Certainly, nowhere outside India and Algeria was such determined and resourceful nationalist opposition offered to continuing colonial rule as in the shape of the Vietnamese and Indonesian revolutions. However, the returning powers attempted more than mere colonial restoration, bringing with them blueprints for the integration of their colonies into a new, rational and reformist imperial order; none of these blueprints was realized, and even the British failed to implement an ambitious plan for Malayan Union, while a 'second colonial occupation' exploiting tin and rubber production was compromised by communist insurgency. Short of wholesale retreat, the French and Dutch were never likely to reach an accommodation with their revolutionary interlocutors, although interim deals were struck in both cases before relations deteriorated beyond repair. The onset of the Asian Cold War had a decisive impact across the region, although with widely differing effects: defeating insurgency in Malaya made the country 'safe for decolonization' (Holland 1985), while in Indonesia the nationalist regime itself destroyed local communists, thus persuading the Americans that a continuing Dutch presence was otiose. In Indochina, by contrast, the French war with the Viet Minh was transformed by Mao's victory in China, and by American involvement: in this sense, *pace* Fanon, French humiliation at Dien Bien Phu was exceptional rather than exemplary, since the war had long since left behind its original 'late colonial' character.

Elsewhere, and particularly in the African empires, the dialectical poles of colonial 'thesis' and nationalist 'antithesis' exerted a more even pull. Here, colonial territories were integrated into the imperial economy through the long-overdue (if still inadequate) injection of development funding and expertise, and the more extensive exploitation of colonial resources. Meanwhile the impact of this intense and often-resented intervention into colonial society was allayed through the gradual extension of systems of political representation, at local, territorial and, in the French case, metropolitan levels. Although initiated by official political reformism, late colonial politics was transformed into a vital process through the dynamic input of political actors, who adopted the forms and modalities of a conventional – and increasingly democratic – politics with enthusiasm. This was a 'time of politics' (Iliffe 1979: 477), as the post-war wave of strikes and disorder set off a chain reaction of party formation, coalition building, and mass mobilization, in counterpoint to official policy and constitution writing. As colonial governments conceded the electoral principle, they confronted an explosion in the growth and activism of political parties and trades unions. Indeed, officials were actors in the political game themselves, whether in a governor's friendly (read 'paternalist') mentoring of suitably moderate politicians, or the more partisan official involvement in party politics that was a trademark of the French proconsular tradition. However, it was far from clear, as Cooper extensively argues (for example, 2002), that the motivation of ordinary Africans need always be interpreted in terms of mobilization in the cause of eventual independence: in the late colonial state, there was much else to mobilize against, not least the impact of its increasingly onerous interventions, both in burgeoning colonial cities and in the countryside.

This late colonial African politics worked itself out differently within the British and French systems, although the two roughly converged, not least in their timetables for decolonization. In effect, the British 'official mind' started out with an idea of controlled, gradual evolution towards eventual self-government, but was jolted into a far more rapid process of concessions, as nationalists such as Nkrumah and Azikiwe couched their demands in terms of 'Self-Government NOW' (Nkrumah's slogan in the 1940s), thus presenting the British 'official mind' with a dilemma when those terms became the platform for a successful election campaign, such as Nkrumah's in 1951. Subsequent iterations of this electoral politics found younger nationalists, such as Nyerere or Kaunda, scrupulously respecting increasingly arcane constitutional rules centring on ultimately fruitless British attempts to disguise settler dominance as 'multi-racialism'; and yet still they won their way through to independence. Conversely, the French system imposed a limited, but expanding conception of political representation, contained within the new French Union, but politics readily jumped the tracks laid down by an explicit and rigid constitutional framework, or even turned the Republican values and democratic institutions of the state against it. Rather than 'self-government NOW', it was the 'mystique of equality' proclaimed by Senghor which prevailed, whether in the prolonged campaigns by African workers for parity with their metropolitan French comrades, or in the political progress towards territorial autonomy and universal suffrage, culminating in the regime established by the 1956 Framework Law. The impact on colonial policy makers was comparable in both empires: while British officials 'seemed to trap themselves into a spiral of constitutional concessions' (Darwin 1991: 116), their French counterparts were 'caught between the threat that imperial citizenship would fail and that it would succeed too well' (Cooper 2005: 177). Both ended up recognizing – and this was part of the logic of the Framework Law, if only implicitly of Macmillan's famous 'profit and loss account' – that the political game in Africa was becoming too costly to sustain.

Typically, this politics remained with the bounds of more or less 'peaceful' activity, although the conception of 'peace' needs to be stretched considerably to encompass a series of disorderly episodes and their attendant 'emergencies' in Gold Coast, Nigeria, Côte d'Ivoire, Cameroun, Nyasaland, Northern and Southern Rhodesia (and many other cases not studied in this volume). The distinction was a fluid one between these episodes and other, more prolonged or intense late colonial conflicts in Madagascar, Kenya, Algeria, Cyprus, alongside those in Southeast Asia (and this list too could be extended). Indeed, a comparative approach allows us to retain some of that fluidity of definition, and to counter, for example, the not uncommon view that 'Britain abandoned its empire skilfully, almost without conflict', though we might concur that France 'fought a string of appalling, unnecessary wars, ending with the Algerian war which nearly destroyed French democracy itself'.[1] Like the Tolstoyan family, each case had its own reasons for the 'unhappiness' that led to conflict. These reasons might include an acute sense of lost independence or national identity, or of social disruption arising from colonial pressures; the dominant presence of settlers or other minorities within colonial society; or the failure or inadequacy of reforms that might have headed off conflict. However, it is difficult not to see the proximate cause of each conflict, if not its deeper roots, in the tensions and contradictions of late colonialism.

Particular emphasis has been placed in this study on the distinctive forms and methods of late colonial warfare. Here too, although combatants on all sides drew on the experience of earlier resistance and its repression, or on a continuous recourse to violence stretching back to conquest, we may nonetheless detect a new seriousness of purpose, a qualitative difference in the nature and outlook of insurgent movements, as also in the responses of the late colonial 'security state' (Darwin 1999). These were self-proclaimed contests for the 'hearts and minds' of civilian non-combatants, as insurgents embraced the strategy and tactics of peasant insurrection but also of 'terror', while colonial armies and official agencies fought back with ever more recondite (if not always more effective) doctrines of counter-insurgency, deployed new technologies (helicopters, electrified barriers, napalm), and refined methods of repression (torture, detention and 'rehabilitation', forced resettlement) which underline the essential modernity of the late colonial state and offer lessons for post-colonial practice.[2]

Meanwhile, shifting metropolitan calculations suggested a recalibrated 'zero-sum' game between growing domestic prosperity and the burden of modern welfare provision, and the apparent demands of outdated and costly imperial commitments. Some of those costs could be counted, in investments 'wasted' overseas, in a potentially open-ended sharing of welfare benefits with new imperial citizens, or in the human and economic costs of conscription. Other costs were incalculable, in the moral opprobrium of late colonial scandals or the 'gangrene' of torture and other abuses. To this must be added, in the French case, the Algerian war's impact on domestic political stability, bringing down the regime in 1958, and wreaking havoc to the last, through the combined effects of military insubordination and settler resistance, which came together in the die-hard terrorism of the OAS.

By the late 1950s, therefore, the colonial powers were poised for the final surge of rapid change which characterized the late colonial endgame. A fundamental part of the background to this change was the recognition of diminishing international options in the face of terminal imperial decline, as reflected in the calamitous diplomatic aftermath of Dien Bien Phu, the Suez expedition or the Sakhiet raid. This was reinforced by a growing international coalition of formerly colonized states, acting in concert in the United Nations and other bodies. At this point also, the more extreme or eccentric experiments in late colonial statehood started to unravel, as the Belgian Congo packed its decolonization into a breathless 18 months, with catastrophic consequences after independence, and the British, with apparent reluctance, abandoned their trials for the establishment of 'multi-racial' constitutions in Central and East Africa. At the very least, this new international environment acted to 'supercharge' the impact of political developments within the colonial state (Darwin 1991), amplifying the wider resonance of each subsequent example of colonial violence or intransigence, and forcing the curtailment of long-cherished timetables for further political development. So in the end, the late colonial project proved too costly to be worth carrying through, and was aborted. Inherent in this terminal pragmatism of the European colonial powers, as Fanon and Macleod both recognized implicitly, was thus the possibility of post-colonial disillusion.

Notes

1   Neal Ascherson, 'As the Queen goes to France this week, the Entente Cordiale remains a fractious, fragile alliance', *Observer*, 4 April 2004. Aside from the 100-year-old Franco-British Entente, the article also drew attention to the fiftieth anniversary of Dien Bien Phu.
2   Cf. the Pentagon's screening of Pontecorvo's (1965) film in August 2003: Patrick Jarreau, 'La direction des opérations spéciales du Pentagone organise une projection de La Bataille d'Alger', *Le Monde*, 9 September 2003. As the Pentagon's flyer put it: 'How to win a battle against terrorism and lose the war of ideas. Children shoot soldiers at point-blank range. Women plant bombs in cafes. Soon the entire Arab population builds to a mad fervor. Sound familiar?': in 'The Battle of Algiers', en.wikipedia.org, accessed 10 January 2007.

Appendix: Dates of Independence of African States

State (as of 2007)	Date of Independence	Name under Colonial Rule, if different (colonial power)
Algeria	1962	(Fr)
Angola	1975	(Port)
Benin	1960	Dahomey (Fr: part of Afrique Occidentale Française (AOF))
Botswana	1966	Bechuanaland Protectorate (Br)
Burkina Faso	1960	Haute-Volta (Fr: part of AOF)
Burundi	1962	Ruanda-Urundi, part of (Be, UN Trusteeship Territory)
Cameroon	1960	Cameroun (Fr) & British Cameroons, part of (Br) (both UN Trusteeship Territories)
Central African Republic	1960	Oubangui-Chari (Fr: part of part of Afrique Équatoriale Française (AEF))
Chad	1960	Tchad (Fr: part of AEF)
Congo-Brazzaville	1960	Moyen-Congo (Fr: part of AEF)
Congo, Democratic Republic	1960	Congo Belge (Be)
Djibouti	1977	Côte Française des Somalis (Fr)
Equatorial Guinea	1968	(Sp)
Eritrea	1941/1991	(It) Federated with Ethiopia 1961–91
Gabon	1960	(Fr: part of AEF)
Gambia, The	1965	(Br)
Ghana	1957	Gold Coast (Br), inc. British Togoland (Br, UN Trusteeship Territory)
Guinea	1958	Guinée (Fr: part of AOF)
Guinea-Bissau	1975	Portuguese Guinea (Port)
Ivory Coast	1960	Côte d'Ivoire (Fr: part of AOF)
Kenya	1963	(Br)
Lesotho	1966	Basutoland (Br)

Libya	1951	(It, then Br/Fr)
Malawi	1964	Nyasaland (Br)
Mali	1960	Soudan Français (Fr: part of AOF)
Mauretania	1960	(Fr: part of AOF)
Morocco	1956	(Fr & Sp) also incorporates disputed former Spanish Sahara (Sp)
Mozambique	1975	Moçambique or Portuguese East Africa (Port)
Namibia	1990	South-West Africa (SAfr, UN Trusteeship Territory)
Niger	1960	(Fr: part of AOF)
Nigeria	1960	(Br), inc part of British Cameroons (Br, UN Trusteeship Territory)
Rwanda	1962	Ruanda-Urundi, part of (Be, UN Trusteeship Territory)
Senegal	1960	(Fr: part of AOF)
Sierra Leone	1961	(Br)
Somalia	1960	(Br), and inc former Italian Somaliland (It)
South Africa	1910	Union of South Africa (Br)
Swaziland	1968	(Br)
Sudan	1956	Anglo-Egyptian Sudan (Br & Egypt)
Tanzania	1961	Tanganyika (Br, UN Trusteeship Territory), inc Zanzibar from 1964 (Br)
Togo	1960	(Fr, UN Trusteeship Territory)
Tunisia	1962	(Fr)
Egypt	1922	(Br)
Uganda	1962	(Br)
Zambia	1964	Northern Rhodesia (Br)
Zimbabwe	1980	Southern Rhodesia (Br), Rhodesia, 1965–80

Bibliography

Ageron, Charles-Robert (1979). *Histoire de l'Algérie contemporaine*, vol. 2. Paris: PUF.

Ageron, Charles-Robert (ed.) (1993). *L'Algérie des Français*. Paris: Seuil.

Ageron, Charles-Robert (1995). 'Les guerres d'Indochine et d'Algérie au miroir des la "guerre révolutionnaire"'. In Ageron & Michel (1995), 47–67.

Ageron, Charles-Robert (2001). 'Une dimension de la guerre d'Algérie: les "regroupements" de population'. In Jauffret & Vaïsse (2001), 327–62.

Ageron, Charles-Robert, & Michel, Marc (eds) (1995). *L'Ère des décolonisations: Actes du Colloque d'Aix-en-Provence*. Paris: Karthala.

Aggoun, Nacéra (2002). 'Psychological propaganda during the Algerian War'. In Alexander et al. (2002a), 193–9.

Aldrich, Robert (1996). *Greater France: A History of French Overseas Expansion*. Basingstoke: Macmillan.

Alexander, Martin S., Evans, Martin & Keiger, John (eds) (2002a). *The Algerian War and the Military: Experiences, Images, Testimonies*. Basingstoke: Palgrave Macmillan.

Alexander, Martin S., Evans, Martin & Keiger, J.F.V. (2002b). 'The "War without a Name": the French army and the Algerians'. In Alexander et al. (2002a), 1–39.

Allman, Jean Marie (1993). *The Quills of the Porcupine: Asante Nationalism in an Emergent Ghana*. Madison, WI: University of Wisconsin Press.

Allman, Jean Marie (2003). 'The Youngmen and the porcupine: class, nationalism and Asante's struggle for self-determination, 1954–57'. In Le Sueur (2003), 204–17.

Amin, Shahid (1988). 'Gandhi as Mahatma: Gorakhpur District, Eastern U.P. 1921–2'. In Guha & Spivak (1988), 288–348.

Anderson, Benedict (1991). *Imagined Communities: Reflections on the Origin and Spread of Nationalism*, rev. edn. Verso, London & New York.

Anderson, David M. (1984). 'Depression, dust bowl, demography, and drought: the colonial state and soil conservation in East Africa during the 1930s'. *African Affairs*, 83, 321–43.

Anderson, David M. (1994). 'Policing and Communal Conflict: The Cyprus Emergency, 1954–60'. In Holland (1994a), 177–207.

Anderson, David M. (2003). 'The Battle of Dandora Swamp, October 1954: Reconstructing the Mau Mau Land Freedom Army, October 1954'. In Atieno Odhiambo & Lonsdale (2003), 155–75.

Anderson, David M. (2005). *Histories of the Hanged: Britain's Dirty War in Kenya and the End of the Empire*. London: Weidenfeld & Nicolson.

Anderson, David M. & Killingray, David (eds) (1992). *Policing and Decolonization: Politics, Nationalism and the Police, 1917–65*. Manchester University Press, Manchester.

Anderson, Lindsay (1969). *If . . .* Film.

Anon. (2000). 'Un fonctionnaire de la torture raconte . . .'. *Nouvel Observateur*, 14–20 December.

Antlöv, Hans, & Tønnesson, Stein (eds) (1995). *Imperial Policy and Southeast Asian Nationalism*. London: Curzon.

Antlöv, Hans (1995). 'Rulers in Imperial Policy. Sultan Ibrahim, Emperor Bao Dai and Sultan Hamengku Buwono IX'. In Antlöv & Tønnesson (1995), 227–60.

Arnold, David (1992). 'Police power and the demise of British rule in India, 1930–47'. In Anderson & Killingray (1992), 42–61.

Ashton, Stephen R. (1999). 'Ceylon', In Louis (1999), 447–64.

Ashton, Stephen R. & Stockwell, Sarah (eds) (1996). *Imperial Policy and Colonial Policy 1925–1945*, British Documents on the End of Empire, vol.1/A. London: HMSO.

Atieno Odhiambo, E.S. (1995). 'The Formative Years 1945–55'. In Ogot & Ochieng' (1995), 25–47.

Atieno Odhiambo, E.S., & Lonsdale, John (eds) (2003). *Mau Mau and Nationhood: Arms, Authority and Narration*. Oxford, Nairobi & Athens: James Currey et al.

Aussaresses, Paul (2001). *Services Secrets*. Paris: Perrin.

Awolowo, Obafemi (1947). *Path to Nigerian Freedom*. London: Faber and Faber.

Bancel, Nicolas, & Mathy, Ghislaine (1993). 'La propagande économique'. In Bancel et al. (1993), 221–31.

Bancel, Nicolas, Blanchard, P. & Gervereau, L. (eds) (1993). *Images et Colonies: Iconographie et propagande coloniale sur l'Afrique française de 1880 à 1962*. Paris: BDIC-ACHAC.

Barthes, Roland (1957). *Mythologies*. Paris: Seuil.

Bayart, Jean-François (1993). *The State in Africa: The Politics of the Belly*.London: Longman. (Originally published as *L'Etat en Afrique: La Politique du ventre*. Paris: Fayard, 1989.)

Beaugé, Florence (2000). 'La torture faisait partie d'une certaine ambiance. On aurait pu faire les choses différemment'. In *Le Monde*, 22 June.

Beaugé, Florence (2005). *Algérie, une guerre sans gloire*. Paris: Calmann-Lévy.

Benoist, Joseph-Roger de (1982). *L'Afrique Occidentale Française de 1944 à 1960*. Dakar: Nouvelles Editions Africaines.

Berman, Bruce, & Lonsdale, John (1992). *Unhappy Valley: Conflict in Kenya and Africa*, 2 vols. London: James Currey.

Bernault, Florence (1996). *Démocraties ambiguës en Afrique Centrale: Congo-Brazzaville, Gabon, 1940–1965*. Paris: Karthala.

Berque, Jacques (1969). *Le Maghreb entre deux guerres*, rev. edn. Paris: Seuil.

Birmingham, David, & Martin, Phyllis (eds) (1998). *History of Central Africa*, vol. III, *The Contemporary Years since 1960*. London: Longman.

Boon Kheng, Cheah (1979). *The Masked Comrades: A Study of the Communist United Front in Malaya, 1945–1948*. Singapore: Time Books.

Bourdet, Claude (1955). 'Votre Gestapo d'Algérie'. In *France-Observateur*, 13 January.

Bourdieu, Pierre (1989). *La noblesse d'État*. Paris: Minuit.

Bourke, Joanna (2000). *An Intimate History of Killing: Face-to-Face Killing in 20th Century Warfare*. London: Granta.

Boyce, D. George (1999). *Decolonisation and the British Empire, 1775–1997*. Basingstoke: Macmillan.

Branche, Raphaëlle (2001). *La Torture et l'armée pendant la guerre d'Algérie, 1954–1962*. Paris: Gallimard.

Braudel, Fernand (1980). 'History and the social sciences: the *Longue Durée*'. In Fernand Braudel, *On History*. London: Weidenfeld & Nicolson, 25–54.

Breuilly, John (1993). *Nationalism and the State*, 2nd edn. Manchester: Manchester University Press.

Brocheux, Pierre, & Hémery, Daniel (1995). *L'Indochine: Une Colonisation ambiguë*. Paris: La Découverte.

Brown, Judith M. (1989). *Gandhi: Prisoner of Hope*. New Haven, CT: Yale University Press.

Brown, Judith M. & Louis, Wm. Roger Louis (eds) (1999). *Oxford History of the British Empire*, vol. IV, *The Twentieth Century*. Oxford: Clarendon.

Brown, Judith M. (1999a). 'India'. In Brown & Louis (1999), 421–46.

Brown, Judith M. (1999b). *Nehru*. London: Longman.

Burton, Richard D.E., & Reno, Fred (eds) (1995). *French and West Indian: Martinique, Guadeloupe and Guiana Today*. Basingstoke: Macmillan.

Brownlie, Ian (1979). *African Boundaries: A Legal and Diplomatic Encyclopaedia*. Oxford: Oxford University Press.

Butler, L.J. (2002). *British and Empire: Adjusting to a Post-Imperial World*. London: I.B. Tauris.

Cain, P.J. & Hopkins, A.G. (1993). *British Imperialism: Crisis and Deconstruction, 1914–1960*. London & New York: Longman.

Carruthers, Susan L. (1995). *Winning Hearts and Minds: British Governments, the Media and Colonial Counter-insurgency, 1944–1960*. London: Leicester University Press.

Cary, Joyce (1939). *Mister Johnson*. London: Victor Gollancz. [Harmondsworth: Penguin, 1962.]

Cell, John (1999). 'Colonial Rule'. In Brown & Louis (1999), 232–54.

Chabal, Patrick (ed.) (1986). *Political Domination in Africa*. Cambridge: Cambridge University Press.

Chafer, Tony, & Sackur, Amanda (eds) (1999). *French Colonial Empire and Popular Front: Hope and Disillusion*. Basingstoke: Macmillan.

Chafer, Tony (2002). *The End of Empire in French West Africa: France's successful Decolonization?* Oxford & New York: Berg.

Chaffard, Georges (1965–7). *Les Carnets secrets de la decolonisation*, 2 vols. Paris: Calmann-Lévy.

Chamberlain, Muriel E. (1998). *The Longman Companion to European Decolonization in the Twentieth Century*. London: Longman.

Chapman, Graham, et al. (1979). *Monty Python's The Life of Brian (of Nazareth)*. London: Eyre Methuen.

Chatterjee, Partha (1986). *Nationalist Thought and the Colonial World: A Derivative Discourse*. London: Zed Books.

Chatterjee, Partha (1992). 'Their own words? An essay for Edward Said'. In Sprinker (1992), 194–220.

Chatterjee, Partha (1993). *The Nation and its Fragments: Colonial and Postcolonial Histories*. Princeton, NJ: Princeton University Press.

Chaturvedi, Vinayak (ed.) (2000). *Mapping Subaltern Studies and the Postcolonial*. London: Verso.

Cheah, Boon Kheng (1988). 'The Erosion of Ideological Hegemony and Royal Power and the Rise of Postwar Malay Nationalism, 1945–46'. *Journal of Southeast Asian Studies*, 19(1), 1–26.

Chenntouf, Tayeb (1986). 'L'assemblée algérienne et l'application des réformes prévues par le statut du 20 septembre 1947'. In Institut d'Histoire du Temps Présent (1986), 367–75.

Chipman, John (1989). *French Power in Africa*. Oxford: Blackwell.

Christie, Clive J. (1996). *A Modern History of Southeast Asia: Decolonization, Nationalism and Separatism*. London: Curzon.

Clarence-Smith, Gervase (1985). 'The impact of the Spanish Civil War and the Second World War on Portuguese and Spanish Africa'. *Journal of African History*, 26, 4.

Clayton, Antony (1992). *Three Marshals of France*. London: Brasseys.

Clayton, Antony (1994). *The Wars of French Decolonization*. Harlow: Longman.

Cmd. 1148 (1960). *Report of the Advisory Commission on the Review of the Constitution of Rhodesia and Nyasaland*. London: HMSO.

Cohen, William B. (1971). *Rulers of Empire: The French Colonial Service in Africa*. Stanford: Hoover Institute Press.

Cohen, William B. (1972). 'The colonial policy of the Popular Front'. *French Historical Studies*, 7(3), 368–93.

Colombani, Olivier (1991). *Mémoires coloniales: La fin de l'Empire français d'Afrique vue par les administrateurs coloniaux*. Paris: La Découverte.

Conklin, Alice L. (1997). *A Mission to Civilize: The Republican Idea of Empire in France and West Africa, 1895–1930*. Stanford: Stanford University Press.

Connelly, Matthew (2002). *A Diplomatic Revolution: Algeria's Fight for Independence and the Origins of the Post-Cold War Era*. Oxford: Oxford University Press.

Cooper, Frederick (1988). 'Mau Mau and the discourses of decolonization'. *Journal of African History* 29, 313–20.

Cooper, Frederick [1994](2003). 'Conflict and Connection: Rethinking colonial African history', In Le Sueur (2003), 23–44. [First published in *American Historical Review* (December 1994), 1515–45.]

Cooper, Frederick (1996a). *Decolonization and African Society: The Labor Question in French and British Africa*. Cambridge: Cambridge University Press.

Cooper, Frederick [1996b](2003). '"Our Strike": Equality, anticolonial politics and the 1947–48 strike in French West Africa'. In Le Sueur (2003), 156–85. (First published in *Journal of African History* 37 (1996), 81–118.)

Cooper, Frederick, & Stoler, Ann Laura (eds) (1997). *Tensions of Empire: Colonial Cultures in a Bourgeois World*. Berkeley, CA: University of California Press.

Cooper, Frederick (1997). 'The dialectics of decolonization: nationalism and labor movements in postwar French Africa'. In Cooper & Stoler (1997), 406–35.

Cooper, Frederick (2002). *Africa since 1940: The Past of the Present*. Cambridge: Cambridge University Press.

Cooper, Frederick (2005). *Colonialism in Question: Theory, Knowledge, History*. Berkeley, CA & London: University of California Press.

Cooper, Nicola (2001). *France in Indochina: Colonial Encounters*. Oxford: Berg.

Copland, Ian (1997). *The Princes of India in the Endgame of Empire, 1917–1947*. Cambridge: Cambridge University Press.

Cornaton, Michel (1998). *Les camps de regroupement de la guerre d'Algérie*. Paris: L'Harmattan. [1st edn, Editions ouvrières, 1967.]

Coupland, Reginald (1945). *The Constitutional Problem in India*. Oxford: Oxford University Press.

Crowder, Michael (1984). *Cambridge History of Africa*, vol. VIII, *From c.1940 to 1975*. Cambridge: Cambridge University Press.

Crozier, Andrew J. (1988). *Appeasement and Germany's Last Bid for Colonies*. Basingstoke: Macmillan.

Crozier, Andrew J. (1997). *The Causes of the Second World War*. Oxford: Blackwell.

Dalloz, Jacques (1987). *La guerre d'Indochine 1945–1954*. Paris: Seuil. [Trans. as: *The French Indochina War, 1945–1954*. London: Hurst, 1991.]

Darwin, John (1988). *Britain and Decolonisation: The Retreat from Empire in the Post-War World*. Basingstoke: Macmillan.

Darwin, John (1991). *The End of the British Empire: The Historical Debate*. Oxford: Blackwell.

Darwin, John (1994). 'The Central African Emergency, 1959'. In Holland (1994a), 217–34.

Darwin, John (1999). 'What was the Late Colonial State?'. *Itinerario*, 23(3/4).

Darwin, John (2005). 'A Fourth British Empire?'. In Lynn (2005), 16–31.

Degras, Jane (ed.) (1956–65). *The Communist International, 1919–1943: documents*, vol. 1: *1919–1922*. London: Oxford University Press.

Delavignette, Robert (1940). *Les Vrais chefs de l'empire*. Paris: Stock.

Delavignette, Robert (1950). *Freedom and Authority in West Africa*. Oxford: Oxford University Press.

Delval, Raymond (1986). 'L'Histoire du PADESM (Parti des Déshérités Malgaches) ou quelques faits oubliés de l'histoire malgache'. In Institut d'Histoire du Temps Présent (1986), 275–88.

Deschamps, Hubert, Decary, R. and Ménard, A. (1948). *Côte des Somalis – Réunion – Inde*. Paris: Berger-Levrault.

Deschamps, Hubert (1975). *Roi de la brousse: Mémoires d'autres mondes*. Paris: Berger-Levrault.

de Silva, K.M. (ed.) (1997). *Sri Lanka*, 2 vols. British Documents on the End of Empire, Series B, vol. 2. London: HMSO.

Devillers, Philippe (1952). *L'Histoire du Viêt-Nam de 1940 à 1952*. Paris: Le Seuil.

Devillers, Philippe (1988). *Paris–Saigon–Hanoi. Les archives de la guerre, 1944–1947*. Paris: Gallimard/Julliard.

Dorward, D.C. (1974). 'Ethnography and Administration: a study of Anglo-Tiv "Working Misunderstanding"'. *Journal of African History*, 15(3), 457–77.

Droz, Bernard, & Lever, Evelyne (re-ed. 1991). *Histoire de la Guerre d'Algérie 1954–1962*. Paris: Seuil [first edn. 1982].

Dunn, Peter (1985). *The First Indochina War*. London: Hurst.

Duroselle, Jean-Baptiste (1982). *Politique étrangère de la France: L'abîme, 1939–1945*. Paris: Imprimerie nationale de la France.

Durrell, Lawrence (1957). *Bitter Lemons of Cyprus*. rev. edn. London: Faber, 2000.

Echenberg, Myron (1985). '"Morts pour la France": the African soldier in France during the Second World War'. *Journal of African History*, 26, 364–5.

Echenberg, Myron (1991). *Colonial Conscripts: The Tirailleurs Sénégalais in French West Africa, 1857–1960*. London & Portsmouth NH: James Currey & Heinemann.

Elkins, Caroline (2003). 'Detention, Rehabilitation and the Destruction of Kikuyu Society'. In Atieno Odhiambo & Lonsdale (2003), 191–226.

Elkins, Caroline (2005). *Britain's Gulag: The Brutal End of Empire in Kenya*. London: Cape.

Ellis, Stephen (1986). *The Rising of the Red Shawls*. Cambdidge: Cambridge University Press.

Ellis, Stephen (1990). *Un complot colonial à Madagascar: L'Affaire Rainandrianampandry*. Paris: Karthala.

Eveno, Patrick, & Planchais, Jean (eds) (1989). *La Guerre d'Algérie*. Paris: La Découverte & Le Monde.

Fanon, Frantz (1952). *Peau Noire Masques Blancs*. Paris: Seuil.

Fanon, Frantz [1961](2002). *Les Damnés de la terre*, préface de Jean-Paul Sartre. Paris: La Découverte. [First published, Paris: Maspero, 1961; trans. as *The Damned of the Earth*, Penguin: Harmondsworth, 1965.]

Feraoun, Mouloud [1962](2000). *Journal, 1955–1962: Reflections on the French–Algerian War*. Lincoln, NE: University of Nebraska Press.

Ferguson, Niall (2003). *Empire: How Britain Changed the Modern World.* London: Penguin.

Flint, John E. (1983). 'The failure of planned decolonisation in Africa'. *African Affairs*, 389–411.

Flint, John E. (1999). '"Managing Nationalism": The Colonial Office and Nnamdi Azikiwe, 1932–1943'. *Journal of Imperial and Commonwealth History*, 27(2), 143–57.

Forster, E.M. (1924). *A Passage to India.* London: Edward Arnold. [Harmondsworth: Penguin, 1989.]

Foster, Anne L. (1995). 'French, Dutch, British and US Reactions to the Nghe Tinh Rebellion of 1930–31'. In Antlöv & Tønnesson (1995), 63–82.

Forsyth, Frederick (1971). *The Day of the Jackal.* London: Hutchinson.

Fourastié, Jean (1979). *Les trente glorieuses, ou, La Révolution invisible de 1946 à 1975.* Fayard, Paris.

Fox, Richard G. (1992). 'East of Said', In Sprinker (1992), 144–56.

Frémeaux, Jacques (2002). 'The Sahara and the Algerian War'. In Alexander et al. (2002), 76–87.

Fukuyama, Francis (1989). 'The End of History?' *The National Interest*, 16 (Summer), 3–18.

Füredi, Frank (1994a). *Colonial Wars and the Politics of Third World Nationalism.* London & New York: I.B. Tauris.

Füredi, Frank (1994b). 'Creating a Breathing Space: The Political Management of Colonial Emergencies'. In Holland (1994a), 89–106.

Furse, Ralph (1962). *Aucuparius: Recollections of a Recruiting Officer.* London: Oxford University Press.

Gallagher, John (1982). *The Decline, Revival and Fall of the British Empire.* Cambridge: Cambridge University Press.

Gallagher, John, & Robinson, R.E. (1962). 'The partition of Africa'. In *The New Cambridge Modern History*, vol. 11. Cambridge: Cambridge University Press.

Gallagher, John, Johnson, G. & Seal, A. (eds) (1973). *Locality, Province and Nation: Essays on Indian Politics 1870–1940.* Cambridge: Cambridge University Press.

Gandhi, Mohandas Karamchand (1926). *The Story of my Experiments with the Truth: An Autobiography.* London: Phoenix Press, 1949 [f.p. 1926].

Gantès, Gilles de (1999). 'Protectorate, Association, Reformism: the roots of the Republican policy pursued by the Popular Front in Indochina'. In Chafer & Sackur (1999), 109–30.

Gardinier, David E. (1963). *Cameroon: United Nations Challenge to French Policy.* Oxford: Oxford University Press.

Gardinier, David E. (1988). 'Les recommandations de la Conférence de Brazzaville sur les problèmes d'éducation'. In Institut Charles-de-Gaulle & Institut d'Histoire du Temps Présent (1988), 170–80.

Gaulle, Charles de (1970a). *Mémoires de guerre.* vol. 1: *L'appel, 1940–1942*; vol. 2: *L'unité, 1942–1944*; vol. 3: *Le salut, 1944–1946.* Paris: Plon.

Gaulle, Charles de (1970b). *Discours et messages.* vol. 1: *Pendant la guerre, juin 1940–janvier 1946*; vol. 2: *Dans l'attente, février 1946–avril 1958*; vol. 3: *Avec le renouveau, mai 1958–juillet 1962.* Paris: Plon.

Gifford, P. & Louis, W.R. (eds) (1971). *France and Britain in Africa.* New Haven, CT: Yale University Press.

Gilmartin, David (2003). 'Democracy, Nationalism and the Public: a speculation on colonial Muslim politics'. In Le Sueur (2003), 191–203.

Goldsworthy, David (1971). *Colonial Issues in British Politics, 1945–1961: From 'Colonial Development' to 'Wind of Change'.* Oxford: Clarendon.

Goldsworthy, David (ed.) (1994). *The Conservative Government and the End of Empire, 1951–1957*. British Documents on the End of Empire, Series A, vol. 3. London: HMSO.

Golsan, Richard J. (ed.) (2000). *The Papon Affair. Memory and Justice on Trial*. London: Routledge.

Goscha, Christopher E. (1995). *Vietnam or Indochina?: Contesting Concepts of Space in Vietnamese Nationalism, 1887–1954*. Copenhagen: NIAS.

Greene, Graham (1948). *The Heart of the Matter*. London: William Heinemann. [London: Penguin, 1971.]

Groen, Petra M.H. (1994). 'Militant Response: The Dutch Use of Military Force and the Decolonization of the Dutch East Indies, 1945–1950'. In Holland (1994a), 30–44.

Guha, Ranajit (1983). *Elementary Aspects of Peasant Insurgency in Colonial India*. New Delhi: Oxford University Press.

Guha, Ranajit, & Spivak, Gayatri Chakravorty (eds) (1988). *Selected Subaltern Studies*. Oxford & New York: Oxford University Press.

Gupta, Amit Kumar (ed.) (1987). *Myth and Reality: The Struggle for Freedom in India, 1945–47*. New Delhi: Manohar.

Gupta, Partha Sarathi (1987). 'Imperial strategy and the Transfer of Power, 1939–51'. In Gupta (1987), 1–53.

Hack, Karl (1995). 'Screwing Down the People: The Malayan Emergency, Decolonisation and Ethnicity'. In Tønnesson & Antlöv (1995), 83–109.

Hailey, Lord (ed.), Kirk-Greene, A. (1980). *Native Administration and Political Development in British Tropical Africa, 1940–1942*. London: Frank Cass.

Haithcox, John P. (1971). *Communism and Nationalism in India: M.N. Roy and Comintern Policy, 1920–1939*. Princeton, NJ: Princeton University Press.

Harbi, Mohamed (1980). *Le FLN, Mirage et Réalité*. Paris: Jeune-Afrique.

Harbi, Mohammed (ed.) (1981). *Les Archives de la Révolution algérienne*. Paris: Jeune-Afrique.

Hargreaves, John (1993). 'The Comintern and anti-colonialism: new research opportunities'. *African Affairs* 92, 255–61.

Hargreaves, John (1996). *Decolonization in Africa*, 2nd edn. Harlow: Longman.

Hazareesingh, Sudhir (1996). *Political Traditions in Modern France*. Oxford: Oxford University Press.

Hémery, Daniel (1977). 'Aux origines des guerres d'indépendance vietnamiennes: pouvoir colonial et phénomène communiste en Indochine avant la Seconde Guerre mondiale'. *Le mouvement social*, no. 101, October–December, 4–35.

Heussler, Robert (1971). 'British rule in Africa'. In Gifford & Louis (1970).

Hintjens, Helen (1995). 'Constitutional and political change in the French Caribbean'. In Burton & Reno (1995), 21–33.

Hobsbawm, Eric (1994). *Age of Extremes: The Short Twentieth Century 1914–1991*. London: Michael Joseph.

Hobsbawm, Eric, & Ranger, Terence O. (eds) (1983). *The Invention of Tradition*. Cambridge: Cambridge University Press.

Hodgkin, Thomas (1956). *Nationalism in Colonial Africa*. Frederick Muller, London.

Holbrook, Wendell P. (1985). 'British propaganda and the mobilization of the Gold Coast war effort, 1939–1945'. *Journal of African History*, 26, 347–61.

Holland, Robert, & Rizvi, Gowher (eds) (1984). *Perspectives on Imperialism and Decolonization: Essays in Honour of A.F. Madden*. Special Issue of *Journal of Imperial and Commonwealth History*, 12(2). London: Frank Cass.

Holland, Robert (1985). *European Decolonization 1918–1981: An Introductory Survey*. Basingstoke: Macmillan.

Holland, Robert (ed.) (1994a). *Emergencies and Disorder in the European Empires after 1945.* London: Frank Cass.

Holland, Robert (1994b). 'Never, Never Land: British Colonial Policy and the Roots of Violence in Cyprus, 1950–54'. In Holland (1994a), 148–76.

Holland, Robert (1995). 'Dirty Wars: Algeria and Cyprus compared'. In Ageron & Michel (1995), 37–46.

Holland, Robert (1998). *Britain and the Revolt in Cyprus, 1954–1959.* Oxford: Clarendon.

Horne, Alistair (1996). *A Savage War of Peace: Algeria, 1954–1962*, rev. edn. Basingstoke: Macmillan. [1st edn. London: Macmillan, 1977.]

Howe, Stephen (1993). *Anticolonialism in British Politics: The Left and the End of Empire, 1918–1964.* Oxford: Clarendon.

Hyam, Ronald (1987). 'The geopolitical origins of the Central African Federation: Britain, Rhodesia and South Africa, 1948–1953'. *Historical Journal*, 30, 145–72.

Hyam, Ronald (ed.) (1992). *The Labour Government and the End of Empire,* British Documents on the End of Empire, Series A, vol. 2. London: HMSO.

Hyam, Ronald (1999). 'Bureaucracy and "Trusteeship" in Colonial Empire'. In Brown & Louis (1999), 255–79.

Hyam, Ronald, & Louis, W. Roger (eds) (2000). *The Conservative Government and the End of Empire, 1957–1964.* British Documents on the End of Empire, Series A, vol. 4. London: Stationery Office.

Ihaddaden, Zahir (2001). 'La désinformation pendant la guerre d'Algérie'. In Jauffret & Vaïsse (2001), 363–82.

Iliffe, John (1979). *A Modern History of Tanganyika.* Cambridge: Cambridge University Press.

Iliffe, John (1988). *The African Poor: A History.* Cambridge: Cambridge University Press.

Institut Charles-de-Gaulle & Institut d'Histoire du Temps Présent (1988). *Brazzaville, aux sources de la décolonisation.* Paris: Plon.

Institut d'Histoire Comparée des Civilisations & Institut d'Histoire du Temps Présent (1995). *Décolonisations comparées: Actes du Colloque international 'Décolonisations comparées'.* Aix-en-Provence: Publications de l'Université de Provence.

Institut d'Histoire du Temps Présent (1986). *Les Chemins de la décolonisation de l'empire français, 1936–1956.* Paris: Editions du CNRS.

Jackson, Ashley (2006). *The British Empire and the Second World War.* London: Hambledon.

Jackson, Julian (1988). *The Popular Front in France: Defending Democracy, 1934–1938.* Cambridge: Cambridge University Press.

Jalal, Ayesha (1985). *The Sole Spokesman: Jinnah and the Muslim League and the Demand for Pakistan.* Cambridge: Cambridge University Press.

Jauffret, Jean-Charles (ed.) (1990). *La Guerre d'Algérie par les documents*, vol. I, *L'Avertissement (1943–1946).* Paris: Service Historique de l'Armée de Terre.

Jauffret, Jean-Charles (1994). 'The Origins of the Algerian War: The Reaction of France and its Army to the Emergencies of 8 May 1945 and 1 November 1954'. In Holland (1994a), 17–29.

Jauffret, Jean-Charles (ed.) (1998). *La Guerre d'Algérie par les documents*, vol. II, *Les Portes de la guerre (10 mars 1946–31 décembre 1954).* Paris: Service Historique de l'Armée de Terre.

Jauffret, Jean-Charles, & Vaïsse, Maurice (eds) (2001). *Militaires et guérilla dans la guerre d'Algérie.* Brussels: Complexe.

Jeffery, Keith (1999). 'The Second World War'. In Brown & Louis (1999), 306–28.

Jennings, Eric (2002). *Vichy in the Tropics: Pétain's National Revolution in Madagascar, Guadeloupe, and Indochina, 1940–44.* Stanford: Stanford University Press.

Jewsiewicki, Bogumil, & Newbury, David (eds) (1986). *African Historiographies: What History for which Africa?* Beverly Hills, CA: Sage.

Johnson, Douglas H. (ed.) (1998). *Sudan*. British Documents on the End of Empire, Series B, vol. 5. London: Stationery Office.

Johnson, Douglas H. (2003). *The Root Causes of Sudan's Civil Wars*. Oxford, Bloomington, IN & Kampala: James Currey, Indiana University Press & Fountain Publishers.

Johnson, R.W. (1972). 'French imperialism in Guinea'. In Owen & Sutcliffe (1972), 230–47.

Joseph, Richard (1977). *Radical Nationalism in Cameroun: Social Origins of the UPC Rebellion*. Oxford: Oxford University Press.

Karnow, Stanley (1994). *Vietnam : A History*, rev. edn. London: Pimlico.

Kedward, Rod (2005). *La Vie en bleu: France and the French since 1900*. London: Penguin.

Kennedy, Dane (1992). 'Constructing the Colonial Myth of Mau Mau'. *International Journal of African Historical Studies*, 25(2), 214–60.

Kent, John (1992). *The Internationalization of Colonialism: Britain, France and Black Africa, 1939–1956*. Oxford: Oxford University Press.

Kent, John (ed.) (1998). *Egypt and the Defence of the Middle East*. British Documents on the End of Empire, Series B, vol. 4. London: Stationery Office.

Kheng, Cheah Boon (1988). 'The erosion of ideological hegemony and royal power and the rise of post-war Malay nationalism'. *Journal of Southeast Asian Studies*, 19(1), 1–26.

Killingray, David, & Rathbone, Richard (eds) (1986). *Africa and the Second World War*. Basingstoke: Macmillan.

Kipling, Rudyard (1901). *Kim*. London: Macmillan. [Edited and with an introduction and notes by Edward Said, Harmondsworth: Penguin, 1987.]

Kirk-Greene, Anthony H.M. (1980). 'The Thin White Line'. *African Affairs*, 79, 25–44.

Kitson, Frank (1960). *Gangs and Counter-Gangs*. London: Barrie and Rockliff.

Kras, Stefan (1999). 'Senghor's rise to power: early roots of French sub-Saharan decolonisation'. *Itinerario*, 23(1), 91–113.

Kratoska, Paul H. (1998). *The Japanese Occupation of Malaya: A Social and Economic History*. London: Hurst.

Lacouture, Jean (1981). *Pierre Mendès-France*. Paris: Le Seuil.

Lacouture, Jean (1984–6). *De Gaulle*, 3 vols: vol. 1. *Le rebelle, 1890–1944*; vol. 2. *Le politique, 1944–1959*; vol. 3. *Le souverain, 1959–1970*. Paris: Le Seuil.

Lan, David (1985). *Guns and Rain: Guerrillas and Spirit Mediums in Zimbabwe*. London & Berkeley, CA: James Currey & University of California Press.

Lanne, Bernard (1995). 'Comparaison de deux formes possibles de décolonisation. Le projet d'Union des Républiques d'Afrique Centrale (URAC), 1960'. In IHCC & IHTP (1995), 163–73.

Lartéguy, Jean (1961). *Les Prétoriens*. Paris: Presses de la Cité.

Le Sueur, James D. (2001). *Uncivil War: Intellectuals and Identity Politics during the Decolonization of Algeria*. Philadelphia: University of Pennsylvania Press.

Le Sueur, James D. (ed.) (2003). *A Decolonization Reader*. London: Routledge.

Léger, Paul-Alain (2002). 'Personal account . . .'. In Alexander et al. (2002a), 237–42.

Leong, Yee Fong (1992). 'The Impact of the Cold War on Trade Unionism in Malaya (1948–1957)'. *Journal of Southeast Asian Studies*, 23, 1, 60–73.

Lever, Evelyne (1993). 'L'OAS et les pieds-noirs'. In Ageron (1993), 223–47.

Lévi-Strauss, Claude (1962). *La Pensée sauvage*. Paris: Plon.

Lewis, James I. (1995). 'The French Colonial Service and the issues of reform, 1944–8'. *Contemporary European History*, 4(2), 153–88.

Lewis, James I. (1998). 'The MRP and the genesis of the French Union, 1944–1948'. *French History*, 12(3), 276–314.

Lewis, James I. (2002). 'Félix Eboué and Late French Colonial Ideology'. *Itinerario*, 25(3/4), 127–44.

Lewis, Joanna (2003). '"Daddy wouldn't buy me a Mau Mau": the British popular press and the demoralisation of empire'. In Atieno Odhiambo & Lonsdale (2003), 227–50.

Liauzu, Claude, & Manceron, Gilles (eds) (2006). *La colonisation, la loi et l'histoire*. Paris: Syllepse.

Longrigg, Stephen (1958). *Syria and Lebanon under French Mandate*. Oxford: Oxford University Press/RIIA.

Lonsdale, John (1986a). 'Political accountability in African History'. In Patrick Chabal (ed.) (1986), *Political Domination in Africa*, Cambridge: Cambridge University Press.

Lonsdale, John (1986b). 'The depression and the Second World War in the transformation of Kenya'. In Killingray & Rathbone (1986), 97–142.

Lonsdale, John (1990). 'Mau Maus of the mind: making Mau Mau and remaking Kenya'. In *Journal of African History*, 31, 393–421. [Also repr. in Le Sueur (2003), 269–90.]

Lonsdale, John (2003). 'Authority, gender and violence: the war within Mau Mau's fight for land & freedom'. In Atieno Odhiambo & Lonsdale (2003), 46–75.

Lorcin, Patricia M. (1995). *Imperial Identities: Stereotyping, Prejudice and Race in Colonial Algeria*. New York: I.B. Tauris.

Louis, W. Roger (1977). *Imperialism at Bay, 1941–1945: The United States and the Decolonization of the British Empire*. Oxford: Oxford University Press.

Louis, W. Roger (1999). 'The dissolution of the British Empire'. In Brown & Louis (1999), 329–56.

Louis, W. Roger, & Robinson, Ronald [1994](2003). 'The imperialism of decolonization'. In Le Sueur (2003), 49–79. [First publ. in *Journal of Commonwealth and Imperial History*, 22(3) (1994), 462–511.]

Low, D.A. (ed.) (1977). *Congress and the Raj: Facets of the Indian Struggle, 1917–1947*. London: Heinemann. [2nd edn: New Delhi & Oxford: Oxford University Press, 2004.]

Low, D.A. & Smith, Alison (eds) (1976). *History of East Africa*, vol. III. Oxford: Clarendon.

Low, D.A. & Lonsdale, John (1976). 'Introduction: towards the new order, 1945–1963'. In Low & Smith (1976), 1–63.

Lumley, E.K. (1976). *Forgotten Mandate: A British District Officer in Tanganyika*. London: Hurst.

Lynn, Martin (ed.) (2001). *Nigeria*. British Documents on the End of Empire, Series B, vol. 7. London: The Stationery Office.

Lynn, Martin (ed.) (2005). *The British Empire in the 1950s: Retreat or Revival?* New York & Basingstoke: Palgrave Macmillan.

M'Bokolo, Elikia (1982). 'French colonial policy in Equatorial Africa in the 1940s and 1950s'. In Gifford & Louis (1982) 172–92.

Macey, David (2000). *Frantz Fanon: A Life*. London: Granta.

MacQueen, Norrie (1997). *The Decolonization of Portuguese Africa*. London: Longman.

Mannoni, Octave (1966). 'The decolonisation of myself'. *Race*, 7(4), 337–45.

Mannoni, Octave (ed.), M. Bloch (1970). *Prospero and Caliban: The Psychology of Colonization*, Manchester: Manchester University Press. [Originally published as. *Psychologie de la Colonisation*. Paris: Minuit, 1950.]

Mansergh, Nicholas (ed.) (1970–82). *The Transfer of Power, 1942–7*. London: HMSO.

Marr, David G. (1983). *Vietnamese Tradition on Trial, 1920–1945*. Berkeley, CA: University of California Press.

Marr, David G. (1995). *Vietnam 1945: The Quest for Power*. Berkeley, CA: University of California Press.

Marseille, Jacques (1984). *Empire colonial et capitalisme français: Histoire d'un divorce*. Paris: Albin Michel.

Marseille, Jacques (1988). 'La Conférence de Brazzaville et l'économie impériale: "des innovations éclatantes" ou des recommandations "prudentes"?'. In Institut Charles-de-Gaulle & Institut d'Histoire du Temps Présent (1988), 107–15.

Marshall, D. Bruce (1973). *The French Colonial Myth and Constitution-Making in the Fourth Republic*. New Haven, CT: Yale University Press.

Martin, Phyllis (1996). *Leisure and Society in Colonial Brazzaville*. Cambridge: Cambridge University Press.

Massu, Jacques (1971). *La Vraie bataille d'Alger*. Paris: Plon.

Mauriac, François (1955). 'La Question'. In *L'Express*, 15 January.

Mazower, Mark (1998). *Dark Continent: Europe's Twentieth Century*. Harmondsworth: Penguin.

McCoy, Alfred W. (ed.) (1980). *Asia under Japanese Occupation: Transition and Transformation*. New Haven: Yale University Press.

McDermott, Kevin & Agnew, Jeremy (1996). *The Comintern: A History of International Communism from Lenin to Stalin*. Basingstoke: Macmillan.

McIntyre, W. David (1998). *British Decolonization, 1946–1997*. Basingstoke: Macmillan.

Messmer, Pierre (1992). *Après tant de batailles: Mémoires*. Paris: Albin Michel.

Messmer, Pierre (1998). *Les blancs s'en vont: Récits de decolonisation*. Paris: Albin Michel.

Meynier, Gilbert (2002). *Histoire intérieure du FLN, 1954–1962*. Paris: Fayard.

Michel, Marc (1982). *Appel à l'Afrique: Contributions et Réactions à l'effort de guerre en A.O.F. 1914–1919*. Paris: Sorbonne.

Michel, Marc (1986). 'Le Togo dans les relations internationales au lendemain de la guerre: prodrome de la décolonisation ou petite "mésentente cordiale"? (1945–1951)'. In Institut d'Histoire du Temps Présent (1986), 96–107.

Michels, Eckard (2002). 'From one crisis to another: the morale of the French Foreign Legion during the Algerian War'. In Alexander et al. (2002a), 88–100.

Ministère des Colonies (1945). *La Conférence Africaine Française: Brazzaville 30 Janvier–8 Février 1944*. Paris.

Mockaitis, Thomas (1990). *British Counterinsurgency 1919–1960*. Basingstoke: Macmillan.

Moneta, Jakob (1971). *La politique du Parti communiste français dans la question coloniale, 1920–1963*. Paris: Maspero.

Moon, Penderel (ed.) (1973). *Wavell: The Viceroy's Journal*. Re-edited 1997. Oxford: Oxford University Press.

Moore, Robin J. (1977). 'The problem of freedom with unity: London's India policy, 1917–47'. In Low (1977), 375–403.

Moore, Robin J. (1999). 'India in the 1940s'. In Winks (1999), 231–42.

Morgenthau, Ruth Schachter (1964). *Political Parties in French-speaking West Africa*. Oxford: Clarendon.

Morlat, Patrice (1990). *La Répression coloniale au Vietnam (1908–1940)*. Paris: L'Harmattan.

Morris-Jones, W.H. & Fischer, Georges (eds) (1980). *Decolonisation and After: The British and French Experience*. London: Frank Cass.

Mortimer, Edward (1969). *France and the Africans, 1940–60: A Political History*. London: Faber.

Mulford, David C. (1967). *Zambia: The Politics of Independence*. London: Oxford University Press.

Murphy, Philip (1995). *Party Politics and Decolonization: the Conservative Party and British Colonial Policy in Tropical Africa, 1951–1964*. Oxford: Clarendon Press.

Murphy, Philip (1999). *Alan Lennox-Boyd: A Biography.* London: I.B. Tauris.

Murphy, Philip (ed.) (2005a). *Central Africa.* British Documents on the End of Empire, Series B, vol. 9. London: Stationery Office.

Murphy, Philip (2005b). '"Government by blackmail": the origins of the Central African Federation reconsidered'. In Lynn (2005), 53–76.

Ndi, Anthony (1986). 'The Second World War in Southern Cameroun and its impact on mission–state relations, 1939–1950'. In Killingray & Rathbone (1986), 204–31.

Nkrumah, Kwame (1957). *The Autobiography of Kwame Nkrumah.* [US edn: *Ghana, the Autobiography of Kwame Nkrumah.*]. Edinburgh & New York: T. Nelson.

Nkrumah, Kwame (1965). *Neo-colonialism: The Last Stage of Imperialism.* London: T. Nelson.

Norindr, Panivong (1999). 'The Popular Front's colonial policies in Indochina: reassessing the Popular Front's "Colonisation altruiste"'. In Chafer & Sackur (1999), 230–48.

Nouschi, André (1962). *La Naissance du nationalisme algérien, 1914–1954.* Paris: Minuit.

Novick, Peter (1968). *The Resistance versus Vichy: The Purge of Collaborators in Liberated France.* London: Chatto & Windus.

Nyerere, Julius (1967). *Freedom and Unity (Uhuru na umoja): A Selection from Writings and Speeches, 1952–65.* London: Oxford University Press.

Ogot, Bethwell A. & Ochieng', William R. (eds) (1995). *Decolonization and Independence in Kenya, 1940–93.* London: James Currey.

Ogot, Bethwell A. (2003). 'Mau Mau and Nationhood: The Untold Story'. In Atieno Odhiambo & Lonsdale (2003), 8–36.

Oliver, Roland (1991). *The African Experience.* London: Weidenfeld & Nicolson.

Omissi, David (1990). *Air Power and Colonial Control.* Manchester: Manchester University Press.

Omouri, Noara (2001). 'Les Sections Administratives Spécialisées et les sciences sociales'. In Jauffret & Vaïsse (2001), 383–97.

Orwell, George (1935). *Burmese Days.* London: Victor Gollancz. [London: Penguin, 2001.]

Orwell, George (1946). 'Politics and the English language'. In Orwell, Sonia, & Angus, Ian (eds) (1968), *The Collected Essays, Journalism and Letters of George Orwell,* vol. 4. *In Front of Your Nose, 1945–1950.* London: Secker & Warburg.

Osterhammel, Jürgen (1997). *Colonialism: A Theoretical Overview.* Princeton, NJ: Markus Wiener.

Ousmane, Sembene (1985). *Thiaroye!* Film.

Owen, Nicholas (2002). 'The Cripps Mission of 1942: a reinterpretation'. *Journal of Imperial and Commonwealth History,* 30(1), 61–98.

Owen, Roger, & Sutcliffe, Bob (eds) (1972). *Studies in the Theory of Imperialism.* London: Longman.

Pandey, Gyan (1988). 'Peasant Revolt and Indian Nationalism: The Peasant Movement in Awadh, 1919–22'. In Guha & Spivak (1988), 234–87.

Parkinson, Cosmo (1947). *The Colonial Office from Within, 1909–1945.* London: Faber.

Patti, Archimedes (1980). *Why Viet Nam? Prelude to America's Albatross.* Berkeley, CA: University of California Press.

Pearce, Robert D. (1982). *The Turning Point in Africa: British Colonial Policy, 1938–1948.* London: Frank Cass.

Pearce, Robert D. (1984). 'The Colonial Office and planned decolonization in Africa'. *African Affairs,* 83, 72–93.

Pervillé, Guy (1986). 'La commission des réformes musulmanes de 1944 et l'élaboration d'une nouvelle politique algérienne de la France'. In Institut d'Histoire du Temps Présent (1986), 357–65.

Pervillé, Guy (1993). 'Guerre d'Algérie: abandon des harkis'. In Ageron (1993), 303–12.

Peterson, Derek (2003). 'Writing in revolution: independent schooling and Mau Mau in Nyeri'. In Atieno Odhiambo & Lonsdale (2003), 76–96.

Pontecorvo, Gillo (1965). *La Bataille d'Alger*. Film.

Porter, Andrew, & Stockwell, Anthony J. (eds) (1989). *British Imperial Policy and Decolonization, 1938–1964*. Basingstoke: Macmillan.

Potter, David C. (1973). 'Manpower shortages and the end of colonialism: the case of the Indian Civil Service'. *Modern Asian Studies*, 7, 47–73.

Potter, David C. (1986). *India's Political Administrators, 1919–1983*. Oxford: Oxford University Press.

Ranger, Terence O. (1968). 'Connexions between "primary resistance" movements and modern mass nationalism in East and Central Africa'. *Journal of African History*, 9, 437–53 & 631–41.

Ranger, Terence O. (1983). 'The invention of tradition in Colonial Africa'. In Hobsbawm & Ranger (1983), 211–61.

Ranger, Terence O. (1985). *Peasant Consciousness and Guerrilla War: A Comparative Study*. London: James Currey.

Ranger, Terence O. (1998). 'Zimbabwe and the long search for independence'. In Birmingham & Martin (1998), 203–29.

Rathbone, Richard (ed.) (1992). *Ghana*. British Documents on the End of Empire, Series B, vol. 1. London: HMSO.

Rathbone, Richard (2000). *Nkrumah and the Chiefs: The Politics of Chieftaincy in Ghana, 1951–1960*. Oxford, Athens, OH & Accra: James Currey, Ohio University Press & F. Reimmer.

Reid, Anthony (1974). *The Indonesian National Revolution 1945–1950*. Hawthorn: Longman.

Roberts, Hugh (2002). 'The image of the French army in the cinematic representation of the Algerian War: the revolutionary politics of the Battle of Algiers'. In Alexander et al. (2002a), 152–63.

Robinson, Ronald E. (1972). 'Non-European foundations of European imperialism: sketch for a theory of collaboration'. In Owen & Sutcliffe (1972), 117–42.

Robinson, Ronald E. (1979). 'The moral disarmament of African Empire, 1919–1947'. *Journal of Imperial and Commonwealth History*, 8(1), 86–104.

Robinson, Ronald E. (1980). 'Andrew Cohen and the Transfer of Power in tropical Africa, 1940–1951'. In Morris-Jones & Fischer (1980), 50–72.

Robinson, Ronald E. (1984). 'Imperial theory and the question of imperialism after Empire'. In Holland & Rizvi (1984), 42–54.

Robinson, Ronald E. & Gallagher, John (1961). *Africa and the Victorians: The Official Mind of Imperialism*. Oxford: Oxford University Press.

Ross, Kristin (1995). *Fast Cars, Clean Bodies: Decolonization and the Reordering of French Culture*. Cambridge, MA: MIT Press.

Rotberg, Richard I. (1966). *The Rise of Nationalism in Central Africa: The Making of Malawi and Zambia, 1873–1964*. Cambridge, MA: Harvard University Press.

Rothschild, D. & Chazan, N. (eds) (1988). *The Precarious Balance: State and Society in Africa*. Boulder, CO: Westview.

Said, Edward (1978). *Orientalism*. Harmondsworth: Penguin.

Said, Edward (1993). *Culture and Imperialism*. London: Chatto & Windus.

Sainteny, Jean (1967). *Histoire d'une paix manqué*, rev. edn. Paris: Fayard.

Salemink, Oscar (1995). 'Primitive partisans: French strategy and the construction of a Montagnard ethnic identity in Indochina'. In Antlöv & Tønnesson (1995), 261–93.

Sanmarco, Louis (1983). *Le colonial colonisé*. Editions ABC, Paris.

Sarkar, Sumit (1989). *Modern India, 1885–1947*, 2nd edn. New Delhi: Oxford University Press.

Sarkar, Sumit (1997). *Writing Social History*. New Delhi: Oxford University Press.

Scott, James C. (1976). *The Moral Economy of the Peasant: Rebellion and Subsistence in Southeast Asia*. New Haven & London: Yale University Press.

Scott, Paul (1976). *The Raj Quartet*. Heinemann, London. [Originally published as: *The Jewel in the Crown* (1966); *The Day of the Scorpion* (1968); *The Towers of Silence* (1971); *A Division of the Spoils* (1975). London: Heinemann.]

Seal, Anil (1973). 'Imperialism and nationalism in India'. In Gallagher, Johnson & Seal (1973), 1–27.

Sellam, Sadek (2001). 'La situation de la wilâya 4 au moment de l'affaire Si Salah'. In Jauffret & Vaïsse (2001), 175–92.

Sellar, W.C. & Yeatman, R.J. (1930). *1066 and All That*. London: Methuen.

Sharkey, Heather (2003). *Living with Colonialism: Nationalism and Culture in the Anglo-Egyptian Sudan*. Berkeley & Los Angeles: University of California Press.

Shennan, Andrew (1989). *Rethinking France: Plans for Renewal 1940–1946*. Oxford: Oxford University Press.

Shimazu, Naoko (1998). *Japan, Race and Equality: The Racial Equality Proposal of 1919*. London: Routledge.

Shipway, Martin (1996a). *The Road to War: France and Vietnam, 1944–1947*. Oxford & Providence, RI: Berghahn.

Shipway, Martin (1996b). 'Madagascar on the eve of insurrection, 1944–1947: the impasse of a liberal colonial policy'. *Journal of Imperial and Commonwealth History*, 24(1), 72–100. [Repr. in Le Sueur (2003), 80–102.]

Shipway, Martin (1999). 'Reformism and the French "official mind": the Brazzaville Conference and the legacy of the Popular Front'. In Chafer & Sackur (1999), 131–51.

Shipway, Martin (2002). 'Algeria and the "official mind": the impact of North Africa on French colonial policy South of the Sahara, 1944–1958'. In Alexander et al. (2002), 61–75.

Shlaim, Avi (1997). 'The Sèvres Protocol, 1956: anatomy of a war plot?'. *International Affairs*, 73(3), 509–29.

Smith, Paul (2005). *A History of the French Senate*, vol. 1. *The Third Republic, 1870–1940*. Lewsiton, NY: Edwin Mellen Press.

Smith, Ralph B. (1972). 'The Vietnamese Elite of French Cochinchina, 1943'. *Modern Asian Studies*, 6(4), 459–82.

Smith, Ralph B. (1988). 'Some contrasts between Burma and Malaya in British policy in Southeast Asia, 1942–1946'. In Smith & Stockwell (1988), 30–76.

Smith, Ralph B. & Stockwell, Anthony J. (eds) (1988). *British Policy and the Transfer of Power in Asia: Documentary Perspectives*. London: India Office & SOAS.

Smith, Simon C. (1995). *British Relations with the Malay Rulers from Decentralization to Malayan Independence 1930–1957*. Kuala Lumpur & Oxford: Oxford University Press.

Sorum, Paul Clay (1977). *Intellectuals and Decolonization in France*. Chapel Hill, NC: University of North Carolina Press.

Soumille, Pierre (1995). 'L'influence des Églises chrétiennes et le rôle des missions dans l'enseignement au Congo belge et dans l'Afrique équatoriale française de 1946 à 1960'. In Ageron & Michel (1995), 393–407.

Spear, Thomas (2003). 'Neo-Traditionalism and the limits of invention in colonial Africa'. In *Journal of African History*, 44, 3–27.

Springhall, John (2001). *Decolonization since 1945*. Basingstoke: Palgrave.

Sprinker, Michael (ed.) (1992). *Edward Said: A Critical Reader*. Oxford: Blackwell.

Stengers, Jean (1995). 'La décolonisation du Congo: un essai de modèle belge'. In Ageron & Michel (1995), 307–17.

Stockwell, Antony J. (1994). 'A widespread and long-concocted plot to overthrow government in Malaya? The origins of the Malayan Emergency'. In Holland (1994a), 66–88.

Stockwell, Antony J. (ed.) (1995). *Malaya.* British Documents on the End of Empire, Series B, vol. 3. London: HMSO.

Stockwell, Antony J. (1999). 'Imperialism and nationalism in South-East Asia'. In Brown & Louis (1999), 465–89.

Stora, Benjamin (1991). *La Gangrène et l'oubli.* Paris: La Découverte.

Stora, Benjamin (1994). 'Algeria: the War without a Name'. In Holland (1994a), 208–16.

Stora, Benjamin (2001). *Algeria, 1830–2000: A Short History.* Ithaca, NY: Cornell University Press.

Stora, Benjamin, & Harbi, Mohammed (eds) (2004). *La guerre d'Algérie: 1954–2004, la fin de l'amnésie.* Paris: Laffont.

Stubbs, Richard (1980). *Hearts and Minds in Guerrilla Warfare: The Malayan Emergency 1948–1960.* Singapore: Oxford University Press.

Talbot, Ian (1999). 'Pakistan's emergence'. In Winks (1999), 253–63.

Thomas, Martin (1998). *The French Empire at War, 1940–1945.* Manchester: Manchester University Press.

Thomas, Martin (2000a). *The French North African Crisis: Colonial Breakdown and Anglo-French Relations, 1945–62.* Basingstoke: Macmillan.

Thomas, Martin (2000b). 'Divisive decolonization: the Anglo-French withdrawal from Syria and Lebanon, 1944–46'. *Journal of Imperial and Commonwealth Studies,* 28, 71–93.

Thomas, Martin (2003). 'The colonial policies of the Mouvement Républicain Populaire, 1944–1954: from reform to reaction'. *English Historical Review,* 476 (April), 380–411.

Thompson, Edward, & Garratt, G.T. (1934). *Rise and Fulfilment of British Rule in India.* London: Macmillan.

Thorne, Christopher (1979). *Allies of a Kind: The United States, Britain and the War against Japan, 1941–1945.* New York: Oxford University Press.

Tinker, Hugh (ed.) (1984–5). *Burma: The Struggle for Independence,* 2 vols. London: HMSO.

Tønnesson, Stein (1991). *The Vietnamese Revolution of 1945: Roosevelt, Ho Chi Minh and de Gaulle in a World at War.* London: Sage.

Tønnesson, Stein (1995). 'Filling the power vacuum: 1945 in French Indochina, the Netherlands East Indies and British Malaya'. In Antlöv & Tønnesson (1995), 83–109.

Tostain, France (1999). 'The Popular Front and the Blum–Viollette Plan'. In Chafer & Sackur (1999), 218–29.

Touchard, Jean (1978). *Le Gaullisme, 1940–1969.* Pasris: Seuil.

Touwen-Bouwsma, Elly (1996). 'The Indonesian nationalists and the Japanese "liberation" of Indonesia: visions and reactions'. *Journal of Southeast Asian Studies* 27(1), 1–18.

Tronchon, Jacques (1986). *L'Insurrection malgache de 1947,* new edn. [f.p. 1974]. Fianarantsoa & Paris: Ambozontany/Karthala.

Twaddle, Michael (1986). 'Decolonization in Africa: a new historiographical debate'. In Jewsiewicki & Newbury (1986), 123–38.

van Bilsen, AAJ (1958). *Vers l'indépendance du Congo et du Ruanda-Urundi: Réflexions sur les devoirs et l'avenir de la Belgique en Afrique centrale.* Brussels: Kraainem.

van den Doel, H.W. (2001). *Afscheid van Indië: Det val van het Nederlandse imperium in Azië.* Amsterdam: Prometheus.

van der Eng, Pierre (2003). 'Marshall Aid as a catalyst in the decolonization of Indonesia, 1947–49'. In Le Sueur (2003), 123–38.

Vergili, Fabrice (2002). *Shorn Women: Gender and Punishment in Liberation France*. Oxford & New York: Berg. [Originally published as *La France 'virile': des femmes tondues à la Libération*, Paris: Payot, 2000.]

Vidal-Naquet, Pierre (1972). *La Torture dans la République: Essai d'histoire et de politique contemporaine*. Paris: Minuit.

Villatoux, Marie-Catherine, & Villatoux, Paul (2001). 'Le 5e Bureau en Algérie'. In Jauffret & Vaïsse (2001), 399–419.

Warburg, Gabriel R. (1992). *Historical Discord in the Nile Valley*. London: Hurst.

Ward, Stuart (ed.) (2001). *British Culture and the End of Empire*. Manchester: Manchester University Press.

Weber, Eugen (1976). *Peasants into Frenchmen*. Stanford: Stanford University Press.

Weber, Jacques (ed.) (2002). *Les Relations entre la France et l'Inde de 1673 à nos jours*. Paris: Les Indes Savantes.

Westcott, Nicholas (1986). 'The impact of the Second World War on Tanganyika, 1939–49'. In Killingray & Rathbone (1986), 143–59.

Williams, Philip (1964). *Crisis and Compromise: Politics in the Fourth Republic*, 3rd edn. London: Longman.

Wilson, H.S. (1994). *African Decolonization*. London: Arnold.

Winks, Robin (ed.) (1999). *Oxford History of the British Empire*, vol. V, *Historiography*. Oxford: Clarendon.

Wolpert, Stanley (1984). *Jinnah of Pakistan*. New York & Oxford: Oxford University Press.

Wolpert, Stanley (2000). *A New History of India*, 6th edn. Oxford: Oxford University Press.

Wright, Gwendolyn (1997). 'Tradition in the service of modernity: architecture and urbanism in French Colonial Policy, 1900–1930'. In Cooper & Stoler (1997), 322–45.

Yong, Mun Cheong (1982). *H.J. van Mook and Indonesian Independence: A Study of his Role in Dutch–Indonesian Relations, 1945–48*. The Hague: Martinus Nijhoff.

Young, Crawford (1965). *Politics in the Congo: Decolonization and Independence*. Princeton, NJ: Princeton University Press.

Young, Crawford (1988). 'The African colonial state and its political legacy'. In Rothschild & Chazan (1988), 25–66.

Young, Crawford (1994). *The African Colonial State in Comparative Perspective*. New Haven & London: Yale University Press.

Zervoudakis, Alexander (2002). 'From Indochina to Algeria: counter-insurgency lessons'. In Alexander et al. (2002a), 43–60.

Zinnemann, Fred (1973). *The Day of the Jackal*. Film.

Zinoman, Peter (2001). *Colonial Bastille: A History of Imprisonment in Vietnam, 1862–1940*. Berkeley: University of California Press.

Index

Note: 'n' after a page number refers to a note on that page.

Printed in Great Britain
by Amazon